COLLEGE SUCCESS SKILLS
at Macomb CSSK 1200
HEATHER MAYERNIK

Customized Version of
Thriving in the Community College & Beyond:
Strategies for Academic Success and Personal Development, Second Edition

by Joseph Cuseo, Aaron Thompson, Julie McLaughlin, and Steady Moono.
Designed specifically for Macomb Community College

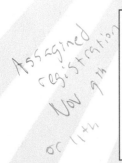

Assigned
registration
Nov 9th
oct 11th

Macomb
Community College

Education • Enrichment • Economic Development

Discover. Connect. *Advance.*

Kendall Hunt
publishing company

Kendall Hunt
publishing company

www.kendallhunt.com
Send all inquiries to:
4050 Westmark Drive
Dubuque, IA 52004-1840

Copyright © 2013 by Kendall Hunt Publishing Company

ISBN 978-1-4652-8626-0

Contents

Chapter 5: Goal Setting, Motivation, and Character 141

Chapter 6: Managing Time and Preventing Procrastination 169

Chapter 7: Higher-Level Thinking
Moving beyond Basic Knowledge to Critical and Creative Thinking 197

Chapter 8: Strategic Learning and Studying
Learning Deeply and Remembering Longer 227

Chapter 9: Test-Taking Skills and Strategies
What to Do before, during, and after Exams 263

Chapter 10: Educational and Career Planning and Decision Making
Making Wise Choices about Your Courses, Major, Degree, and Career Plans 291

Chapter 11: Diversity and the Community College Experience
Appreciating the Value of Human Differences for Promoting Learning and Personal Development 349

Chapter 12: Social and Emotional Intelligence
Relating to Others and Regulating Emotions 381

Macomb Community College
Education • Enrichment • Economic Development

Discover. Connect. *Advance.*

Welcome to Macomb Community College.

My name is Jim Jacobs, and I have been the president of the college since 2008. I started my college career a long time ago—before there were computers, electronic gadgets, even before anyone even thought about how to be successful in college. We just had books and the professors to lecture to us, and every six weeks we took tests. But, I learned a few things that may still be useful today.

First—establish a routine—try to study at the same time each day. I played sports in college, so I knew that every afternoon during the season I could not study from 3:00 to 6:00 p.m. So, I compensated by getting up early before classes, or right after dinner, going straight to the library. That discipline served me very well, because I was able to balance my school work with my other activities.

Second, I used a three-step process for reading of materials. When I had an assignment, particularly one that would be a textbook chapter, I did three things. First, I looked over the material and just read the sub-headings and then looked at the graphs and pictures to see what the book was about. Then, I would read it carefully—take notes and identify the words I did not know—which I would look up and try to make sense out of the material. Then, right before class I would go over the material so I knew what the teacher was covering in the class. This made me better prepared.

Finally, I did something else that I felt was important—studying in the library of the college. This was a neutral space, and, in those days, a library was very quiet. You could concentrate on what you were doing with few diversions.

Today, things are different—but, concentrating and doing a little each day is a key to being successful. One of the great things about Macomb is the attention you receive from the dedicated instructors in small-sized classes.

I am Jim Jacobs and I am Macomb.

Courtesy of Jim Jacobs

History and Overview

The Michigan Superintendent of Public Instruction approved the establishment of South Macomb Community College as an extension of the traditional K–12 system in the Van Dyke Public School District on May 22, 1953. Through assistance from faculty and administrators at the University of Michigan, Michigan State University, and Wayne State University, curriculum and a catalog were developed.

Classes officially began at South Macomb Community College on September 16, 1954, with 84 students in Lincoln High School. On August 7, 1962, Macomb County voters approved the creation of the Community College District of the County of Macomb and authorized a one-mil property tax to support its operation. Commonly known as Macomb County Community College (MCCC), the institution took form and began offering classes under the governance of its own elected Board of Trustees. Land was subsequently purchased in Warren and Clinton Township for two campus sites.

Macomb Community College has developed into a nationally prominent institution. With a staff of more than 1,800, an operating budget over $120 million, three campuses encompassing 40 buildings with over 1.5 million square feet, situated on over 400 acres, and providing learning experiences to more than 59,000 students annually, Macomb Community College is the largest grantor of associate's degrees in the State of Michigan and consistently ranks in the top 2% nationally. Fully accredited by the Higher Learning Commission of the North Central Association of Colleges and Schools since 1970, with locations throughout the county, Macomb Community College meets the needs of the community it serves by adhering to the vision and mission approved by the Board of Trustees.

Vision

Macomb will continue to be a leading edge community college and the community's preferred choice for lifelong learning, cultural enrichment, and community development opportunities.

Mission

As a publicly funded and community-based institution of higher education, Macomb Community College provides a comprehensive program of high-quality educational, enrichment, and economic development experiences designed to promote individual growth and social improvement.

Organizational Goals and Purposes

Macomb Community College endeavors to maintain open, affordable, and lifelong access to an integrated continuum of learner-centered educational opportunities, personal enrichment experiences, and community development programs, including:

Transfer Education, designed to offer courses that parallel university curricula and prepare students successfully to pursue a baccalaureate degree.

Career Preparation, designed to prepare and qualify students for immediate employment and ongoing success in the world of work.

Learning Outreach, designed to provide alternative delivery systems, personalized options, and community-based learning opportunities.

Advanced Studies, designed to enable students to complete baccalaureate degrees, graduate programs, and continuing professional education experiences through affiliations with colleges, universities, and professional associations.

Center Campus

44575 Garfield Road • Clinton Twp., MI 48038-1139 • 1.866.Macomb1 • www.macomb.edu

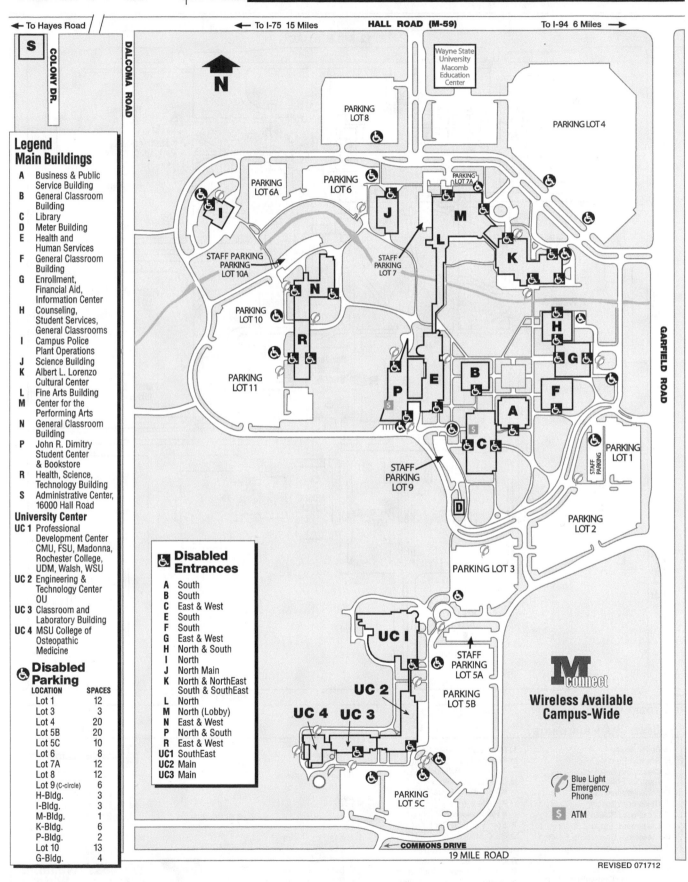

Legend
Main Buildings

A   Business & Public Service Building
B   General Classroom Building
C   Library
D   Meter Building
E   Health and Human Services
F   General Classroom Building
G   Enrollment, Financial Aid, Information Center
H   Counseling, Student Services, General Classrooms
I   Campus Police Plant Operations
J   Science Building
K   Albert L. Lorenzo Cultural Center
L   Fine Arts Building
M   Center for the Performing Arts
N   General Classroom Building
P   John R. Dimitry Student Center & Bookstore
R   Health, Science, Technology Building
S   Administrative Center, 16000 Hall Road

University Center

UC 1   Professional Development Center CMU, FSU, Madonna, Rochester College, UDM, Walsh, WSU
UC 2   Engineering & Technology Center OU
UC 3   Classroom and Laboratory Building
UC 4   MSU College of Osteopathic Medicine

♿ Disabled Parking

LOCATION	SPACES
Lot 1	12
Lot 3	3
Lot 4	20
Lot 5B	20
Lot 5C	10
Lot 6	8
Lot 7A	12
Lot 8	12
Lot 9 (C-circle)	6
H-Bldg.	3
I-Bldg.	3
M-Bldg.	1
K-Bldg.	6
P-Bldg.	2
Lot 10	13
G-Bldg.	4

♿ Disabled Entrances

A   South
B   South
C   East & West
E   South
F   South
G   East & West
H   North & South
I   North
J   North Main
K   North & NorthEast South & SouthEast
L   North
M   North (Lobby)
N   East & West
P   North & South
R   East & West
UC1   SouthEast
UC2   Main
UC3   Main

← To Hayes Road

COLONY DR.

DALCOMA ROAD

← To I-75 15 Miles   HALL ROAD (M-59)   To I-94 6 Miles →

N

Wayne State University Macomb Education Center

PARKING LOT 8

PARKING LOT 4

PARKING LOT 6A

PARKING LOT 6

PARKING LOT 7A

STAFF PARKING PARKING LOT 10A

STAFF PARKING LOT 7

PARKING LOT 10

PARKING LOT 11

STAFF PARKING LOT 9

PARKING LOT 1

PARKING LOT 2

GARFIELD ROAD

PARKING LOT 3

UC 1

UC 2

UC 4   UC 3

STAFF PARKING LOT 5A

PARKING LOT 5B

PARKING LOT 5C

M connect
Wireless Available Campus-Wide

♿ Blue Light Emergency Phone

S   ATM

← COMMONS DRIVE

19 MILE ROAD

REVISED 071712

South Campus

14500 E. 12 Mile Road • Warren, Michigan 48088-3896 • 1.866.Macomb1

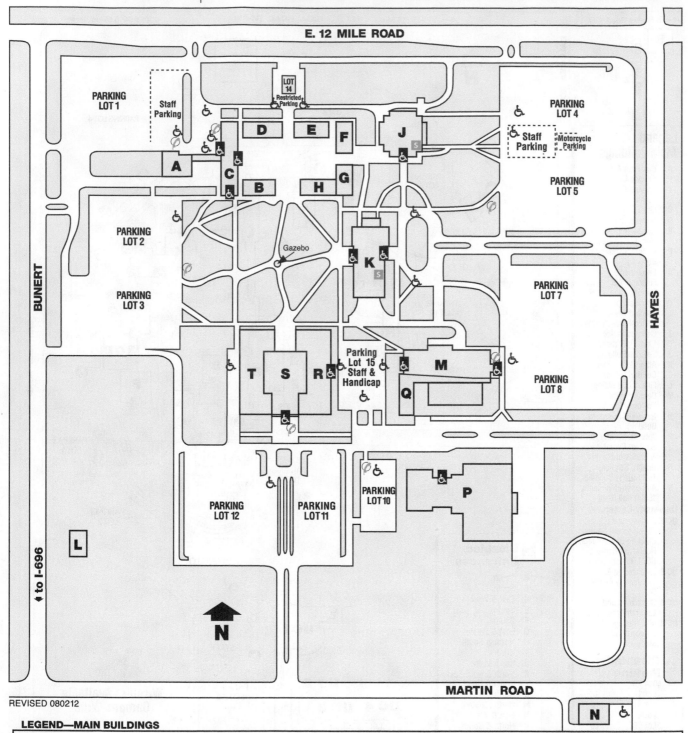

E. 12 MILE ROAD

PARKING LOT 1

Staff Parking

LOT 14 Restricted Parking

PARKING LOT 4

Staff Parking — Motorcycle Parking

PARKING LOT 5

D   E   F   J

A   C   B   H   G

BUNERT

PARKING LOT 2

Gazebo

PARKING LOT 3

K

PARKING LOT 7

T   S   R

Parking Lot 15 Staff & Handicap

M

Q

PARKING LOT 8

HAYES

PARKING LOT 12

PARKING LOT 11

PARKING LOT 10

P

L

← to I-696

N

MARTIN ROAD

N

REVISED 080212

LEGEND—MAIN BUILDINGS

A Boiler House
B Science Building
C Classroom Building
   Campus Police Dept.
D Administration Building
E Classroom Building
F Classroom Building
G Classroom, Student Services
H Classroom Counseling Building
J Max Thompson Learning
   Media Center
K John Lewis Student
   Community Center/Bookstore

L Bunert Conference Center
M Transportation and Energy
   Technology Building
N College Park Annex
   ■ Institutional Research
   ■ Marketing
   ■ Publications
P Sports & Expo Center
Q Boiler House
Robert E. Turner Complex
R Graphic Technical Building
S Walter E. Bradley Auditorium
T Mechanical Technical Building

♿ Disabled Parking

Location	Spaces
Lot 1A Staff	3
Lot 2	7
Lot 4	8
Lot 4 Staff	4
Lot 8	14
Lot 10	18
Lot 14	1
Lot 15 Staff	8
C-Bldg	19
K-Bldg	12

Location	Spaces
P-Bldg	18
T-Bldg	8
N-Bldg	6

🕿 Blue Light Emergency Phone

Ⓢ ATM

♿ Disabled Entrances

C	East, West & South
J	Main
K	East & West
M	East & West
R	East Middle
P	North
M-TEC	Main

 Wireless Available Campus-Wide

Student and Community Enrichment, designed to provide artistic, athletic, cultural, co-curricular and personal enrichment experiences, and related community development programs.

Economic and Workforce Development, designed to deliver customized learning experiences, specialized business support services, and continuing education offerings that rapidly respond to business and community needs.

Student Success Services, designed to improve academic achievement, persistence, and the attainment of educational goals.

Master Student Qualities*

Mastery means attaining a level of skill that goes beyond technique. For a master, work is effortless; struggle evaporates. The master carpenter is so familiar with her tools that they are part of her. To a master chef, utensils are old friends. Because these masters don't have to think about the details of the process, they bring more of themselves to their work.

Mastery can lead to flashy results: an incredible painting, for example, or a gem of a short story. In basketball, mastery might result in an unbelievable shot at the buzzer. For a musician, it might be the performance of a lifetime, the moment when everything comes together. You could describe the experience as "flow" or being "in the zone."

Often, the result of mastery is a sense of profound satisfaction, well-being, and timelessness. Distractions fade. Time stops. Work becomes play. After hours of patient practice, after setting clear goals and getting precise feedback, the master has learned to be fully in control.

At the same time, he lets go of control. Results happen without effort, struggle, or worry. Work seems self-propelled. The master is in control by being out of control. He lets go and allows the creative process to take over. That's why after a spectacular performance by an athlete or performer, observers often say, "He played full out—and made it look like he wasn't even trying."

Likewise, the master student is one who makes learning look easy. She works hard without seeming to make any effort. She's relaxed *and* alert, disciplined *and* spontaneous, focused *and* fun-loving.

You might say that those statements don't make sense. Actually, mastery does *not* make sense. It cannot be captured with words. It defies analysis. Mastery cannot be taught. It can only be learned and experienced.

By design, you are a learning machine. As an infant, you learned to walk. As a toddler, you learned to talk. By the time you reached age 5, you'd mastered many skills needed to thrive in the world. And you learned all these things without formal instruction, without lectures, without books, without conscious effort, and without fear.

Shortly after we start school, however, something happens to us. Somehow we start forgetting about the master student inside us. Even under the best teachers, we experience the discomfort that sometimes accompanies learning. We start avoiding situations that might lead to embarrassment. We turn away from experiences that could lead to mistakes. We accumulate a growing list of ideas to defend, a catalog of familiar experiences that discourages us from learning anything new. Slowly, we restrict our possibilities and potentials.

However, the story doesn't end there. You can open a new chapter in your life, starting today. You can rediscover the natural learner within you. Each chapter of this book is about a step you can take on this path.

Master students share certain qualities. These are attitudes and core values. Though they imply various strategies for learning, they ultimately go beyond what you do. Master student qualities are ways of *being* exceptional.

Following is a list of master student qualities. Remember that the list is not complete. It merely points in a direction.

As you read the following list, look to yourself. Put a check mark next to each quality that you've already demonstrated. Put another mark, say an exclamation point, next to each quality you want to actively work on possessing. This is not a test. It is simply a chance to celebrate what you've accomplished so far—and start thinking about what's possible for your future.

- **Inquisitive.** The master student is curious about everything. By posing questions, she can generate interest in the most mundane, humdrum situations. When she is bored during a biology lecture, she thinks to herself, "I always get bored when I listen to this Instructor. Why is that? Maybe it's because he reminds me of my boring Uncle Ralph, who always tells those endless fishing stories. He even looks like Uncle Ralph. Amazing! Boredom is certainly interesting." Then she asks herself, "What can I do to get value out of this lecture, even though it seems boring?" And she finds an answer.

- **Able to focus attention.** Watch a 2-year-old at play. Pay attention to his eyes. The wide-eyed look reveals an energy and a capacity for amazement that keep his attention absolutely focused in the here and now. The master student's focused attention has a childlike quality. The world, to a child, is always new. Because the master student can focus attention, to him the world is always new too.

- **Willing to change.** The unknown does not frighten the master student. In fact, she welcomes it—even the unknown in herself. We all have pictures of who we think we are, and these pictures can be useful. But they also can prevent learning and growth. The master student is open to changes in her environment and in herself.

- **Able to organize and sort.** The master student can take a large body of information and sift through it to discover relationships. He can play with information, organizing data by size, color, function, timeliness, and hundreds of other categories. He has the guts to set big goals—and the precision to plan carefully so that those goals can be achieved.

- **Competent.** Mastery of skills is important to the master student. When she learns mathematical formulas, she studies them until they become second nature. She practices until she knows them cold, then puts in a few extra minutes. She also is able to apply what she learns to new and different situations.

- **Joyful.** More often than not, the master student is seen with a smile on his face— sometimes a smile at nothing in particular other than amazement at the world and his experience of it.

- **Able to suspend judgment.** The master student has opinions and positions, and she is able to let go of them when appropriate. She realizes she is more than her thoughts. She can quiet her internal dialogue and listen to an opposing viewpoint. She doesn't let judgment get in the way of learning. Rather than approaching discussions with a "Prove it to me, and then I'll believe it" attitude, she asks herself, "What if this is true?" and explores possibilities.

- **Energetic.** Notice the student with a spring in his step, the one who is enthusiastic and involved in class. When he reads, he often sits on the very edge of his chair, and he plays with the same intensity. He is determined and persistent. He is a master student.

- **Well.** Health is important to the master student, though not necessarily in the sense of being free of illness. Rather, she values her body and treats it with respect. She tends to her emotional and spiritual health as well as her physical health.

- **Self-aware.** The master student is willing to evaluate himself and his behavior. He regularly tells the truth about his strengths and those aspects that could be improved.

- **Responsible.** There is a difference between responsibility and blame, and the master student knows it well. She is willing to take responsibility for everything in her life—even for events that most people would blame on others. For example, if a master student takes a required class that most students consider boring, she chooses to take responsibility for her interest level. She looks for ways to link the class to one of her goals. She sees the class as an opportunity to experiment with new study techniques that will enhance her performance in any course. She remembers that by choosing her thoughts and behaviors, she can create interesting classes, enjoyable relationships, fulfilling work experiences, or just about anything else she wants.

- **Willing to take risks.** The master student often takes on projects with no guarantee of success. He participates in class dialogues at the risk of looking foolish. He tackles difficult subjects in term papers. He welcomes the risk of a challenging course.

- **Willing to participate.** Don't look for the master student on the sidelines. She's in the game. She is a team player who can be counted on. She is engaged at school, at work, and with friends and family. She is willing to make a commitment and to follow through on it.

- **A generalist.** The master student is interested in everything around him. In the classroom, he is fully present. Outside the classroom, he actively seeks out ways to deepen his learning—through study groups, campus events, student organizations, and team-based projects. Through such experiences, he develops a broad base of knowledge in many fields that can apply to his specialties.

- **Willing to accept paradox.** The word *paradox* comes from two Greek words, *para* ("beyond") and *doxen* ("opinion"). A paradox is something that is beyond opinion or, more accurately, something that might seem contradictory or absurd yet might actually have meaning. For example, the master student can be committed to managing money and reaching her financial goals. At the same time, she can be totally detached from money, knowing that her real worth is independent of how much money she has. The master student recognizes the limitations of the mind and is at home with paradox. She can accept that ambiguity.

- **Courageous.** The master student admits his fear and fully experiences it. For example, he will approach a tough exam as an opportunity to explore feelings of anxiety and tension related to the pressure to perform. He does not deny fear; he embraces it. If he doesn't understand something or if he makes a mistake, he admits it. When he faces a challenge and bumps into his limits, he asks for help. And he's just as willing to give help as to receive it.

- **Self-directed.** Rewards or punishments provided by others do not motivate the master student. Her desire to learn comes from within, and her goals come from herself. She competes like a star athlete—not to defeat other people, but to push herself to the next level of excellence.

- **Spontaneous.** The master student is truly in the here and now. He is able to respond to the moment in fresh, surprising, and unplanned ways.

- **Relaxed about grades.** Grades make the master student neither depressed nor euphoric. She recognizes that sometimes grades are important. At the same time, grades are not the only reason she studies. She does not measure her worth as a human being by the grades she receives.

- **"Tech" savvy.** A master student defines "technology" as any tool that's used to achieve a human purpose. From this point of view, computers become tools for deeper learning, higher productivity, and greater success in the workplace. When faced with a task to accomplish, the master student chooses effectively from the latest options in hardware and software. He searches for information efficiently, thinks critically about data, and uses technology to create online communities. If he isn't familiar with a type of technology, he doesn't get overwhelmed. Instead, he embraces learning about the new technology and finding ways to use the technology to help him succeed at the given task. He also knows when to go "offline" and fully engage with his personal community of friends, family members, classmates, instructors, and coworkers.

- **Intuitive.** The master student has an inner sense that cannot be explained by logic alone. She trusts her "gut instincts" as well as her mind.

- **Creative.** Where others see dull details and trivia, the master student sees opportunities to create. He can gather pieces of knowledge from a wide range of subjects and put them together in new ways. The master student is creative in every aspect of his life.

- **Willing to be uncomfortable.** The master student does not place comfort first. When discomfort is necessary to reach a goal, she is willing to experience it. She can endure personal hardships and can look at unpleasant things with detachment.

- **Optimistic.** The master student sees setbacks as temporary and isolated, knowing that he can choose his response to any circumstance.

- **Willing to laugh.** The master student might laugh at any moment, and her sense of humor includes the ability to laugh at herself. While going to school is a big investment, with high stakes, you don't have to enroll in the deferred-fun program. A master student celebrates learning, and one of the best ways of doing that is to laugh now and then.

- **Hungry.** Human beings begin life with a natural appetite for knowledge. In some people, it soon gets dulled. The master student has tapped that hunger, and it gives him a desire to learn for the sake of learning.

- **Willing to work.** Once inspired, the master student is willing to follow through with sweat. She knows that genius and creativity are the result of persistence and work. When in high gear, the master student works with the intensity of a child at play.

- **Caring.** A master student cares about knowledge and has a passion for ideas. He also cares about people and appreciates learning from others. He collaborates on projects and thrives on teams. He flourishes in a community that values win-win outcomes, cooperation, and love.

The Master Student in You

The purpose of this exercise is to demonstrate to yourself that you truly are a master student. Start by remembering a time in your life when you learned something well or demonstrated mastery. This experience does not have to relate to school. It might be a time when you aced a test, played a flawless soccer game, created a work of art that won recognition, or burst forth with a blazing guitar solo. It might be a time when you spoke from your heart in a way that moved someone else. Or it might be a time when you listened deeply to another person who was in pain, comforted him, and connected with him at a level beyond words.

Describe the details of such an experience in your life. Include the place, time, and people involved. Describe what happened and how you felt about it.

When my friend was doing a photoshoot and asked me to do her freinds makeup. It was after school and she was taking photos of her friend. It made me feel happy because I want to be a makeup artist in life. Even though I'm good doing mine not others.

Now, review the article "Master student qualities" and take a look at the master student qualities that you checked off. These are the qualities that apply to you. Give a brief example of how you demonstrated at least one of those qualities.

Willing to take risks. I am very bad at doing others make up but I'm good at mine. I took a risk because I could have been awful.

Now think of other qualities of a master student—characteristics that were not mentioned in the article. List those qualities here, along with a one-sentence description of each.

Confidence: I was confident that I could do it.

Reasonable- I was reasonable to do this, it gave me practice.

Celebrate Mistakes*

The title of this article is no mistake. And, it is not a suggestion that you purposely set out to *make* mistakes. Rather, the goal is to shine a light on mistakes so that we can examine them and fix them. Mistakes that are hidden cannot be corrected and are often worth celebrating for the following reasons.

Mistakes are valuable feedback. Mistakes are part of the learning process. In fact, mistakes are often more interesting and more instructive than are successes.

Mistakes demonstrate that we're taking risks. People who play it safe make few mistakes. Making mistakes can be evidence that we're stretching to the limit of our abilities—growing, risking, and learning.

Celebrating mistakes gets them out into the open. When we celebrate a mistake, we remind ourselves that the person who made the mistake is not bad—just human. Everyone makes mistakes. And hiding mistakes takes a lot of energy that could be channeled into correcting errors. This is not a recommendation that you purposely set out to make mistakes. Mistakes are not an end in themselves. Rather, their value lies in what we learn from them. When we make a mistake, we can admit it and correct it.

Mistakes happen only when we're committed to making things work. Imagine a school where teachers usually come to class late. Residence halls are never cleaned, and scholarship checks are always late. The administration is in chronic debt, students seldom pay tuition on time, and no one cares. In this school, the word *mistake* would have little meaning. Mistakes become apparent only when people are committed to quality.

"F" Is for Feedback*

When some students get an "F" on an assignment, they interpret that letter as a message: "You are a failure." That interpretation is not accurate. Getting an "F" means only that you failed a test—not that you failed your life.

From now on, imagine that the letter "F" when used as a grade represents another word: *feedback.* An "F" is an indication that you didn't understand the material well enough. It's a message to do something differently before the next test or assignment. If you interpret "F" as *failure,* you don't get to change anything. But if you interpret "F" as *feedback,* you can change your thinking and behavior in ways that promote your success. You can choose a new learning strategy, or let go of an excuse about not having the time to study.

Getting prompt and meaningful feedback on your performance is a powerful strategy for learning *anything.* Tests are not the only source of feedback. Make a habit of asking for feedback from your instructors, advisors, classmates, coworkers, friends, family members, and anyone else who knows you. Just determine what you want to improve and ask, "How am I doing?"

*From Ellis, Annotated Instructor's Edition for Ellis' Becoming a Master Student, 14th, 14E. © 2013 Wadsworth, a part of Cengage Learning, Inc. Reproduced by permission. www.cengage.com/permission

Succeeding in School—At Any Age*

Being an adult learner puts you on a strong footing. With a rich store of life experiences, you can ask meaningful questions and make connections between course work and daily life. Any abilities that you've developed to work on teams, manage projects, meet deadlines, and solve problems are assets. Many instructors will especially enjoy working with you.

Following are some suggestions for adult learners who want to ease their transition to higher education. If you're a younger student, commuting student, or community college student, look for useful ideas here as well.

Acknowledge your concerns. Adult learners might express any of the following fears:

- *I'll be the oldest person in all my classes.*
- *I've been out of the classroom too long.*
- *I'm concerned about my math, reading, and writing skills.*
- *I'm worried about making tuition payments.*
- *How will I ever make the time to study, on top of everything else I'm doing?*
- *I won't be able to keep up with all the new technology.*

Those concerns are understandable. Now consider some facts:

- College classrooms are more diverse than ever before. According to the U.S. Census Bureau, 37 percent of students in the nation's colleges are age 25 and older. The majority of these older students attend school part-time.
- Adult learners can take advantage of evening classes, weekend classes, summer classes, distance learning, and online courses. Also look for classes in off-campus locations, closer to where you work or live.
- Colleges offer financial aid for students of all ages, including scholarships, grants, and low-interest loans.
- You can meet other students and make new friends by taking part in orientation programs. Look for programs that are targeted to adult learners.
- You are now enrolled in a course that can help boost your skills at math, reading, writing, note taking, time management, and other key skills.

Ease into it. If you're new to higher education, consider easing into it. You can choose to attend school part-time before making a full-time commitment. If you've taken college-level classes in the past, find out if any of those credits will transfer into your current program.

Plan ahead. By planning a week or month at a time, you get a bigger picture of your multiple roles as a student, an employee, and a family member. With that awareness, you can make conscious adjustments in the number of hours you devote to each domain of activity in your life. For example:

- If your responsibilities at work or home will be heavy in the near future, then register for fewer classes next term.
- Choose recreational activities carefully, focusing on those that relax you and recharge you the most.

- Don't load your schedule with classes that require unusually heavy amounts of reading or writing.

Delegate tasks. If you have children, delegate some of the household chores to them. Or start a meal co-op in your neighborhood. Cook dinner for yourself and someone else one night each week. In return, ask that person to furnish you with a meal on another night. A similar strategy can apply to child care and other household tasks.

Get to know other returning students. Introduce yourself to other adult learners. Being in the same classroom gives you an immediate bond. You can exchange work, home, or cell phone numbers and build a network of mutual support. Some students adopt a buddy system, pairing up with another student in each class to complete assignments and prepare for tests.

In addition, learn about student services and organizations. Many schools have a learning assistance center with workshops geared to adult learners. Sign up and attend. Meet people on campus. Personal connections are key to your success.

Find common ground with traditional students. Traditional and nontraditional students have many things in common. They seek to gain knowledge and skills for their chosen careers. They desire financial stability and personal fulfillment. And, like their older peers, many younger students are concerned about whether they have the skills to succeed in higher education.

Consider pooling resources with younger students. Share notes, edit one another's papers, and form study groups. Look for ways to build on one another's strengths. If you want help with using a computer for assignments, you might ask a younger student for help. In group projects and case studies, you can expand the discussion by sharing insights from your experiences.

Enlist your employer's support. Let your employer in on your educational plans. Point out how the skills you gain in the classroom will help you meet work objectives. Offer informal seminars at work to share what you're learning in school. You might find that your company reimburses its employees for some tuition costs or even grants time off to attend classes.

Get extra mileage out of your current tasks. Look for ways to relate your schoolwork to your job. For example, when you're assigned a research paper, choose a topic that relates to your current job tasks. Some schools even offer academic credit for work and life experience.

Review your subjects before you start classes. Say that you've registered for trigonometry and you haven't taken a math class since high school. Consider brushing up on the subject before classes begin. Also, talk with future instructors about ways to prepare for their classes.

"Publish" your schedule. After you plan your study and class sessions for the week, write up your schedule and post it in a place where others who live with you will see it. If you use an online calendar, print out copies to put in your school binder or on your refrigerator door, bathroom mirror, or kitchen cupboard.

Enroll family and friends in your success. School can cut into your social life. Prepare friends and family members by discussing this issue ahead of time.

You can also involve your spouse, partner, children, or close friends in your schooling. Offer to give them a tour of the campus, introduce them to your instructors and classmates, and encourage them to attend social events at school with you. Share ideas from this book, and from your other courses.

Take this process a step further, and ask the key people in your life for help. Share your reason for getting a degree, and talk about what your whole family has to gain from this change in your life. Ask them to think of ways that they can support your success in school and to commit to those actions. Make your own education a joint mission that benefits everyone.

Enroll Your Instructor in Your Success*

Faced with an instructor you don't like, you have two basic choices. One is to label the instructor a "dud." When you make this choice, you endure class and complain to other students. This choice gives your instructor sole responsibility for the quality of your education and the value of your tuition payments.

There is another option. Don't give away your power. Instead, take responsibility for your education.

The word *enroll* in this headline is a play on words. Usually we think of students as the people who enroll in school. Turn this idea on its head. See whether you can enlist instructors as partners in getting what you want from higher education.

Research the instructor. When deciding what classes to take, you can look for formal and informal sources of information about instructors. One source is the school catalog. Alumni magazines or newsletters or the school newspaper might run articles on teachers. At some schools, students post informal evaluations of instructors on Web sites. Also talk to students who have taken courses from the instructor you're researching.

Or introduce yourself to the instructor. Set up a visit during office hours, and ask about the course. This conversation can help you get the flavor of a class and the instructor's teaching style. Other clues to an instructor's style include the *types* of material he presents (ranging from theory or fact) and the *ways* that the material is presented (ranging from lectures to discussion and other in-class activity).

Show interest in class. Students give teachers moment-by-moment feedback in class. That feedback comes through posture, eye contact, responses to questions, and participation in class discussions. If you find a class boring, recreate the instructor through a massive display of interest. Ask lots of questions. Sit up straight, make eye contact, take detailed notes. Your enthusiasm might enliven your instructor. If not, you are still creating a more enjoyable class for yourself.

Release judgments. Maybe your instructor reminds you of someone you don't like—your annoying Aunt Edna or a rude store clerk. Your attitudes are in your own head and beyond the instructor's control. Likewise, an instructor's beliefs about politics, religion, or feminism are not related to teaching ability. Being aware of such things can help you let go of negative judgments.

Instructors are a lot like you. They have opinions about politics, sports, and music. They worry about their health, finances, and career path. They're sometimes in a good mood and sometimes sad or angry. What distinguishes them is a lifelong passion for the subject that they teach.

Get to know the instructor. Meet with your instructor during office hours. Teachers who seem boring in class can be fascinating in person. Prepare to notice your pictures and let them go. An instructor that someone told you to avoid might become one of your favorite teachers. You might hear conflicting reports about teachers from other students. The same instructor could be described by two different students as a riveting speaker and as completely lacking in charisma. Decide for yourself what descriptions are accurate.

Students who do well in higher education often get to know at least one instructor outside of class. In some cases, these instructors become mentors and informal advisors.

Open up to diversity. Sometimes students can create their instructors by letting go of pictures about different races and ethnic groups. According to one picture, a Hispanic person cannot teach English literature. According to other pictures, a white teacher cannot have anything valid to say about African music, and a teacher in a wheelchair cannot command the attention of a hundred people in a lecture hall. All of those pictures can clash with reality. Releasing them can open up new opportunities for understanding and appreciation.

Separate liking from learning. You don't have to like an instructor to learn from her. See whether you can focus on content instead of form. *Form* is the way something is organized or presented. If you are irritated at the sound of an instructor's voice, you're focusing on form. When you put aside your concern about her voice and turn your attention to the points she's making, you're focusing on *content*.

Seek alternatives. You might feel more comfortable with another teacher's style or method of organizing course materials. Consider changing teachers, asking another teacher for help outside class, or attending an additional section taught by a different instructor.

If you cannot change instructors, then take charge of your learning. Actively use the suggestions in this article. You can also learn from other students, courses, tutors, study groups, books, and DVDs. Be a master student, no matter who teaches your classes. Your education is your own creation.

Avoid excuses. Instructors know them all. Most teachers can see a snow job coming before the first flake hits the ground. Accept responsibility for your own mistakes, and avoid thinking that you can fool the teacher.

Submit professional work. Prepare papers and projects as if you were submitting them to an employer. Imagine that your work will determine whether you get a promotion and raise. Instructors often grade hundreds of papers during a term. Your neat, orderly, well-organized paper can stand out and lift a teacher's spirits.

Accept criticism. Learn from your teachers' comments about your work. It is a teacher's job to give feedback. Don't take it personally.

Use course evaluations. In many classes, you'll have an opportunity to evaluate the instructor. Respond honestly. Write about the aspects of the class that did not work well for you. Offer specific ideas for improvement. Also note what *did* work well.

Communicate effectively by phone and e-mail. Ask your instructors how they prefer to be contacted. If they take phone calls, leave a voice mail message that includes your first and last name, course name, section, and phone number.

If your instructor encourages contact via e-mail, then craft your messages with care. Start by including your name, course title, and section number in the subject line. Keep the body of your message brief and get to the point immediately.

Remember that the recipient of online communication is a human being whose culture, language, and humor may have different points of reference from your own.

Write clearly, and keep the tone positive. Do not type in FULL CAPS, which is equivalent to shouting.

If there's a problem to solve, focus on solutions rather than blame. For example, avoid: "Why do you grade so unfairly?" Instead, write, "I'd like to understand your criteria for grading our assignments so that I can raise my scores."

Also proofread your message carefully and fix any errors. Write with full words and complete sentences. Avoid the abbreviations that you might use in a text message.

Finally, remember that instructors are busy people with personal lives. Don't expect them to be online at the same time as you.

Take further steps, if appropriate. Sometimes severe conflict develops between students and instructors. In such cases, you might decide to file a complaint or ask for help from an administrator.

Be prepared to document your case in writing. Describe specific actions that created problems. Stick to the facts—events that other class members can verify. Your school has grievance procedures to use in these cases. Use them. You are a consumer of education and have a right to fair treatment.

Meeting with Your Instructor*

Meeting with an instructor outside class can save hours of study time and help boost your grade. Instead of trying to resolve a conflict with an instructor in the few minutes before or after class, schedule a time during office hours. During this meeting, state your concerns in a respectful way. Then focus on finding solutions. To get the most from these meetings, consider doing the following:

- Schedule a meeting time during the instructor's office hours. These are often listed in the course syllabus and on the instructor's office door.
- If you need to cancel or reschedule an appointment, let your instructor know well in advance.
- During the meeting, relax. This activity is not graded.
- Come prepared with a list of questions and any materials you'll need. During the meeting, take notes on the instructor's suggestions.
- Show the instructor your class notes to see whether you're capturing essential material.
- Get feedback on outlines that you've created for papers.
- Go over items you missed on exams.
- Get overall feedback on your progress.
- Ask about ways to prepare for upcoming exams.
- If the course is in a subject area that interests you, ask about the possibilities of declaring a major in that area and the possible careers associated with that major.
- Avoid questions that might offend your instructor—for example, "I missed class on Monday. Did we do anything important?"
- Ask whether your instructor is willing to answer occasional short questions via e-mail or a phone call.
- When the meeting is over, thank your instructor for making time for you.
- Remember that meeting during office hours is something that you do in addition to attending class regularly.

*From Ellis, Annotated Instructor's Edition for Ellis' Becoming a Master Student, 14th, 14E. © 2013 Wadsworth, a part of Cengage Learning, Inc. Reproduced by permission. www.cengage.com/permission

Introduction

We applaud your decision to continue your education. You've made it to college, also known as "higher education," where you'll be learning and thinking at a higher level than you did in high school and work situations. You're about to begin a new and exciting journey in your life, joining approximately 12 million students who are now enrolled at more than 1,000 community colleges in the United States today. America's community college system embodies the nation's ideal of equal educational opportunity for all people, regardless of their age, gender, race, ethnicity, prior educational history, family history, or family income. Community colleges in the United States represent the most diverse system of college education in the world. (See Snapshot Summary 1.1 for a list of community college students in America today.)

It's probably safe to say that after your college experience, you'll never again be a member of an organization or community with as many resources and services that are intentionally designed to promote your learning, development, and success. Your time in college has the potential to be the most enriching experience of your life. If you capitalize on the numerous resources available to you and use effective college-going strategies (such as those suggested in this book), you can create an experience that will transform your life.

Snapshot Summary

1.1 Student Diversity in America's Community Colleges

- There are 13 million students currently enrolled in approximately 1,150 community colleges in the United States; they account for almost half of all first-year college students in America today.
- More than 630,000 community college students will earn an associate degree this year, and more than 425,000 will earn a certificate.
- Most first-year community college students are employed either part or full time and attend college part time.
- The average age of the American community college student is 28.
- Almost 42 percent of all community college students are the first in their family to attend college.
- More than 37 percent of community college students are members of minority racial or ethnic groups.

- Close to 6 percent of international students attend America's community colleges.

Source: American Association of Community Colleges (2012).

There are two other groups of students that are growing in number and adding to the student diversity found in America's community colleges:

- Veterans returning from the war in the Middle East who have been afforded the opportunity to attend college with the help of generous financial aid provided by a GI Bill passed in 2009.
- Displaced workers over the age of 20 who have lost full-time jobs due to job layoffs and company closings triggered by the current economic recession.

Ready for take off,
On my adventure today,
As I take a seat in my chair
And clear the way.
Eager people around,
With destinations to go,
As a woman at the front says,
"Please find a seat in any
    row."
Some people are anxious,
Waiting to take flight,
To soar above the rest
With aspirations in sight
Our first day of college,
A chance to start anew,
To find out who we are,
And learn what is true.

—"Waiting to Take Flight," a poem by
Kimberly Castaneda, first-year student

Your previous enrollment in school was required; however, your decision to continue your education in college is entirely your choice. You have made a choice that will improve the quality of your life for the remainder of your life. (See **Snapshot Summary 1.1** for a list of the multiple lifetime benefits of a college education and college degree.)

Think About It ——————————— *Journal Entry* 1.1

1. How did you feel on your first day of college?

My first day of college made me think how can I get through this.

2. Why did you feel this way?

Because it was more different than highschool. I had more help.

Snapshot Summary

1.2 Why College Is Worth It: The Economic and Personal Benefits of a College Education

Less than 30 percent of Americans have earned a four-year college degree (U.S. Census Bureau). When individuals who attend college are compared with people from similar social and economic backgrounds who did not continue their education beyond high school, research reveals that college is well worth the investment. College graduates experience multiple benefits, such as those summarized in the following list:

1. **Career Benefits**
   - Security and stability—lower rates of unemployment
   - Versatility and mobility—more flexibility to move out of a position and into other positions
   - Advancement—more opportunity to move up to higher professional positions
   - Interest—more likely to find their work stimulating and challenging

- Autonomy—greater independence and opportunity to be their own boss
- Satisfaction—more enjoyment of their work and the feeling that it allows them to use their special talents
- Prestige—higher-status positions (i.e., careers that are more socially desirable and respected)

"A bachelor's degree continues to be a primary vehicle of which one gains an advantaged socioeconomic position in American society."

—Ernest Pascarella and Patrick Terenzini, *How College Affects Students*

2. **Economic Advantages**
   - Make better consumer choices and decisions
   - Make wiser long-term investments
   - Receive greater pension benefits
   - Earn higher income

The gap between the earnings of high school graduates and those of college graduates is growing. Individuals with a bachelor's (or baccalaureate) degree now earn an average annual salary of about $50,000 per year, which is 40 percent higher than that of high school graduates, whose average salary is less than $30,000 per year. When these differences are calculated over a lifetime, families headed by people with a bachelor's degree take in about $1.6 million more than families headed by people with a high school diploma.

"I am coming from a household that does not have a high standard of living—I want to do better than just getting by."

—First-year student (Franklin, 2002)

"If you think education is expensive, try ignorance."

—Derek Bok, former president of Harvard University

3. **Advanced Intellectual Skills**
   * Greater knowledge
   * More effective problem-solving skills
   * Better ability to deal with complex and ambiguous (uncertain) problems
   * Greater openness to new ideas
   * More advanced levels of moral reasoning
   * Clearer sense of self-identity and greater awareness and knowledge of personal talents, interests, values, and needs
   * Greater likelihood to continue learning throughout life

4. **Better Physical Health**
   * Better health insurance—more comprehensive coverage and greater likelihood of being covered
   * Better dietary habits
   * More regular exercise
   * Lower rates of obesity
   * Longer and healthier life

5. **Social Benefits**
   * Higher social self-confidence
   * Better understanding and more effective communication with others
   * Greater popularity
   * More effective leadership skills
   * Greater marital satisfaction

Student
Perspective

"I noticed before when I wasn't going to college, they [my family] didn't look at me as highly as a person. But now since I have started college, everybody is lifting me up and saying how proud they [are] of me."

—First-year student (Franklin, 2002)

6. **Emotional Benefits**
   * Lower levels of anxiety
   * Higher levels of self-esteem
   * Greater sense of self-efficacy and belief that they have more influence and control over their lives
   * Higher levels of psychological well-being
   * Higher levels of personal happiness

Student
Perspective

"My 3-month-old boy is very important to me, and it is important that I graduate from college so my son, as well as I, live a better life."

—First-year student responding to the question "What is most important to you?"

7. **Effective Citizenship**
   * Greater interest in national issues, both social and political
   * Greater knowledge of current affairs
   * Higher voting participation rates
   * Higher rates of participation in civic affairs and community service

8. **Higher Quality of Life for Their Children**
   * Less likelihood of smoking during pregnancy
   * Better health care for their children
   * More time spent with their children
   * More likely to involve their children in educational activities that stimulate their mental development
   * More likely to save money for their children to go to college
   * More likely that their children will graduate from college
   * More likely that their children will attain high-status and higher-paying careers

Student
Perspective

"Being a first-generation college student, seeing how hard my parents worked these past 18 years to give all that they can to get me to where I am now, I feel I cannot let them down. It is my responsibility to succeed in school and life and to take care of them in their old age."

—First-year college student (Nunez, 2005)

Sources: Astin (1993); Bowen (1977, 1997); College Board (2006); Dee (2004); Feldman & Newcomb (1969/1994); Pascarella & Terenzini (1991, 2005); Tomasho (2009); U.S. Census Bureau (2008).

Think About It ─────────────── *Journal Entry* **1.2**

1. Why have you decided to attend college?

    My dad made me go to community college first then beauty school.

2. Why are you are attending the college you're enrolled in now?

    Because University was to much money and I wouldant survive

The Importance of the First Year of College

Your movement into higher education represents an important life transition. Somewhat like an immigrant moving to a new country, you're moving into a new culture with different expectations, regulations, customs, and language (Chaskes, 1996). (See the Glossary and Learning the Language of Higher Education: A Dictionary of College Vocabulary at the end of this book for translations of the new language that is used in the college culture.)

The first year of college is undoubtedly the most important year of the college experience because it's a stage of *transition*. During the first year of college, students report the most change, the most learning, and the most development (Doyle, Edison, & Pascarella, 1998; Flowers, Osterlind, Pascarella, & Pierson, 2001; Light, 2001). Other research suggests that the academic habits students establish in their first year of college are likely to persist throughout their remaining years of college (Schilling, 2001). When graduating seniors look back at their college experience, many of them say that the first year was the time of greatest change and the time during which they made the most significant improvements in their approach to learning. Here is how one senior put it during a personal interview (Chickering & Schlossberg, 1998, p. 47):

Interviewer: What have you learned about your approach to learning [in college]?

Student: I had to learn how to study. I got to the university and there was no structure. No one checked my homework. No one took attendance to make sure I was in class. No one told me I had to do something. There were no quizzes on the readings. I did not work well with this lack of structure. It took my first year and a half to learn to deal with it. But I had to teach myself to manage my time. I had to teach myself how to study. I had to teach myself how to learn in a different environment.

In many ways, the first-year experience in college is similar to surfing or downhill skiing; it can be filled with many exciting thrills, but there's also a risk of taking some dangerous spills. The first year is also the stage of the college experience during which students experience the most stress, the most academic difficulties, and the highest withdrawal rate (American College Testing, 2009; Bartlett, 2002; Sax, Bryant, & Gilmartin, 2004). The goal of surfing and downhill skiing is to experience the thrills, avoid the spills, and finish the run while you're still standing. The same is true for the first year of college; studies show that if you can complete your first-year experience in good standing, your chances for successfully completing college improve dramatically (American College Testing, 2009).

In a nutshell, your college success will depend on taking advantage of what your college does to help you and what you do to help yourself. You'll find that the research cited and the advice provided in this book point to one major conclusion: Success in college depends on *you*—you make it happen by what you do and how well you capitalize on resources available to you.

After reviewing 40 years of research on how college affects students, two distinguished researchers (Pascarella & Terenzini, 2005, p. 602) concluded the following:

> *The impact of college is largely determined by individual effort and involvement in the academic, interpersonal, and extracurricular [cocurricular] offerings on a campus. Students are not passive recipients of institutional efforts to "educate" or "change" them, but rather bear major responsibility for any gains they derive from their postsecondary [college] experience.*

> "What students do during college counts more than who they are or where they go to college."
>
> —George Kuh et al., *Student Success in College* (2005)

Compared to your previous schooling, college will provide you with a broader range of courses, more resources to capitalize on, more freedom of choice, and more decision-making opportunities. Your own college experience will differ from that of any other college student because you have the freedom to actively shape or create it in a way that is uniquely your own. Don't let college happen *to* you; make it happen *for* you—take charge of your college experience and take advantage of the college resources that are at your command.

> "Some people make things happen, while others watch things happen or wonder what has happened."
>
> —Author unknown

Think About It — Journal Entry 1.3

To succeed in college, what do you think you'll have to do differently from what you've done in the past?

Study at the library, make note cards.
Study at home, actually try.

Importance of a Student Success Course (a.k.a. First-Year Experience Course)

If you're reading this book, you are already beginning to take charge of your college experience because you are probably enrolled in a course that's designed to promote your college success. Research strongly indicates that new students who participate in student success courses (such as the one that's using this text) are more likely to stay in college, complete their degrees, and achieve higher grades. These positive effects have been found for:

- all types of students (underprepared and well prepared, minority and majority, residential and commuter, male and female);
- students at all types of colleges (two- and four-year, public and private);
- students attending colleges of different sizes (small, midsized, and large); and
- students attending colleges in different locations (urban, suburban, and rural).

Sources: Barefoot, Warnock, Dickinson, Richardson, & Roberts (1998); Boudreau & Kromrey (1994); Cuseo & Barefoot (1996); Fidler & Godwin (1994); Glass & Garrett (1995); Grunder & Hellmich (1996); Hunter & Linder (2005); Porter & Swing (2006); Shanley & Witten (1990); Sidle & McReynolds (1999); Starke, Harth, & Sirianni (2001); Thomson (1998); Tobolowski (2005).

There has been more carefully conducted research on student success and college success courses, and more evidence supporting their effectiveness for promoting success, than for any other type of course in the college curriculum. You're fortunate to be enrolled in this course, so give it your best effort and take full advantage of what it has to offer. If you do, you'll be taking an important first step toward thriving in community college and beyond.

Enjoy the trip!

Chapter 1 Reflection

After reading the Introduction, how do you feel this course can benefit you?

I can talk to my instructor and help my self become a better student in and outside of school.

List and explain three things you hope to learn or accomplish as a result of successfully completing this course.

1. Writing Notes. What is important and what is not.

2. Study techiques. What will stick in your head.

3. Organization. Im horrible with this

Welcome to Macomb Community College!

My name is Don Hutchison, and I am the Associate Dean of Engineering Technology. I oversee many of the exciting programs related to the STEM (Science, Technology, Engineering, and Mathematics) fields.

My major responsibility is to ensure that our students are well prepared to start, or enhance their careers, by training them on some of the most technologically advanced equipment and software available anywhere. The fields of study include many popular programs such as Robotics, Computer-Aided Design, Computer Graphics, Renewable Energy, and Mechatronics. It's great to play such an important role in such exciting programs!

The strange thing is, as a young man, I never envisioned myself going to college at all, much less working for one of the best institutions in the country. In fact, for me, the thought of graduating from college was about as likely as having a conversation with the President of the United States over lunch. Unfortunately, statistics for those in my demographic did not trend in my favor. Don't misunderstand me, I wanted what higher education offered, I just didn't think I'd ever be able to obtain it. Honestly, I had little hope that my academic skills would ever take me where I wanted to be. Regrettably, this mindset is common for those who, like me, were raised in an urban environment where college degrees are not the norm.

Clearly, I had a poor educational foundation. But, what I lacked in educational prowess, I made up for in hard work, tenacity, and discipline (by the grace of God). I also had the support of people who believed in me before I believed in myself.

Is college tough at times? Yes. Can it be intimidating? Yes. Is it worth the effort? A thousand times, YES! What I've found is that a few, small successes early on provide a good deal of motivation for the future. The first year is the hardest. Statistics show that the first year of college is also the most critical. If you can get through the initial growing pains and survive, you'll have a much better chance of finishing. I encourage you to look for the little victories and build on them. You'll be surprised what you can accomplish if you keep your focus. For me, with each successive class, I began to recognize more and more that I wasn't as far behind my classmates as I thought. In fact, in some areas, I excelled!

I remember at the end of every college semester, as I walked out of my last final exam, I would raise my hands high above my head in victory and shout "YES!" It was important for me to celebrate the fact that I had overcome my fears and took another step closer to my goal. Eventually, I finished a bachelor's degree, and, ultimately, a master's degree; all to the chagrin of my biggest doubter—me.

I look forward to seeing you celebrate on your way across the stage on graduation day!

I am Don Hutchison and I am Macomb.

Courtesy of Don Hutchison

28

Four Key Components of CSSK-1200

This chapter consists of the four key components of the CSSK-1200 course. These four big ideas are campus explorations, technology, investigation, and reading to learn. This chapter is meant to be used throughout the course. Each week you will be introduced to a technology. Your teacher will model the assignment. After the introduction, the technology activity will be completed for the assignment.

Also, included in this chapter are the directions to completing the final assessment piece of this course: the Macomb Binder. This is where you will keep evidence of each completed assignment.

CSSK Macomb Binder

Organization is important to your success at Macomb Community College. Teachers expect their students to come prepared for class with materials that will help them be successful. In CSSK-1200, we will use some tools that will be useful for learning how to organize class materials.

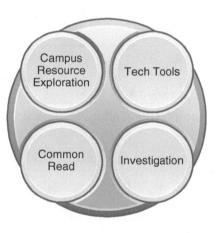

You will be responsible for keeping a Macomb Binder organized throughout the semester. The Macomb Binder will include a schedule of our Campus Explorations along with the contact information for Campus Exploration locations. This way, if you are late for class and you show up to the classroom after the class has already left, you will be able to look in your binder to find the location on campus.

In CSSK-1200 we will keep Student Success calendars in the Macomb Binders. This calendar is provided by the Macomb Learning Center. It will help you manage your time throughout this year at Macomb. Your teacher will expect you to keep this calendar updated at all times with coursework obligations for all of your classes (test dates, homework, and project due dates), study hours, employment, and family obligations. In this calendar you will also find the dates for Student Success Seminars at Macomb. These seminars will give you an opportunity to learn strategies such as Stress Management, Memory Skills, and Critical Thinking Skills. These events are free.

Handouts from each Campus Exploration will also be located in your Macomb Binder. During our Campus Explorations we will learn a lot of information about how to be successful with campus resources. The speakers often give out valuable handouts in their presentations. You will want to be able to locate these services and learning resources throughout your career at Macomb.

To create your Macomb Binder you will first need a way to divide the sections. Your instructor will give you dividers for this class, which will be labeled with each binder section. You can purchase dividers for other class binders in the bookstore.

1. **Class Materials.** CSSK course syllabus and materials.
2. **Calendar.** Student Success Calendar provided by the Learning Center.
3. **Explorations.** Campus Explorations materials and campus maps.
4. **Tests.** LASSI test results and assessments.
5. **Technology.** Evidence of Technology Workshop activities.
6. **Notes and Journals.** Book reflection log and book group responses.
7. **Investigations.** Investigation project requirements, brainstorming ideas for topics of interest, project plans, and information.
8. **My Future.** Goals, career plan, and degree requirements, coursework plan from counseling or academic advising, and transfer college information.

The Macomb Binder Table of Contents will list the sections in your binder as well as a short description of each. An Information section is included, which you should fill out with your personal information as well as class information. This can help you organize your class information and help others locate you if you lose your binder.

Information

Student Name: Amanda Noble	**E-mail:** amandanobleCSSK@gmail.com
School: Macomb community college	**Phone:** 586-703-8736
Course Name: College Success Skills	**Section Number:** 1200 - 1414
Time: 6:00 Pm ~ 8:55 Pm	**Building and Room:** B 107
Instructor: Dr. Jeffers	**Instructor Phone:** 586-286-2187
Instructor E-mail: Jeffers@macomb.edu	**Instructor Office Location:** Center G-110
School Web Address: http://www.macomb.edu	**Semester:** 1

Throughout the semester we will work on staying organized. Your teacher and various campus departments are here to help you manage your time and make sure you have access to materials and services that will help you achieve success at Macomb.

Campus Explorations

It is important that students explore different resources at Macomb Community College. Throughout the semester classes will go on explorations around campus. These resources can help you be a successful student. Additional information about campus resources is located in your "New Student Orientation Guide."

Exploration 1: Bookstore

Pre Questions

1. What do you expect the bookstore to sell other than books? *Food, Clothing, Scantions, Paper, drinks and medicine*

2. What reasons would you have to go to the bookstore at Macomb?
   To get supplys, scantrons, pencils, snacks, etc .

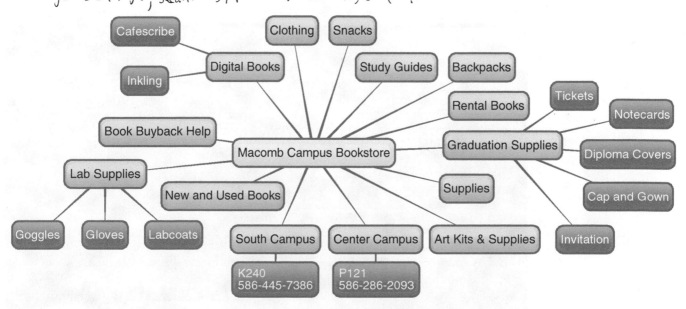

Post Questions

Books that are not there. (handwritten)

1. Search the Online Bookstore at macomb.edu. What differences did you find between what you can order online and what we saw at the bookstore?

Course Section (handwritten)

8am – 9pm (handwritten)

2. What do you use to find books for a specific course?

So you can take them back or sell them. (handwritten)

3. What are the hours for the bookstore?

4. Why should you keep your receipts from the bookstore?

Renting, used, or new. Or financial aid. (handwritten)

5. What are the different options for purchasing your books and course materials?

Exploration 2: Learning Center

Pre Questions

1. Have you ever been to the Learning Center? *Yes* (handwritten)

2. What do you expect the Learning Center will be like? *Very open to teaching* (handwritten)

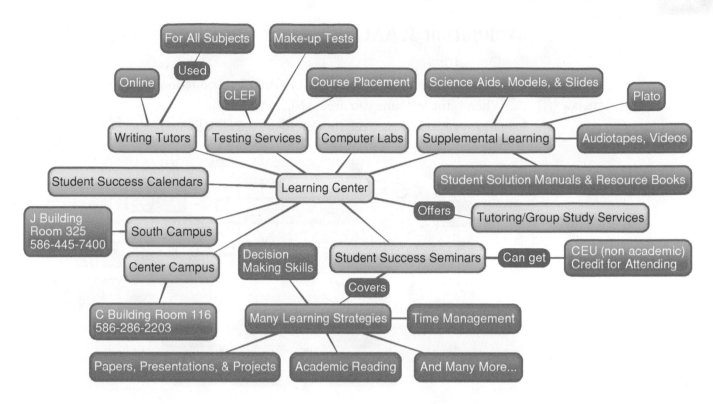

Post Questions

1. What was the most valuable resource in the Learning Center? *The tutors/writing center*
2. Was there anything that surprised you at the Learning Center? *Lots of people so*
3. Where do you go for help in the Learning Center? *Writing center*
4. What areas of the Learning Center do you think you will use most this semester? *Writing center*
5. Where can you find the tutoring schedule? *online*
6. When do you need a Macomb ID or picture ID at the Learning Center? *None.*

Exploration 3: ANGEL/Canvas

Pre Questions

Yes

1. Have you completed the ANGEL or Canvas Introduction?

Today 9/12

2. When is the last time you used ANGEL or Canvas?

Yes.

3. Do any of your classes require you to use ANGEL this semester?

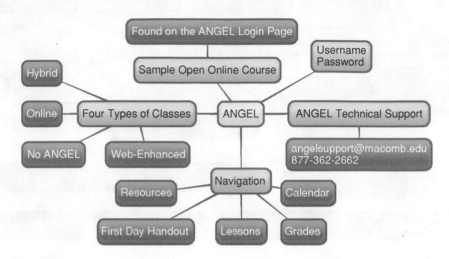

Post Questions

Angel is more clustered
Academic advising, calendar
lessons   Learning center

1. How have your thoughts about ANGEL or Canvas changed after the Exploration?
2. What tabs did you find in ANGEL or Canvas?
3. What was the most interesting thing you found under Student Resources?
4. What was a challenge with ANGEL or Canvas?

I liked using blackboard then switching to angel/canvas got me mad.

Exploration 4 : Reading and Writing Studio

Pre Questions

1. What kind of help do you think you generally need with your writing?
2. Can you go to the Reading and Writing Studio without anything written? *Everything about it*
   Do you feel confident about your reading and writing?

Yes and yes

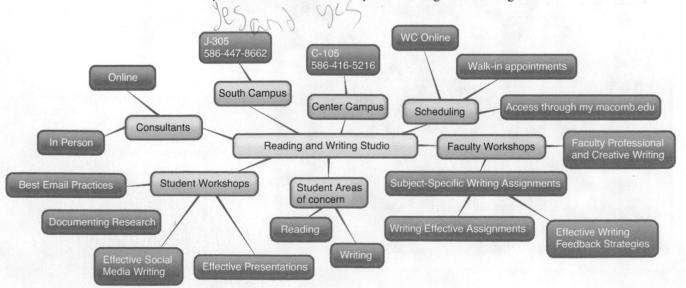

Post Questions

1. What services does the Reading and Writing Studio provide? *help with papers, grammar, reading*
2. How can you make an appointment at the Studio? *walk in or online*
3. How can you cancel an appointment at the Studio? *call them or online*
4. At what point in the writing process is it best to go to the Reading and Writing Studio? *anytime*
5. What stood out to you as surprising or interesting about the Reading and Writing Studio? *The help*
6. What can you expect during a meeting with a consultant? *Help. and getting work done.*

Exploration 5: Student Life and Leadership

Pre Questions

1. What services do you think Student Life and Leadership will offer? *Organizations*
2. Do you have your Macomb One Card? *yes*
3. Where do you go to unwind from studying? *Cafeteria*
4. In the past, what community service activities have you participated in? *Optimist Club*

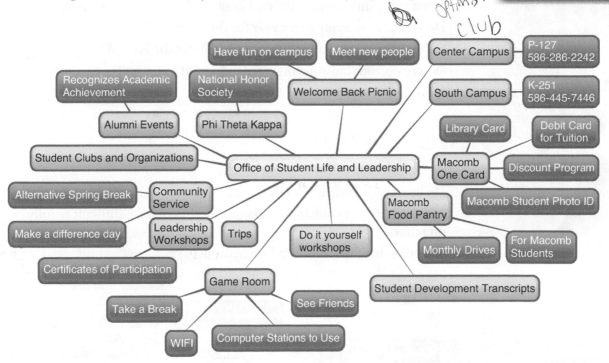

Post Questions

1. What is offered at the Office of Student Life and Leadership? *clubs, trips, etc.*
2. How does the Office of Student Life and Leadership develop a leader? *They pick you*
3. How will you get involved at Macomb? *join clubs*
4. What other things would you like the Office of Student Life and Leadership to offer? *More field trips*

Exploration 6: Financial Aid

Pre Questions

1. Have you been to the FAFSA.gov website to apply for federal financial aid? *Yes*
2. Do you have a budget? *Yes*
3. Do you track your borrowing? *No*

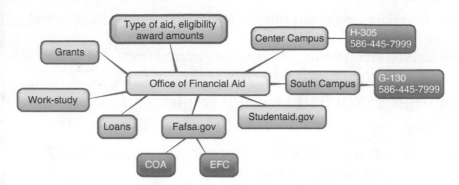

© Shutterstock, Inc.

Post Questions

1. What is the difference between a grant and a loan? *grant - you dont pay back / loan - pays back*
2. Do you have to apply every year for financial aid?
3. Do you need your parents' tax info to fill out the FAFSA? *yes new faster*
4. Where do you find your financial aid award letter on the Macomb website?
5. How do you lose financial aid? *Not on time or loaned enough*

Exploration 7: SOS

Pre Questions

1. Do you know anyone who may need help with Public Benefit Assistance? *No*
2. Are there barriers outside the classroom that make it difficult to fully focus on school? *Yes,*
3. How can these barriers be addressed? *Maybe if I go to the root of the problem and deal with it.*

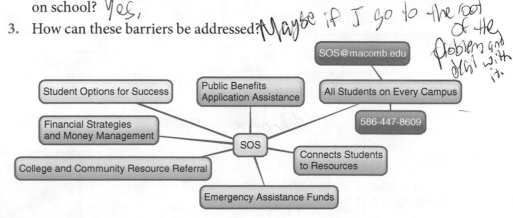

Post Questions

1. What does SOS stand for? *Students options for success*
2. How do you think these services could help someone stay in college?
3. What is the best way to contact SOS? *visit/call/email*
4. What advice would you give a friend who was nervous about getting help from SOS? *Dont be embarresed. Natural problem*

Exploration 8: Library

Pre Questions

1. What would you expect to find in the library? *Books, Magazines, help, Students, computers*
2. Have you used the electronic resources in the library before? *yes*

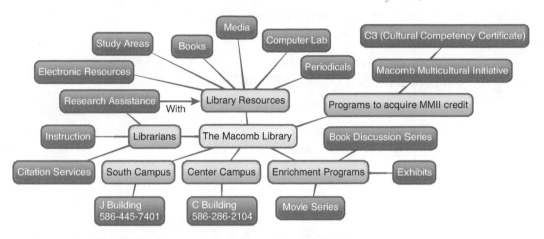

Post Questions

1. Where are the journals? *up stairs*
2. What are Citation Services? *over due feis*
3. What is the mission of the Macomb Library? *To help you*
4. How do the library events support the mission? *to cater your needs*

© Shutterstock, Inc.

Exploration 9: Counseling and Academic Advising Services

Pre Questions

1. Have you been to the Counseling and Advising Center? *Yes*
2. Have you thought about class selection for next semester? *No*
3. Have you selected a program plan? *No*

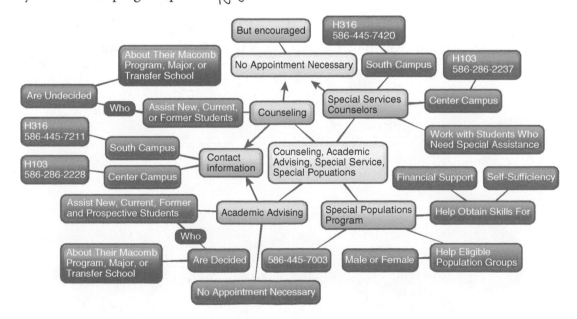

Post Questions

1. What services are offered at the Counseling and Academic Advising Center? *Special services*

2. What time do you think would be best to visit the Counseling and Academic Advising Center? *early before rush*

3. If you have not visited the Counseling and Academic Advising Center since orientation, what has kept you from going? *Time*

© Shutterstock, Inc.

Exploration 10: Career Services

Pre Questions

1. What types of career exploration have you done in the past? *Job finds*

2. Do you have a job? *No*

3. What are your expectations from the Career Services visit? *What this was*

Post Questions

1. What are your plans after Macomb Community College? *Beauty school*

2. How do you think Career Services will help you in the future? *Help me find something I Like*

Personal Technology Reflection

Macomb teachers know that technology changes the dynamic of the classroom and helps engage students in active learning situations. Macomb offers a number of technology courses, certifications, and degree programs for students to take as part of course selection. Students acquire skills while using technology to enhance projects, and to research and create assignments in other courses as well. CSSK-1200 is designed to help students explore using some beginning online tools, and learn to locate and share helpful learning resources. As we begin this course, we will reflect on some of our experiences while working with technology.

1. How do you feel about technology?

   I'm ok with it.

2. What success have you had with technology?

   I have had 90% success with it.

3. Explain any difficulties you have had with technology in the past.

   Either things not working, breaking, or not know how to use them.

4. How have you responded to technology issues in the past?

   Try to figure it out or get help.

5. What do you think the hardest technological task will be in college?

   How to start something.

6. How will you cope if you are unsure of the technology you are using in this course?

   Make sure of what I am doing.

7. What different technologies are available for students today?

   Computer, phone, TV.

USE TECHNOLOGY TO . . .

Communicate with instructors and classmates.

Technology: Gmail: www.gmail.com

Terms:

E-mail: Electronic Mail. A tool you can use to send messages. It is also the name for a message sent using an e-mail provider.

E-mail Address: The name that makes sure an e-mail reaches the right user.

Inbox: The term for the location that collects incoming e-mails. This is used to sort incoming e-mails from e-mails you have sent out.

Compose: To make or form the basis of. This is the term that is usually used when writing e-mails.

Mnemonic Device: A memory technique that uses a series of letters to stand for a phrase that you want to remember. This can also help you remember a series of letters that stand for a phrase. An example of this is ROY G. BIV, which stands for the colors of the rainbow.

reCaptcha: A tool that websites use to make sure the user is not a computer program. It is useful, because it prevents hacking and the creation of spam e-mails, and is usually found when a user is creating a new account or enters the incorrect password too many times. A reCaptcha uses a picture comprised of two words, which the computer user must type in.

Terms of Service: A list of agreements that explain what a website and its user can and cannot do with information passing through the website.

Assignment: Welcome to the first of many technology activities that will be completed during CSSK-1200. For this activity, you will create an e-mail account. As you may know, there are many e-mail service providers. The one that will be used for this activity is called Gmail. This is a free service offered by Google.

You must still complete this assignment if you already have a Gmail account. This e-mail is meant for professional use, and should be used for school and work purposes only, to prevent having an inbox full of unneeded messages mixed in with important school or work messages.

To begin, go to www.gmail.com, and click on create an account. Type in your first and last name, and pick a username. The username will become your e-mail address, and you should use your name, or something similar to your name, so your instructors can recognize it.

Examples include:

JSmith@Gmail.com

JohnSmith@Gmail.com

Smith.John@Gmail.com

Smith987@Gmail.com

If the username you would like is not available, add a number or change the format of the username. Next, select a password. Passwords must have at least 8 characters. Do not select a password that is too obvious, but make sure it is something you will remember. One way to create a password is create a mnemonic device such as the password ilmccsvm. This would stand for I Love Macomb Community College So Very Much. Passwords that contain a number or symbol are stronger, and you should use at least one number while selecting yours.

Enter your birthday and gender, as well as mobile phone number. If you have another e-mail address enter this as well. If you do not have another e-mail, Gmail will still allow you to make an account. The phone number and additional address are used for password recovery in case you forget it. Enter the reCaptcha, refreshing it if you are unable to identify the letters. Make sure your location is set to United States, and click the box that allows you to agree to the Terms of Service. Click the button to move on to the next step.

Skip the next step, which requests that you add a profile picture by clicking the next step button. Write your username and password on a piece of paper, but do not share it with anyone. Read through Google's quick, automatic tour. Then, click the "Compose" button, and compose an e-mail to your instructor. Type your instructor's e-mail into the "To" box, then write the subject "Practice E-mail" in the subject bar. Send a file to your instructor, using the paper clip icon box. Type a fact about yourself into the e-mail's body, then sign it with your name. Click the send button.

Click on, and read, the automated e-mails already in your inbox. Then, make a list of the e-mail addresses of your instructors this semester and add the list to your Macomb Binder.

Reflection

What e-mail provider, if any, have you used in the past?

Yahoo, gmail, and my computer website.

How is Gmail different from that provider?

Its a lot easier to use. Not a lot of pop ups.

Do you plan on using Gmail in the future for personal use?

Yes I do.

What is your Gmail username?

Amandanoblecssh@gmail.com

Why is having an e-mail address in college important?

To get important info sent to you or contacted.

Self-Monitoring

(Agree)	Disagree	1.	I have my own e-mail account.
(Agree)	Disagree	2.	I know my e-mail username.
(Agree)	Disagree	3.	I know my Gmail password.
(Agree)	Disagree	4.	I can compose and send e-mail messages to my teacher.
(Agree)	Disagree	5.	I can send attachments by e-mail to my teacher.
(Agree)	Disagree	6.	I can read e-mails sent to me.

USE TECHNOLOGY TO . . .

Assess skills, self-regulation, and learning attitudes.

Technology: LASSI (Learning and Study Stategies Inventory): www.hhpubco.com/LASSI

> **Terms:**
>
> *Sign Up:* The location on a website where you can create an account.
>
> *Log In:* The location on a website that allows you to access an account after it has been created by typing in a username and password.
>
> *Pre-Test:* The first time you take a test.
>
> *Post-Test:* The final test, which allows you to look at how your results change.

Assignment: Today you are going to take a LASSI Inventory. You will need access to the Web and your LASSI envelope to complete this activity.

Use the password in the instruction package to create a LASSI account. You will use this account on the first and last days of class to measure your attitudes and skills toward learning. When signing up on the first day, type in your school number and the password found in the envelope.

WWW.HHPUBCO.COM/LASSI

Take the pre-test. Do not take the post-test. The post-test will be this class's final exam on the last day of class.

This test uses drop down menus. To use these, click the menu and then your choice. You can find a sample menu on the sign up page, along with an explanation key for the various options.

After looking over your pre-test, e-mail the results to your new Gmail account. Print your LASSI results and put them in your Macomb Binder. Remember that it may take a few minutes to complete this process. The computer may load slowly. Only push the buttons once and wait for the computer to complete your request.

In order to pass CSSK-1200, you must be present on the last day of class and take the LASSI post-test.

Reflection

Do you agree or disagree with your LASSI results and why?

I agree. I have a hard time with my strategies and trying to succeed in school...

In which areas did you score well?

Motivation, info processing, study aids

In which areas do you have the most difficulty?

Studying (Retaing info) and concentration

List three of your strengths.

Motivation, Attitude & interests, and Time managments

List three goals for the improvement of your challenge areas.

Better information proceesing, To have better concentration, and better Retaing info.

What surprised you about your test results?

My motavation. I have no motavation at all.

Self-Monitoring

Agree	(Disagree)	1.	I have a LASSI account.
Agree	(Disagree)	2.	I know my LASSI password.
(Agree)	Disagree	3.	I can read and interpret my LASSI results.
(Agree)	Disagree	4.	I went into Gmail to retrieve my LASSI results.

USE TECHNOLOGY TO . . .

Get to know Macomb.

Technology: The Macomb Website: www.macomb.edu

Terms:

Websites: Sites on the World Wide Web that contain a home page and material for public use.

Web Pages: Pages within a website containing links and information.

Browse: Explore the web page by following links to gain information.

Control Key (CTRL): The key that allows a shortcut to print on a PC computer (CTRL +P).

Command Key: The key that allows a shortcut to print on a MAC (command +P).

Browser: This is a software application that allows you to access the Internet. Firefox, Internet Explorer, and Google Chrome are some examples.

URL: Uniform Resource Locator. This is the address of a website. Macomb.edu is the URL for Macomb Community College.

Assignment: For Activity 3 you will explore the Macomb Community College Website. You will need to locate specific pages on the website and answer questions about what you find.

The Macomb Community College Website is available to help students learn about the college and its resources. It contains information about the campus and the community. It also has links to helpful areas involving admissions and enrollment, educational offerings, student services, student life, transfer information, and financial aid.

Go to the URL for Macomb's website: www.macomb.edu. Please take some time to look around the website. This gives you an opportunity to learn more about the college. Answer the following questions for class discussion, and print a web page screen using the shortcut your instructor showed in class. Remember, CTRL + P for a PC, and Command + P for a Mac, will help you.

Use the search bar to locate key words and explore the website.

Reflection

What links are located on the Macomb home page?

Future students, Current students, Business, Community, Alumni & dooble, etc.

What programs are being offered at the Lorenzo Cultural Center this semester?

American Art, Hegrey V, Day of dead, museums secrets.

Select one that you can attend.

Day of dead.

Why does this program interest you?

different culture

What art exhibits are being offered by the Macomb Center for the Performing Arts in the art gallery?

American art, museum

Select one that interests you.

American Art

Why does this program interest you?

Its the DIA's

What is the Macomb University Center?

the college

Read about one of Macomb University Center partners. What did you find most interesting about the school?

That More than 4 schools.

Read about the athletics at Macomb. What athletic teams does Macomb have?

Baseball, basket ball, etc.

Have you ever played a sport?

No

What athletic events could you attend this semester?

Baseball

Use what you have learned about websites to look up another topic you have questions about.

Ok

What is this topic?

Peforming arts

What interesting information did you find out? Be prepared to report back to the class.

What shows these with be

What URLs are you familiar with besides the school website?

Not sure

Self-Monitoring

(Agree)	Disagree	1.	I can locate the Macomb website.
Agree	Disagree	2.	I have used the Macomb website to get to know Macomb Community College.
Agree	Disagree	3.	I am confident to find what I need on the Macomb website.
(Agree)	Disagree	4.	I can print a page from the Macomb website.
Agree	Disagree	5.	I can use URLs to go to another website.

Technology Activity ④

USE TECHNOLOGY . . .

In the Online Classroom Environment

Technology: ANGEL: https://macomb.angellearning.com

Canvas: https://macomb.instructure.com

Terms:

ANGEL: A New Global Environment for Learning. It is a website Macomb uses to allow instructors and students to communicate about course material.

Canvas: As of 2016 Macomb will be transitioning to Canvas as the main LMS. You may have classes in both Angel and Canvas until Summer 2016.

Learning Management System (LMS): A computer platform that provides Web access to grades and course material.

Tabs: Major navigational aids that take you to a different section on a website.

Hyperlinks: Buttons with words that take you to a new page.

Discussion Board: A place where students can post comments to discussion topics.

Grade Book: An online grade book where teachers who have an ANGEL course site post grades.

Assignment:

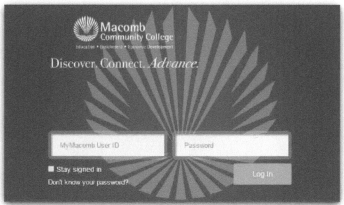

Your first time login information is:

Username: Your MyMacomb User ID.
Password: Your MyMacomb Password.

ANGEL is Macomb's Learning Management System. At Macomb, instructors often use ANGEL to Web-enhance courses or teach online. Instructors assist their students by adding resources, lectures, and assignments to an ANGEL page. Students have access during the semester to this learning environment. Often teachers use the announcement features to post messages to the class about the course. Some instructors also have students take online quizzes and tests in ANGEL. While not all instructors at Macomb use ANGEL, many do. To be successful in a Web-enhanced or online course, you must become familiar with ANGEL.

An "H" in the course section in the Macomb Schedule book identifies hybrid courses (e.g., MKTG-1210-H0802).

A "V" in the course section identifies online courses (e.g., MKTG-1210 VO801). Web-enhanced courses do not have a designation, because they do not replace scheduled on-campus time like hybrid or online courses.

Before you take an online or hybrid course you should complete the introduction to online learning.

This assignment includes completing the introduction to the ANGEL course and exploring the sample online course on the ANGEL page.

Project 1

Go to Macomb's website. Click on the ANGEL link that brings you to the ANGEL log in page. Next, click on the "view a sample online course" button. View and explore the sample online course.

Project 2

Complete the introduction to ANGEL on the ANGEL site, found on Macomb's website. If you have trouble, Frequently Asked Questions (FAQs) are located on Macomb's website and the ANGEL login page. If the FAQs do not cover your problem, call 1-877-362-2662 or e-mail onlinesupport@macomb.edu.

To log in, go to macomb.angellearning.com. Your username is your My Macomb User ID, and your password is your My Macomb password. After logging in, you are able to change your password. You should use the same password that you did for your WebAdvisor.

Project 3—Optional

Log on to Canvas at https://macomb.instructure.com. Complete the introduction to Canvas training. You will find this training under Courses and Groups.

Reflection

Do any of your instructors this semester use ANGEL to web enhance their courses? If yes, then for what subjects?

Yes, college success skills and early childhood development

What parts of ANGEL do you think will be most useful?

Grades I think will be the most useful.

Where would you find the link to ANGEL on the Macomb website?

You first click: current students. Then you log in. Then after that you put academics and then click angel.

What did you find most helpful about the sample online course?

It shows you the hang of angel.

Self-Monitoring

Agree	Disagree	1.	I have explored the ANGEL sample online course.
Agree	Disagree	2.	I can log into ANGEL.
Agree	Disagree	3.	I have completed the introduction to ANGEL Training.
Agree	Disagree	4.	I found student resources in ANGEL.
Agree	Disagree	5.	I viewed the videos in the sample online course.
Agree	Disagree	6.	I have completed the introduction to Canvas.

USE TECHNOLOGY TO . . .

Share learning and resources.

Technology: Delicious: www.delicious.com

Terms:

Social Bookmarking: A Web tool used to save links to web pages on an Internet website to share with others or collect for future use.

Tag: A key word used to organize information and create a link that allows the user to revisit a specific type of website.

Followers: Friends and classmates that follow your work (i.e., links that you find important).

@: A symbol that needs to go in front of someone's name when you search them.

Assignment:

Go to www.delicious.com. Click the sign in button, and then go to the button that says "Create an Account." When it asks you to sign in with Facebook or Twitter, deny the request. Type your first and last name into "Display Name," and use your new Gmail account as your e-mail. Choose a username similar to, if not the same as, your e-mail. Fill in the rest of the form, using the same password you did for e-mail and filling in the reCaptcha.

Go to "Add Link" and type in Macomb's website URL. Add the tags "CSSK" and "Macomb." Always press return after typing in a key word. You may add multiple key words to one link.

Go to the search bar. Locate your instructor by typing in the username you received in class. Always remember to include an @ sign before the username you are searching for. You can also add @heathermayernik to see another example. Follow your instructor by clicking the follow button.

Reflection

What have you used to save websites in the past?

My web browser

What challenges did you face while setting up a Delicious account?

I was confused on how to use this.

How does Delicious help you collect and organize websites?

you add them so you wont lose them

Did you find any interesting websites on your teacher's Delicious site? What were they?

New movie Releases atredbox

Self-Monitoring

(Agree)	Disagree	1.	I can bookmark Macomb's website.
Agree	Disagree	2.	I can bookmark other websites to use for my investigation project.
Agree	Disagree	3.	I can follow my instructor in Delicious.
Agree	Disagree	4.	I can search in Delicious.
Agree	Disagree	5.	I can use tags successfully.

USE TECHNOLOGY TO . . .

Express yourself.

Technology: Animoto: www.animoto.com

Terms:

Templates: Premade styles for a video that offer a range of different appearances.

Captions: Words that emphasize the images (in this case in a video).

Thumbnail: A small picture used to represent a video when it is not playing.

Assignment:

Animoto is an online video creation software tool that blends music, pictures, and text to produce a professional looking video. While more lengthy videos require a subscription, for this assignment you will be creating a free 30-second video.

Go to www.animoto.com and click the sign up button. Enter your e-mail from the first Activity, as well as your name and the same password you used previously. Choose a template from the options given. Click on the desired style, then click on "make a 30 second video for free."

Your video will be about a college success theme. Some options include:

Persistence, questioning, new situations, thinking, responsibility, creating, listening, fear, continuous learning, risk taking, speaking, knowledge, clear vision, graduation, self-evaluation, emotion, differences, jealousy, patience, assessment, portfolio, honor, clarity, problem solving, collaboration, imagination, humor, intelligence, destination, success, critical thinking, determination, goals, dream, helping others, service, self-confidence, self-motivation, time management, thank you, a journey, ups and downs, innovation, student-success, truth, leaders.

Use the image grabbing software to collect pictures from either your computer, or a variety of online sources. Software tools to the side of the video layout allow you to add videos, music, text, and pictures. If you decide you don't like the video style, you can also use these to change it. When you finish, go up to the settings and change the thumbnail. Then click the button to preview your video. If you aren't satisfied, click "continue editing." If you are, change your title and add a description. Click the button to finish.

Once your video is published, click the option to share using e-mail. First you must type in your teacher's e-mail into the "to" section, and then write "This is _____'s Animoto video" in the subject bar. Be prepared to share your video in class.

Reflection

What tools have you used to edit videos or photos in the past?

Instagram, Photoshop, Apps.

What could you use Animoto for in your other classes?

Video making, slide shows

How was your experience with Animoto?

Very easy!

What other topics could you use to make videos?

Social life, school topics, yourself, etc

Self-Monitoring

(Agree)	Disagree	1.	I can log into my Animoto account.
(Agree)	Disagree	2.	I know how to pick a theme in Animoto.
(Agree)	Disagree	3.	I know how to upload an image to my video.
(Agree)	Disagree	4.	I know how to add music to my video.
(Agree)	Disagree	5.	I completed my video.
(Agree)	Disagree	6.	I e-mailed my video to my teacher.
(Agree)	Disagree	7.	I was able to share my video with my classmates.

USE TECHNOLOGY TO . . .

Represent understanding.

Technology: Bubbl.us: www.bubbl.us

Terms:

Brainstorm: To think of as many possible ideas about a topic.

Concept Map: A type of graphic organizer that allows people to visualize a topic; thoughts and ideas are organized by arranging key words to show relationships.

Cursor: The arrow on a computer screen.

Assignment:

Go to Bubbl.us, then to "Create Account." Make your username the same as your e-mail, and use the same password as your e-mail. Next, type in your name and e-mail from the first activity. Then click the button to make an account. Your username and password will automatically move into the sign in options. Click sign in. If Bubbl.us requests data in your computer, and you are on a school computer, deny this option. Click the button to start brainstorming. With this free account you can save three concept maps. Type a key word into the box. Click the small box located at the bottom of the center bubble to make a child bubble. Type a new word or idea into the child bubble. Play with the features.

Project 1: Concept Map a Textbook

In the first portion of this assignment, you will create a concept map for a textbook. This requires a book from another class you are currently taking, or have previously taken.

Read the headings and several sections of text. Determine what key words are important. Write a key word, then box or circle it. Draw arrows linking the boxes of key words. The map should make sense to you and help you organize your understanding. Print your finished map.

Project 2: Brainstorm Using Bubbl.us

In the next part, you will brainstorm ideas around a general topic: your Investigation Poster Project ideas. Create a bubble. Type your general topic inside this bubble. As you brainstorm, create bubbles that contain the terms around your general topic using child bubbles. Keep adding more specific terms and branch around the center circle. Add colors and text differences to make important words stand out. Print your finished map.

Reflection

What was your first response to making a concept map?

It was kinda easy and gave ideas.

What subject did you use to make your concept map?

ADHd, thinking, time

What other things can you make a concept map for?

Brainstorming, info, subjects

What big ideas stood out in your textbook and why?

None

What ideas have you come up with for your investigation project?

ADHD

Self-Monitoring

~~Agree~~	Disagree	1.	I can log into my Bubbl.us account.
~~Agree~~	Disagree	2.	I can decide what parts of a text are most important to map.
~~Agree~~	Disagree	3.	I can create a concept map of a textbook section.
~~Agree~~	Disagree	4.	I can create a concept map to plan for a project.
~~Agree~~	Disagree	5.	I can print my concept map.

USE TECHNOLOGY TO . . .

Play with vocabulary.

Technology: Wordle: www.wordle.net

Terms:

Context: The text that surrounds a word that influences a person's understanding of the meaning.

Word Cloud: Words arranged in a pattern with different colors and sizes.

Randomize: To arrange words without a specific pattern.

Assignment:

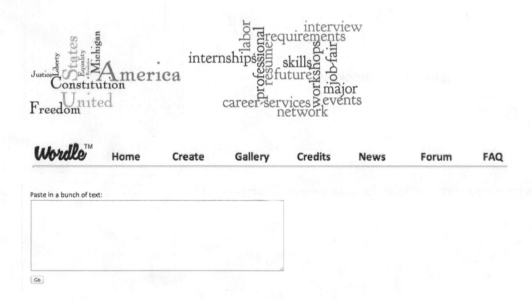

Wordle is a website that highlights key words by taking them out of the context of a website or textbook. You can use it to present concepts in an interesting and engaging pattern. Wordle can also help reinforce key vocabulary about a subject. The wordle that you create will be eye-catching if you choose to add it to your poster investigation project.

To begin this assignment, create a list of meaningful words related to your investigation poster project topic. Next, go to wordle.net, and click on "create your own." Then, click on the "create" tab on the menu bar across the top of the website. Paste or type your list of words about your topic into the box. After you are done, press the green "go" button. Another option is to take some of the text off of a website and paste it in the box, but you should not use this option for this assignment. If you would like, you can go back later and experiment with this or other advanced options available on the top of the screen. Do not do this until after your project is finished.

Your wordle will appear. Change the look of your wordle by using the "randomize" button. Try changing the order and font of your wordle in the dropdown menu across the top. Wordle does not have a user log in option so you must copy and paste your finished wordle into a Word document.

Print your wordle. Wordle also has the option to save your wordle. If you save a wordle, it goes to a public gallery and others may view it. If you do not save a wordle, you may print it out without saving it. Look through the public gallery to see if any other wordles have been done about your topic.

Wordle may not work in all browsers, such as Internet Explorer, Firefox or Google Chrome. If it does not work in the one you are using, switch to another browser.

Reflection

How could Wordle be used to share ideas?

By putting words down and randomizing.

Did you find any other interesting wordles in the gallery? What did you like about them?

that they were all creative

Where online could someone place a wordle?

Anywhere. Magazines, Bookes, articles, etc.

How can you use Wordle to reinforce your knowledge of vocabulary?

By using new words

Self-Monitoring

Agree   Disagree   1.   I can create a wordle.

Agree   Disagree   2.   I can print my wordle.

Agree   Disagree   3.   I can choose important words about my topic for my Investigation Poster Project.

USE TECHNOLOGY TO . . .

Research careers.

Technology: O∗net: http://www.onetonline.org/

> **Terms:**
>
> *Job Profile:* Contains a list of skills and qualifications needed to perform a specific job.
>
> *Recruitment Fair:* Also known as a Career Fair. A place where a person can go and meet with companies looking for employees.

Assignment:

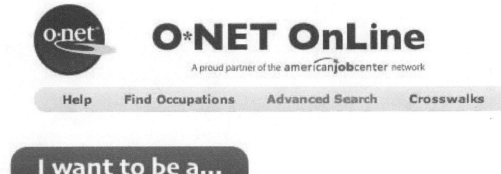

Click the "I want to be a . . ." option. This leads you to three options. Choose the option to take a test to discover what types of careers you may enjoy. Use the "next" buttons and follow the instructions on the screen. You can use this website to examine careers that may interest you. You will go into further detail about careers in the Educational and Career Planning chapter of this book.

Write down your interest results.

Realistic: 5
Investigative: 7
Artistic: 22
Social: 21
Enterprising: 26
Conventional: 4

Actor
Public announcer
Singer

Reflection

What careers have you considered in the past?

Modeling, Actress, and Sinser.

Which careers in your results interest you the most?

Public speaker.

Do you think your results are accurate?

Eh. Yes.

Self-Monitoring

(Agree) Disagree   1. I can complete the interest profiler.

(Agree) Disagree   2. I can interpret my results.

USE TECHNOLOGY TO . . .

Assess improvement.

Technology: LASSI

In order to pass CSSK-1200, you must retake the LASSI test and evaluate your improvement. To do this, turn back to the instructions from Activity 1. This time you only need your school number and student key. Your student key is located on your results sheet from Activity 1. You should enter these into the box labeled second administration.

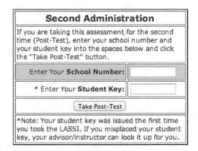

Print out the new LASSI results. Take a marker or highlighter and dot your fall results for each area on the final LASSI result sheet. Celebrate your success.

Reflection

What area have you improved the most since the initial test?

Self testing

Why do you think this area shows the most improvement?

Because I was struggling realized and got better and I

What surprised you most about your results?

It went up a lot More than I expected

Self-Monitoring

(Agree)   Disagree   1. I completed the second LASSI test.

(Agree)   Disagree   2. I compared my results to the first test from the beginning of the semester.

64

Investigation Poster Project

In CSSK-1200 you are required to do a poster presentation project. This poster project will involve the process of investigating and sharing your knowledge about a topic. This is an opportunity to use your skills to incorporate text and images into a poster presentation.

After completing your project, you will share your poster with the school community at the knowledge fair poster session located at the Macomb Library. Your instructor will give you more details about the topic and grading rubric. To design the layout of your poster, use the following poster plan template:

NAME _____ TOPIC _____

Side One	Center	Side Two

Reading in CSSK-1200

In CSSK-1200 you will have two reading texts. We will refer to them as the textbook, and a book we will call our "common read." As you read through *College Success at Macomb*, you will complete all journal reflections in the book. This way you will be able to reflect on your learning as you read. This will also prepare you for all class discussions.

The other book we use in this course is, *What the Best College Students Do*. Ken Bain, the author, tells about incredible learners and how they succeed. He shows through examples various learning strategies and attitudes that help lead to deeper learning and understanding. Our hope is that this book will inspire you to find your passion and keep on learning everywhere you go.

While you read this "common read" book, you should focus on asking "good questions," participating in open discussions, and listening to other students talk about their ideas and learning. The goal is to remember to reflect about this book, as you participate in activities. The main focuses in this course are your understanding and the connections you make.

You must come prepared for class ready to discuss, so that you can share your learning with others in CSSK-1200. You should take notes as you go through *What the Best College Students Do*. You can do this in different forms. One way to clarify thinking is to annotate, or talk to the text, and write notes or underline in the margins of a book. Using symbols and underlining, which clarify thinking, helps when you need to go back to the text to review. Practice annotating the reading, listening, and speaking articles included in the chapter.

Another strategy involves answering questions, or creating your own, on a two-column notebook sheet of paper. On the left side you put what you find interesting, confusing, or new from the text. This can be a vocabulary word, sentence, topic, idea, or question. On the right side, jot down a reaction to what you know about the text, concept clarification, explanation, or definition. This strategy helps you extract important information and highlight key concepts and vocabulary.

Another way to dig deep into the text to understand connections and concepts is to use advanced organizers or concept maps that pull facts and terms from the text and allow you to organize them. These maps can be handwritten or typed using a concept mapping tool.

While keeping notes, you should include page numbers. If you organize notes like this, it becomes easier for you to find evidence to support your ideas quickly while discussing the book. You can also consolidate your notes into key points that you feel are most important. Then you can include these key points in the book discussion group forms in this chapter. Use these forms to guide your thoughts during group discussions.

Before you read the first chapter in *What the Best College Students Do*, please answer these questions. After you discuss the answers with your class, find out what Ken Bain thinks by reading Chapter 1.

Anticipation Guide Chapter 1

Pre-Reading Activity

Agree	Disagree	Surviving a college class is the primary goal.
Agree	Disagree	Best students focus and concentrate on getting good grades.
Agree	Disagree	High marks in college tell us a lot about how a person thinks.
Agree	Disagree	You should always brush aside failure.
Agree	Disagree	Good ideas and results come quickly.
Agree	Disagree	To do well you must believe that you can do it and visualize yourself doing it.
Agree	Disagree	I would hang up on the phone if someone called and said that I won a half a million dollars to do whatever I wanted.

When Reading Is Tough*

Sometimes ordinary reading methods are not enough. It's easy to get bogged down in a murky reading assignment. The solution starts with a First Step: When you are confused, tell the truth about it. Successful readers monitor their understanding of reading material. They do not see confusion as a mistake or a personal shortcoming. Instead, they take it as a cue to change reading strategies and process ideas at a deeper level.

Read it again. Somehow, students get the idea that reading means opening a book and dutifully slogging through the text—line by line, page by page—moving in a straight line from the first word until the last. Actually, this method can be an ineffective way to read much of the published material you'll encounter in college.

Feel free to shake up your routine. Make several passes through tough reading material. During a preview, for example, just scan the text to look for key words and highlighted material. Next, skim the entire chapter or article again, spending a little more time and taking in more than you did during your preview. Finally, read in more depth, proceeding word by word through some or all of the text. Difficult material—such as the technical writing in science texts—is often easier the second time around. Isolate difficult passages and read them again, slowly.

This suggestion comes with one caution. If you find yourself doing a lot of re-reading, then consider a change in reading strategies. For example, you might benefit from reciting after each paragraph or section rather than after each chapter. For more ideas, review the steps of Muscle Reading and consider the following suggestions.

Look for essential words. If you are stuck on a paragraph, mentally cross out all of the adjectives and adverbs, and then read the sentences without them. Find the important words—usually verbs and nouns.

Hold a mini-review. Pause briefly to summarize—either verbally or in writing—what you've read so far. Stop at the end of a paragraph and recite, in your own words, what you have just read. Jot down some notes, or create a short outline or summary.

Read it out loud. Make noise. Read a passage out loud several times, each time using a different inflection and emphasizing a different part of the sentence. Be creative. Imagine that you are the author talking.

Talk to someone who can help. Admit when you are stuck. Then bring questions about reading assignments to classmates and members of your study group. Also make an appointment with your instructor. Most teachers welcome the opportunity to work individually with students. Be specific about your confusion. Point out the paragraph that you found toughest to understand.

Stand up. Changing positions periodically can combat fatigue. Experiment with standing as you read, especially if you get stuck on a tough passage and decide to read it out loud.

Skip around. Jump to the next section or to the end of a tough article or chapter. You might have lost the big picture. Simply seeing the next step, the next main point, or a summary might be all you need to put the details in context. Retrace the steps in a chain of ideas, and look for examples. Absorb facts and ideas in whatever order works for you—which may be different than the author's presentation.

Find a tutor. Many schools provide free tutoring services. If your school does not, other students who have completed the course can assist you.

Use another text. Find a similar text in the library. Sometimes a concept is easier to understand if it is expressed another way.

Children's books—especially children's encyclopedias—can provide useful overviews of baffling subjects.

Note where you get stuck. When you feel stuck, stop reading for a moment and diagnose what's happening. At these stop points, mark your place in the margin of the page with a penciled *S* for *Stuck*. A pattern to your marks over several pages might indicate a question you want to answer before going further.

Stop reading. When none of the above suggestions work, do not despair. Admit your confusion and then take a break. Catch a movie, go for a walk, study another subject, or sleep on it. The concepts you've already absorbed might come together at a subconscious level as you move on to other activities. Allow some time for that process. When you return to the reading material, see it with fresh eyes.

Word Power—Expanding Your Vocabulary*

Having a large vocabulary makes reading more enjoyable and increases the range of materials you can explore. In addition, building your vocabulary gives you more options for self-expression when speaking or writing. With a larger vocabulary, you can think more precisely by making finer distinctions between ideas. And you won't have to stop to search for words at crucial times—such as a job interview.

Strengthen your vocabulary by taking delight in words. Look up unfamiliar terms. Pay special attention to words that arouse your curiosity.

Before the age of the Internet, students used two kinds of printed dictionaries: the desk dictionary and the unabridged dictionary. A desk dictionary is an easy-to-handle abridged dictionary that you can use many times in the course of a day. You can keep this book within easy reach (maybe in your lap) so you can look up unfamiliar words while reading.

In contrast, an unabridged dictionary is large and not made for you to carry around. It provides more complete information about words and definitions not included in your desk dictionary, as well as synonyms, usage notes, and word histories. Look for unabridged dictionaries in libraries and bookstores.

You might prefer using one of several online dictionaries, such as Dictionary. com. Another common option is to search for definitions by using a search engine such as Google.com. If you do this, inspect the results carefully. They can vary in quality and be less useful than the definitions you'd find in a good dictionary or thesaurus.

Construct a word stack. When you come across an unfamiliar word, write it down on a 3 x 5 card. Below the word, copy the sentence in which it was used, along with the page number. You can look up each word immediately, or you can accumulate a stack of these cards and look up the words later. Write the definition of each word on the back of the 3 x 5 card, adding the diacritics—marks that tell you how to pronounce it.

To expand your vocabulary and learn the history behind the words, take your stack of cards to an unabridged dictionary. As you find related words in the dictionary, add them to your stack. These cards become a portable study aid that you can review in your spare moments.

Learn—even when your dictionary is across town. When you are listening to a lecture and hear an unusual word or when you are reading on the bus and encounter a word you don't know, you can still build your word stack. Pull out a 3 x 5 card and write down the word and its sentence. Later, you can look up the definition and write it on the back of the card.

Divide words into parts. Another suggestion for building your vocabulary is to divide an unfamiliar word into syllables and look for familiar parts. This strategy works well if you make it a point to learn common prefixes (beginning syllables) and suffixes (ending syllables). For example, the suffix -*tude* usually refers to a condition or state of being. Knowing this makes it easier to conclude that *habitude* refers to a usual way of doing something and that *similitude* means being similar or having a quality of resemblance.

Infer the meaning of words from their context. You can often deduce the meaning of an unfamiliar word simply by paying attention to its context—the surrounding words, phrases, sentences, paragraphs, or images. Later, you can confirm your deduction by consulting a dictionary.

Practice looking for context clues such as these:

- *Definitions.* A key word might be defined right in the text. Look for phrases such as *defined as* or *in other words.*
- *Examples.* Authors often provide examples to clarify a word meaning. If the word is not explicitly defined, then study the examples. They're often preceded by the phrases *for example, for instance,* or *such as.*
- *Lists.* When a word is listed in a series, pay attention to the other items in the series. They might define the unfamiliar word through association.
- *Comparisons.* You might find a new word surrounded by synonyms—words with a similar meaning. Look for synonyms after words such as *like* and *as.*
- *Contrasts.* A writer might juxtapose a word with its antonym. Look for phrases such as *on the contrary* and *on the other hand.*

Choosing to Listen*

Effective listening is not easy. It calls for concentration and energy. But it's worth the trouble. People love a good listener. The best salespeople, managers, coworkers, teachers, parents, and friends are the best listeners.

Through skilled listening, you can gain insight into other people and yourself. You can also promote your success in school through more powerful notes, more productive study groups, and better relationships with students and instructors.

To listen well, begin from a clear intention. *Choose* to listen well. Once you've made this choice, you can use the following techniques to be even more effective at listening. Notice that these techniques start with suggestions for nonverbal listening, which involves remaining silent while another person talks. The second set of sug-

*From Ellis, *Annotated Instructor's Edition for Ellis' Becoming a Master Student, 14th*, 14E. © 2013 Wadsworth, a part of Cengage Learning, Inc. Reproduced by permission. www.cengage.com/permission

gestions is about verbal listening, where you occasionally speak up in ways that help you fully receive a speaker's message.

Nonverbal Listening

Be quiet. Silence is more than staying quiet while someone is speaking. Allowing several seconds to pass before you begin to talk gives the speaker time to catch her breath and gather her thoughts. She might want to continue. Someone who talks nonstop might fear she will lose the floor if she pauses.

If the message being sent is complete, this short break gives you time to form your response and helps you avoid the biggest barrier to listening—listening with your answer running. If you make up a response before the person is finished, you might miss the end of the message, which is often the main point.

In some circumstances, pausing for several seconds might be inappropriate. Ignore this suggestion completely in an emergency, where immediate action is usually necessary.

Maintain eye contact. Look at the other person while he speaks. Maintaining eye contact demonstrates your attentiveness and helps keep your mind from wandering. Your eyes also let you observe the speaker's body language and behavior. If you avoid eye contact, you can fail to see *and* fail to listen.

This idea is not an absolute. Maintaining eye contact is valued more in some cultures than others. Also, some people learn primarily by hearing; they can listen more effectively by turning off the visual input once in a while.

Display openness. You can display openness through your facial expression and body position. Uncross your arms and legs. Sit up straight. Face the other person, and remove any physical barriers between you, such as a pile of books.

Send acknowledgments. Let the speaker know periodically that you are still there. Words and nonverbal gestures of acknowledgment convey to the speaker that you are interested and that you are receiving his message. These words and gestures include "Umhum," "Okay," "Yes," and head nods.

These acknowledgments do not imply your agreement. When people tell you what they don't like about you, your head nod doesn't mean that you agree. It just indicates that you are listening.

Release distractions. Even when your intention is to listen, you might find your mind wandering. Thoughts about what *you* want to say or something you want to do later might claim your attention. There's a simple solution: Notice your wandering mind without judgment. Then bring your attention back to the act of listening.

You can also set up your immediate environment to release distractions. Turn off or silence your cell phone. Stash your laptop and other digital devices. Send the message that your sole intention in the moment is to listen.

Another option is to ask for a quick break so that you can make a written note about what's on your mind. Tell the speaker that you're writing so that you can clear your mind and return to full listening.

Suspend judgments. Listening and agreeing are two different activities. As listeners, our goal is to fully receive another person's message. This does not mean that we're obligated to agree with the message. Once you're confident that you accurately understand a speaker's point of view, you are free to agree or disagree with it. The key to effective listening is understanding *before* evaluating.

Verbal Listening

Choose when to speak. When we listen to another person, we often interrupt with our own stories, opinions, suggestions, and comments. Consider the following dialogue:

> "Oh, I'm so excited! I just found out that I've been nominated to be in *Who's Who in American Musicians.*"

> "Yeah, that's neat. My Uncle Elmer got into *Who's Who in American Veterinarians.* He sure has an interesting job. One time I went along when he was treating a cow, and you'll never believe what happened next . . ."

To avoid this kind of one-sided conversation, delay your verbal responses. This does not mean that you remain totally silent while listening. It means that you wait for an *appropriate* moment to respond.

Watch your nonverbal responses too. A look of "Good grief!" from you can deter the other person from finishing his message.

Feed back meaning. Sometimes you can help a speaker clarify her message by paraphrasing it. This does not mean parroting what she says. Instead, briefly summarize. Psychotherapist Carl Rogers referred to this technique as *reflection.*

Feed back what you see as the essence of the person's message: "Let me see whether I understood what you said . . ." or "What I'm hearing you say is . . ." Often, the other person will say, "No, that's not what I meant. What I said was . . ."

There will be no doubt when you get it right. The sender will say, "Yeah, that's it," and either continue with another message or stop sending when he knows you understand.

When you feed back meaning, be concise. This is not a time to stop the other person by talking on and on about what you think you heard.

Notice verbal and nonverbal messages. You might point out that the speaker's body language seems to convey the exact opposite of what her words do. For example: "I noticed you said you are excited, but you look bored."

Keep in mind that the same nonverbal behavior can have various meanings across cultures. Someone who looks bored might simply be listening in a different way.

Listen for requests and intentions. An effective way to listen to complaints is to look for the request hidden in them. "This class is a waste of my time" can be heard as "Please tell me what I'll gain if I participate actively in class." "The instructor talks too fast" might be asking "What strategies can I use to take notes when the instructor covers material rapidly?"

We can even transform complaints into intentions. Take this complaint: "The parking lot by the dorms is so dark at night that I'm afraid to go to my car." This complaint can result in having a light installed in the parking lot.

Viewing complaints as requests gives us more choices. Rather than responding with defensiveness ("What does he know anyway?"), resignation ("It's always been this way and always will be"), or indifference ("It's not my job"), we can decide whether to grant the request (do what will alleviate the other's difficulty) or help the person translate his own complaint into an action plan.

Allow emotion. In the presence of full listening, some people will share things that they feel deeply about. They might shed a few tears, cry, shake, or sob. If you feel uncomfortable when this happens, see whether you can accept the discomfort for a little while longer. Emotional release can bring relief and trigger unexpected insights.

Ask for more. Full listening with unconditional acceptance is a rare gift. Many people have never experienced it. They are used to being greeted with resistance, so they habitually stop short of saying what they truly think and feel. Help them shed this habit by routinely asking, "Is there anything more you want to say about that?" This question sends the speaker a message that you truly value what she has to say.

Be careful with questions and advice. Questions are directive. They can take conversations in a new direction, which may not be where the speaker wants to go. Ask questions only to clarify the speaker's message. Later, when it's your turn to speak, you can introduce any topic that you want.

Also be cautious about giving advice. Unsolicited advice can be taken as condescending or even insulting. Skilled listeners recognize that people are different, and they do not assume that they know what's best for someone else.

Take care of yourself. People seek good listeners, and there are times when you don't want to listen. You might be distracted with your own concerns. Be honest. Don't pretend to listen. You can say, "What you're telling me is important, but I'm pressed for time right now. Can we set aside another time to talk about this?" It's okay not to listen.

Stay open to the adventure of listening. Receiving what another person has to say is an act of courage. Listening fully—truly opening yourself to the way another person sees the world—means taking risks. Your opinions may be challenged. You may be less certain or less comfortable than you were before.

Along with the risks come rewards. Listening in an unguarded way can take your relationships to a new depth and level of honesty. This kind of listening can open up new possibilities for thinking, feeling, and behaving. And when you practice full listening, other people are more likely to receive when it's your turn to send.

Choosing to Speak*

We all have this problem. Sometimes we feel wonderful or rotten or sad or scared, and we want to express it. Emotions, though, can get in the way of the message. And although you can send almost any message through tears, laughter, fist pounding, or hugging, sometimes words are better. Begin with a sincere intention to reach common ground with your listener. Then experiment with the suggestions that follow.

Replace "you" messages with "I" messages. It can be difficult to disagree with someone without his becoming angry or your becoming upset. When conflict occurs, we often make statements about the other person, or "you" messages:

> "You are rude."
> "You make me mad."
> "You must be crazy."
> "You don't love me anymore."

This kind of communication results in defensiveness. The responses might be similar to these:

"I am not rude."
"I don't care."
"No, *you* are crazy."
"No, *you* don't love *me!*"

"You" messages are hard to listen to. They label, judge, blame, and assume things that may or may not be true. They demand rebuttal. Even praise can sometimes be an ineffective "you" message. "You" messages don't work.

Psychologist Thomas Gordon suggests that when communication is emotionally charged, consider limiting your statements to descriptions about yourself. Replace "you" messages with "I" messages:

"You are rude" might become "I feel upset."
"You make me mad" could be "I feel angry."
"You must be crazy" can be "I don't understand."
"You don't love me anymore" could become "I'm afraid we're drifting apart."

Suppose a friend asks you to pick him up at the airport. You drive 20 miles and wait for the plane. No friend. You decide your friend missed her plane, so you wait 3 hours for the next flight. No friend. Perplexed and worried, you drive home. The next day, you see your friend downtown.

"What happened?" you ask.
"Oh, I caught an earlier flight."
"You are a rude person," you reply.

Look for and talk about the facts—the observable behavior. Everyone will agree that your friend asked you to pick her up, that she did take an earlier flight, and that you did not receive a call from her. But the idea that she is rude is not a fact—it's a judgment.

She might go on to say, "I called your home, and no one answered. My mom had a stroke and was rushed to Valley View. I caught the earliest flight I could get." Your judgment no longer fits.

When you saw your friend, you might have said, "I waited and waited at the airport. I was worried about you. I didn't get a call, I feel angry and hurt. I don't want to waste my time. Next time, you can call me when your flight arrives, and I'll be happy to pick you up."

"I" messages don't judge, blame, criticize, or insult. They don't invite the other person to counterattack with more of the same. "I" messages are also more accurate. They report our own thoughts and feelings.

At first, "I" messages might feel uncomfortable or seem forced. That's okay. Use the "Five Ways to Say 'I'" explained on page 75.

Remember that questions are not always questions. You've heard these "questions" before. A parent asks, "Don't you want to look nice?" Translation: "I wish you'd cut your hair, lose the blue jeans, and put on a tie." Or how about this question from a spouse: "Honey, wouldn't you love to go to an exciting hockey game tonight?" Translation: "I've already bought tickets."

We use questions that aren't questions to sneak our opinions and requests into conversations. "Doesn't it upset you?" means "It upsets me," and "Shouldn't we hang the picture over here?" means "I want to hang the picture over here."

Communication improves when we say, "I'm upset" and "Let's hang the picture over here."

Choose your nonverbal messages. How you say something can be more important than what you say. Your tone of voice and gestures add up to a silent message that you send. This message can support, modify, or contradict your words. Your posture, the way you dress, how often you shower, and even the poster hanging on your wall can negate your words before you say them.

Most nonverbal behavior is unconscious. We can learn to be aware of it and choose our nonverbal messages. The key is to be clear about our intention and purpose. When we know what we want to say and are committed to getting it across, our inflections, gestures, and words work together and send a unified message.

Notice barriers to sending messages. Sometimes fear stops us from sending messages. We are afraid of other people's reactions, sometimes justifiably. Being truthful doesn't mean being insensitive to the impact that our messages have on others. Tact is a virtue; letting fear prevent communication is not.

Assumptions can also be used as excuses for not sending messages. "He already knows this," we tell ourselves.

Predictions of failure can be barriers to sending too. "He won't listen," we assure ourselves. That statement might be inaccurate. Perhaps the other person senses that we're angry and listens in a guarded way. Or perhaps he is listening and sending nonverbal messages we don't understand.

Or we might predict, "He'll never do anything about it, even if I tell him." Again, making assumptions can defeat your message before you send it.

It's easy to make excuses for not communicating. If you have fear or some other concern about sending a message, be aware of it. Don't expect the concern to go away. Realize that you can communicate even with your concerns. You can choose to make them part of the message: "I am going to tell you how I feel, but I'm afraid that you will think it's stupid."

Talking to someone when you don't want to could be a matter of educational survival. Sometimes a short talk with an advisor, a teacher, a friend, or a family member can solve a problem that otherwise could jeopardize your education.

Speak candidly. When we brood on negative thoughts and refuse to speak them out loud, we lose perspective. And when we keep joys to ourselves, we diminish our satisfaction. A solution is to share regularly what we think and feel. Psychotherapist Sidney Jourard referred to such openness and honesty as *transparency* and wrote eloquently about how it can heal and deepen relationships.

Sometimes candid speaking can save a life. For example, if you think a friend is addicted to drugs, telling her so in a supportive, nonjudgmental way is a sign of friendship.

Imagine a community in which people freely and lovingly speak their minds—without fear or defensiveness. That can be your community.

This suggestion comes with a couple of caveats. First, there is a big difference between speaking candidly about your problems and griping about them. Gripers usually don't seek solutions. They just want everyone to know how unhappy they are. Instead, talk about problems as a way to start searching for solutions.

Second, avoid bragging. Other people are turned off by constant references to how much money you have, how great your partner is, how numerous your social successes are, or how much status your family enjoys. There is a difference between sharing excitement and being obnoxious.

Offer "feedforward." Giving people feedback about their past performance can be a powerful way to help them learn. Equally useful is "feedforward," which means exploring new options for the future.

Marshall Goldsmith, a management consultant, suggests a way to do this. First, talk about a specific, high-impact behavior that you'd like to change—for example, "I want to be a better listener."

Five Ways to Say "I"*

An "I" message can include any or all of the following five elements. Be careful when including the last two elements, though, because they can contain hidden judgments or threats.

Observations. Describe the facts—the indisputable, observable realities. Talk about what you—or anyone else—can see, hear, smell, taste, or touch. Avoid judgments, interpretations, or opinions. Instead of saying, "You're a slob," say, "Last night's lasagna pan was still on the stove this morning."

Feelings. Describe your own feelings. It is easier to listen to "I feel frustrated" than to "You never help me." Stating how you feel about another's actions can be valuable feedback for that person.

Wants. You are far more likely to get what you want if you say what you want. If someone doesn't know what you want, she doesn't have a chance to help you get it. Ask clearly. Avoid demanding or using the word *need*. Most people like to feel helpful, not obligated. Instead of saying, "Do the dishes when it's your turn, or else!" say, "I want to divide the housework fairly."

Thoughts. Communicate your thoughts, but use caution. Beginning your statement with the word "I" doesn't automatically make it an "I" message. "I think you are a slob" is a "you" judgment in disguise. Instead, say, "I'd have more time to study if I didn't have to clean up so often."

Intentions. The last part of an "I" message is a statement about what you intend to do. Have a plan that doesn't depend on the other person. For example, instead of "From now on, we're going to split the dishwashing evenly," you could say, "I intend to do my share of the housework and leave the rest."

*From Ellis, *Annotated Instructor's Edition for Ellis' Becoming a Master Student,* 14th, 14E. © 2013 Wadsworth, a part of Cengage Learning, Inc. Reproduced by permission. www.cengage.com/permission

Book Discussion Group Chapter 1: The Roots of Success

What did you learn?	What do you think about it?
Just because you get good grades Doesn't mean you always understand it.	It has a lot of pages but true.

Questions?	Key Vocabulary
None	grades Passing Flunking

Chapter 1: The Roots of Success

Write down the following:

1. What is your passion? Use two words or less!

   Doing Makeup

2. Why?

   I love it.

3. How could you incorporate this as a type of career?

   Makeup artist,

Let's share within small groups and then present to the class as a whole.

- You need presentation skills in college and in the workplace.
- This is a safe environment, all must be respectful!

The key is to mix in a balance between passion (writing, NFL) and reality!

What do you expect out of life?

Good and Bad

What is your favorite "golden line" from this chapter?

Just because you get good grades doesn't mean you understand it.

Book Discussion Group Chapter 2: What Makes You an Expert

What did you learn?	What do you think about it?
Surface learners focus only on passing the exam, not ever using anything they read	Very true.

Questions?	Key Vocabulary
What am I?	Surface learner Deep learner Strategic learners

Chapter 2: What Makes You an Expert?

1. What does the author mean when he states that "the problem in college is that your interests don't always line up with what you've been assigned to do"?

   Just because your intrested in this its not always interesting

2. There are three types of learners: Surface, Deep, and Strategic. Describe the differences.

   Surface focuses on passing
   Strategic- Uses Strategys   Deep- use all Info

3. Which type of learner are you and why?

   Surface - thats they way I always have been

4. Some students are "task-oriented" and some are "ego-oriented." What is the difference?

   Told what to do and personality.

5. Intrinsic people look within themselves for ideas, solutions, and motivation ("I get good grades for myself and to learn"). Extrinsic people are moved by factors or people outside of themselves ("I want to graduate with honors", "I get good grades because grades matter" or "my parents expect me to get good grades"). Which one sounds more like you?

   My Parents expect me to get good grades

Now . . . Stand up everyone!

Find someone like you by combining your response to questions 2 and 5.

Surface Intrinsics
Surface Extrinsics
Deep Intrinsics
Deep Extrinsics
Strategic Intrinsics
Strategic Extrinsics

What is your favorite "golden line" from this chapter?

Surface learners intrested in only passing

Book Discussion Group Chapter 3: Managing Yourself

What did you learn?	What do you think about it?
myside bias vividness bias	People do think from there perspective

Questions?	Key Vocabulary
No	Bias myside biss vividness bias Foolish

Chapter 3: Managing Yourself

1. Is it reasonable to believe that others will think the same way that you do? Why or why not?

Well not everything, but somthings yes.
Because we are all alike.

2. Students that had lived in a foreign country and had adapted to the culture of that society were able to do what better? (read: page 69)

They can allways lear n somthing   Problem Solve

3. Why is your "alligator brain" called "alligator," according to the author? (read: page 72)

Pleasure enthusiasm / enjoys life

4. The author explains the difference between "myside bias" and "vividness bias." (read: pages 77–79). As an example of vividness bias, he says that it was "foolish" that so many people decided to drive, rather than fly, after the tragedies of September 11, 2001. Why was it foolish?

Because Flying takes less time and driving takes more!

5. This chapter discusses how society influences our thinking (read: pages 85–88). Tell me three stereotypes you have seen in the media that are unfair judgments to make. Here's an example (please choose 3 of your own): Women aren't as good at sports as men because they primarily show men's athletic competitions on ESPN and during primetime network TV.

1) Example: Men cant wear makeup | Men make more money then women

2) Example: Women need to stay in the kitchen | homeless people are lazy because no job

3) Example: All guys are messy

6. What is your favorite "golden line" from this chapter?

People tend to think from there own perspective

Book Discussion Group Chapter 4: Learning How to Embrace Failure

What did you learn?	What do you think about it?
IQ is not fixed at Birth	Very interesting Chapter.

Questions?	Key Vocabulary
None	IQ

Chapter 4: Learning How to Embrace Failure

1. People who are highly ___creative___ and ___productive___ learn to acknowledge their failures, even to embrace them! (read: page 100).

2. The author says that sometimes we do things to ensure that we will __not__ succeed, even if we are able to succeed. Why would we do that to ourselves? (read: pages 104–105).

   So we dont have to do it.

   To protect yourself from potential failures

3. Did you know that intelligence (IQ) is __not__ fixed at birth? What do you think of this idea? (read: pages 109–111).

   That is true - You dont fix it.

   You have to try and you grow from there

4. Adults often become "disenchanted." This means that as you "grow up," you learn that life is not easy and you begin to feel realistic, or even negative, about the world we live in. Perhaps your dream of being a ballerina or a baseball pitcher as a child is now out-of-reach to you. We see people living in poverty, getting divorced, struggling with many things in life, and we may feel "disenchanted," as though the world is not as sweet and wonderful as a child may see it. Write down five things you thought were "special" or "easy" as a child that you now realize as difficult or, worse yet, near-impossible. For one of my examples, I thought as a child that anyone who looks healthy, probably is, failing to realize that someone can be extremely ill, or near-death, and you may not even know it. So appreciate the time you have with people!

   1) *That everybody is happy*

   2) *living on your own isnt easy*

   3) *Studying hard*

   4) *everybody can have kids*

   5) *every marriage is happy*

5. What is your favorite "golden line" from this chapter?

   None.

Book Discussion Group Chapter 5: Messy Problems

What did you learn?	What do you think about it?
They think on higher levels but never when they were born	Very Interesting

Questions?	Key Vocabulary
nope	prereflective thinking quasi-reflective reflective thinking

Chapter 5: Messy Problems

This chapter addresses whether a college education can help you think better . . . and aid you in problem solving throughout your life.

The author lists on pages 135–136 five different patterns (steps) for people to learn how to handle problems. They are:

1. Surround yourself with diverse sets of people and talk about the problems.
2. Welcome the opportunity to discuss ideas with someone who may disagree with you, or see things differently.
3. Maintain a child-like fascination with the world.
4. Engage in your research and self-questioning regarding your problems.
5. Get the support of a mentor.

Write a problem that you are facing: _Procrastination_

Now, give an example of what you will do to solve this problem, using each of the five patterns (steps) listed above.

1. Plan an agenda

2. Pick a time to do it

3. Stick to the time

4. do it ~~as~~ as planned

5. have extra time to do it

What is your favorite "golden line" from this chapter?

Work

Book Discussion Group Chapter 6: Encouragement

What did you learn?	What do you think about it?
How to relate	Very important

Questions?	Key Vocabulary
no	Compassion understanding Relate.

Chapter 6: Encouragement

Please pair up with someone in class. Discuss an area where each of you needs encouragement when it comes to college.

The author says that encouragement can come from the following sources:

1. Be kind to yourself
2. Keep in mind that other people have faced the same problems
3. Be mindful of what may be causing your problem, but don't obsess over it

Now, write down some ways that you will show understanding and compassion to your classmate regarding his/her specific issue, by completing these phrases below. Offer thorough answers, i.e. more than one word!

1. Understanding: "I can help you think of a solution to your problem by . . ."

   Not giving up, keep trying trying to solve the problem

2. Compassion: "I'm sorry you are facing this. Please know . . ."

   It will get better to keep trying.

3. Relate: "I have/haven't faced that exact issue, but I felt similarly when . . ."

   this has happend to my self

What is your favorite "golden line" from this chapter?

None

Book Discussion Group Chapter 7: Curiosity and Endless Education

What did you learn?	What do you think about it?
You could go to so many classes and they can be pointless.	Interesting

Questions?	Key Vocabulary
No	Major Degrees

Chapter 7: Curiosity and Endless Education

1. "An important part of the creative process is the ability to recognize _good ideas when_ _you encounter them_." (read: page 202)

2. What subject is "the broadest of disciplines because it encompasses all of human affairs?" (read: page 204).

   History

3. Why is it important, in your opinion, to let students choose their own majors?

   Because they will be board out of their mind and miserable

   Should colleges only offer majors/degrees in areas that have definite jobs? Why or why not?

   Well in some things because that maybe will waste your time

4. You should be interested in more subject areas than only your intended major, according to the author. Write down five college subjects, whether you have taken classes in them or not, *and* why they would be of interest to you to take a course in. Consult the Macomb web site if you need ideas.

   1) _Infants_
   2) _Child development_
   3) _Childs arts & crafts_
   4) _Kids learning_
   5) _Developmental needs_

   — They all have to do with children

5. What is your favorite "golden line" from this chapter?

   None

Book Discussion Group Chapter 8: Making the Hard Choices

What did you learn?	What do you think about it?
Do you, you dont have to listan to your Parents	very Interestns with the Harry Potter

Questions?	Key Vocabulary
No	College reading semester Jk Rowing

Chapter 8: Making the Hard Choices

1. What did author J.K. Rowling choose to study in college, to her parents' disappointment? (read: page 221).

    Classics not modern language

    What do your parents (or your relatives) wish you would major in? Why?

    My dad wants me to be in the service.

2. On page 222, what does the author say that he's "written little about" in the book?

    Failure taught me

3. Who said "Failure taught me things about myself that I could have learned no other way." (read: page 223).

    Jo Rowling

4. Much of chapter 8 talks about how reading can make a difference in college and, more importantly, in life. Give three brief examples (read: pages 233–238).

    1) _Better understanding_

    2) _Read faster_

    3) _Better reading skills_

5. How will you approach your classes next semester?

    With no procrastination at 100%

6. How have you changed over this semester?

    I actually tried.

7. What is your favorite "golden line" from this chapter?

    None

Thank you to Cassandra Spieles for helping create these review activities.

Discover. Connect. *Advance.*

Welcome to Macomb Community College!

My name is Dr. Michael Balsamo, and I am the Dean of Learning Resources and Libraries. I also teach business courses as a part-time instructor at the college. I manage online learning, instructional technologies, academic development, and the libraries. I have an Associate's Degree from Macomb Community College, a Bachelor's Degree from Oakland University, a Master's Degree from Walsh College, and a Doctoral Degree from Walden University.

I am responsible for the training and development of the entire faculty at the College, and the quality of the course curriculum. Additionally, I oversee the quality and format of all of the online and hybrid courses. I also manage the libraries, which include all of the computers, books, magazines, journals, and on-line databases that students use to complete their course requirements. What I like most about my position is that I get to work with all parts of the college on many interesting projects that help our students succeed. I am very proud to work at the institution that shaped my career.

In 1985 I graduated from Utica High School. I was an average high school student. I did do very well in drafting and thought of becoming an architect, but wasn't certain. I came to Macomb in the fall of that year to start my college education, unsure of what I wanted to do. That first year, I took all of my classes at Center Campus during the day. It was close to home, and many of my friends also had classes there. Unfortunately, I didn't do very well that year. I struggled with managing my time, and my friends became a distraction. I was very discouraged and wondered if college was for me. I went to speak to a college advisor, and after listening to me about what I was interested in, she informed me of a program at South Campus called Construction Technology. This turned out to be very good advice and changed the path of my life. Being at the other campus removed many of the distractions. Most of the program's courses were at night, and I found myself with older students. And, because I was now in a program, I had a goal to work toward. I started to do well and gain confidence. Without this important moment in my educational journey, I would not be where I am today.

The most important factor in my college success was learning time management skills. Unlike high school, college classes do not meet every day. Some of my classes only met one day a week. I started to put off my homework, and studying until the last moment. Other things, like my social life and work, always seemed to come first. I found myself falling behind, and my grades showed it. As a result of my poor time management, I had to drop or withdraw from a few courses. I was very upset at the time about the money I wasted. I made a commitment to work on my studies in better ways. I developed a calendar that listed all of my course requirements (homework, projects, quizzes, and tests), along with my work schedule. This calendar helped me "see" how much work I needed to do and when. I was able to plan my other activities so that it didn't take time away from my school priorities. I also started spending more time on campus to work in the library where there were no distractions. My grades improved and I felt much better about my ability to do college level work!

I am Michael Balsamo and I am Macomb.

Courtesy of Michael Balsamo

The Game Plan

Appropriate Online and In-Class Behavior

THOUGHT STARTER | *Journal Entry* **3.1**

LEARNING GOAL

To equip you with a set of fundamental skills that all college students need to get off to a fast and good start in college and that will ease your adjustment to college.

1. What are the differences between college and high school?

   Highschool is required and college is not.

2. What tools do you have that will help you succeed in college? Explain.

   the library, tutor, writing center.

Think About It — *Journal Entry* **3.2**

Look at the list of differences between high school and college in Snapshot Summary 3.1. Which differences were you most unaware of or most surprised to see?

School year is 36 weeks long and college is divided in semesters or periods

(continued)

Why? Because school is required. College is not.

Snapshot Summary

3.1 Birds of a Different Feather: High School vs. College

High School	College
Your classes are mostly arranged for you.	You arrange your own schedule in consultation with your advisor. Schedules tend to look lighter than they really are.
Your time is structured by others.	You manage your own time.
You go from one class directly to another, spending six hours per day—30 hours per week—in class.	You have free time between classes; class times vary throughout the day and evening; and you spend 12–16 hours each week in class if you are a full-time student.
The school year is 36 weeks long; some classes extend over both semesters, and some do not.	The academic year may be divided into separate semesters or quarters.
Teachers monitor class attendance.	Professors may not formally monitor class attendance; you're expected to have the self-discipline to show up and get down information that's presented in class.
Teachers often write information on the board for you to put in your notes.	Professors may lecture nonstop, expecting you to identify and write down important information in your notes. Notes that professors write on the board are used to supplement or complement the lecture, not to summarize or substitute for the lecture.
Teachers provide you with information you missed when you were absent.	Professors expect you to get information you missed from classmates.
You are given short reading assignments that are then discussed, and often reviewed, in class.	You're assigned substantial amounts of reading and writing that may not be directly addressed in class.
You seldom need to read anything more than once, and sometimes listening in class is enough.	You need to review class notes and read material regularly.
Teachers present material to help you understand the textbook.	Professors may not follow the textbook, but you may be expected to relate class sessions to textbook readings.

You may have studied outside of class for zero to two hours per week.	You need to study for at least two to three hours outside of class for each hour spent in class.
Teachers remind you of assignments and due dates.	Professors expect you to consult the course syllabus for assignments and deadlines.

Source: Southern Methodist University (2006).

Think About It ——————————— Journal Entry 3.3

1. How do you think college will be different from high school?

   Periods of break and choosing whatever you want.

2. What do you think it will take to be successful in college? (What personal characteristics, qualities, or strategies do you feel are most important for college success?)

   Actually trying and self control.

3. How well do you expect to do in your first term of college? Why?

   I hope hopefully dcent. Because I cant flunk.

Time Spent in Class

Since the total amount of time you spend on learning is associated with how much you learn and how successfully you learn, this association leads to a straightforward recommendation: Attend all class sessions in all your courses. It may be tempting to skip or cut classes because college professors are less likely to monitor your attendance or take roll than your teachers were in high school. However, don't let this new freedom fool you into thinking that missing classes will have no effect on your grades. Over the past 75 years, many research studies in many types of courses have shown a direct relationship between class attendance and course grades—as one goes up or down, so does the other (Anderson & Gates, 2002; Devadoss & Foltz, 1996; Grandpre, 2000; Launius, 1997; Moore, 2003, 2006; Moore, et al., 2003; Shimoff & Catania, 2001; Wiley, 1992; Wyatt, 1992). Figure 3.1 represents the results of a study conducted at the City Colleges of Chicago, which shows the relationship between students' class attendance during the first five weeks of the term and their final course grades.

Student *Perspective*

"My biggest recommendation: GO TO CLASS. I learned this the hard way my first semester. You'll be surprised what you pick up just by being there. I wish someone would have informed me of this before I started school."

—Advice to new students from a college sophomore (Walsh, 2005)

FIGURE 3.1

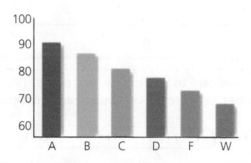

Percentage of Classes Attended and Final Course Grades

Time Spent on Coursework outside the Classroom

You will spend fewer hours per week sitting in class in college than you did in high school. However, you will be expected to spend more time on your own on academic work. Studies clearly show that when college students spend more time on academic work outside of class, the result is better learning and higher grades. For example, one study of more than 25,000 college students found that the percentage of students receiving mostly A grades was almost three times higher for students who spent 40 or more hours per week on academic work than it was for students who spent between 20 and 40 hours. Among students who spent 20 or fewer hours per week on academic work, the percentage receiving grades that were mostly Cs or below was almost twice as high as it was for students who spent 40 or more hours on academic work (Pace, 1990a, 1990b).

"If you are going to achieve excellence in big things, you develop the habit in little matters. Excellence is not an exception, it is a prevailing attitude."

—Colin Powell

Unfortunately, less than 40 percent of beginning college students report having studied for six or more hours per week during their final year in high school (Pryor et al., 2012), only one-third expect to spend more than 20 hours per week preparing for class in college (National Survey of Student Engagement, 2009), and less than 10% say they will study at least two hours out of class for every hour spent in class—which is what most college faculty believe is necessary to do well in college (Kuh, 2005). This has to change if new college students are to earn good grades. Just as successful athletes need to put in time and often work hard to improve their physical performance, successful students need to do the same to improve their academic performance.

Think About It —   Journal Entry 3.4

How are you going to make sure you have the time needed to study in college?

I am going make a time to study and stick to it no putting it off.

If you need further motivation to achieve good grades, keep in mind that higher grades during college result in higher chances of career success after college. Research on college graduates indicates that the higher their college grades, the higher:

- The status (prestige) of their first job;
- Their job mobility (ability to change jobs or move into different positions); and
- Their total earnings (salary).

The more you learn, the more you'll earn. This relationship between college grades and career success exists for students at all types of colleges and universities regardless of the reputation or prestige of the institution that the students are attending (Pascarella & Terenzini, 1991, 2005). In other words, how well you do academically in college matters more to your career success than where you go to college and what institutional name appears on your diploma.

Student Perspective

"In high school, you were a dork if you got good grades and cared about what was going on in your class. In college, you're a dork if you don't."

—College sophomore (Appleby, 2008)

Think About It — Journal Entry 3.5

In high school, how many hours per week did you spend on schoolwork outside of class during your senior year? What do you think you will need to do differently in college?

Not alot because high school wasn't that serias to me as college. I need to sourly try.

Author's Experience

When I went to college, I had to work to assist my family and to assist in paying for college. Although I was an 18-year-old, I came from a very poor family and it was part of my obligation to assist them financially, while it was more important for me to go to school and graduate so I could have a higher standard of living in comparison to my mother and father. Juggling my work life and school life quickly became a reality to which I had to adjust. Thus, I made sure I made the time to study and attend class as my first priority and worked with my employer to adjust my work hours around my classes. By placing my future above my immediate present, I was able to get my college degree and increase my earnings substantially beyond the earnings I had in college and way beyond my parents' earnings.

Aaron Thompson

Classroom Basics (or Fundamentals)

You are now in college and there will be expectations for appropriate behavior both in and out of the classroom. Depending on what kind of course (traditional face-to-face, online, technology-enhanced, or hybrid) you are taking, there will be different expectations for which you are held responsible. Other than a few exceptions (i.e., you can wear pajamas in your house to do an online course but you should not in class), most of the following expectations apply to all.

Snapshot Summary

3.2 Types of Classrooms

Traditional (face-to-face) instruction classrooms offer students and instructors an opportunity to see each other and have interaction. This kind of classroom setting and experience enhances the opportunity for collaborative and social learning.

Technology-enhanced courses use traditional (face-to-face) instruction but also use some Web-based learning tool (i.e., Blackboard) to enhance the course. You are expected to attend all class sessions and also to check the course Web site regularly. You may even be required to do some of your assignments through the course Web site.

Online courses are designed to bring campus-based classes to students' computers. The instructor provides information posted on a course Web site that guides the student through course content, prompts discussions, and helps students keep pace with assignments. Online courses offer flexibility for many working adults; they can offer an accelerated opportunity to a certificate and/or degree. However, they provide less face-to-face social interaction and fewer degree options in comparison to traditional face-to-face classrooms. You will need to pay special attention to when assignments are due and where to turn them in for the instructor's review. In addition, you may have to go to a central location to take proctored exams or do other assessments (e.g., placement tests). Students who are not disciplined often struggle in online courses. These courses are not as easy as many commercials make them out to be. Sometimes an online class can be more difficult than a traditional course.

Web-hybrid (blended) courses blend on-campus instruction with Web-based instruction. Students meet on campus according to the published schedule of classes with approximately half of the course instruction and/or activities occurring online. The hybrid classroom incorporates characteristics from both the traditional and the online classroom: hybrid classrooms have access to the Internet in order to enhance the learning process. Students have the benefit of having face-to-face interactions along with having assignments available to them online at any time. Web-hybrid courses create flexible learning options while allowing students to meet face-to-face with instructors and other students.

Source: http://www.csmd.edu/OnlineLearning/WhatisOnlineLearning.htm

No matter how you take your classes, the first day of class is often the most important and is full of hustle and bustle. There are students of all ages, ethnicities, races, and genders walking with backpacks and energy drinks, looking for their classrooms, or sitting down in front of the computer. Most of these students will be like you, full of newfound curiosities and apprehensions. Questions are being asked of new faces and soon new friends. When you find your classroom (in person or virtually), hopefully the first person you sit next to will become a new friend or study partner. Here you go on your college trip, so please enjoy the ride!

Classroom Top Strategies

1. **Adopt a seating location that maximizes your focus of attention and minimizes sources of distraction.** Many years of research show that students who sit in the front and center of class tend to earn higher exam scores and course grades (Benedict & Hoag, 2004; Rennels & Chaudhair, 1988; Tagliacollo, Volpato, & Pereira, 2010). These results are found even when students are assigned seats by their instructor, so it's not just a matter of more motivated and studious students tending to sit in the front of the room: instead, the better academic performance achieved by students sitting in the front and center of the room likely results from a learning advantage provided by this seating location. Front-and-center seating benefits students' academic performance by improving their vision of

material written on the board or screen and their ability to hear the instructor's lectures. In addition, this seating position allows for better eye contact with the instructor, which can increase students' level of attention, reduce their feeling of anonymity, and heighten their sense of involvement in the classroom. Sitting in the front of class can also reduce your level of anxiety about speaking up in class because, when you speak, you will not have numerous classmates sitting in front of you turning around to look at you while you speak.

2. **Sit by people who will enable (not disable) your ability to learn.** Intentionally sit near classmates who will not distract you or interfere with the quality of your note taking. Attention comes in degrees or amounts; you can give all of your attention or part of it to whatever task you're performing. Trying to grasp complex information in class is a task that demands your undivided attention.

3. **Adopt a seating posture that screams attention.** Sitting upright and leaning forward increases your attention because these bodily signals will reach your brain and increase mental alertness. If your body is in an alert and ready position, your mind tends to pick up these physical cues and follow your body's lead by also becoming alert and ready (to learn). Just as baseball players assume a ready position in the field before a pitch is delivered to put their bodies in position to catch batted balls, learners who assume a ready position in the classroom put themselves in a better position to catch ideas batted around in the classroom. Studies show that when humans are mentally alert and ready to learn, greater amounts of the brain chemical C-kinase are released at the connection points between brain cells, which increases the likelihood that a learning connection will form between them (Howard, 2000).

There's another advantage to being attentive in class: you send a clear message to your instructor that you're a conscientious and courteous student. This can influence your instructor's perception and evaluation of your academic performance, which can earn you the benefit of the doubt at the end of the term if you're on the border between a lower and higher course grade.

Expectations: Classroom Behavior

"For success, attitude is equally as important as ability."
—Walter Scott

Research indicates that one key characteristic of successful learners is that they monitor or watch themselves and maintain self-awareness of the following:

- Whether they are using effective learning strategies. For example, they're aware of their level of attention or concentration in class.
- Whether they comprehend what they are attempting to learn. For example, they're aware of whether they're understanding it at a deep level or merely memorizing it at a surface level.
- How to self-regulate or self-adjust their learning strategies to meet the different demands of different tasks or subjects. For example, when reading technical material in a science textbook, they read more slowly and stop to test their understanding more frequently than when they're reading a novel (Pintrich, 1995; Weinstein, 1994; Weinstein & Meyer, 1991).

"Successful students know a lot about themselves."
—Claire Weinstein and Debra Meyer, professors of educational psychology, University of Texas

For instance, studies show that students who self-monitor their thought processes when solving math and science problems are more effective problem solvers than those who just go through the motions (Resnick, 1986). Effective problem solvers ask themselves such questions as "How did I go about solving this problem correctly?" and "What were the key steps I took to arrive at the correct solution?"

Snapshot Summary

3.3 Reading and Understanding a Syllabus

What's in a syllabus? A course syllabus is a document created by instructors that will probably be given to you on the first day of class. The syllabus has been called a contract between the student and the instructor. Please pay careful attention to all parts of the syllabus and make a copy to keep with you at all times. You are responsible for adhering to this contract. However, your instructor can change the syllabus as he/she deems necessary. A syllabus usually contains the following components (not necessarily in this order):

1. Course department, prefix, number, title, credit hours, semester and year, and course reference number.
2. Meeting times and location, instructor information (name, office location, office hours, contact information).
3. Catalog course description, including prerequisites and/or corequisites (courses students need to have taken before this one or at the same time); prerequisite skill sets (e.g., programming languages, familiarity with software).
4. Text(s) with dates, supplemental text(s), other required readings, and references readings (books, reserve readings, course readers, software, and supplies with information about where they can be obtained). You are expected to have these on the first day or soon after the first day.
5. Student learning outcomes and/or course objectives (this is what the instructor is telling you that he or she will work the lectures around, and you will have learning opportunities around them throughout the course). The tests, quizzes, papers, etc., are based on these objectives.
6. Skills and knowledge students will gain. These are the new items you will have learned after the course is completed. You may hear these referred to as competencies.
7. Course organization. This tells you step-by-step how this course will be taught.
8. Explanation of the topical organization of the course. This will give you an idea of the specific topics that will be covered in class.
9. Course requirements (what students will have to do in the course: assignments, exams, projects, performances, attendance, participation, etc.). Usually the nature and format of assignments and the expected length of written work, as well as due dates for assignments and dates for exams, will be explained.
10. Evaluation and grading policy: what grades are based on, especially your final grade. Always keep up on what grade you have in class and discuss how to improve it with the instructor on a regular basis.
11. Course policies and expectations: may include policies on attendance, participation, tardiness, academic integrity, missing homework, missed exams, recording classroom activities, food in class, laptop use, cell phone use, etc.
12. Other expectations such as student behavior (e.g., respectful consideration of one another's perspectives, open-mindedness, creative risk-taking).
13. Course calendar/schedule (sometimes the instructor will put "tentative" before these words, letting you know it is subject to change). However, this is a class-to-class breakdown of topics and assignments (readings, homework, project due dates).

As a college student, you are responsible for knowing the contents of the course syllabus. It is not the instructor's responsibility to go over it with you. Be sure you read and understand your syllabi for all your courses. If you have any questions, be sure to ask your instructor right away.

You can begin to establish good self-monitoring habits now by getting into a routine of periodically pausing to reflect on how you're going about learning and how you're "doing" college. For instance, consider these questions:

- Are you listening attentively to what your instructor is saying in class?
- Do you comprehend what you are reading outside of class?
- Are you effectively using campus resources that are designed to support your success?

- Are you interacting with campus professionals who can contribute to your current success and future development?
- Are you interacting and collaborating with peers who can contribute to your learning and increase your level of involvement in the college experience?
- Are you effectively implementing the key success strategies identified in this book?

Inappropriate Classroom Behaviors

The following behaviors indicate to the instructor and to your fellow classmates that you are not as committed to your education as they are. In addition, they create confusion in the classroom and disturb the education process. More specifically, they cut down on your opportunity to learn all that you could.

"Behavior is a mirror in which everyone displays his own image."

—Johann Wolfgang von Goethe

- Coming in class late and/or leaving early
- Walking in and out of the classroom during class
- Talking with classmates while the instructor is lecturing
- Disregarding the deadlines set by your instructor or study partners
- Interrupting class with electronic devices or other distractions
- Disrespecting your classmates and/or instructor
- Acting uninterested or sleeping during class
- Working on homework during class
- Cheating on tests, quizzes, papers, or other homework

Technology Is for Learning

Guidelines for Civil and Responsible Use of Personal Technology in the College Classroom

Technology as a Partner

- Turn your cell phone completely off or leave it out of the classroom. In the rare case of an emergency when you think you need to leave it on, inform your instructor.
- Don't check your cell phone during the class period by turning it off and on.
- Don't text message during class.
- Don't surf the Web during class.
- Don't touch your cell phone during any exam, because this may be viewed by the instructor as a form of cheating.

Insensitive Use of Personal Technology in the Classroom: A Violation of Civility

Behavior that interferes with the rights of others to learn or teach in the college classroom is a violation of civility. Listed below are behaviors illustrating classroom incivility that involve student use of personal technology. These behaviors are increasing in college, as is the anger of college instructors who witness them, so be sure not to engage in them.

Using Cell Phones

Keeping a cell phone on in class is a clear example of classroom incivility because if it rings, it will interfere with the right of others to learn. In a study of college students who were exposed to a cell phone ringing during a class session and were later tested for their recall of information presented in class, they scored approximately 25 percent worse when attempting to recall information that was presented at the time a cell phone rang. This attention loss occurred even though the material was covered by the professor before the cell phone rang and was projected on a slide during the call. This study also showed that students were further distracted when classmates frantically searched through handbags or pockets to find and silence a ringing (or vibrating) phone (Shelton, Elliot, Eaves, & Exner, 2009). These findings clearly suggest that the civil thing to do is turn your cell phone off before entering the classroom or keep it out of the classroom altogether.

Sending and Receiving Text Messages

Just as answering a cell phone during class is a violation of civility because it interferes with the learning of other members of the classroom community, so too is text messaging. Although messaging is often viewed as a quick and soundless way to communicate, it can momentarily disrupt learning if it takes place when the instructor is covering critical or complex information. Text messaging while driving a car can take your eyes and mind off the road, thereby putting yourself and others in danger. Similarly, messaging in the classroom takes your eyes and mind off the instructor and any visual aids being displayed at the time. It's also discourteous or disrespectful to instructors when you put your head down and turn your attention from them while they're speaking to the class. Finally, it can be distracting or disturbing to classmates who see you messaging instead of listening and learning.

Correct Use of the Internet

There are common rules for the use of the Internet (see Snapshot Summary 3.4), colloquially referred to as *netiquette* [nétti kèt]. These rules hold true for social media sites such as Facebook, LinkedIn, or MySpace.

Plagiarism: A Violation of Academic Integrity

What Is Plagiarism?

Plagiarism is deliberate or unintentional use of someone else's work without acknowledging it, giving the reader the impression that it's your own work.

Various Forms of Plagiarism

1. Submitting an entire paper, or portion thereof, that was written by someone else
2. Copying sections of someone else's work and inserting it into your own work
3. Cutting paragraphs from separate sources and pasting them into the body of your own paper
4. Paraphrasing (rewording) someone else's words or ideas without citing that person as a source; for examples of acceptable paraphrasing versus plagiarism, go to www.princeton.edu/pr/pub/integrity/pages/plagiarism.html

Student
Perspective

"My intent was not to plagiarize. I realize I was unclear [about] the policy and am actually thankful for now knowing exactly what I can and cannot do on assignments and how to prevent academic dishonesty in the future."

—First-year student's reflection on a plagiarism violation

Snapshot Summary

3.4 Top 20 Rules to Follow for Appropriate Netiquette

Internet etiquette

1. The Internet is not private. What goes out on the airwaves stays on the airwaves! Do not post pictures to the Internet that you would not want your mom or younger cousin to see.
2. Avoid saying anything that could be interpreted as derogatory (e.g., no cursing).
3. Do not say harsh or mean things to someone over e-mail or text (this could be considered cyber bullying) and do not post nasty, mean, or insulting items about someone.
4. Do not respond to nasty e-mails sent to you.
5. Do not break up with a significant other via text or e-mail.
6. When you receive an e-mail that says to forward it to everyone you know, please don't.
7. Do not use ALL CAPITALS. IT IMPLIES YOU ARE SHOUTING!!!
8. When you send messages online, make sure you proofread and correct mistakes before sending.
9. Do not forward other people's e-mails without their permission.
10. Do not forward virus warnings. They are generally hoaxes.
11. Ask before you send huge attachments.
12. Keep your communications short and to the point.
13. Do not leave the subject field blank in e-mails.
14. Avoid posting personal messages to a listserv.
15. Avoid using texting language for e-mails or social media sites (use correct spellings and correct language mechanics).
16. Remember to treat others online as you would like to be treated.
17. Use the Internet in ways that do not take away from your learning, but add to it.
18. Allow an appropriate amount of time for a person to respond to a message (24–48 business hours).
19. Be sure to have an appropriate salutation (i.e., *good morning, hello*) and closing (i.e., *goodbye, see you tomorrow*, etc.) in your e-mails.
20. Avoid slang (i.e., *wha's up, yo*, etc.) and acronyms (*btw, lol*, etc.)

Student Perspective

5. Not placing quotation marks around someone else's exact words that appear in the body of your paper
6. Failing to cite the source of factual information included in your paper that's not common knowledge

Note: If the source for information included in your paper is listed at the end of your paper in your reference (works cited) section but is not cited in the body of your paper, this still qualifies as plagiarism.

Sources: Academic Integrity at Princeton (2003); Pennsylvania State University (2005); Purdue University Online Writing Lab (2004).

Think About It ———————— Journal Entry 3.6

Look back at the definition and forms of plagiarism. List any form of plagiarism contained in that box that you were not already aware of.

Rewording is a form of plagarism

_____

_____

_____

_____

_____

People with integrity have the courage to admit when they're wrong and when they haven't done what they should have done. They don't play the role of victim and look for something or someone else to blame; they're willing to accept the blame and "take the heat" when they're wrong and to take responsibility for making it right. They feel remorse or guilt when they haven't lived up to their own ethical standards, and they use this guilt productively to motivate them to do what's right in the future.

Summary and Conclusion

Research reviewed in this chapter points to the conclusion that successful students are able to:

1. Understand the differences between high school and college;
2. Understand responsible classroom personal behaviors;
3. Understand the dos and don'ts of Internet usage; and
4. Understand the syllabus and class policies.

Learning More through the World Wide Web

Internet-Based Resources for Further Information on Academic Integrity

For additional information related to the ideas discussed in this chapter, we recommend the following Web site:

www.academicintegrity.org/useful_links/index.php

3.1 Personal Traits of a Responsible Student

Construct a master list of personal traits you need to be a responsible student.

1. _Self control_
2. _Responsible_
3. _Productive_
4. _Reasonable_
5. _Successfull_

3.2 Is It or Is It Not Plagiarism?

Following are four incidents that were actually brought to a judicial review board to determine if plagiarism had occurred and, if so, what the penalty should be. After you read each case, answer the questions listed below it.

Case 1. A student turned in an essay that included substantial material copied from a published source. The student admitted that he didn't cite the sources properly, but argued that it was because he misunderstood the directions, not because he was attempting to steal someone else's ideas.

Is this plagiarism?

Copying, stealing, or using anybody work.

How severe is it? (Rate it on a scale from 1 = low to 10 = high)

10, you cangot in big trouble

What should the consequence or penalty be for the student?

I think they should fail whatever they plagecize.

How could the suspicion of plagiarism have been avoided in this case?

Use your own worke

Case 2. A student turned in a paper that was identical to a paper submitted by another student for a different course.

Is this plagiarism?

Yes it could be.

How severe is it? (Rate it on a scale from 1 = low to 10 = high)

10 if copied.

What should the consequence or penalty be for the student?

Fail the assignment

How could the suspicion of plagiarism have been avoided in this case?

Use your own work

Case 3. A student submitted a paper he wrote in a previous course as an extra-credit paper for a course.

Is this plagiarism?

No. It's his work.

How severe is it? (Rate it on a scale from 1 = low to 10 = high)

0

What should the consequence or penalty be for the student?

Nothing

How could the suspicion of plagiarism have been avoided in this case?

There should be none

Case 4. A student submitted a paper in an art history course that contained some ideas from art critics that she read about and whose ideas she agreed with. The student claimed that not citing these critics' ideas wasn't plagiarism because their ideas were merely their own subjective judgments or opinions, not facts or findings, and, furthermore, they were opinions that she agreed with.

Is this plagiarism?

No

How severe is it? (Rate it on a scale from 1 = low to 10 = high)

3

What should the consequence or penalty be for the student?

No one,

Looking back at these four cases, which of them do you think are the most severe and least severe violations of academic integrity? Why?

1 and 2. They copied.

Crime and Punishment: Plagiarism and Its Consequences

In an article that appeared in an Ohio newspaper, titled "Plagiarism Persists in Classrooms," an English professor is quoted as saying, "Technology has made it easier to plagiarize because students can download papers and exchange information and papers through their computers. But technology has also made it easier to catch students who plagiarize." This professor's college subscribes to a Web site that matches the content of students' papers with content from books and online sources. Many professors now require students to submit their papers through this Web site. If students are caught plagiarizing, for a first offense, they typically receive an F for the assignment or the course. A second offense can result in dismissal or expulsion from college, which has already happened to a few students.

Source: Mariettatimes.com (March 22, 2006).

Discussion Questions

1. Why do you think students plagiarize? What do you suspect are the primary motives, reasons, or causes?

   Because they are lazy or busy.

2. What do you think is a fair or just penalty for those found guilty of a first plagiarism violation? What is fair for those who commit a second violation?

   How do you think plagiarism could be most effectively reduced or prevented from happening in the first place?

   They fail paper/assignment. For people keep doing it get kicked out/fired.

   Make punishment more severe

Chapter 3 Reflection

List and describe at least five principles discussed in this chapter that you can use to be a successful college student.

1. No Plagerism
2. Do your own work
3. Responsibility
4. focus
5. Preparation

Now explain HOW you can put these principles into practice.

Do them all and not fail.

In college, like any other meaningful endeavor, there is no short cut to success. In order to be successful in college, students must make the commitment to put forth whatever effort is required to master new knowledge. No one else can do it for you, but rest assured we are here to help you.

We recognize that students come to Macomb with various levels of skill and academic preparedness. Some students come to us directly from high school, and are used to a highly structured learning environment. We also have older adults returning to school for the first time in many years, and they do not know what to expect. We strive to meet all students at their current level, whatever that may be.

In order to help you be successful in college, Macomb has established the College Success Skills course. This course will address several different topics that will help you be successful in your academic career while at Macomb, as well as any other colleges you may attend. Macomb is committed to helping you achieve your educational goal.

Some of the specific topics the College Success Skills course will address to help you be successful include:

- Time management
- Organization
- Effective reading and writing
- Understanding the college process
- Utilizing the support services available to help you

What we have learned from both successful and unsuccessful community college students is that they found deadlines and managing multiple priorities to be a challenge. By learning time management and organization techniques, you will be better able to handle the multiple demands on your time. These skills will help you in college as well as in your personal life.

Successful college students must be able to effectively read, write, communicate, and understand math. These traits are not only required to be successful in college, but they are also required to be a contributing citizen in today's society. The College Success Skills course will help prepare you to further develop your skills in these areas as you take other courses in college.

We have found far too often that students do not take advantage of the resources that are available at Macomb to help them. In many instances students are unfamiliar with the registration process, how to apply for financial aid, or how to know what courses they need to select. Although you have found your way through some of these processes since you are in this course, I suspect some of you may have found it challenging to get to this point.

In this course you will develop a better understanding of how the college process works, and the various resources that are available to assist you. Probably the most important thing you can do is to reach out to the faculty when you are having difficulty with your coursework. Faculty members want you to be successful, and they will do what they can to help you. You will also learn about counseling and advising, tutoring, student success seminars, and career services; all services Macomb has put into place for you to utilize to help you be successful. I cannot stress enough how important it is for you to make use of these services.

By attending college, you are taking one of the steps necessary to create a better life for you and those who are important to you. Congratulations to you in taking that step. If you apply yourself and put forth your best effort, nothing can stop you from being successful. Please utilize the college support services available, and let us help you achieve your educational goal. I look forward to seeing you at a future commencement!

Dr. James O. Sawyer IV
Provost and Vice President for the Learning Unit

Touching All the Bases

An Overview and Preview of the Most Powerful Principles of Community College Success

Journal Entry **4.1**

To equip you with a set of powerful success strategies that you can use immediately to get off to a fast start in college and use continually throughout your college experience to achieve success.

1. What concerns do you have about starting college?

   I have concerns about failing.

2. What excites you about starting college?

   Being on ADA. Starting my life.

The Most Powerful Research-Based Principles of Community College Success

Research on human learning and student development indicates four powerful principles of college success:

1. Active involvement
2. Use of campus resources
3. Interpersonal interaction and collaboration
4. Personal reflection and self-awareness (Astin, 1993; Kuh et al., 2005; Light, 2001; Pascarella & Terenzini, 1991, 2005; Tinto, 1993).

FIGURE 4.1

□ =Supporting Bases for College Success
▼ =Primary ("Home") Base for College Success

© Kendall Hunt

The Diamond of College Success

These four principles represent the key bases of college success. They are introduced and examined carefully in this chapter for two reasons:

1. You can put them into practice to establish good habits for early success in college.
2. These principles represent the foundational bases for all success strategies recommended throughout this book.

The four bases of college success can be represented visually by a baseball diamond (see Figure 4.1).

Touching the First Base of Community College Success: Active Involvement

Research indicates that active involvement may be the most powerful principle of human learning and college success (Astin, 1993; Kuh, 2005). It could be considered the first base of college success, because if it's not touched or covered, you can't advance to any other base. This principle is the gateway to implementing all other principles of college success. The bottom line is that to maximize your success in college, you cannot be a passive spectator: you need to be an active player in the learning process.

The principle of active involvement includes the following pair of processes:

- The amount of personal time you devote to learning in the college experience
- The degree of personal effort or energy (mental and physical) you put into the learning process

Think of something you do with intensity, passion, and commitment. If you were to approach academic work in the same way, you would be faithfully implementing the principle of active involvement.

"Tell me and I'll listen. Show me and I'll understand. Involve me and I'll learn."
—Teton Lakota Indian saying

Student *Perspective*

"You don't have to be smart to work hard."
—24-year-old first-year student who has returned to college

One way to ensure that you're actively involved in the learning process and putting forth high levels of energy or effort is to *act* on what you are learning. Engage in some physical action with respect to what you're learning. You can engage in any of the following actions to ensure that you are investing a high level of effort and energy:

- **Writing.** Express what you're trying to learn in print.
- Action: Write notes when reading rather than passively underlining sentences.
- **Speaking.** Express what you're trying to learn orally.
- Action: Explain a course concept to a study-group partner rather than just looking over it silently.
- **Organizing.** Group or classify ideas you're learning into logical categories.
  Action: Create an outline, diagram, or concept map to visually connect ideas.

The following section explains how you can apply both components of active involvement—spending time and expending energy—to the major learning challenges that you will encounter in college.

Active Listening and Note Taking

You'll find that college professors rely heavily on the lecture method: they profess their knowledge by speaking for long stretches of time, and the students' job is to listen and take notes on the knowledge they dispense. This method of instruction places great demands on the ability to listen carefully and take notes that are both accurate and complete.

Student
Perspective

"I never had a class before when the teacher just stands up and talks to you. He says something and you're writing it down, but then he says something else."

—First-year college student
(Erickson & Strommer, 1991)

Remember

Research shows that, in all subject areas, most test questions on college exams come from the professor's lectures and that students who take better class notes get better course grades (Brown, 1988; Kiewra, 2000).

The best way to apply the principle of active involvement during a class lecture is to engage in the physical action of writing notes. Writing down what your instructor is saying in class "forces" you to pay closer attention to what is being said and reinforces your retention of what was said. By taking notes, you not only hear the information (auditory memory) but also see it on paper (visual memory) and feel it in the muscles of your hand as you write it (motor memory).

Remember

Your role in the college classroom is not to be a passive spectator or an absorbent sponge that sits back and simply soaks up information through osmosis. Instead, your role is more like that of an aggressive detective or investigative reporter who's on a search-and-record mission. You need to actively search for information by picking your instructor's brain, picking out your instructor's key points, and recording your "pickings" in your notebook. See Do It Now! 4.1 for top strategies on classroom listening and note taking, which you should put into practice immediately. Compared to high school, achieving academic success in college will require you to work harder (by investing more time and energy) and to work smarter (by using more effective learning strategies). Academic success will depend not only on the quantity of your work time, but also on its quality; you need to work hard and you need to work smart—by using effective learning strategies and methods (such as those discussed in this text) that enable you to learn more efficiently and more deeply.

4.1   DO IT **NOW** !

Top Strategies for Listening and Note Taking

One of the tasks that you will be expected to perform at the start of your first term in college is to take notes in class. Studies show that professors' lecture notes are the number one source of test questions (and test answers) on college exams. So, get off to a fast start by using the following strategies to improve the quality of your note taking:

1. **Get to every class.** Whether or not your instructors take roll, you're still responsible for all material covered in class. Remember that a full load of college courses (12 units) only requires that you be in class for about 12 hours per week. If you consider your classwork to be a full-time job that only requires you to show up for about 12 hours a week, that's a sweet deal, and it's a deal that allows more educational freedom than you had in high school. To miss a session when you're required to spend so little time in class per week is an abuse of your educational freedom. It's also an abuse of the money you pay, your family pays, or taxpaying American citizens pay to support your college education.

2. **Get to every class on time.** The *first few minutes* of a class session often contain valuable information, such as reminders, reviews, and previews. It is also rude and disruptive to come in late.

3. **Get organized.** Arrive at class with the right equipment; get a separate notebook for each class, write your name on it, date each class session, and store all class handouts in it. Bring your textbook, a writing utensil, paper to take notes, and the right attitude.

4. **Get in the right position.**
   - The ideal place to sit—front and center of the room, where you can hear and see most effectively
   - The ideal posture—upright and leaning forward, because your body influences your mind: if your body is in an alert and ready position, your mind is likely to follow
   - The ideal position socially—near people who will not distract you or detract from the quality of your note taking

5. **Get in the right frame of mind.** Get psyched up; come to class with attitude—an attitude that you're going to pick your instructor's brain, pick up answers to test questions, and pick up your grade.

6. **Get it down (in writing).** Actively look, listen, and record important points at all times in class. Pay special attention to whatever information instructors put in writing, whether it is on the board, on a slide, or in a handout.

7. **Don't let go of your pen.** When in doubt, write it out; it's better to have it and not need it than to need it and not have it.

> **Remember**
>
> *Most college professors do not write all important information on the board for you: instead, they expect you to listen carefully to what they're saying and write it down for yourself.*

8. **Finish strong.** The *last few minutes* of class often contain valuable information, such as reminders, reviews, and previews.

9. **Stick around.** As soon as class ends, don't immediately bolt: instead, hang out for a few moments to briefly review your notes (by yourself or with a classmate). If you find any gaps, check them out with your instructor before he or she leaves the classroom. This quick end-of-class review will help your brain retain the information it just received.

Note: More detailed information on listening and note taking is provided in Chapter 7.

Finish class with a rush of attention, not a rush out the door!

"Learning is something students do, NOT something done to students."
—Alfie Kohn

Think About It —————— Journal Entry 4.2

1. When you enter a classroom, where do you usually sit?

   In the back usually.

2. Why do you think you sit there? Is it a conscious choice or more like an automatic habit?

   Conscious choice, I dont want to be called on.

Active Class Participation

You can become actively involved in the college classroom by arriving at class prepared (e.g., having done the assigned reading), by asking relevant questions, and by contributing thoughtful comments during class discussions. When you communicate orally, you elevate the level of active involvement you invest in the learning process because speaking requires you to exert both mental energy (thinking about what you are going to say) and physical energy (moving your lips to say it). Thus, class participation will increase your ability to stay alert and attentive in class. It also sends a clear message to the instructor that you are a motivated student who takes the course seriously and wants to learn. Since class participation accounts for a portion of your final grade in many courses, your attentiveness and involvement in class can have a direct, positive effect on your course grade.

Active Reading

Writing not only promotes active listening in class, but also can promote active reading out of class. Taking notes on information that you're reading, or on information you've highlighted while reading, helps keep you actively involved in the reading process because it requires more mental and physical energy than merely reading the material or passively highlighting sentences with a highlighter. (See Do It Now! 4.2 for top strategies for reading college textbooks that you should put into practice immediately.)

4.2　　　　　　　　　　　　　　　　　　　　DO IT **NOW** !

Top Strategies for Improving Textbook Reading Comprehension and Retention

If you haven't already acquired textbooks for your courses, get them immediately and get ahead on your reading assignments. Information from reading assignments ranks right behind lecture notes as a source of test questions on college exams. Your professors are likely to deliver class lectures with the expectation that you have done the assigned reading and can build on that knowledge when they're lecturing. If you haven't done the reading, you'll have more difficulty following and taking notes on what your instructor is saying in class. Thus, by not doing the reading you pay a double penalty. College professors also expect you to relate or connect what they talk about in class to the reading they have assigned. Thus, it's important to start developing good reading habits now. You can do so by using the following strategies to improve your reading comprehension and retention.

Student
Perspective

"I recommend that you read the first chapters right away because college professors get started promptly with assigning certain readings. Classes in college move very fast because unlike high school, you do not attend class five times a week but two or three times a week."

—Advice from a first-year student to new college students

1. **Come fully equipped.**
   - **Writing tool and storage.** Always bring a writing tool (pen, pencil, or keyboard) to record important information and a storage space (notebook or computer) to save and later retrieve information acquired from your reading for use on tests and assignments.
   - **Dictionary.** Have a dictionary nearby to quickly find the meaning of unfamiliar words that may interfere with your ability to comprehend what

you're reading. Looking up definitions of unfamiliar words does more than help you understand what you're reading: it's also an effective way to build your vocabulary. Building your vocabulary will improve your reading comprehension in all college courses, as well as your performance on standardized tests, such as those required for admission to graduate and professional schools.

- **Glossary of terms.** Check the back of your textbook for a list of key terms included in the book. Each academic subject or discipline has its own special vocabulary, and knowing the meaning of these terms is often the key to understanding the concepts covered in the text. Don't ignore the glossary; it's more than an ancillary or afterthought to the textbook. Use it regularly to increase your comprehension of course concepts.

2. **Get in the right position.** Sit upright and have light coming from behind you, over the opposite side of your writing hand. This will reduce the distracting and fatiguing effects of glare and shadows.

3. **Get a sneak preview.** Approach the chapter by first reading its boldface headings and any chapter outline, summary, or end-of-chapter questions that may be provided. This will supply you with a mental map of the chapter's important ideas before you start your reading trip and provide an overview that will help you keep track of the chapter's major ideas (the "big picture"), thereby reducing the risk that you'll get lost among the smaller, more specific details you'll encounter along the way.

4. **Use boldface headings and subheadings.** These are cues for important information. Turn these headings into questions, and then read to find their answers. This will launch you on an answer-finding mission that will keep you mentally active while reading and enable you to read with a purpose. Turning headings into questions is also a good way to prepare for tests because you're practicing exactly what you'll be expected to do on tests—answer questions.

5. **Pay special attention to the first and last sentences.** Absorb those in sections of the text that lie beneath the chapter's major headings and subheadings. These sentences often contain an important introduction and conclusion to the material covered within that section of the text.

6. **Finish each of your reading sessions with a short review.** Recall what you have highlighted or noted as important information (rather than trying to cover a few more pages). It's best to use the last few minutes of reading time to "lock in" the most important information you've just read because most forgetting takes place immediately after you stop processing (taking in) information and start doing something else (Underwood, 1983).

Remember

Your goal while reading should be to discover or uncover the most important information contained in what you're reading; when you finish reading, your final step should be to reread (and lock in) the most important information you discovered while reading.

Touching the Second Base of Community College Success: Use of Campus Resources

Your campus environment contains multiple resources designed to support your quest for educational and personal success. Studies show that students who use campus resources report higher levels of satisfaction with college and get more out of the college experience (Pascarella & Terenzini, 1991, 2005).

Remember

Involvement with campus services is not just valuable, it's free; the cost of these services has already been covered by your college tuition. By investing time and energy in campus resources, you not only increase your prospects for personal success but also maximize the return on your financial investment in college—that is, you get a bigger bang for your buck.

"Do not be a PCP (Parking Lot → Classroom → Parking Lot) student. The time you spend on campus will be a sound investment in your academic and professional success."

—Dr. Drew Appleby, professor of psychology

Your Key Campus Resources

Using your campus resources is an important, research-backed principle of college success, and it is a natural extension of the principle of active involvement. Successful students are active learners inside and outside the classroom, and this behavior extends to active use of campus resources. An essential first step toward putting this principle into practice is to become fully aware of all key support services that are available on campus. You can find this information in three major forms:

1. **In print.** Information published in written form. For in-print information on campus resources, consult your college catalog (also known as the college bulletin) and your student handbook. If you do not have a copy of the college catalog, you should be able to obtain one from the Office of Admissions or Center for Academic Advising. If you do not have a copy of the student handbook, you should be able to obtain one from the Office of Student Life or Student Affairs.
2. **Online.** Information posted electronically on the Internet. For online information on campus resources, check your college's Web site. Your college may have its entire catalog and student handbook available online.
3. **In person.** Information communicated directly to you by a knowledgeable person. For in-person information on campus resources, speak with professionals in different offices or centers on your campus, such as those listed here:
   - **Academic Support Services (Tutoring/Writing Center).** Ask about the type of support the tutoring center provides for improving course learning and increasing academic success (e.g., study and test-taking strategies).
   - **College Library.** Ask about the type of support the library provides for finding information and completing research assignments (e.g., term papers and group projects). Librarians are professional educators who provide instruction outside the classroom. You can learn from them just as you can learn from faculty inside the classroom. Furthermore, the library is a place where you can acquire skills for locating, retrieving, and evaluating information that you may apply to any course you are taking or will ever take.
   - **Academic Advisement.** An academic advisor is a personal resource who can help guide you through the educational planning and decision-making process. Studies show that college students who have developed clear educational and career goals are more likely to continue their college education and complete their degrees (Willingham, 1985; Wyckoff, 1999). However, most beginning college students need help clarifying their educational goals, selecting an academic major, and exploring careers (Cuseo, 2005; Frost, 1991). As a first-year college student, being undecided or uncertain about your educational and career goals is nothing to be embarrassed about. However, you should start thinking about your future now. Connect early and often with an academic advisor to help you clarify your educational goals and choose a field that best complements your personal interests, talents, and values.
   - **Student Development Services (Student Affairs).** Ask about the type of support provided on issues relating to social and emotional adjustment, involvement in campus life outside the classroom, and leadership development.
   - **Disability Services.** If you have a physical or learning disability that is interfering with your performance in college, or think you may have such a disability, Disability Services would be the resource on your campus to consult

for assistance and support. Programs and services typically provided by this office include:

- Assessment for learning disabilities;
- Verification of eligibility for disability support services;
- Authorization of academic accommodations for students with disabilities; and
- Specialized counseling, advising, and tutoring.

- **Financial Aid.** If you have questions concerning how to obtain assistance in paying for college, the staff of your Financial Aid Office is there to guide you through the application process. Upon first glance, the materials that need to be submitted may seem confusing or overwhelming. Don't let this intimidate you; seek assistance with this process from the knowledgeable staff in this office on your campus.

- **Counseling Center.** Counseling services can provide you with a valuable source of support in college, not only helping you cope with college stressors that may be interfering with your academic success but also helping you realize your full potential. Personal counseling can promote your self-awareness and self-development in social and emotional areas of your life that are important for mental health, physical wellness, and personal growth.

Think About It ——————————— Journal Entry 4.3

Take a minute to look back at the major campus resources that have been mentioned in this section, and identify two or three of them that you think you should use immediately. Briefly explain why you have identified these resources as your top priorities at this time. Consider asking your course instructor or academic advisor for recommendations about what campus resources you should consult during your first term on campus.

The library - it could help me a lot.

Disability services - this could change my whole life.

Touching the Third Base of Community College Success: Interpersonal Interaction and Collaboration

Learning is strengthened when it takes place in a social context that involves interpersonal interaction. As some scholars put it, human knowledge is socially constructed, or built through interaction and dialogue with others. According to these scholars, your interpersonal conversations become mentally internalized (represented in your mind) and are shaped by the dialogue you've had with others (Bruffee,

1993). Thus, by having frequent, intelligent conversations with others, you broaden your knowledge and deepen your thinking.

Four particular forms of interpersonal interaction have been found to be strongly associated with student learning and motivation in college:

1. Student-faculty interaction
2. Student interaction with academic advisors
3. Student interaction with a mentor
4. Student-student (peer) interaction

Student-Faculty Interaction

Studies repeatedly show that college success is influenced heavily by the quality and quantity of student-faculty interaction *outside the classroom.* Such contact is associated with the following positive outcomes for college students:

- Improved academic performance
- Increased critical thinking skills
- Greater satisfaction with the college experience
- Increased likelihood of completing a college degree
- Stronger desire to seek further education beyond college (Astin, 1993; Pascarella & Terenzini, 1991, 2005)

These positive results are so strong and widespread that we encourage you to seek interaction with college faculty outside of class time. Here are some of the most manageable ways to increase your out-of-class contact with college instructors during the first year of college:

1. **Seek interaction with your instructors immediately after class.** This is when you may be interested in talking about something that was just discussed in class, and it may be when your instructor is interested in discussing it with you. Furthermore, interaction with your instructor immediately after class can help the professor get to know you as an individual, which should increase your confidence and willingness to seek subsequent contact.

2. **Seek interaction with your course instructors during their office hours.** One of the most important pieces of information on the course syllabus is your instructor's office hours. Make specific note of these office hours, and make an earnest attempt to capitalize on them. College professors spend most of their professional time outside the classroom preparing for class, grading papers, conducting research, and serving on college committees. However, some of their out-of-class time is reserved specifically for office hours, during which they are expected to be available.

   You can schedule an office visit with your instructor during the early stages of the course. You can use this time to discuss course assignments, term-paper topics, and career options in your instructor's field. Try to make at least one visit to the office of each of your instructors, preferably early in the term, when quality time is easier to find, rather than at midterm, when major exams and assignments begin to pile up.

   Even if your early contact with instructors is only for a few minutes, it can serve as a valuable icebreaker that helps your instructors get to know you as a person and helps you feel more comfortable interacting with them in the future.

Student *Perspective*

"I wish that I would have taken advantage of professors' open-door policies when I had questions, because actually understanding what I was doing, instead of guessing, would have saved me a lot of stress and re-doing what I did wrong the first time."

—Advice to new students from a college sophomore (Walsh, 2005)

3. **Seek interaction with your instructors through e-mail.** Electronic communication is another effective way to interact with an instructor, particularly if that professor's office hours conflict with your class schedule, work responsibilities, or family commitments. If you are a commuter student who does not live on campus, or if you are an adult student who is juggling family and work commitments along with your academic schedule, e-mail communication may be an especially effective and efficient mode of interaction for you. If you're shy or hesitant about "invading" your professor's office space, e-mail can provide a less threatening way to interact and may give you the self-confidence to seek face-to-face contact with an instructor.

Student-Advisor Interaction

An academic advisor can be an effective referral agent who can direct you to, and connect you with, campus support services that best meet your needs. An advisor can also help you understand college procedures and help you navigate the bureaucratic maze of college policies and politics.

Your academic advisor should be someone whom you feel comfortable speaking with, someone who knows your name, and someone who's familiar with your personal interests and abilities. Give your advisor the opportunity to get to know you personally, and seek your advisor's advice about courses, majors, and personal issues that may be affecting your academic performance.

Think About It ——————————— *Journal Entry* 4.4

Do you know where your advisor or counselor is located on campus? Stop by and meet with an advisor or counselor in the next two weeks to discuss a general education plan. When do you think you can go to advising and counseling?

Whenever I want ~~and~~ while its open.

Interaction with Peers (Student-Student Interaction)

Studies repeatedly point to the power of the peer group as a source of social and academic support during the college years (Pascarella, 2005). One study of more than 25,000 college students revealed that when peers interact with one another while learning, they achieve higher levels of academic performance and are more likely to persist to degree completion (Astin, 1993). In another study that involved in-depth interviews with more than 1,600 college students, it was discovered that almost all

Top Strategies for Making Connections with Key Members of Your College Community

Here is a list of 10 tips for making important interpersonal connections in college. Start making these connections now so that you can begin constructing a base of social support that will strengthen your performance during your first term and, perhaps, throughout your college experience.

1. Connect with a favorite peer or student development professional that you may have met during orientation.
2. Connect with peers who live near you or who commute to school from the same community in which you live. If your schedules are similar, consider carpooling together.
3. Join a college club, student organization, campus committee, intramural team, or volunteer service group whose members may share the same personal or career interests as you.
4. Connect with a peer leader who has been trained to assist new students (e.g., peer tutor, peer mentor, or peer counselor) or with a peer who has more college experience than you.
5. Look for and connect with a motivated classmate in each of your classes and try working as a team to take notes, complete reading assignments, and study for exams. (Look especially to team up with a peer who may be in more than one class with you.)
6. Connect with faculty members in a field that you're considering as a major by visiting them during office hours, conversing briefly with them after class, or communicating with them via e-mail.
7. Connect with an academic support professional in your college's Learning Center for personalized academic assistance or tutoring related to any course in which you'd like to improve your performance.
8. Connect with an academic advisor to discuss and develop your educational plans.
9. Connect with a college librarian to get early assistance and a head start on any research project that you've been assigned.
10. Connect with a personal counselor or campus minister to discuss any college adjustment or personal life issues that you may be experiencing.

students who struggled academically had one particular study habit in common: they always studied alone (Light, 2001).

Peer interaction is especially important during the first term of college. At this stage of the college experience, new students have a strong need for belonging and social acceptance because many of them have just left the lifelong security of family and hometown friends. As a new student, it may be useful to view the early stages of your college experience through the lens of psychologist Abraham Maslow's hierarchy of human needs (see Figure 4.2). According to Maslow's hierarchy of needs, humans cannot reach their full potential and achieve peak performance until their more basic emotional and social needs have been met (e.g., their needs for personal safety, social acceptance, and self-esteem). Making early connections with your peers helps you meet these basic human needs, provides you with a base of social support to ease your integration into the college community, and prepares you to move up to higher levels of the need hierarchy (e.g., achieving educational excellence and fulfilling your potential).

Getting involved with campus organizations or activities is one way to connect you with other students. Also, try to interact with students who have spent more time at college than you. Sophomores can be valuable social resources for a new student. You're likely to find that they are willing to share their experiences with you because you have shown an interest in hearing what they have to say. You may be the first person who has ever asked them what their experiences have been like on your campus. You can learn from their experiences by asking them which courses and instructors they would recommend or what advisors they found to be most well informed and personable.

FIGURE 4.2

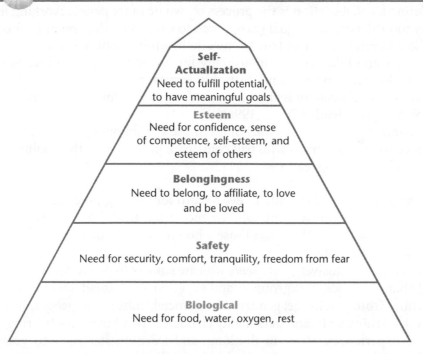

Abraham Maslow's Hierarchy of Needs

Remember

Your peers can be more than competitors or a source of negative peer pressure: they can also be collaborators, a source of positive social influence, and a resource for college success. Be on the lookout for classmates who are motivated to learn and willing to learn with you, and keep an eye out for advanced students who are willing to assist you. Start building your social support network by surrounding yourself with success-seeking and success-achieving students. They can be a stimulating source of positive peer power that can drive you to higher levels of academic performance and heighten your drive to complete college.

Think About It ——————————— *Journal Entry* **4.5**

Think about the students in your classes this term. (1) Are there any students who might be good to connect with and form learning teams? (2) Do you have any classmates who are currently in more than one class with you and who might be good peer partners to team up with and work together on the courses you have in common?

I guess they could be but I am shy.

Collaboration with Peers

Simply defined, collaboration is the process of two or more people working interdependently toward a common goal (as opposed to working independently or competitively). Collaboration involves true teamwork, in which teammates support one another's success and take equal responsibility for helping the team move toward its shared goal. Research on students from kindergarten through college shows that when students collaborate in teams, their academic performance and interpersonal skills improve dramatically (Cuseo, 1996).

To maximize the power of collaboration, use the following guidelines to make wise choices about teammates who will contribute positively to the quality and productivity of your learning team:

1. Observe your classmates with an eye toward identifying potentially good teammates. Look for fellow students who are motivated and who should contribute to your team's success, rather than those who you suspect may just be hitchhikers looking for a free ride.

2. Don't team up exclusively with peers who are similar to you in terms of their personal characteristics, backgrounds, and experiences. Instead, include teammates who differ from you in age; gender; ethnic, racial, cultural, or geographical background; learning style; and personality characteristics. Such variety brings different life experiences, styles of thinking, and learning strategies to your team, which enrich not only its diversity but its quality as well. If your team consists only of friends or classmates whose interests and lifestyles are similar to your own, this familiarity can interfere with your team's focus and performance because your common experiences can get you off track and on to topics that have nothing to do with the learning task (e.g., what you did last weekend or what you are planning to do next weekend).

"TEAM = Together Everyone Achieves More"
—Author unknown

"Surround yourself with only people who are going to lift you higher."
—Oprah Winfrey, actress and talk-show host

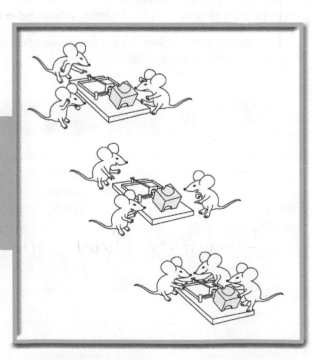

Research shows that when peers work collaboratively to reach a common goal, they learn more effectively and reach "higher levels" of thinking.

Remember

Seek diversity; capitalize on the advantages of collaborating with peers with varied backgrounds and lifestyles. Simply stated, studies show that we learn more from people who are different from us than we do from people who are similar to us (Pascarella, 2001).

Keep in mind that learning teams are not simply study groups formed the night before an exam. Effective learning teams collaborate more regularly and work on a wider variety of academic tasks than late-night study groups. In the following series of important academic tasks and situations, learning teams may be formed to improve your performance.

Note-Taking Teams

Immediately after class sessions end, take a couple of minutes to compare and share notes with other students. Since listening and note taking are demanding tasks, one student often picks up an important point that the others overlooked, and vice versa. By teaming up immediately after class to review your notes, your team has the opportunity to consult with your instructor about any missing or confusing information before the instructor leaves the classroom.

Author's Experience   During my first term in college, I was having difficulty taking complete notes in my biology course because the instructor spoke rapidly and with an unfamiliar accent. I noticed another student (Alex) sitting in the front row who was trying to take notes the best he could, but he was experiencing the same difficulty. Following one particularly fast and complex lecture, we looked at each other and began to share our frustrations. We decided to do something about it by pairing up immediately after every class and compare our notes to identify points we missed or found confusing. First, we helped each other by comparing and sharing our notes in case one of us got something that the other missed. If there were points that we both missed or couldn't figure out, we went to the front of class together to consult with the instructor before he left the classroom. At the end of the course, Alex and I finished with the highest grades in the course.

Joe Cuseo

Reading Teams

After completing your reading assignments, you can compare your highlighting and margin notes with classmates. Consult with one another and share what you thought were the most important points in the reading that should be studied for upcoming exams.

Writing Teams

Teammates can provide one another with feedback that can be used to revise and improve the quality of their individual writing. You can form writing teams with peers at any or all of the following stages in the writing process:

- **Topic selection and refinement.** To help generate a list of potential topics and subtopics
- **Prewriting.** To clarify your purpose and audience
- **First draft.** To improve your general style and tone
- **Final draft.** To proofread and correct mechanical errors before submitting your work

Library Research Teams

Many first-year students are unfamiliar with the process of conducting library research, and some experience "library anxiety" and try to avoid even stepping into the library, particularly if it's large and intimidating (Malvasi, Rudowsky, & Valencia, 2009). Forming library research teams is an effective way for you to develop a social support group that can make trips to the library less intimidating and transform library research from a "flying solo" experience into a collaborative experience.

> **Remember**
>
> *It is ethical and acceptable for you to team up with others to search for and share resources. This is not cheating or plagiarizing, as long as your final product is completed individually and what you turn in to your instructor represents your own work.*

Team-Instructor Conferences

Visiting course instructors outside of class with other classmates is an effective way to get additional assistance in preparing for exams and completing assignments for several reasons:

- You may feel more comfortable about seeing instructors on their turf if you are accompanied by peers, rather than entering this unfamiliar territory on your own. As the old expression goes, "There's safety in numbers."
- When you make an office visit as a team, the information shared by the instructor is heard by more than one person, so your teammates may pick up some useful information that you may have missed, misinterpreted, or forgotten, and you may do the same for them.
- You save instructors time by allowing them to help multiple students at the same time rather than requiring them to engage in repeat "performances" for students who visit individually at different times.
- You send a message to instructors that you're serious about the course and are a motivated student because you've taken the time—ahead of time—to connect with your peers and prepare for the office visit.

"Two heads are better than one, not because either is infallible, but because they are unlikely to go wrong in the same direction."

—C. S. Lewis, English novelist and essayist

Study Teams

Research clearly demonstrates that college students learn from peers as much as, or more than, they do from instructors and textbooks (Astin, 1993; Pascarella, 2005). When seniors at Harvard University were interviewed, nearly everyone who had been part of a study group considered this experience to be crucial to their academic progress and success (Light, 1990, 1992).

Research on study groups also indicates that they are effective only if each member has done required coursework in advance of the team meeting; for example, if each group member has done the required reading and other course assignments (Light, 2001). Thus, to fully capitalize and maximize the power of study teams, each member should study individually *before* studying in a group. Each member should come prepared with specific information or answers to share with teammates, as well as specific questions or points of confusion about which they hope to receive help from the team. This ensures that all team members are individually accountable and equally responsible for doing their own learning, as well as for contributing to the learning of their teammates.

Test-Review and Assignment-Review Teams

After you receive the results of your course exams and assignments, you can collaborate with peers to review your results as a team. By comparing answers, you can better identify the sources of your mistakes. By observing the answers of teammates who may have received maximum credit on particular questions, you can get a clearer picture of where you went wrong and what you need to do better next time.

Teaming up after tests and assignments given early in the term is especially effective, because it enables you to get a better idea of what the instructor expects from students throughout the remainder of the course. What you learn from your peers can be used as early feedback to diagnose your mistakes, improve your next performance, and raise your grade while there's still plenty of time left in the course to do so.

Touching the Fourth (Home) Base of Community College Success: Personal Reflection and Self-Awareness

The final steps in the learning process, whether it be learning in the classroom or learning from experience, are to step back from the process, thoughtfully review it, and connect it to what you already know. Reflection may be defined as the flip side of active involvement; both processes are necessary for learning to be complete. Learning requires not only effortful action, but also thoughtful reflection. Active involvement gets and holds your focus of attention, which enables information to reach your brain, and personal reflection promotes consolidation, which "locks" that information into your brain's long-term memory (Bligh, 2000; Broadbent, 1970).

Brain research reveals that two different brain-wave patterns are associated with the mental states of involvement and reflection (Bradshaw, 1995; see Figure 4.3). The brain waves on the left reveal faster activity, indicating that the person is actively involved in the learning task and attending to it. The slower brain-wave pattern on the right indicates that the person is thinking deeply about information taken in, which will help consolidate or lock that information into long-term memory. Thus, effective learning combines active mental involvement (characterized by faster, shorter brain waves) with thoughtful reflection (characterized by slower, longer brain waves).

FIGURE 4.3

High-Amplitude Brain Waves Associated with a Mental State of *Active Involvement.*

High-Frequency Brain Waves Associated with a Mental State of *Reflective Thinking.*

© Kendall Hunt

Brain Wave Patterns

Personal reflection involves introspection—turning inward and inspecting yourself to gain deeper self-awareness of what you've done, what you're doing, or what you intend to do. Two forms of self-awareness are particularly important for success in college:

> "We learn to do neither by thinking nor by doing; we learn to do by thinking about what we are doing."
>
> —George Stoddard, former professor of psychology and education, University of Iowa

1. Self-assessment
2. Self-monitoring

Self-Assessment

Simply defined, self-assessment is the process of reflecting on and evaluating your personal characteristics, such as your personality traits, learning habits, and personal strengths or weaknesses. Self-assessment promotes self-awareness, which is the critical first step in the process of self-improvement, personal planning, and effective decision making. The following are important target areas for self-assessment and self-awareness because they reflect personal characteristics that play a pivotal role in promoting success in college and beyond:

- **Personal interests.** What you like to do or enjoy doing
- **Personal values.** What is important to you and what you care about doing
- **Personal abilities or aptitudes.** What you do well or have the potential to do well
- **Learning habits.** How you go about learning and the usual approaches, methods, or techniques you use to learn
- **Learning styles.** How you prefer to learn; that is, the way you like to:
  - Receive information—which learning format you prefer (e.g., reading, listening, or experiencing)
  - Perceive information—which sensory modality you prefer (e.g., vision, sound, or touch)
  - Process information—how you mentally deal with information once you have taken it in (e.g., think about it on your own or discuss it with others)
- **Personality traits.** Your temperament, emotional characteristics, and social tendencies (e.g., whether you lean toward being outgoing or reserved)
- **Academic self-concept.** Your personal beliefs about what kind of student you think you are and how you perceive yourself as a learner (e.g., your level of self-confidence and whether you believe success is within your control or depends on factors beyond your control)

Think About It ———————————————— Journal Entry 4.6

1. How would you rate your academic self-confidence at this point in your college experience? (Circle one)

   very confident   (somewhat confident)   somewhat unconfident   very unconfident

2. Why did you make this choice?

   Because Im afraid to still fail.

   _____

   _____

   _____

   _____

Self-Monitoring

Research indicates that one key characteristic of successful learners is that they monitor or watch themselves and maintain self-awareness of the following:

- Whether they are using effective learning strategies. For example, they're aware of their level of attention or concentration in class.
- Whether they are comprehending what they are attempting to learn. For example, they're aware of whether they're understanding it at a deep level or merely memorizing it at a surface level.
- How to self-regulate or self-adjust their learning strategies to meet the different demands of different tasks or subjects. For example, they read technical material in a science textbook more slowly and stop to test their understanding more frequently than when they're reading a novel (Pintrich, 1995; Weinstein, 1994; Weinstein & Meyer, 1991).

Summary and Conclusion

Research reviewed in this chapter points to the conclusion that successful students are:

"Successful students know a lot about themselves."

—Claire Weinstein and Debra Meyer, professors of educational psychology, University of Texas

1. **Involved.** They invest time and effort in the college experience;
2. **Resourceful.** They capitalize on their surrounding resources;
3. **Interactive.** They interact and collaborate with others; and
4. **Reflective.** They are self-aware learners who assess and monitor their own performance.

Successful students are students who could honestly check almost every box in the following self-assessment checklist of success-promoting principles and practices.

A Checklist of Success-Promoting Principles and Practices

1. **Active Involvement**
   Inside the classroom, I:
   - ☑ **Get to class.** Treat it like a job; if you cut, your pay (grade) will be cut.
   - ☑ **Get involved in class.** Come prepared, listen actively, take notes, and participate.

   Outside the classroom, I:
   - ☑ **Read actively.** Take notes while you read to increase attention and retention.
   - ☑ **Double up.** Spend twice as much time on academic work outside the classroom than you spend in class—if you're a full-time student, that makes it a 40-hour academic workweek (with occasional "overtime").

2. **Use of Campus Resources**
   I capitalize on academic and student support services, such as the following:
   - ☑ Learning Center
   - ☑ Writing Center
   - ☑ Disability Services
   - ☑ College Library
   - ☑ Academic Advisement
   - ☑ Career Development Center

☑ Financial Aid Office
☑ Counseling Center
☑ Experiential Learning Resources

3. **Interpersonal Interaction and Collaboration**
    I interact with the following people:

    ☑ **Peers.** Join student clubs and participate in campus organizations.
    ☑ **Faculty members.** Connect with them immediately after class, in their offices, or via e-mail.
    ☑ **Academic advisors.** See them for more than just a signature to register; find an advisor you can relate to and with whom you can develop an ongoing relationship.
    ☑ **Mentors.** Try to find experienced people on campus who can serve as trusted guides and role models.

    I collaborate by doing the following:

    ☑ **Form learning teams.** Join not only last-minute study groups but also teams that collaborate more regularly to work on such tasks as taking lecture notes, completing reading and writing assignments, conducting library research, and reviewing results of exams or course assignments.
    ☑ **Participate in learning communities.** Enroll in two or more classes with the same students during the same term.

4. **Personal Reflection and Self-Awareness**
    I engage in:

    ☑ **Self-assessment.** Reflect on and evaluate your personal traits, habits, strengths, and weaknesses.
    ☑ **Self-monitoring.** Maintain self-awareness of how you're learning, what you're learning. and whether you're learning.

Think About It ———   *Journal Entry* **4.7**

Before exiting this chapter, look back at the Checklist of Success-Promoting Principles and Practices and see how these ideas compare with those you recorded at the start of this chapter, when we asked you how you thought college would be different from high school and what it would take to be successful in college.

Tutors / library etc.

_____

_____

_____

_____

_____

1. What ideas from your list and our checklist tend to match?

   Learning teams, library, and tutors

2. Were there any ideas on your list that were not on ours, or vice versa?

   Nope.

Learning More through the World Wide Web

Internet-Based Resources for Further Information on College Success

For additional information relating to the ideas discussed in this chapter, we recommend the following Web sites:

www.dartmouth.edu/~acskills/success/index.html

www.uni.edu/walsh/linda7.html

www.lifehack.org/article/lifehack/from-a-freshman-five-tips-for-success-in-college.html

Alone and Disconnected: Feeling Like Calling It Quits

Josephine is a first-year student in her second week of college. She doesn't feel like she fits in with other students on her campus. She feels that by going to college she's taking time away from her family and longtime friends who are not in college, and she fears that her ties with them will be weakened or broken if she continues to spend so much time on school and schoolwork. Josephine is feeling so torn between college and her family and old friends that she's beginning to have second thoughts about whether she should have even begun college.

Discussion Questions

1. What might you say to Josephine that might persuade her to stay in college?

   Just stay, your family wants you to succede.

2. Could the college have done more during her first two weeks on campus to make Josephine (and other students) feel more connected with college and less disconnected from family?

   Nope, its on her.

3. Do you see anything that Josephine could do now to minimize the conflict or balance the tension she's experiencing between her commitment to college and her ties to family and friends?

   Visit her friends/family more.

Chapter 4 Reflection

WHAT do you believe is the most important principle of community college success?

To succede and lean.

WHY do you believe this is the most important one?

Because if you dont succede and learn there is nopoint of going to college

Explain HOW you will use this principle to assist you in being successful in college.

I will learn and succede.

Welcome to Macomb Community College!

I am Lou Aquino. I am a Counselor in the Special Services Office at the Center Campus. I work with students with disabilities, students whose first language is not English, and students who place into remedial courses on the COMPASS placement test. Over the years I have seen many students come in and out of my office. Some students are on the road to success, and some students have not found the road yet. For the ones who have, they decided to make an investment in themselves and worked on their fundamental academic skills in English and reading. Many students don't realize the importance of strong reading and writing skills in college-level classes. By starting out with a strong foundation in these areas, students are often better prepared for the reading and writing demands throughout their college careers.

Goal setting is an activity that I encourage students to think about and utilize. There are a variety of goals that are important to think about. Educational goals, employment goals, financial goals, and personal goals are a few common goals that students may be thinking about. Within each of those goals, there are also long-term objectives and short-term objectives. It takes some time to establish goals, and they can be changed or modified as you go through life. Goals should be specific, realistic, measurable, achievable, and time-targeted. I often recommend that students write down their goals and periodically look at them to measure their progress or make adjustments.

Goal setting is a great way to create motivation. When you are able to see your long-term and short-term goals and track your progress toward reaching them, it helps keep you motivated to continue your pursuit of those goals. Being a motivated student can lead to better attendance, better grades, and a better attitude. It can turn into a positive cycle where motivation feeds success and success feeds motivation.

When students set goals and are motivated to attain them, they push themselves to seek better ways to study, make connections with other students and instructors, and utilize available resources to improve their chances of success. Though engaging in these activities may put students out of their comfort zone, it helps them build strong character and gain confidence in themselves. They begin to change the way they think about challenging classes and difficult assignments, viewing them as learning situations and opportunities for growth.

I hope you find your experience at Macomb Community College rewarding and exciting. I hope you make lasting connections with faculty and other students. I hope you engage in setting goals for yourself and develop the motivation to work toward them. I also hope that you begin to view the challenges in your classes as growth opportunities, and begin to develop the strong character qualities of successful students.

Please stop by the Counseling and Academic Advising Office if you would like to discuss goal setting, motivation, programs of study at Macomb Community College, and campus resources. We look forward to working with you.

I am Lou Aquino and I am Macomb.

Courtesy of Lou Aquino

Goal Setting, Motivation, and Character

5

LEARNING GOAL

To develop meaningful goals to strive for, along with strategies for maintaining motivation and building character to achieve those goals.

How would you define the word *successful*?

To get to where you need to be or where you want to be

What Does "Being Successful" Mean to You?

The word *success* means "to achieve a desired outcome"; it derives from the Latin root *successus,* which means "to follow or come after" (as in the word *succession*). Thus, by definition, success involves an order or sequence of actions that lead to a desired outcome. The process starts with identifying an end (goal) and then finding a means (sequence of steps) to reach that goal (achieving success). Goal setting is the first step in the process of becoming successful because it gives you something specific to strive for and ensures that you start off in the right direction. Studies consistently show that setting specific goals is a more effective self-motivational strategy than to simply tell yourself that you should "try hard" or "do your best" (Boekaerts, Pintrich, & Zeidner, 2000; Locke & Latham, 1990).

By setting goals, you show initiative—you work to gain control of your future and take charge of your life. By taking initiative, you demonstrate what psychologists call an internal locus of control—you believe that the locus (location or source) of control for events in your life is *internal,* and thus within you and your control, rather than *external,* or outside of you and beyond your control (controlled by such factors as luck, chance, or fate; Rotter, 1966).

Research reveals that individuals with a strong internal locus of control display the following characteristics:

1. Greater independence and self-direction (Van Overwalle, Mervielde, & De Schuyer, 1995)

"You've got to be careful if you don't know where you're going because you might not get there."

—Yogi Berra, Hall of Fame baseball player

"There is perhaps nothing worse than reaching the top of the ladder and discovering that you're on the wrong wall."

—Joseph Campbell, American professor and writer

"Success is getting what you want. Happiness is wanting what you get."

—Dale Carnegie, author of the bestselling book *How to Win Friends and Influence People* (1936) and founder of the Dale Carnegie Course, a worldwide program for business based on his teachings

"I'm a great believer in luck, and I find the harder I work the more I have of it."

—Thomas Jefferson, third president of the United States

2. More accurate self-assessment (Hashaw, Hammond, & Rogers, 1990; Lefcourt, 1982)
3. Higher levels of learning and achievement (Wilhite, 1990)
4. Better physical health (Maddi, 2002; Seligman, 1991)

An internal locus of control also contributes to the development of another positive trait, which psychologists call *self-efficacy*—the belief that you have the power to produce a positive effect on the outcomes of your life (Bandura, 1994). People with low self-efficacy tend to feel helpless, powerless, and passive; they allow things to happen *to* them rather than taking charge and making things happen *for* them. College students with a strong sense of self-efficacy believe they're in control of their educational success, regardless of their past or current circumstances.

If you have a strong sense of self-efficacy, you initiate action, put forth effort, and sustain that effort until you reach your goal. If you encounter setbacks or bad breaks along the way, you don't give up or give in: you persevere or push on (Bandura, 1986, 1997).

Students with a strong sense of academic self-efficacy have been found to:

1. Put great effort into their studies;
2. Use active-learning strategies;
3. Capitalize on campus resources; and
4. Persist in the face of obstacles (Multon, Brown, & Lent, 1991; Zimmerman, 1995).

> "What lies behind us and what lies in front of us are small matters compared to what lies within us."
>
> —Ralph Waldo Emerson, 19th-century American essayist and lecturer

> "Control your own destiny or someone else will."
>
> —Jack Welch, chemical engineer, author, and successful CEO of the General Electric Company

Think About It ———————————————————— Journal Entry 5.2

You are not required by law or by others to attend college; you've made the decision to continue your education. Do you believe you are in charge of your educational destiny?

Yes, grades are not given you earn them.

Why or why not?

Grades are not given, you earn them.

Students with self-efficacy also possess a strong sense of personal responsibility. As the breakdown of the word *responsible* implies, they are "response" "able"—i.e., they believe they are able to respond effectively to personal challenges, including educational challenges.

Students with self-efficacy do not have a false sense of entitlement. They don't feel they're entitled to, or owed, anything; they believe that success is earned and is theirs for the taking. For example, studies show that students who convert their college degrees into successful careers have two common characteristics: personal initiative and a positive attitude (Pope, 1990). They don't take a passive approach and assume good positions will fall into their laps, nor do they believe they are owed positions simply because they have college degrees or credentials. Instead, they become actively involved in the job-hunting process and use various job-search strategies (Brown & Krane, 2000).

> "The price of greatness is responsibility."
>
> —Winston Churchill, British prime minister during World War II and Nobel Prize winner in literature

> "You miss 100 percent of the shots you never take."
>
> —Wayne Gretzky, Hall-of-Fame hockey player, nicknamed "The Great One" and considered by many to be the greatest hockey player of all time

Think About It — Journal Entry 5.3

1. In what area or areas of your life do you feel that you've been able to exert the most control and achieve the most positive results?

   What I want to do during my life and passions!

2. In what area or areas of your life do you wish you had more control and were achieving better results?

   If I could go to beauty school and do what I want to do

3. What have you done in the area or areas of your life where you've taken charge and gained control that might be transferred or applied to the area or areas in which you need to gain more control?

   Telling my Dad no and not going into the service.

Strategies for Effective Goal Setting

Motivation begins with goal setting. Studies show that people who neglect to set and pursue life goals are prone to feelings of "life boredom" and a belief that life is meaningless (Bargdill, 2000). Goals may be classified into three general categories: long-range, mid-range, and short-range, depending on the length of time it takes to reach them and the order in which they are to be achieved. Short-range goals need to be completed before a mid-range goal can be reached, and mid-range goals must be reached before a long-range goal can be achieved. For example, if your long-range goal is a successful career, you must complete the courses required for a degree (mid-range goal) that will allow your entry into a career; to reach your mid-range goal of a college degree, you need to successfully complete the courses you're taking this term (short-range goal).

This process is called *means-end analysis*, which involves working backward from your long-range goal (the end) and identifying the order and timing of the mid-range and short-range subgoals (the means) that need to be taken to reach your long-range goal (Brooks, 2009; Newell & Simon, 1959).

Setting Long-Range Goals

Setting effective long-range goals involves two processes: (1) self-awareness, or insight into who you are now, and (2) self-projection, or a vision of what you want to become in the future. When you engage in both of these processes, you're able to see a connection between your short- and your long-range goals.

"To fail to plan is to plan to fail."

—Robert Wubbolding, internationally known author, psychologist, and teacher

Long-range goal setting enables you to take an approach to your future that is proactive—acting beforehand to anticipate and control your future life rather than putting it off and being forced to react to it without a plan. Research shows that people who neglect to set goals for themselves are more likely to experience boredom with life (Bargdill, 2000). Setting long-range goals and planning ahead also help reduce feelings of anxiety about the future because you've given it forethought, which gives you greater power to control it (i.e., it gives you a stronger sense of self-efficacy). As the old saying goes, "To be forewarned is to be forearmed."

"You have brains in your head. You have feet in your shoes. You can steer yourself any direction you choose."

—Theodore Seuss Giesel, a.k.a. Dr. Seuss, famous author of children's books including *Oh, the Places You'll Go!*

Remember that setting long-range goals and developing long-range plans doesn't mean you can't adjust or modify them. Your goals can undergo change as you change, develop new skills, acquire new knowledge, and discover new interests or talents. Finding yourself and your path in life is one of the primary purposes of a college education. Don't think that the process of setting long-range goals means you will be locked into a premature plan and reduced options. Instead, it will give you something to reach for and some momentum to get you moving in the right direction.

Steps in the Goal-Setting Process

Effective goal setting involves a four-step sequence:

1. **Awareness of yourself.** Your personal interests, abilities and talents, and values;
2. **Awareness of your options.** The choices available to you;
3. **Awareness of the options that best fit you.** The goals most compatible with your personal abilities, interests, values, and needs;
4. **Awareness of the process.** The steps that you need to take to reach your chosen goal.

Discussed in the next sections are strategies for taking each of these steps in the goal-setting process.

Step 1. Self-Awareness

The goals you choose to pursue say a lot about who you are and what you want from life. Thus, self-awareness is a critical first step in the process of goal setting. You must know yourself before you can choose the goals you want to achieve. While this may seem obvious, self-awareness and self-discovery are often overlooked aspects of the goal-setting process. Deepening your self-awareness puts you in a better position to select and choose goals and to pursue a personal path that's true to who you are and what you want to become.

"Know thyself, and to thine own self be true."

—Plato, ancient Greek philosopher

© Kendall Hunt

> **Remember**
>
> *Self-awareness is the first, most important step in the process of making any important life choice or decision.*

No one is in a better position to know who you are, and what you want to be, than *you*. One effective way to get to know yourself more deeply is through self-questioning. You can begin to deepen your self-awareness by asking yourself questions that can stimulate your thinking about your inner qualities and priorities. Effective self-questioning can launch you on an inward quest or journey to self-discovery and self-insight, which is the critical first step to effective goal setting. For example, if your long-range goal is career success, you can launch your voyage toward achieving this goal by asking yourself thought-provoking questions relating to your personal:

- **Interests.** What you like to do;
- **Abilities.** What you're good at doing; and
- **Values.** What you believe is worth doing.

"In order to succeed, you must know what you are doing, like what you are doing, and believe in what you are doing."

—Will Rogers, Native American humorist and actor

Know Thyself

Self-awareness is the first and most important step in the process of making effective choices or decisions.

The following questions are designed to sharpen your self-awareness with respect to your interests, abilities, and values. As you read each question, briefly note what thought or thoughts come to mind about yourself.

Your Personal Interests

makeup
makeup
go to concerts
music
makeup
fan girl

1. What tends to grab your attention and hold it for long periods?
2. What sorts of things are you naturally curious about or tend to intrigue you?
3. What do you enjoy and do as often as you possibly can?
4. What do you look forward to or get excited about?
5. What are your favorite hobbies or pastimes?
6. When you're with your friends, what do you like to talk about or spend time doing together?

learning new
price taging
chilling
romance
notification
harry styles

7. What has been your most stimulating or enjoyable learning experience?
8. If you've had previous work or volunteer experience, what jobs or tasks did you find most enjoyable or stimulating?
9. When time seems to "fly by" for you, what are you usually doing?
10. What do you like to read about?
11. When you open a newspaper or log on to the Internet, what do you tend to read first?
12. When you find yourself daydreaming or fantasizing about your future life, what do you most find yourself doing?

Think About It ——————————— *Journal Entry* **5.4**

From your responses to the preceding questions, identify a long-range goal you could pursue that's compatible with your personal interests. In the space that follows, note the goal and the interests that are compatible with it.

I could be a makeup artiste.
Go to beauty school.

Your Personal Abilities and Talents

1. What seems to come easily or naturally to you? *Makeup*
2. What would you say is your greatest talent or personal gift? *myself*
3. What do you excel at when you apply yourself and put forth your best effort? *Style*
4. What are your most advanced or well-developed skills? *creativeness*
5. What would you say has been the greatest accomplishment or achievement in your life thus far? *Doing a modeling shoot.*
6. What about yourself are you most proud of, or what do you take the most pride in doing? *I dont listen to any negative*
7. When others come to you for advice or assistance, what is it usually for?

Makeup.

"Never desert your line of talent. Be what nature intended you for and you will succeed."

—Sydney Smith, 18th-century English writer and defender of the oppressed

8. What would your best friend or friends say is your best quality, trait, or characteristic? *they, that im very loving and talkative*

9. What things have you done that gave you a strong feeling of being successful? *Making People happy.*

10. If you've received awards or other forms of recognition, what have you received them for? *Being good at somthing*

11. On what types of learning tasks or activities have you experienced the most success? *Doing stuff onmyself*

12. In what types of courses do you tend to earn the highest grades?

English, etc.

Think About It ——————————————— Journal Entry 5.5

From your responses to the preceding questions, identify a long-range goal you could pursue that's compatible with your personal abilities. In the space that follows, note the goal and the abilities that are compatible with it.

Make more friends and start getting more people to know my name.

Your Personal Values

1. What matters most to you? *family*
2. If you were to single out one thing you stand for or believe in, what would it be? *Love*
3. What would you say are your highest priorities in life? *being successful*
4. What makes you feel good about what you're doing when you're doing it? *Makeup*
5. If there were one thing in the world you could change, improve, or make a difference in, what would it be? *to be Smarter and better*
6. When you have extra spending money, what do you usually spend it on? *Makeup*
7. When you have free time, what do you usually find yourself doing? *hanging w/ friends*
8. What does living a "good life" mean to you? *living the fullest*
9. How would you define success? (What would it take for you to feel that you were successful?) *To be widely known*
10. How do you define happiness? (What would it take for you to feel happy?) *to not be upset*
11. Do you have any heroes or anyone you admire, look up to, or feel has set an example worth following? If yes, who and why? *Desi perkins, Lustrelux, Kathleen lights*
12. Which of the following four personal qualities would you want to be known for? Rank them in order of priority to you (1 = highest, 4 = lowest).
    ____4__ Smart
    ____3__ Wealthy
    ____1__ Creative
    ____2__ Caring

> "Do what you value; value what you do."
>
> —Sidney Simon, *Values Clarification* and *In Search of Values* (1993)

From your responses to the preceding questions, identify a long-range goal you could pursue that's compatible with your personal values. In the space that follows, note the goal and the values that are compatible with it.

To become known in this world.

Become youtuber.

Step 2. Awareness of Your Options

The second critical step in the goal-setting process is to become aware of your long-range goal choices. For example, to effectively choose a career goal, you need to be aware of what career options are available to you and have a realistic understanding of the types of work done in these careers. To gain this knowledge, you'll need to capitalize on available resources, such as the following:

1. Reading books about different careers
2. Taking career development courses
3. Interviewing people in different career fields
4. Observing (shadowing) people working in different careers

One characteristic of effective goal setting is to create goals that are realistic. In the case of careers, getting firsthand experience in actual work settings (e.g., shadowing, internships, volunteer services, and part-time work) would give you a realistic view of what work is like in certain careers, as opposed to the idealized or fantasized way careers are portrayed on TV and in the movies.

"Students [may be] pushed into careers by their families, while others have picked one just to relieve their anxiety about not having a career choice. Still others may have picked popular or lucrative careers, knowing nothing of what they're really like or what it takes to prepare for them."

—Lee Upcraft, Joni Finney, and Peter Garland, student development specialists

Step 3. Awareness of the Options That Best Fit You

In college, you'll have many educational options and career goals from which to choose. To deepen your awareness of whether a field may be a good fit for you, take a course in that field to test out how well it matches your interests, values, talents, and learning style. Ideally, you want to select a field that most closely taps into, or builds on, your strongest skills and special talents. Choosing a field that's compatible with your strongest abilities should enable you to master the skills required by that field more deeply and efficiently. You're more likely to succeed or excel in a field that taps your talents, and the success you experience will, in turn, strengthen your self-esteem, self-confidence, and drive to continue with it. You've probably heard of the old proverb "If there's a will, there's a way" (i.e., when you're motivated, you're more likely to succeed). However, it's also true that "If there's a way, there's a will" (i.e., when you know the way to do something well, you're more motivated to do it).

| Think About It —————— Journal Entry 5.7 |

Think about a career you're considering and answer the following questions:

1. Why are you considering this career? (What led or caused you to become interested in this choice?)

   Cosmotologist, because I love beauty.

2. Would you say that your interest in this career is motivated primarily by intrinsic factors (i.e., factors "inside" of you, such as your personal abilities, interests, needs, and values)? Or, would you say that your interest in the career is motivated more heavily by extrinsic factors (i.e., factors "outside" of you, such as starting salary, pleasing parents, meeting family expectations, or societal expectations for your gender or ethnicity)? Explain.

   Factors inside me. I want to be happy with my life.

Step 4. Awareness of the Process

The fourth and final step in an effective goal-setting process is becoming aware of the steps needed to reach your goal. For example, if you've set the goal of achieving a college degree in a particular major, you need to be aware of the course requirements that need to be completed for you to graduate in that major. Similarly, to set a career goal, you need to know what major or majors lead to that career, because some careers require a specific major but other careers may be entered through various majors.

Remember

The four-step process for effective goal setting applies to more than just educational goals. It's a strategic process that could and should be applied to any goal you set for yourself in life, at any stage of your life.

Snapshot Summary

5.1   The SMART Method of Goal Setting

A popular mnemonic device for remembering the key components of a well-designed goal is the acronym "SMART" (Doran, 1981; Mayer, 2003).

A SMART goal is one that is:

Specific: States exactly what the goal is and what will be done to achieve it.

Example: I'll achieve at least a "B" average this term by spending 25 hours per week on my course work outside of class and by using the effective learning strategies described in this book. (As opposed to the non-specific goal "I'm really going to work hard.")

Meaningful (and Measurable): The goal really matters to the individual, and progress toward reaching it can be steadily measured or tracked.

Example: I will achieve at least a "B" average this term because it will enable me to get into a field that I really want to pursue as a career, and I will measure my progress toward this goal by keeping track of the grades I'm earning in all my courses throughout the term.

Actionable: Identifies the concrete actions or behaviors that will be engaged in to reach the goal.

Example: I will achieve at least a "B" average this term by (1) attending all classes, (2) taking detailed notes in all my classes, (3) completing all reading assignments before

their due dates, and (4) avoiding cramming by studying in advance of all my major exams.

Realistic: The individual is capable of achieving or attaining the goal.

Example: Achieving a "B" average this term will be a realistic goal for me because my course load is manageable and I will not be working at my part-time job for more than 15 hours per week.

Timed: The goal is broken down into a timeline that includes short-range, mid-range, and long-range steps.

Example: To achieve at least a "B" average this term, first I'll acquire the information I need to learn by taking complete notes in class and on my assigned readings (short-range step). Second, I'll study the information I've acquired from my notes and readings in short study sessions held in advance of major exams (mid-range step). Third, I'll hold a final review session for all information previously studied on the day before my exams, and after exams I'll review my test results as feedback to determine what I did well and what I need to do better in order to maintain at least a "B" average (long-range step).

Note: The strategy for setting SMART goals is a transferable process that can be applied to goals in any aspect or dimension of your life, including health-related goals such as losing weight, social goals such as meeting new people, and fiscal goals such as saving money.

Strategies for Maintaining Motivation and Progress toward Your Goals

Reaching your goals requires will and energy; it also requires skill and strategy. Listed here are strategies for maintaining your motivation and commitment to reaching your goals.

1. **Visualize reaching your long-range goals.** Imagine vivid images of being successful, including not only what success looks like, but also what it feels like. For

example, if your goal is to achieve a college degree, imagine a crowd of cheering family, friends, and faculty at your graduation. Visualize how you'll be able to cherish and carry this proud memory with you for the rest of your life and how the benefits of a college degree will last a lifetime. Imagine yourself in the career that college enabled you to enter and your typical workday going something like this: You wake up in the morning and hop out of bed enthusiastically, looking forward to your day at work. When you're at work, time flies by, and before you know it, the day's over. When you return to bed that night and look back on your day, you feel good about what you did and how well you did it.

You can also use negative imagery to motivate yourself by imagining the worst-case scenario: failing to reach your goal and suffering the consequences. For example, vividly imagine yourself without any alternative other than a poor-paying, backbreaking job that you have to do to survive for the rest of your working life.

Author's Experience

My father, who spent 50 years working in the coal mines of eastern Kentucky, always had a simple motivating statement for me to gain more education than he had. He would always say, "Son, I did not have the chance to go to school, so I have to write my name with an X and work in the coal mines. You have the opportunity to get an education and you do not have to break your back in those mines." What my father was telling me was that education would give me options in life that he did not have and that I should take advantage of those options by going to college. My dad's lack of education supplied me with drive and dedication to pursue education. My experience suggests that when you are developing your goals and motivating yourself to achieve them, it may be as important to know what you don't want as it is to know what you do want.

Aaron Thompson

---

2. **Put your goals in writing.** When you put your goals in writing, you remain aware of them and remember them. This can stimulate your motivation to put your plan into action by serving almost like a written contract that holds you accountable to following through on your commitment. Place your written goals where you see them regularly. Consider writing them on sticky notes and posting them in multiple places that you encounter on a daily basis (e.g., your laptop, refrigerator, and bathroom mirror). If you keep them constantly in sight, you'll keep them constantly in mind.

3. **Create a visual map of your goals.** Lay out your goals in the form of a flowchart to show the flow of steps you'll be taking from your short- through mid- to long-range goals. Visual diagrams can help you "see" where you want to go, enabling you to connect where you are now and where you want to be. Diagramming can be energizing because it gives you a sneak preview of the finish line and a map-like overview of how to get you there.

4. **Keep a record of your progress.** Research indicates that the act of monitoring and recording progress toward goals can increase motivation to continue pursuing them (Locke & Latham, 2005; Matsui, Okada, & Inoshita, 1983). The act of keeping records of your progress probably increases your motivation by giving you frequent feedback on your progress and positive reinforcement for staying on track and moving toward your target (long-range goal) (Bandura & Cervone, 1983; Schunk, 1995). For example, mark your accomplishments in red on your calendar, or keep a journal of the goals you've reached; your entries will keep you

motivated by supplying you with concrete evidence of your progress and commitment. You can also chart or graph your progress, which provides a powerful visual display of your upward trends and patterns. Keep the chart where you can see it on a daily basis so you can use it as an ongoing source of inspiration and motivation. You can add musical inspiration by playing a motivational song in your head to keep you going (e.g., "We Are the Champions" by Queen).

5. **Develop a "skeletal resume" of your goals.** Include your goals as separate sections or categories that will be progressively fleshed out as you complete them. Your to-be-completed resume can provide a framework or blueprint for organizing, building, and tracking progress toward your goals. It can also serve as a visual reminder of the things you plan to accomplish and eventually showcase to potential employers. Furthermore, every time you look at your growing resume, you're reminded of your past accomplishments, which can energize and motivate you to reach your future goals. As you fill in and build up your resume, you can literally see how much you've achieved, which boosts your self-confidence and motivation to continue achieving. (See Chapter 10, p. 323, for a sample skeletal resume.)

6. **Reward yourself for making steady progress toward your long-range goals.** Reward is already built into reaching your long-range goal because it represents the end of your trip, which lands you at your desired destination (e.g., in a successful career). However, short- and mid-range goals may not be desirable ends in themselves but rather the means to a desirable end (your long-range goal). Consequently, you need to intentionally reward yourself for landing on these smaller stepping stones on the way to your long-range goal. When you complete these short- and mid-range goals, record and reward your accomplishment (e.g., celebrate your successful completion of midterms or finals by treating yourself to something you enjoy).

   A habit of perseverance and persistence through all intermediate steps is needed to reach a long-range goal, and like any other habit, is more likely to continue if it's followed by a reward (positive reinforcement). Setting small goals, moving steadily toward them, and rewarding yourself for reaching them are components of a simple but powerful strategy. This strategy will help you maintain motivation over the extended period needed to reach a long-range goal.

7. **Capitalize on available campus resources that can help you stay on track and move toward your goal.** Research indicates that college success results from a combination of what students do for themselves (personal responsibility) and what they do to capitalize on resources that are available to them (resourcefulness; Pascarella & Terenzini, 1991, 2005). Successful college students are resourceful students: they seek out and take advantage of college resources to help them reach their goals.

   For example, a resourceful student who's having trouble deciding what field of study to pursue for a degree or credential will seek assistance from an academic advisor on campus. A resourceful student who's interested in a particular career but is unclear about the best educational path to take toward that career will use the Career Development Center as a resource.

8. **Use your social resources.** The power of social support groups for helping people achieve personal goals is well documented by research in various fields (Ewell, 1997; Moeller, 1999). You can use the power of people by surrounding yourself with peers who are committed to successfully achieving their educational goals and by avoiding "toxic" people who are likely to poison your plans or dampen your dreams.

"Life isn't a matter of milestones but of moments."

—Rose Fitzgerald Kennedy, philanthropist and mother of John F. and Robert F. Kennedy

"Willpower is the personal strength and discipline, rooted in strong motivation, to carry out your plans. 'Waypower' is the exertion of willpower that helps you find resources and support."

—Jerry Pattengale, historian, author, and advocate for first-year student success

"Develop an inner circle of close associations in which the mutual attraction is not sharing problems or needs. The mutual attraction should be values and goals."

—Denis Waitley, former mental trainer for U.S. Olympic athletes and author of *Seeds of Greatness* (XXXX)

For example, find a supportive and motivating friend and make a mutual pact to help each other reach your respective goals. This step could be taken to a more formal level by drawing up a "social contract" whereby you and your partner are "cowitnesses" or designated social-support agents whose role is to help each other stay on track and move toward long-range goals. Studies show that making a public commitment to a goal increases your commitment to it, probably because it becomes a matter of personal pride and integrity that's seen not only through your own eyes but also through the eyes of others (Hollenbeck, Williams, & Klein, 1989).

> "I make progress by having people around who are smarter than I am."
>
> —Henry Kaiser, successful industrialist, known as the father of American shipbuilding

Think About It ——————————————— Journal Entry 5.8

1. What would you say is the biggest setback or obstacle you've overcome in your life thus far?

   My Dad threatening to kick me out.

   _____

   _____

   _____

   _____

   _____

2. How did you overcome it? (What enabled you to get past it or prevented you from being blocked by it?)

   I listened to what he said and

   forced into it.

   _____

   _____

   _____

   _____

9. **Convert setbacks into comebacks.** The type of thoughts you have after experiencing a setback can affect your emotional reaction to it and the action you take in response. For instance, what you think about a poor performance (e.g., a poor test grade) can affect your emotional reaction to that grade and what action, or lack of action, you take in response to it. You can react to the poor grade by knocking yourself down with self-putdowns ("I'm a loser") or by building yourself back up with positive pep talk ("I'm going to learn from my mistakes on this test and rebound with a stronger performance on the next one").

It's noteworthy that the root of the word *failure* is *fallere*, which means to "trip or fall," while the root word for *success* is *successus*, which means "to follow or come after." Thus, when we fail at something, it doesn't mean we've been defeated: it just means we've stumbled and fallen. Success can still be achieved after the fall by getting up, not giving up, and continuing to take the succession of steps need to successfully reach our goal.

If a poor past performance is seen not as a personal failure but as a learning opportunity, the setback may be turned into a comeback. Here are some notable people who turned early setbacks into successful comebacks:

- Louis Pasteur, famous bacteriologist, who failed his admission test to the University of Paris;
- Albert Einstein, Nobel Prize–winning physicist, who failed math in elementary school;
- Thomas Edison, prolific inventor, who was once expelled from school as "uneducable";
- Johnny Unitas, Hall-of-Fame football player, who was cut twice from professional football teams early in his career

In response to their early setbacks, these successful people didn't get bitter: they got better. Getting mad or sad about a setback will likely make you stressed or depressed and leave you focused on a past event that you can no longer control. Reacting rationally to a poor performance by focusing on how the results can be used as feedback to improve your future performance allows you to gain control of it and gives you the opportunity to convert the setback into a comeback.

This can be a challenging task because when you have an experience, your response to it passes through emotional areas of the brain before it reaches areas of the brain involved in rational thinking and reasoning (LeDoux, 1998). (See Figure 5.1.)

Thus, your brain reacts to events emotionally before it does rationally. If the experience triggers intense emotions (e.g., anger, anxiety, or sadness after receiving a bad test grade), your emotional reaction has the potential to "short-circuit"

FIGURE 5.1

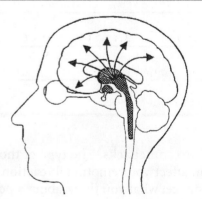

Information passes through the emotional center of the brain (lower, shaded area) before reaching the centers responsible for rational thinking (upper area). Thus, we need to counteract our tendency to respond emotionally and irrationally to personal setbacks by making a conscious attempt to respond rationally and reflectively.

© Kendall Hunt

The Brain's Human Attention System

or wipe out rational thinking. If you find yourself beginning to feel overwhelmed by negative emotions following a setback, you need to consciously and quickly block them with rational thoughts (e.g., thinking or saying to yourself, "Before I get carried away emotionally, let me think this through rationally"). This involves more than simply saying, "I have to think positively." Instead, you should develop a set of specific counterthinking strategies ready to use as soon as you begin to think negatively. Described here are thinking strategies that you can use to maintain motivation and minimize negative thinking in reaction to setbacks.

Remember

Don't let past mistakes bring you down emotionally or motivationally, but don't ignore or neglect them. Instead, inspect them, reflect on them, and correct them so that they don't happen again.

- **Develop self-awareness of your thinking patterns and habits.** Becoming aware of the nature of your thoughts is the first step to controlling them. Thinking often involves silent self-talk (i.e., talking silently to yourself). Thus, negative thinking often involves negative self-talk (e.g., "I'm a loser," "What's happening to me is just horrible," or "There's absolutely nothing I can do"). One of the best ways to become more aware of your self-talk, particularly negative self-talk, is to periodically write down your thoughts in a "thought journal" and review it with an eye for patterns of negative self-talk that you tend to use in certain situations (e.g., setbacks).

- **Substitute positive thoughts for negative thoughts.** Once you've become aware of your negative thoughts and the situations in which they occur, replace them with positive alternative thoughts. Let's say that one situation in which you experience negative thinking is during exams, especially when you see students turning in their tests well before you're finished. You think, "I must be doing terribly on this exam because others are getting through it so quickly. They must be smarter and better prepared than I am." You can stop this negative thinking by immediately substituting the following thought: "They're getting up and getting out because the test was difficult for them and they're giving up." Or, you can think to yourself, "They're rushing out because they're not taking the time to review their tests carefully before turning them in." The key to this thought-substitution strategy is to have specific, positive self-talk statements ready to use in situations where you tend to think negatively. Practice them so well that you think of them automatically and immediately. If those situations include personal setbacks or disappointing performances, your positive self-talk statements could include expressions such as "This isn't the end of the world," "Tomorrow's another day," or "I'll turn this setback into a comeback." By choosing and repeatedly using these positive self-talk statements, you train your mind to develop the habit of thinking in ways that are self-motivating rather than self-defeating.

> "The greatest weapon against stress is our ability to choose one thought over another."
>
> —William James, philosopher and one of the founders of American psychology

Whatever you do, don't let setbacks make you mad or sad, particularly at early stages in your college experience, because you're just beginning to learn what it takes to be successful in college. Look at mistakes in terms of what they can do *for* you, not *to* you. A bad performance can be turned into a good learning experience by using the results as an error detector for identifying sources or causes of your mistakes and as feedback for improving your future performance.

> **Remember**
>
> *Don't let past mistakes bring you down emotionally or motivationally; however, don't ignore or neglect them either. Instead, inspect them, reflect on them, and correct them so that they don't happen again.*

10. **Maintain positive expectations.** Just as your thoughts in reaction to something that's already taken place can affect your motivation, so can thoughts about what you *expect* to happen next. Your expectations of things to come can be either positive or negative. For example, before a test you could think, "I'm poised, confident, and ready to do it." Or you could think, "I know I'm going to fail this test; I just know it."

"Whether you think you can or you can't, you're right."

—Henry Ford, founder of Ford Motor Co. and one of the richest people of his generation

Expectations can lead to what sociologists and psychologists have called a self-fulfilling prophecy—a positive or negative expectation leads you to act in ways that are consistent with your expectation, which, in turn, make your expectation come true. For instance, if you expect you're going to fail an exam, you're less likely to put as much effort into studying for it. ("What's the use? I'm going to fail anyway.") During the test, your negative expectation is likely to reduce your test confidence and elevate your test anxiety: for example, if you experience difficulty with the first item on a test, you get anxious and begin to think you're going to have difficulty with all remaining items and flunk the entire exam. All of this negative thinking is likely to increase the probability that your expectation of doing poorly on the exam will become a reality.

In contrast, positive expectations can lead to a positive self-fulfilling prophecy: If you expect to do well on an exam, you're more likely to demonstrate higher levels of effort, confidence, and concentration, all of which combine to increase the likelihood that you'll earn a higher test grade. Research shows that learning and practicing positive self-talk increases a sense of hope—a belief in the ability to reach goals and the ability to actually reach them (Snyder, 1994).

Think About It ———————————— *Journal Entry* 5.9

1. Would you consider yourself to be an optimist or a pessimist?

   I am an optimist

2. In what situations are you more likely to think optimistically and pessimistically?

   I always try to be an optimist in situations but its hard in bad.

Why?
Because things never go my way.

11. **Keep your eye on the prize.** Don't lose sight of the long-term consequences of your short-term choices and decisions. Long-range thinking is the key to reaching long-range goals. Unfortunately, however, humans are often more motivated by short-range thinking because it produces quicker results and more immediate gratification. It's more convenient and tempting to think in the short term ("I like it; I want it; I want it now.") Studies show that the later consequences occur, the less likely people are to consider those consequences when they make their decisions (Ainslie, 1975; Elster & Lowenstein, 1992; Lewin, 1935). For example, choosing to do what you feel like doing instead of working to meet a future deadline and choosing to buy something with a credit card instead of saving money for future use cause people to suffer the negative long-term consequences of procrastination and credit-card debt, respectively.

To be successful in the long run, you need to keep your focus on the big picture—your long-range goals and dreams that provide your motivation. At the same time, you need to focus on the details—the due dates, to-do lists, and day-to-day duties that require your perspiration.

Thus, setting an important life goal and steadily progressing toward that long-range goal require two focus points. One is a narrow-focus lens that allows you to view the details immediately in front of you. The other is a wide-focus lens that gives you a big-picture view of what's farther ahead of you (your long-range goal). Success involves seeing the connection between the small, short-term chores and challenges (e.g., completing an assignment that's due next week) and the large, long-range picture (e.g., college graduation and a successful future). Thus, you need to periodically shift from a wide-focus lens that gives you the bigger, more distant picture to a narrow-focus lens that shifts your attention to completing the smaller tasks immediately ahead of you and keeping on the path to your long-range goal: future success.

Author's Experience When I was an assistant coach for a youth soccer team, I noticed that many of the less successful players tended to make either one of two mistakes when they were trying to move with the ball. Some spent too much time looking down, focusing on the ball at their feet, trying to be sure that they did not lose control of it. By not lifting their heads and looking ahead periodically, they often missed open territory, open teammates, or an open goal. Other unsuccessful players made the opposite mistake: They spent too much time with their heads up, trying to see where they were headed. By not looking down at the ball immediately in front of them, they often lost control of the ball, moved ahead without it, or sometimes stumbled over it and fell flat on their faces. Successful soccer players were in the habit of shifting their focus between looking down to maintain control of the ball immediately in front of them and lifting their heads to see where they were headed.

The more I thought about how successful players alternated between handling the ball in front of them and viewing the goal farther ahead, the more it struck me that this was a metaphor for success in life. Successful people alternate between both of these perspectives so that they don't lose sight of how the short-range tasks in front of them connect with the long-range goal ahead of them.

— Joe Cuseo

> "We are what we repeatedly do. Excellence, then, is not an act, but a habit."
>
> —Aristotle, ancient Greek philosopher

> "Sow an act and you reap a habit; sow a habit and you reap a character; sow a character and you reap a destiny."
>
> —Frances E. Willard, 19th-century American educator and women's rights activist

> "As gold which he cannot spend will make no man rich, so knowledge which he cannot apply will make no man wise."
>
> —Dr. Samuel Johnson, famous English literary figure and original author of the *Dictionary of the English Language* (1747)

> "Mere knowledge is not power; it is only possibility. Action is power; and its highest manifestation is when it is directed by knowledge."
>
> —Francis Bacon, English philosopher, lawyer, and champion of modern science

> "You can lead a horse to water, but you can't make him drink."
>
> —Proverb

> "Education is not the filling of a pail, but the lighting of a fire."
>
> —William Butler Yeats, Irish poet and playwright

Remember

Keep your future dreams and current tasks in clear focus. Integrating these two perspectives will produce an image that can provide you with the inspiration to complete your college education and the determination to complete your day-to-day tasks.

Motivation: Moving toward Your Long-Range Goals

The word *motivation* derives from the Latin *movere*, meaning "to move." Success comes to those who exert effort to move toward their goals. Knowledge of all kinds of success-promoting strategies, such as those discussed in this text, provides only the potential for success; turning this potential into reality requires motivation, which converts knowledge into action. If you have all the knowledge, strategies, and skills for being successful but don't have the will to succeed, there's no way you will succeed. Studies show that without a strong personal commitment to attain a goal, it will not be reached, no matter how well designed the goal and the plan to reach it are (Locke & Latham, 1990).

Motivation consists of three elements that may be summarized as the "three Ds" of motivation:

1. Drive
2. Discipline
3. Determination

Drive

Drive is the force within you that supplies you with the energy needed to overcome inertia and initiate action. Much like shifting into the drive gear is necessary to move your car forward, it takes personal drive to move forward and toward your goals.

People with drive aren't just dreamers: they're dreamers and doers. They take action to convert their dreams into reality, and they hustle—they go all out and give it their all, all of the time, to achieve their goals. College students with drive approach college with passion and enthusiasm. They don't hold back and work halfheartedly: they give 100 percent and put their whole heart and soul into the experience.

Think About It	Journal Entry 5.10

"Success comes to those who hustle."

—Abraham Lincoln, 16th American president and author of the Emancipation Proclamation, which set the stage for the abolition of slavery in the United States

1. Think about something that you do with drive, effort, and intensity. What thoughts, attitudes, and behaviors do you display when you do it?

   I try to became something of myself.
   Never give up on my dreams.

2. Do you see ways in which you could apply the same approach to your college experience?

   Yes I could.

Discipline

Discipline includes such positive qualities as commitment, devotion, and dedication. These personal qualities enable you to keep going over an extended period. Successful people think big, but start small—they take all the small steps and diligently do all the little things that need to be done, which in the long run, add up to a big accomplishment: the achievement of their long-range goal.

People who are self-disciplined accept the day-to-day sweat, toil, and perspiration needed to attain their long-term aspirations. They're willing to tolerate short-term strain or pain for long-term gain. They have the self-control and self-restraint needed to resist the impulse for instant gratification or the temptation to do what they feel like doing instead of what they need to do. They're willing to sacrifice their immediate needs and desires in the short run to do what is necessary to put them where they want to be in the long run.

"I long to accomplish some great and noble task, but it is my chief duty to accomplish small tasks as if they were great and noble."

—Helen Keller, seeing- and hearing-impaired author and activist for the rights of women and the handicapped

Student
Perspective
"Why is it so hard when I *have* to do something and so easy when I *want* to do something?"

—First-year student

Remember

Sacrifices that are made for a short time can bring benefits that last a lifetime.

"Self-discipline is the ability to make yourself do the thing you have to do, when it ought to be done, whether you like it or not."

—Thomas Henry Huxley, 19th-century English biologist

Remember

Sometimes you've got to do what you have to do in order to get to do what you want to do.

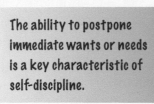

The ability to postpone immediate wants or needs is a key characteristic of self-discipline.

Studies show that individuals with dedication—who are deeply committed to what they do—are more likely to report that they are healthy and happy (Maddi, 2002; Myers, 1993).

Author's Experience

When I entered college in the mid-1970s, I was a first-generation student from an extremely impoverished background. Not only did I have to work to pay for part of my education, but I also needed to assist my family financially. I stocked grocery store shelves at night during the week and waited tables at a local country club on the weekends. Managing my life, time, school, and work required full-time effort. However, I always understood that my purpose was to graduate from college and all of my other efforts supported that goal. Thus, I went to class and arrived on time even when I did not feel like going to class. One of my greatest successes in life was to keep my mind and body focused on the ultimate prize: getting a college education. That success has paid off many times over.

Aaron Thompson

Determination

"If you are going through hell, keep going."

—Winston Churchill, British prime minister during World War II and Nobel Prize winner in literature

People who are determined pursue their goals with a relentless tenacity. They have the fortitude to persist in the face of frustration and the resiliency to bounce back after setbacks. When the going gets tough, they keep going. If they encounter something on the road to their goal that's hard to do, they work harder and longer to do it. They don't give up or give in: they dig deeper and give more.

People with determination are also more likely to seek out challenges. Research indicates that people who continue to pursue opportunities for personal growth and self-development throughout life are more likely to report feeling happy and healthy (Maddi, 2002; Myers, 1993). Rather than remaining stagnant and simply doing what's safe, secure, or easy, they stay hungry and display an ongoing commitment to personal growth and development; they keep striving and driving to be the best they can possibly be in all aspects of life.

> **Remember**
>
> *On the highway to success, you can't be a passive passenger; you're the driver and at the wheel. Your goal setting will direct you there, and your motivation will drive you there.*

"Success is peace of mind which is a direct result of self-satisfaction in knowing you made the effort to become the best that you are capable of becoming."

—John Wooden, college basketball coach and creator of the Pyramid of Success (XXXX)

Summary and Conclusion

Goal setting only becomes meaningful if you have motivation to reach the goals you set. Motivation may be said to consist of three Ds: drive, dedication, and determination. Drive is the internal force that gives you the energy to overcome inertia and initiate action. Discipline consists of positive personal qualities such as commitment, devotion, and dedication that enable you to sustain your effort over time. Determination enables you to relentlessly pursue your goals, persist in the face of frustration, and bounce back after any setback.

Reaching your goals requires all three Ds; it also involves the use of effective self-motivational strategies, such as:

- Visualizing reaching your long-range goals;
- Putting goals in writing;
- Creating a visual map of your goals;
- Keeping a record of your progress;
- Developing a skeletal resume;
- Rewarding yourself for progress toward long-range goals;
- Capitalizing on available campus and social resources;
- Converting setbacks into comebacks by using positive self-talk, maintaining positive expectations, and avoiding negative self-fulfilling prophecies; and
- Keeping your eye on the long-term consequences of your short-term choices and decisions.

Studies of highly successful people, whether they are scientists, musicians, writers, chess masters, or basketball stars, consistently show that achieving high levels of skill and success requires practice (Levitin, 2006). This is true even of people whose success is thought to be to be due to natural gifts or talents. For example, during the Beatles' first four years as a band and before they burst into musical stardom, they performed live an estimated 1,200 times, and many of these performances lasted five or more hours a night. They performed (practiced) for more hours during those first four years than most bands perform during their entire career. Similarly, before Bill Gates became a computer software giant and creator of Microsoft, he logged almost 1,600 hours of computer time during one seven-month period alone, averaging eight hours a day, seven days a week (Gladwell, 2008).

Reaching long-range goals means making small steps; they aren't achieved in one quick, quantum leap. If you are patient and persistent and consistently practice effective strategies, their positive effects will accumulate gradually and eventually have a significant impact on your success in college and beyond.

Remember

Success isn't a short-range goal; it's not a sprint but a long-distance run that takes patience and perseverance to complete. What matters most is not how fast you start but where you finish.

Learning More through the World Wide Web

Internet-Based Resources for Further Information on Goal Setting

For additional information related to the ideas discussed in this chapter, we recommend the following Web sites:

www.siue.edu/SPIN/activity.html

www.selfmotivationstrategies.com

5.1 Prioritizing Important Life Goals

Consider the following life goals. Rank them in the order of their priority for you (1 = highest, 5 = lowest):

___1___ Emotional well-being

___5___ Spiritual growth

___4___ Physical health

___3___ Social relationships

___2___ Rewarding career

Self-Assessment Questions

1. What was the primary reason behind your choices of first- and last-ranked goals? *Your emotional well being is important and spiritual growth is not.*
2. Have you established any short- or mid-range goals for reaching your highest-ranked choice? If yes, what are they? If no, what could they be? *Yes, clearing my acne.*

5.2 Setting Goals for Reducing the Gap between the Ideal Scenario and the Current Reality

Think of an aspect of your life with a gap between what you hoped it would be (the ideal) and what it is (the reality).

On the lines that follow, identify goals you could purse that would reduce this gap:

Long-range goal: _Be great in beauty_

Mid-range goal: _graduate college_

Short-range goal: ~~getting~~ _Get through school_

(For information on long-, mid-, and short-range goals, see p. 136.) Use the form below to identify more strategies for reaching each of these three goals. Consider the following areas for each goal:

- Actions to be taken: *Be known*
- Available resources: *have great products*
- Possible roadblocks: *No money*
- Potential solutions to roadblocks: *Work harder*

Long-range goal: *Be great in beauty*

- Actions to be taken:
- Available resources:
- Possible roadblocks:
- Potential solutions to roadblocks:

Mid-range goal: _Graduate college_

- Actions to be taken: _pass_
- Available resources: _tutor_
- Possible roadblocks: _failing_
- Potential solutions to roadblocks: _passing_

Short-range goal: _getting through school_

- Actions to be taken: _try_
- Available resources: _tutor_
- Possible roadblocks: _not passing_
- Potential solutions to roadblocks: _study hard_

5.3 Converting Setbacks into Comebacks: Transforming Pessimism into Optimism

In *Hamlet,* Shakespeare wrote, "There is nothing good or bad, but thinking makes it so." His point was that experiences have the potential to be positive or negative, depending on how people interpret them and react to them.

Listed here is a series of statements representing negative interpretations and reactions to a situation or experience:

1. "I'm just not good at this," _But I will try_
2. "There's nothing I can do about it," _but try_
3. "Things will never be the same," _if I don't try_
4. "Nothing is going to change," _if I don't try_
5. "This always happens to me," _if I don't try_
6. "This is unbearable." _for me_
7. "Everybody is going to think I'm a loser," _if I don't try._
8. "I'm trapped, and there's no way out." _But I can do it_

For each of the preceding statements, replace the negative statement with a statement that represents a more positive interpretation or reaction.

(For help in constructing these positive statements, see the discussion of thought-substitution strategies on p. 147.)

Goals and Motivation

Lorraine has decided to go to her local community college to become an RN. She knows that nurses make good money and it is easy to get a job in the profession right now. All she really cares about is having a good job and making money. She did not realize the classes would be difficult and she has a hard time getting through them since she really is not that interested in them. She started her clinicals and HATED what she was being asked to do. She was not prepared for all the bodily fluids she would see in one day. Lorraine decides nursing is not for her and is angry that no one told her she would hate it this much! She has to find a different major now that will still make a lot of money, but she is angry that she wasted more than a year of her life as well as the money she has spent on her education.

Discussion Questions

1. Why do you think Lorraine is really unhappy with the events that have unfolded during the past year?

2. What could Lorraine have done differently to avoid this situation?

3. What goals would you suggest Lorraine set for herself?

   Lorraine is clearly motivated by money; is that what is going to make her happy? Why or why not?

Chapter 5 Reflection

What is the one thing that motivates you the most in college?

HOW and WHY does this motivate you?

What is the one obstacle that gets in the way of your success?

How can you use your motivation to overcome your obstacle(s)?

Discover. Connect. *Advance.*

Welcome to Macomb Community College and College Success Skills!

I am Lois McGinley, and I am the Director of Student Success Services at Macomb. The areas I supervise are Placement Testing and the Learning Centers. I love my job, because I have learned that students can be successful when they are determined, when they have support, and when they manage their time. This area of the college tries to give students multiple ways to become more academically successful. I think that is one of the things that makes Macomb great . . . not many schools have this high level of academic support.

I know academic support is important, because when I started college, I floundered. I came from a very small high school where I got good grades. I was very shy, so I studied by myself and read chapters over and over to remember the information. When I arrived at college, I did not know that the pace of classes would be so fast. Like many of our students, I worked part time on-campus at the bookstore. I needed that job and I needed to get good grades. The first two years were very hard. My grade point average changed from a 3.8 in high school to a 2.8 in college! I was not happy about that. Over time, I learned more about managing my time. I also took a lot of notes and reviewed them, instead of reading a chapter two or three times. I was learning how to find out what was important. It is a good thing that I learned some study skills, because by the time I finished my bachelor's degree, I had "stopped out" twice, gotten married, and my oldest son was born. I kept plugging away and I finished my degree in teaching in five years.

I later pursued a Master's degree in reading. I'd always loved to read, but I learned there were special techniques to use to get the information out of a difficult textbook. Good readers typically make good students, but all students can improve skills in reading textbooks, which will help their test taking abilities. During that period, I had two children, was working full time teaching middle school, and finished a three year program in two years. Guess what; my grade point average went up to 3.3, because I learned to study more efficiently. I was thrilled!

As time went on, our family moved to several different states because of my husband's business. When I lived in Massachusetts, the only teaching job I could find was in the state prison system. It didn't pay much, but guess what . . . I learned a great deal about learning and student success! I figured out that if 17, 18, and 19 year old men in a state prison, who haven't been to school since the 5th or 6th grade can learn, then those who have more opportunity should be able to learn. I wanted to know how these young men could be successful. How could they get a GED (high school equivalency diploma) and then go on to college? How could they keep their minds on learning? Prison is a difficult place. Actually, it is a horrible place. These young men had challenges most of us do not face. From that experience, I learned that some things are critical for learning:

- You have to have a **goal**. Many of these young men would be released in a year or two or three. The ones who concentrated on their classes wanted skills for the next stage of their life. Most people do not want to return to prison, so many of them had the **goal** of getting an education so they would not make the same mistakes.

- You have to **attend** classes. In order to get the information, you need to be there. In this school, students did not have to attend. Those who did often got their GED within three months to a year. That is quite an accomplishment for those who had not been to school for several years. Students who **attended** class built skills.
- You have to have **determination**. Even in prison, things get in your way. You have to make the time to study. There are times you are called to the office, you are locked down, and you go to mandatory meetings. Or, you go to your job. There are always reasons not to study, but those who are **determined** will find a way.

I learned that I love it when those who aren't supposed to succeed do succeed. Some of my students went on to the prison college program after finishing their GED and got their Bachelor's degree. I became eager to learn more about learning, because I knew wishing did not make it happen. I realized there were skills all could learn.

A few years later, I found out there was an educational program to assist students who were struggling at college. It is called Developmental Education. I went back to college and got a degree in that area. I learned so much more about studying and student success. I loved that program. Teachers at colleges across the country were trying to implement good study strategies into their curriculum. Because I learned so much, I did a two year program in one year. It actually did not seem that hard. That was partially because I loved what I was doing, and everything we love comes easier. But, it was also because as I learned skills, I implemented them into my own study. I learned that **time management** is crucial. You see, I worked 20 hours a week and got the best grades I had ever had. I had my **time management** skills down. I knew when I was in class, I knew when I was working and I planned study time for each class, and I stuck to my schedule.

When I came to Macomb, I was delighted to be part of something called Student Success Services. I have tried to impart what I had learned all these years into all aspects of our work in the Learning Centers. We offer free seminars in Time Management, Academic Reading, Test Taking Skills, as well as many others. These are the skills it took me three degrees to learn . . . and they are here at Macomb just for you. I urge you to take advantage of these seminars and other resources in the Learning Centers. Macomb Community College has one of the finest support systems for students in the country. You will become an independent learner and develop your own success strategies. You will learn to "Study Smarter, Not Harder!"

See you in the Learning Centers!

I am Lois McGinley and I am Macomb.

Courtesy of Lois McGinley

Managing Time and Preventing Procrastination

Study 6 & 7 (handwritten annotation)

THOUGHT STARTER | *Journal Entry* **6.1**

LEARNING GOAL

To help you appreciate the significance of managing time and supply you with a powerful set of time-management strategies that can be used to promote your success in college and beyond.

Complete the following sentence with the first thought that comes to your mind.

For me, time is . . .

Important and ment to be used Wisely - (handwritten response)

The Importance of Time Management

For many first-year students, the beginning of college means the beginning of more independent living and self-management. Even if you've lived on your own for some time, managing time is an important skill to possess because you're likely juggling multiple responsibilities, including school, family, and work. Studies show that most first-year community college students are attending classes while working either part-time or full-time (American Association of Community Colleges, 2009). In college, the academic calendar and your class schedule will differ radically from those during high school. You will have less "seat time" in class each week and more "free time" outside of class, which you will have the freedom to self-manage; it will not be closely monitored by school authorities or family members, and you will be expected to do more academic work on your own outside of class. Personal time-management skills grow in importance when a person's time is less structured or controlled by others, leaving the individual with more decision-making power about how personal time will be spent. Thus, it is no surprise that research shows the ability to manage time effectively as playing a crucial role in college success (Erickson, Peters, & Strommer, 2006).

Simply stated, college students who have difficulty managing their time have difficulty managing college. In one study, sophomores who had an outstanding first year in college (both academically and socially) were compared with another group of sophomores who struggled during their freshman year. Interviews conducted with these students revealed one key difference between the two groups: The sophomores who experienced a successful first year repeatedly brought up the topic of time during the interviews. The successful students said they had to think carefully about how they spent their time and budget their time because it was a scarce resource. In contrast, the sophomores who experienced difficulty in their first year of

Student
Perspective

"The major difference [between high school and college] is time. You have so much free time on your hands that you don't know what to do for most of the time."

—First-year college student (Erickson & Strommer, 1991)

Student
Perspective

"I cannot stress enough that you need to intelligently budget your time."

—Words written by a first-year student in a letter of advice to students who are about to begin college

169

college hardly talked about the topic of time during their interviews, even when they were specifically asked about it (Light, 2001).

Studies also indicate that managing time plays a pivotal role in the lives of working adults. Setting priorities and balancing multiple responsibilities (work, family, and school) that compete for limited time and energy can be a juggling act and a source of stress for people of all ages (Harriott & Ferrari, 1996).

For these reasons, time management should be viewed not only as a college-success strategy but also as a life-management and life-success skill. Studies show that people who manage their time well report being more in control of their lives and happier (Myers, 1993). In short, when you gain greater control of your time, you become more satisfied with your life.

Author's Experience   I started the process of earning my doctorate a little later in life than other students. I was a married father with a preschool daughter (Sara). Since my wife left for work early in the morning, it was always my duty to get up and get my daughter's day going in the right direction. In addition, I had to do the same for me—which was often harder than doing it for my daughter. Three days of my week were spent on campus in class or in the library. (We did not have quick access to research on computers then as you do now.) The other two days of the workweek and the weekend were spent on household chores, family time, and studying. I knew that if I was going to have any chance of finishing my Ph.D. in a reasonable amount of time and have a decent family life, I had to adopt an effective schedule for managing my time. Each day of the week, I held to a very strict routine. I got up in the morning, drank coffee while reading the paper, took a shower, got my daughter ready for school, and took her to school. Once I returned home, I put a load of laundry in the washer, studied, wrote, and spent time concentrating on what I needed to do to be successful from 8:30 a.m. to 12:00 p.m. every day. At lunch, I had a pastrami and cheese sandwich and a soft drink while rewarding myself by watching *Perry Mason* reruns until 1:00 p.m. I then continued to study until it was time to pick up my daughter from school. Each night I spent time with my wife and daughter and prepared for the next day. I lived a life that had a preset schedule. By following this schedule, I was able to successfully complete my doctorate in a decent amount of time while giving my family the time they needed. (By the way, I still watch *Perry Mason* reruns.)

— Aaron Thompson

Strategies for Managing Time

Effective time management involves three key mental processes:

1. **Analysis.** Breaking down time into specific segments and work into smaller tasks;
2. **Itemizing.** Identifying all key tasks that need to be done and by what dates; and
3. **Prioritizing.** Organizing and attacking tasks in order of their importance.

The following steps can help you apply these skills to find more time in your schedule and use this time more productively.

1. **Break down your time and become more aware of how it's spent.** Have you ever asked yourself, "Where did all the time go?" or told yourself, "I just can't seem to find the time"? One way to find out where your time went is by taking a time inventory (Webber, 1991). To do this, you conduct a time analysis by breaking down and tracking your time, recording what you do and when you do it. By mapping out how you spend time, you become more aware of how much total time you have available to you and how its component parts are used up, including patches of wasted time in which you get little or nothing accomplished. You don't have to do this time analysis for more than a week or two. This should be long enough to give you some sense of where your time is going and allow you to start developing strategies for using your time more effectively and efficiently.

Think About It ———————— *Journal Entry* **6.2**

1. What is your greatest time waster?

   Being lazy all day

2. Is there anything you can do right now to stop or eliminate it?

   Just actually doing my work

> "Dost thou love life? Then do not squander time, for that is the stuff life is made of."
>
> —Benjamin Franklin, 18th-century inventor, newspaper writer, and signer of the *Declaration of Independence*

2. **Identify which key tasks you need to accomplish and when you need to accomplish them.** We make lists to be sure we don't forget items we need from the grocery store or people we want to be sure are invited to a party. We can use the same list-making strategy for work tasks so that we don't forget to do them or forget to do them on time. Studies of effective people show that they are list makers and they write out lists not only for grocery items and wedding invitations, but also for things they want to accomplish each day (Covey, 1990).

   You can itemize your tasks by listing them in one of the following time-management tools:

   - **Personal digital assistant (PDA) or cell phone.** You can use these to do a lot more than check social networking sites and send and receive text messages. Use the calendar tools in these devices to record due dates and set up the alert functions to remind you of these deadlines. Many PDAs and smartphones will also allow you to set up task or "to-do" lists and to set priorities for each item you enter.
   - **Small, portable planner.** List all your major assignments and exams for the term, along with their due dates. If you pull all work tasks from different courses into one place, it is easier to keep track of what you have to do and when you have to do it.

© Gary Woodward, 2013. Under license from Shutterstock, Inc.

Using a personal planner is an effective way to itemize your academic commitments.

- **Large, stable calendar.** Record in the calendar's date boxes your major assignments for the academic term and when they are due. Place the calendar in a position or location where it's in full view and you can't help but see it every day (e.g., on your bedroom or refrigerator door). If you regularly and literally "look" at the things you have to do, you're less likely to "overlook" them, forget about them, or subconsciously push them out of your mind.

Think About It — Journal Entry 6.3

1. Do you have a calendar for the current academic term that you carry with you?

   Nope.

2. If yes, why? If no, what do you use instead?

   I use my camera for my agenda.

3. How does that work for you?

   I look at it and do my work.

Author's Experience

My mom was the person who ensured I got up for school on time. Once I got to school, the bell would ring to let me know to move on to the next class. When I returned home, I had to do my homework and chores. My daily and weekly schedules were dictated by others.

When I entered college, my mom quickly realized that I needed to develop my own system for being organized, focused, and productive without her assistance. Since I came from a modest background, I had to work my way through college. Juggling schedules became an art and science for me. I knew the things that I could not miss, such as work and school, and the things I could miss—TV and girls. (OK, TV, but not girls.)

After college, I spent 10 years in business—a world where I was measured by being on time and a productive "bottom line." It was during this time that I discovered a scheduling book. When I became a professor, I had other mechanisms to make sure I did what I needed to do when I needed to do it. This was largely based on when my classes were offered. Other time was dedicated to working out and spending time with my family. Now, as an administrator, I have an assistant who keeps my schedule for me. She tells me where I am going, how long I should be there, and what I need to accomplish while I am there. Unless you take your parents with you or have the luxury of a personal assistant, it's important to determine which activities are required and to allow time in your schedule for fun. Use a planner!

Aaron Thompson

3. **Rank your tasks in order of their importance.** Once you've itemized your work by listing all tasks you need to do, prioritize them—determine the order in which you will do them. Prioritizing basically involves ranking your tasks in terms of their importance, with the highest-ranked tasks appearing at the top of your list to ensure that they are tackled first. How do you determine which tasks are most important and should be ranked highest? Two key criteria or standards of judgment can be used to help determine which tasks should be your priorities:

- **Urgency.** Tasks that are closest to their deadline or due date should receive high priority. For example, finishing an assignment that's due tomorrow should receive higher priority than starting an assignment that's due next month.

- **Gravity.** Tasks that carry the heaviest weight (count the most) should receive highest priority. For example, if an assignment worth 100 points and another worth 10 points are due at the same time, working on the 100-point task should receive higher priority. You want to be sure you invest your work time on work tasks that matter most. Just like investing money, you want to invest your time on tasks that yield the greatest dividends or payoff.

One strategy for prioritizing your tasks is to divide them into A, B, and C lists (Lakein, 1973). The A list is for *essential* tasks—what you *must* do now. The B list is for *important* tasks—what you *should* do soon. Finally, the C list is for *optional* tasks—what you *could* or *might* do later if there is time remaining after you've completed the tasks on the A and B lists. Organizing your tasks in this fashion can help you decide how to divide your labor in a way that ensures you put first things first. What you don't want to do is waste time on unimportant things and deceive yourself into thinking that you're keeping busy and getting things done when actually you're doing things that just take your time (and mind) away from the more important things.

At first glance, itemizing and prioritizing may appear to be rather boring chores. However, if you look at these mental tasks carefully, they require many higher-level thinking skills, such as:

1. **Analysis.** Breaking down time into its component elements or segments and breaking down work into specific tasks;

2. **Evaluation.** Critically evaluating the relative importance or value of tasks; and
3. **Synthesis.** Organizing individual tasks into classes or categories based on their level of priority.

Thus, developing self-awareness about how you spend time is more than a menial clerical task: when done with thoughtful reflection, it's an exercise in higher-level thinking. It's also a good exercise in values clarification, because what people choose to spend their time on is a more accurate indicator of what they truly value than what they *say* they value.

Develop a Time-Management Plan

"Time = Life. Therefore waste your time and waste your life, or master your time and master your life."

—Alan Lakein, international expert on time management and author of the bestselling book *How to Get Control of Your Time and Your Life* (1973)

Humans are creatures of habit. Regular routines help us organize and gain control of our lives. Doing things by design, rather than leaving them to chance or accident, is the first step toward making things happen for us rather than allowing them to happen to us by chance or accident. By developing an intentional plan for how you're going to spend your time, you're developing a plan to gain greater control of your life.

Don't buy into the myth that you don't have time to plan because it takes too much time that could be spent on getting started and getting things done. Time-management experts estimate that the amount of time you spend planning your work reduces your total work time by a factor of three (Lakein, 1973). In other words, for every one unit of time you spend planning, you save three units of work time. Thus, five minutes of planning time will typically save you 15 minutes of total work time, and 10 minutes of planning time will save you 30 minutes of work time. This saving of work time probably occurs because you develop a clearer game plan or plan of attack for identifying what needs to be done and the best order in which to get it done. A clearer sense of direction reduces the number of mistakes you may make due to false starts—starting the work but then having to restart it because you started off in the wrong direction. If you have no plan of attack, you're more likely to go off track and in the wrong direction; when you discover this at some point after you've started, you're then forced to retreat and start over.

As the old proverb goes, "A stitch in time saves nine." Planning your time represents the "stitch" (in time) that saves you nine additional stitches (units of time). Like successful chess players, successful time managers plan ahead and anticipate their next moves.

Elements of a Comprehensive Time-Management Plan

Once you've accepted the notion that taking the time to plan your time saves you time in the long run, you're ready to design a time-management plan. The following are the key elements of a comprehensive, well-designed plan for managing time:

1. **A good time-management plan should have several time frames.** Your academic time-management plan should include:
   - A *long-range* plan for the entire academic term that identifies deadline dates for reports and papers that are due toward the end of the term;
   - A *mid-range* plan for the upcoming month and week; and
   - A *short-range* plan for the following day.

The preceding time frames may be integrated into a total time-management plan for the term by taking the following steps:

a. Identify deadline dates of all assignments, or the time when each of them must be completed (your long-range plan).

b. Work backward from these final deadlines to identify dates when you plan to begin taking action on these assignments (your short-range plan).

c. Identify intermediate dates when you plan to finish particular parts or pieces of the total assignment (your mid-range plan).

This three-stage plan should help you make steady progress throughout the term on college assignments that are due later in the term. At the same time, it will reduce your risk of procrastinating and running out of time.

Here's how you can put this three-stage plan into action this term. Develop a long-range plan for the academic *term*.

- Review the *course syllabus (course outline)* for each class you are enrolled in this term, and highlight all major exams, tests, quizzes, assignments, and papers and the dates on which they are due.

Remember

College professors are more likely than high school teachers to expect you to rely on your course syllabus to keep track of what you have to do and when you have to do it. Your instructors may not remind you about upcoming papers, tests, quizzes, assignments, etc.

- Obtain a *large calendar* for the academic term (available at your campus bookstore or Learning Center) and record all your exams, assignments, and so on, for all your courses in the calendar boxes that represent their due dates. To fit this information within the calendar boxes, use creative abbreviations to represent different tasks, such as E for exam and TP for term paper (not toilet paper). When you're done, you'll have a centralized chart or map of deadline dates and a potential master plan for the entire term.

- Activate the calendar and task list functions on your PDA or cell phone. Enter your schedule, important dates, and deadlines, and set alert reminders. Since you carry your PDA or cell phone with you regularly, you will always have this information at your fingertips.

- **Plan your *week*.**

a. Make a map of your *weekly schedule* that includes times during the week when you are in class, when you typically eat and sleep, and if you are employed, when you work.

b. If you are a full-time college student, find *at least 25 total hours per week* when you can do academic work outside the classroom. (These 25 hours can be pieced together in any way you like, including time between daytime classes and work commitments, evening time, and weekend time.) When adding these 25 hours to the time you spend in class each week, you will end up with a 40-hour workweek, similar to any full-time job. If you are a part-time student, you should plan on spending at least two hours on academic work outside of class for every hour that you're in class.

c. Make good use of your *free time between classes* by working on assignments and studying in advance for upcoming exams. See Do It Now! 6.1 for a summary of how you can make good use of your out-of-class time to improve your academic performance and course grades.

Student
Perspective

"The amount of free time you have in college is much more than in high school. Always have a weekly study schedule to go by. Otherwise, time slips away and you will not be able to account for it."

—First-year college student
(Rhoads, 2005)

- **Plan your *day*.**
  a.   Make a *daily to-do list*.

  Remember

  If you write it out, you're less likely to block it out and forget about it.

  b.   Attack daily tasks in *priority order*.

  Remember

  "First things first." Plan your work by placing the most important and most urgent tasks at the top of your list, and work your plan by attacking tasks in the order in which you have listed them.

- Carry a *small calendar, planner, or appointment book* with you at all times. This will enable you to record appointments that you may make on the run during the day and will allow you to jot down creative ideas or memories of things you need to do, which sometimes pop into your mind at the most unexpected times.
- Carry *portable work* with you during the day—that is, work you can take with you and do in any place at any time. This will enable you to take advantage of "dead time" during the day. For example, carry material with you that you can read while sitting and waiting for appointments or transportation, allowing you to resurrect this dead time and convert it to "live" work time.
- Wear a *watch* or carry a cell phone that can accurately and instantly tell you what time it is and what date it is. You can't even begin to manage time if you don't know what time it is, and you can't plan a schedule if you don't know what date it is. Set the time on your watch or cell phone slightly ahead of the actual time; this will help ensure that you arrive to class, work, or meetings on time.

| Think About It | Journal Entry | 6.4 |

1.   Do you make a to-do list of things you need to get done each day?

    never   (seldom)   often   almost always

2.   If you selected "never" or "seldom," why don't you?

    I never go by that in my day

6.1   DO IT NOW!

Making Productive Use of Free Time Outside the Classroom

Unlike in high school, homework in college often does not involve turning things in to your instructor daily or weekly. The academic work you do outside the classroom may not even be collected and graded. Instead, it is done for your own benefit to help prepare yourself for upcoming exams and major assignments (e.g., term papers or research reports). Rather than formally assigning work to you as homework, your professors expect that you will do this work on your own and without supervision. Listed below are strategies for working independently and in advance of college exams and assignments. These strategies will increase the quality of your time management in college and the quality of your academic performance.

Working Independently in Advance of Exams

Use the following strategies to use out-of-class time wisely to prepare for exams:

- **Complete reading assignments** relating to lecture topics before the topic is discussed in class. This will make lectures easier to understand and will prepare you to participate intelligently in class (e.g., ask meaningful questions of your instructor and make informed comments during class discussions).
- **Review your class notes** between class periods so that you can construct a mental bridge from one class to the next and make each upcoming lecture easier to follow. When reviewing your notes before the next class, rewrite any class notes that may be sloppily written the first time. If you find notes related to the same point all over the place, reorganize them by combining them into one set of notes. Lastly, if you find any information gaps or confusing points in your notes, seek out the course instructor or a trusted classmate to clear them up before the next class takes place.
- **Review information** you highlighted in your reading assignments to improve your retention of the information. If certain points are confusing to you, discuss them with your course instructor during office hours or with a fellow classmate outside of class.
- **Integrate key ideas** in your class notes with information that you have highlighted in your assigned reading that relates to the same major point or general category. In other words, put related information from your lecture notes and your reading in the same place (e.g., on the same index card).
- **Use a part-to-whole study method** whereby you study material from your class notes and assigned reading in small pieces during short, separate study sessions that take place well in advance of the exam; then make your last study session before the exam a longer review session during which you restudy all the small parts together as a whole. It's a myth that studying in advance is a waste of time because you'll forget it all anyway by test time. As you'll see in Chapter 8, information studied in advance of an exam remains in your brain and is still there when you later review it. Even if you cannot recall the previously studied information when you first start reviewing it, you will relearn it faster than you did the first time, thus proving that some memory of it was retained from your earlier study sessions.

Work Independently Well in Advance of Due Dates for Term Papers and Research Reports

Work on large, long-range assignments by breaking them into the following smaller, short-term tasks:

- Search for and select a topic.
- Locate sources of information on the topic.
- Organize the information obtained from these sources into categories.
- Develop an outline of the report's major points and the order or sequence in which you plan to discuss them.
- Construct a first draft of the paper (and, if necessary, a second draft).
- Write a final draft of the paper.
- Proofread the final draft of your paper for minor mechanical mistakes, such as spelling and grammatical errors, before submitting it to your instructor.

Murphy's Laws:
1. Nothing is as simple as it looks.
2. Everything takes longer than it should.
3. If anything can go wrong, it will.

—Author unknown; named after Captain Edward Murphy, naval engineer, in 1949

2. **A good time-management plan should include reserve time to take care of the unexpected.** You should always hope for the best but should always be prepared for the worst. Your time-management plan should include a buffer zone or safety net, building in extra time that you can use to accommodate unforeseen developments or unexpected emergencies. Just as you should plan to save money in your bank for unexpected extra costs (e.g., emergency medical expenses), you should plan to save time in your schedule for unexpected events that cost you time (e.g., dealing with unscheduled tasks or taking longer than expected to complete already-planned tasks).

3. **A good time-management plan should capitalize on your biological rhythms.** When you plan your daily schedule, be aware of your natural peak periods and down times. Studies show that individuals differ in terms of the time of day when their bodies naturally tire and prefer to sleep or become energized and prefer to wake up. Some people are "early birds" who prefer to go to sleep early and wake up early; others are "night owls" who prefer to stay up late at night and get up late in the morning (Natale & Ciogna, 1996). (Teenagers are more likely to fall into the category of night owls.) Individuals also vary with respect to the times of day when they are at their highest and lowest levels of energy. Naturally, early birds are more likely to be morning people whose peak energy period occurs before noon; night owls are likely to be more productive in the late afternoon and evening. Also, most people experience a post-lunch dip in energy in the early afternoon (Monk, 2005).

   Be aware of your most productive hours of the day and schedule your highest-priority work and most challenging tasks for when you tend to work at peak performance levels. For example, schedule out-of-class academic work so that you're tackling academic tasks that require intense thinking (e.g., technical writing or complex problem solving) when you are most productive; schedule lighter work (e.g., light reading or routine tasks) at the times when your energy level tends to be lower. Also, keep your natural peak and down times in mind when you schedule your courses. Try to arrange your class schedule in such a way that you experience your most challenging courses at the times of the day when your body (brain) is most ready and able to accept that challenge.

4. **A good time-management plan should include a balance of work and recreation.** Don't only plan work time: plan time to relax, refuel, and recharge. Your overall plan shouldn't turn you into an obsessive-compulsive workaholic. Instead, it should represent a balanced blend of work and play, which includes activities that promote your mental and physical wellness, such as relaxation, recreation, and reflection. You could also arrange your schedule of work and play as a self-motivation strategy by using your play time to reward your work time.

Student
Perspective

"It is just as important to allow time for things you enjoy doing because this is what will keep you stable."

—Words written by a first-year college student in a letter of advice to new students

Remember

A good time-management plan should help you stress less, learn more, and earn higher grades while leaving you time for other important aspects of your life. A good plan not only enables you to get your work done on time, but also enables you to attain and maintain balance in your life.

A good time-management plan includes a balanced blend of time planned for both work and recreation.

Author's Experience

My mom is a schoolteacher, and when my sister and I were growing up she had a strict policy: when we came home from school we could have a snack, but after that we were not allowed to do anything else until our homework was finished. I remember that on days when it was really nice outside, I would beg and plead (and sometimes even argue) with my mom about going outside to play. She always won, and often I had wasted so much time arguing that I completely missed out on the opportunity to play at all. At the time I thought my mom was really mean. As I grew older (in high school and college), though, it became easy to put my homework first. My mom had taught me the importance of prioritizing and completing important things (like homework) before things that were not as important.

Julie McLaughlin

Think About It — Journal Entry 6.5

1. What activities do you engage in for fun or recreation?

   Concerts, hanging with friend, Netflix TBM.

2. What do you do to relax or relieve stress?

   Netflix, Sleep, Read, lay in bed internet.

3. Brainstorm a list of activities you could do to relieve stress:

   Sleep, read, Netflix

5. **A good time-management plan should have some flexibility.** Some people are immediately turned off by the idea of developing a schedule and planning their time because they feel it overstructures their lives and limits their freedom. It's only natural for you to prize your personal freedom and resist anything that appears to restrict your freedom in any way. A good plan preserves your freedom by helping you get done what must be done, reserving free time for you to do what you want and like to do.

6. **A good time-management plan shouldn't enslave you to a rigid work schedule.** It should be flexible enough to allow you to occasionally bend it without having to break it. Just as work commitments and family responsibilities can crop up unexpectedly, so, too, can opportunities for fun and enjoyable activities. Your plan should allow you the freedom to modify your schedule so that you can take advantage of these enjoyable opportunities and experiences. However, you should plan to make up the work time you lost. In other words, you can borrow or trade work time for play time, but don't "steal" it; you should plan to pay back the work time you borrowed by substituting it for a play period that existed in your original schedule.

Remember

When you create a personal time-management plan, remember that it is your plan—you own it and you run it. It shouldn't run you.

Converting Your Time-Management Plan into an Action Plan

Once you've planned the work, the next step is to work the plan. A good action plan is one that gives you a preview of what you intend to accomplish and an opportunity to review what you actually accomplished. You can begin to implement an action plan by constructing a daily to-do list, bringing that list with you as the day begins, and checking off items on the list as you get them done. At the end of the day, review your list and identify what was completed and what still needs to be done. The uncompleted tasks should become high priorities for the next day.

At the end of the day, if you find yourself with many unchecked items still remaining on your daily to-do list, this could mean that you're are spreading yourself too thin by trying to do too many things in a day. You may need to be more realistic about the number of things you can reasonably expect to accomplish per day by shortening your daily to-do list.

Being unable to complete many of your intended daily tasks may also mean that you need to modify your time-management plan by adding work time or subtracting activities that are drawing time and attention away from your work (e.g., taking cell-phone calls during your planned work times).

Think About It ——————————————— *Journal Entry* **6.6**

1. By the end of a typical day, how often do you find that you accomplished most of the important tasks you hoped to accomplish?

   never   seldom   (often)   almost always

2. Why?

   Because if I need to do it I have too.

Dealing with Procrastination

Procrastination Defined

The word *procrastination* derives from two roots: *pro* (meaning "forward") plus *crastinus* (meaning "tomorrow"). As these roots suggest, procrastinators don't abide by the proverb "Why put off to tomorrow what can be done today?" Their philosophy is just the opposite: "Why do today what can be put off until tomorrow?" Adopting this philosophy promotes a perpetual pattern of postponing what needs to be done until the last possible moment, which results in rushing frantically to get it done (and compromising its quality), getting it only partially done, or not finishing it.

Research shows that 80 to 95 percent of college students procrastinate (Steel, 2007) and almost 50 percent report that they procrastinate consistently (Onwuegbuzie, 2000). Furthermore, the percentage of people reporting that they procrastinate is on the rise (Kachgal, Hansen, & Nutter, 2001).

Procrastination is such a serious issue for college students that some colleges and universities have opened "procrastination centers" to provide help exclusively for students who are experiencing problems with procrastination (Burka & Yuen, 1983).

Student *Perspective*

"I believe the most important aspect of college life is time management. DO NOT procrastinate because, although this is the easy thing to do at first, it will catch up with you and make your life miserable."

—Advice from a first-year student to new college students

A procrastinator's idea of planning ahead and working in advance often boils down to this scenario.

Author's Experience During my early years in college, I was quite a procrastinator. During my sophomore year, I waited to do a major history paper until the night before it was due. Back then, I had a word processor that was little more than a typewriter; it allowed you to save your work to a floppy disk before printing. I finished writing my paper around 3:00 a.m. and hit "print," but about halfway through the printing I ran out of paper. I woke up my roommate to ask if she had paper, but she didn't. So, at 3:00 a.m. I was forced to get out of my pajamas, get into my street clothes, get into my car, and drive around town to find someplace open at three in the morning that sold typing paper. By the time I found a place, got back home, printed the paper, and washed up, it was time to go to class. I could barely stay awake in any of my classes that day, and when I got my history paper back, the grade wasn't exactly what I was hoping for. I never forgot that incident. My procrastination on that paper caused me to lose sleep the night before it was due, lose attention in all my other classes on the day it was due, and lose points on the paper that I managed to do. Thereafter, I was determined not to let procrastination get the best of me.

Julie McLaughlin

Procrastination is by no means limited to college students. It is a widespread problem that afflicts people of all ages and occupations (Harriott & Ferrari, 1996). This is why you'll find many books on the subject of time management in the self-help section of any popular bookstore. It's also why you see so many people at the post office on April 15 every year, mailing their tax returns at the last possible moment ("Haven't Filed Yet," 2003).

Myths That Promote Procrastination

Before there can be any hope of putting a stop to procrastination, procrastinators need to let go of two popular myths (misconceptions) about time and performance.

Myth 1. "I work better under pressure" (e.g., on the day or night before something is due). Procrastinators often confuse desperation with motivation. Their belief that they work better under pressure is often just a rationalization to justify or deny the truth, which is that they *only* work when they're under pressure—that is, when they're running out of time and are under the gun to get it done just before the deadline.

It's true that some people will only start to work and will work really fast when they're under pressure, but that does not mean they're working more *effectively* and producing work of better *quality*. Because they're playing "beat the clock," procrastinators' focus is no longer on doing the job *well* but on doing the job *fast* so that it gets done before they run out of time. This typically results in a product that turns out to be incomplete or inferior to what could have been produced if the work process began earlier.

Confusing rapidity with quality is a sin. It's an indisputable fact that it takes more time to do higher-quality work, particularly if that job requires higher-level thinking skills such as thinking critically and creatively (Ericsson & Charness, 1994). Academic work in college often requires deep learning and complex thinking, which require time for reflection. Deep thoughts and creative ideas take time to formulate, incubate, and eventually "hatch," which is not likely to happen under time pressure (Amabile, Hadley, & Kramer, 2002). Working under pressure on tasks that require higher-level thinking would be similar to trying to complete a long, challenging test within a short time frame. What happens is people have less time to think, to attend to fine details, to double-check their work, and to fine-tune their final product. Research indicates that most procrastinators admit that the work they produce is of poorer quality because they procrastinate (Steel, Brothen, & Wambach, 2001; Wesley, 1994) and that they experience considerable anxiety and guilt about their procrastination habit (Tice & Baumeister, 1997).

Myth 2. "Studying in advance is a waste of time because you will forget it all by test time." This misconception is commonly used to justify procrastinating with respect to preparing for upcoming exams. As will be discussed in Chapter 8, studying that is distributed (spread out) over time is more effective than massed (crammed) studying. Furthermore, last-minute studying that takes place the night before exams often results in lost sleep time due to the need to pull late-nighters or all-nighters. This fly-by-night strategy interferes with retention of information that has been studied and elevates test anxiety because of lost dream (a.k.a. rapid eye movement, or REM) sleep, which enables the brain to store memories and cope with stress (Hobson, 1988; Voelker, 2004). Research indicates that procrastinators experience higher rates of stress-related physical disorders, such as insomnia, stomach problems, colds, and flu (McCance & Pychyl, 2003).

Working under time pressure adds to performance pressure because procrastinators are left with no margin of error to correct mistakes, no time to seek help on their work, and no chance to handle random catastrophes that may arise at the last minute (e.g., an attack of the flu or a family emergency).

"Haste makes waste."

—Benjamin Franklin, 18th-century inventor, newspaper writer, and signer of the *Declaration of Independence*

| Think About It ———————————————— | *Journal Entry* **6.7** |

Have you ever put off work for so long that getting it done turned into an emergency situation?

Explain:

No I have not.

_____

_____

_____

_____

_____

Psychological Causes of Procrastination

Sometimes, procrastination has deeper psychological roots. People may procrastinate for reasons related not directly to poor time-management habits but more to emotional issues involving self-esteem or self-image. For instance, studies show that procrastination is sometimes used as a psychological strategy to protect one's self-esteem, which is referred to as self-handicapping. This strategy may be used by some procrastinators (consciously or unconsciously) to give themselves a "handicap" or disadvantage. Thus, if their performance turns out to be less than spectacular, they can conclude (rationalize) that it was because they were performing under a handicap—lack of time (Smith, Snyder, & Handelsman, 1982).

For example, if the grade they receive on a test or paper turns out to be low, they can still "save face" (self-esteem) by concluding that it was because they waited until the last minute and didn't put much time or effort into it. In other words, they had the ability or intelligence to earn a good grade; they just didn't try very hard. Better yet, if they happened to luck out and get a good grade despite doing it at the last minute, then the grade just shows how intelligent they are! Thus, self-handicapping creates a fail-safe scenario that's guaranteed to protect the procrastinator's self-image. If the work performance or product is less than excellent, it can be blamed on external factors (e.g., lack of time); if it happens to earn them a high grade, they can attribute the result to their extraordinary ability, which enabled them to do so well despite doing it all at the last minute.

In addition to self-handicapping, other psychological factors have been found to contribute to procrastination, including the following:

- **Fear of failure.** Feeling that it's better to postpone the job, or not do it, than to fail at it (Burka & Yuen, 1983; Soloman & Rothblum, 1984).
- **Perfectionism.** Having unrealistically high personal standards or expectations, which leads to the belief that it's better to postpone work or not do it than to risk doing it less than perfectly (Flett, Blankstein, Hewitt, & Koledin, 1992; Kachgal et al., 2001).

"We didn't lose the game; we just ran out of time."

—Vince Lombardi, legendary football coach

"Procrastinators would rather be seen as lacking in effort than lacking in ability."

—Joseph Ferrari, professor of psychology and procrastination researcher

"Striving for excellence motivates you; striving for perfection is demoralizing."

—Harriet Braiker, psychologist and bestselling author

- **Fear of success.** Fearing that doing well will show others that the procrastinator has the ability to achieve success and others will expect the procrastinator to maintain those high standards by doing "repeat performances" (Beck, Koons, & Milgram, 2000; Ellis & Kraun, 1977).
- **Indecisiveness.** Having difficulty making decisions, including decisions about what to do or how to begin doing it (Anderson, 2003; Steel, 2003).
- **Thrill seeking.** Enjoying the adrenaline rush triggered by rushing to get things done just before a deadline (Szalavitz, 2003).

If these or any other issues are involved, their underlying psychological causes must be dealt with before procrastination can be overcome. Because they have deeper roots, it may take some time and professional assistance to uproot them. A good place to get such assistance is the Personal Counseling Office. Personal counselors on college campuses are professional psychologists who are trained to deal with psychological issues that can contribute to procrastination.

Think About It ——————————————— Journal Entry 6.8

1. How often do you procrastinate?

   rarely   occasionally   ⟨frequently⟩   consistently

2. When you do procrastinate, what is the usual reason?

   Lazy, I forget or I dont
   want to do it.

Self-Help Strategies for Beating the Procrastination Habit

Once inaccurate beliefs or emotional issues underlying procrastination have been identified and dealt with, the next step is to move from gaining self-insight to taking direct action on the procrastination habit itself. Listed here are our top strategies for minimizing or eliminating the procrastination habit.

1. **Continually practice effective time-management strategies.** If effective time-management practices, such as those previously cited in this chapter, are implemented consistently, they can turn into a habit. Studies show that when people repeatedly practice effective time-management strategies, they gradually become part of their routine and develop into habits. For example, when procrastinators repeatedly practice effective time-management strategies with respect to tasks that they procrastinate on, their procrastination tendencies begin to fade and are gradually replaced by good time-management habits (Ainslie, 1992; Baumeister, Heatherton, & Tice, 1994).

For many procrastinators, getting started *is often their biggest obstacle.*

2. **Make the start of work as inviting or appealing as possible.** Getting started can be a key stumbling block for many procrastinators. They experience what's called "start-up stress" when they're about to begin a task they expect will be unpleasant, difficult, or boring (Burka & Yuen, 1983). If you have trouble starting your work, one way to give yourself a jump-start is to arrange your work tasks in an order that allows you to start on tasks that you're likely to find most interesting or most likely to experience success with. Once you overcome the initial inertia and get going, you can ride the momentum you've created to attack the tasks that you find less appealing and more daunting.

You're also likely to discover that the dreaded work wasn't as difficult, boring, or time-consuming as it appeared to be. When you sense that you're making some progress toward getting work done, your anxiety begins to decline. As with many experiences in life that are dreaded and avoided, the anticipation of the event turns out to be worse than the event itself. Research on students who hadn't started a project until it was about to be due indicates that these students experience anxiety and guilt about delaying their work, but once they begin working, these negative emotions decline and are replaced by more positive feelings (McCance & Pychyl, 2003).

3. **Make the work manageable.** Work becomes less overwhelming and less stressful when it's handled in small chunks or pieces. You can conquer procrastination for large tasks by using a "divide and conquer" strategy: divide the large task into smaller, more manageable units, and then attack and complete them one at a time.

Don't underestimate the power of short work sessions. They can be more effective than longer sessions because it's easier to maintain momentum and concentration for shorter periods. If you're working on a large project or preparing for a major exam, dividing your work into short sessions will enable you to take quick jabs and poke small holes in it, reducing its overall size with each successive punch. This approach will also give you the sense of satisfaction that comes with knowing that you're making steady progress toward completing a big task—continually chipping away at it in short strokes and gradually taking away the pressure associated with having to go for a big knockout punch right before the final bell (deadline).

Author's Experience   The two biggest projects I've had to complete in my life were writing my doctoral thesis and writing this textbook! The strategy that enabled me to keep going until I completed both of these large tasks was to make up short-term deadlines for myself (e.g., complete 5–10 pages each week). I psyched myself into thinking that these were real "drop-dead" deadlines and that if I didn't meet them and complete these small, shorter-term tasks, I was going to drop the ball and fail to get the whole job done. I think these self-imposed deadlines worked for me because they gave me short, more manageable tasks to work on that allowed me to make steady progress toward my larger, long-term task. It was as if I took a huge, hard-to-digest meal and broke it up into small, bite-sized pieces that I could easily swallow and gradually digest over time, as opposed to trying to consume a large meal right before bedtime (the final deadline).

Joe Cuseo

4. **Organization matters.** Research indicates that disorganization is a factor that contributes to procrastination (Steel, 2003). How well we organize our workplace and manage our work materials can reduce our risk of procrastination. Having the right materials in the right place at the right time can make it easier to get to our work and get going on our work. Once we've made a decision to get the job done, we don't want to waste time looking for the tools we need to begin doing it. For procrastinators, this time delay may be just the amount of time they need to change their minds and not start their work.

One simple yet effective way to organize your college work materials is by developing your own file system. You can begin to create an effective file system by filing (storing) materials from different courses in different colored folders or notebooks. This will allow you to keep all materials related to the same course in the same place and give you direct and immediate access to the materials you need as soon as you need them. Such a system helps you get organized, reduces stress associated with having things all over the place, and reduces the risk of procrastination by reducing the time it takes for you to start working.

5. **Location matters.** *Where* you work can influence when or whether you work. Research demonstrates that distraction is a factor that can contribute to procrastination (Steel, 2003). Thus, it may be possible for you to minimize procrastination by working in an environment whose location and arrangement prevent distraction and promote concentration.

Distractions tend to come in two major forms: social distractions (e.g., people nearby who are not working) and media distractions (e.g., cell phones, e-mails, text messages, iPods, Internet, and TV). Research indicates that the number of hours per week that college students spend watching TV is *negatively* associated with academic success: more TV leads to lower college grade point averages, less likelihood of graduating college with honors, and lower levels of personal development (Astin, 1993).

Remember

Select a workplace and arrange your workspace to minimize distraction from people and media. Try to remove everything from your work site that's not directly relevant to your work.

Think About It ———————————————————— *Journal Entry* **6.9**

List your two most common sources of distraction while working. Next to each distraction, identify a strategy that you might use to reduce or eliminate it.

Source of Distraction   Strategy for Reducing This Distraction

1. _____phone_____   ___Turn it off_____

2. ___everything around me_____   ___Zone it out_____

Lastly, keep in mind that you can arrange your work environment in a way that not only disables distraction, but also enables concentration. You can enable or empower your concentration by working in an environment that allows you easy access to work support materials (e.g., class notes, textbooks, and a dictionary) and social support (e.g., working with a group of motivated students who will encourage you to get focused, stay on task, and keep on track to complete your work tasks).

6. **Arrange the order or sequence of your work tasks to intercept procrastination when you're most likely to experience it.** While procrastination often involves difficulty starting work, it can also involve difficulty continuing and completing work (Lay & Silverman, 1996). As previously mentioned, if you have trouble starting work, it might be best to first do tasks that you find most interesting or easiest. However, if you have difficulty maintaining or sustaining your work until it's finished, you might try to schedule work tasks that you find easier and more interesting *in the middle or toward the end* of your planned work time. If you're performing tasks of greater interest and ease at a point in your work when you typically lose interest or energy, you may be able to sustain your interest and energy long enough to continue working until you complete them, which means that you'll have completed your entire list of tasks. Also, doing your most enjoyable and easiest tasks later can provide an incentive or reward for completing your less enjoyable tasks first.

7. **If you're close to completing a task, don't stop until you complete it.** It's often harder to restart a task than it is to finish a task that you've already started, because once you've overcome the initial inertia associated with getting started, you can ride the momentum that you've already created. Furthermore, finishing a task can give you a sense of closure—the feeling of personal accomplishment and self-satisfaction that comes from knowing that you "closed the deal." Placing a checkmark next to a completed task and seeing that it's one less thing you have to do can motivate you to continue working on the remaining tasks on your list.

Summary and Conclusion

Mastering the skill of managing time is critical for success in college and in life beyond college. Time is a valuable personal resource; the better you use it, the greater control you have over your life. On the other hand, if you ignore or abuse this resource, you run the risk of reducing the quality of your work and the quality of your life. Once you let go of the pervasive and pernicious procrastination-promoting myth that you work better under pressure (e.g., on the day or night before something is due), you can begin planning how to manage your time and control your future.

Managing time involves three key processes:

1. Analysis of how we spend time, which will allow us to become more consciously aware of our time-spending habits and enable us to know where all our time actually goes.
2. Development of a plan that connects our short-range, mid-range, and long-range tasks (i.e., for the next day, the next week, and the end of the term).
3. Evaluation of our priorities to ensure that we put most of our time into what's most important or matters the most.

These are the three keys to effective time management; they are also likely to be the keys to managing any personal resource, such as your money or your relationships.

Learning More through the World Wide Web
Internet-Based Resources for Further Information on Time Management

For additional information related to the ideas discussed in this chapter, we recommend the following Web sites:

www.time-management-guide.com/procrastination.html

www.studygs.net/timman.htm

www.essortment.com/lifestyle/timemanagement_sjmu.htm
(This site includes time-management strategies designed specifically for adult or non-traditional-aged students.)

6.1 Who's in Charge?

You have a paper due tomorrow for your 10:00 a.m. class. You stay up late writing the paper, and then your friends call and ask you to go out. The paper is finished, and you decide you can print it off when you get to school tomorrow. You have a great time with your friends and oversleep, waking at 9:45 a.m. You go straight to the computer lab and experience difficulties printing off your paper. You find a lab technician to help you, but it takes him 40 minutes to retrieve the paper. You run into class (45 minutes late) and give the paper to your instructor, who informs you that she will take the paper for late credit because the class policy states that any papers handed in after the beginning of class are considered late.

1. Who is primarily responsible for this paper being late? Why?

    Myself, I didn't print the paper.

2. How could the situation have been avoided or handled differently?

    Print the paper.

6.2 Term at a Glance

Review the syllabus (course outline) for each course you're enrolled in this term, and complete the following information for each:

Term _____, Year __*2015*__

Course	Professor	Exams	Projects & Papers	Other Assignments	Attendance Policy	Late & Makeup Assignment Policy
english	Shoverman	7	6	2	2 days	No
wills	Idk	12	3	yes	Idk	yes

1. Is the overall workload what you expected? Are you surprised by the amount of work required in any particular course or courses?

    No I am not surprised.

2. At this point in the term, what do you see as your most challenging or demanding course or courses? Why?

    child development. Definitions

3. Do you think you can handle the total workload required for the full set of courses you're enrolled in this term?

    yes if i put myself to it.

4. What adjustments or changes could you make to your personal schedule that would make it easier to accommodate your academic workload this term?

study more.

6.3 Your Week at a Glance

On the blank grid that follows, map out your typical week for this term. Start by recording what you usually do on these days, including when you have class, when you work, and when you relax or recreate. You can use abbreviations or write tasks out in full if you have enough room in the box (J = job, R&R = rest/relaxation, etc.). List the abbreviations you create at the bottom of the page so that your instructor can follow them.

If you're a *full-time* student, find *25 hours* in your week that you can devote to homework (HW). These 25 hours could be found between classes, during the day, in the evenings, or on the weekends. If you can find 25 hours per week for homework, in addition to your class schedule, you'll have a 40-hour schoolwork week, which research has shown to result in good grades and success in college.

If you're a *part-time* student, find *two hours* you can devote to homework *for every hour* that you're in class (e.g., if you're in class nine hours per week, find 18 hours of homework time).

	Sunday	Monday	Tuesday	Wednesday	Thursday	Friday	Saturday
7:00 a.m.	S	S	S	S	Sleep	S	S
8:00 a.m.	l		E				
9:00 a.m.	e	e	get ready	e	get ready		
10:00 a.m.	P	e	Class	e	Class		
11:00 a.m.		P		P			
12:00 p.m.			Lunch		Lunch		
1:00 p.m.			class		class		
2:00 p.m.							
3:00 p.m.		homework					
4:00 p.m.			R				
5:00 p.m.			R				
6:00 p.m.		Class	R				
7:00 p.m.			R				
8:00 p.m.							
9:00 p.m.		Come home					
10:00 p.m.							
11:00 p.m.							

191

6.4 Personal Time Inventory

1. Go to the following Web site:

   www.ulc.psu.edu/studyskills/time_management.html#monitoring_your_time

2. Complete the time management exercise at this site. The exercise asks you to estimate the number of hours per day or week that you spend doing various activities (e.g., sleeping, employment, and commuting). As you enter the amounts of time you engage in these activities, the total number of remaining hours available in the week for academic work will be automatically computed.

3. After completing your entries, answer the following questions:
   - How many hours per week do you have available for academic work? *16*
   - Do you have two hours available for academic work outside of class for each hour you spend in class? *yes*
   - What time wasters do you detect that might be easily eliminated or reduced to create more time for academic work outside of class? *Internet, nap, Lazyness*

6.5 Ranking Priorities

Look at the tasks below and decide if they are A, B, or C priorities:

__C__ Going for a run

__A__ Writing a paper that is due tomorrow

__A__ Paying your electric bill that is due next week

__C__ Checking out what your friends are doing on Facebook

__B__ Getting your haircut

__B__ Making an appointment with your academic advisor to register for classes

__C__ Playing your favorite video game

__B__ Making it to your doctor's appointment

__B__ Helping your sister plan her wedding

__A__ Picking up your child's prescription from the pharmacy

__A__ Studying for your final exams

__C__ Calling your cousin to catch up on family gossip

__C__ Making reservations for your vacation

__C__ Going to see the hot new movie that has come out

__B__ Getting your oil changed in your car

__B__ Getting your car washed

Procrastination: The Vicious Cycle

Delilah has a major paper due at the end of the term. It's now past midterm and she still hasn't started to work on her paper. She tells herself, "I should have started sooner."

However, Delilah continues to postpone starting her work on the paper and begins to feel anxious and guilty about it. To relieve her growing anxiety and guilt, she starts doing other tasks instead, such as cleaning her room and returning e-mails. This makes Delilah feel a little better because these tasks keep her busy, take her mind off the term paper, and give her the feeling that at least she's getting something accomplished. Time continues to pass; the deadline for the paper is growing dangerously close. Delilah now finds herself in the position of having lots of work to do and little time in which to do it.

Source: Burka & Yuen (1983)

Discussion Questions

1. What do you predict Delilah will do at this point?

2. Why did you make the above prediction?

3. What grade do you think Delilah will receive on her paper?

4. What do you think Delilah will do on the next term paper she's assigned?

5. Other than starting sooner, what recommendations would you have for Delilah (and other procrastinators like her) to break this cycle of procrastination and prevent it from happening repeatedly?

Chapter 6 Reflection

Looking back on suggestions from this chapter, what are three things you can do to start managing your time better?

1.

2.

3.

Explain how you are going to make this happen.

Welcome to Macomb Community College!

My name is Carl Weckerle, and I am the Director of Instructional Technology and Online Learning. I oversee the College's Learning Management System, and instructional technologies used by faculty to support learning in and out of the classroom.

The interesting part about being in my position is that I did not set out to have a career dealing with technology. I actually avoided it early on, because I did not want to sit at a desk and stare at a computer all day. My focus in college and throughout my career has been on education. It was only through small opportunities and being slightly more comfortable in using computers, that I became more interested and passionate about how technology, combined with education, can provide opportunities where they may not otherwise exist.

We don't all start off with the same advantages. I saw this firsthand as a student in the Hamtramck and Detroit Public Schools, and eventually as a teacher in the Detroit Public Schools. While going through school, I knew there were many things that I could not control, but I always kept in mind two things that I could control that allowed me to be successful. **The first was having a goal, so that I knew where I wanted to go; and second, was remaining positive in the face of difficulties.**

Everyone runs into barriers in life, and I was no different. What helped keep me going was knowing that I was going to graduate and become a teacher, and keeping a positive attitude even during difficult times. By having that goal and remaining positive, I was able to keep pushing toward it. Without that goal, I probably would have floundered.

You will run into difficult times; some more than others. There may be situations you can control and others where you cannot. You may have a course that is challenging, a loved one who is sick, a car that won't start, or going to class with no sleep. By having that goal, big or small, you have a purpose to help keep you going. By remaining positive, you rise above the negativity that tries to pull you down.

Keep focused and keep your head held high. You never know if your small interests will turn into great opportunities.

I am Carl Weckerle and I am Macomb.

Courtesy of Carl Weckerle

Higher-Level Thinking
Moving beyond Basic Knowledge to Critical and Creative Thinking

| THOUGHT STARTER | *Journal Entry* 7.1 | LEARNING GOAL |

LEARNING GOAL

To increase awareness of what it means to think at a higher level and how higher-level thinking can be used to achieve excellence in college and beyond.

To me, critical thinking means . . .

(At a later point in this chapter, we'll discuss critical thinking and ask you to flash back to the response you made here.)

To ~~~~~~~~~~ Makeing ~~~~~ critical thinking ↱ Chellange

Think About It — *Journal Entry* 7.2

To me, thinking is . . .

Useing your brain and Knowledge

What Is Higher-Level Thinking?

The term *higher-level thinking* (or *higher-order thinking*) refers to a more advanced level of thought than that used for learning basic skills and acquiring factual knowledge. Higher-level thinking involves reflecting on the knowledge you've acquired and taking additional mental action on it, such as evaluating its validity, integrating it with something else you've learned, or creating new ideas.

Student
Perspective

"To me, thinking at a higher level means deep thought. It is when you have to put your time and effort into whatever you are thinking or writing."

—First-year college student

Contestants performing on TV quiz shows such as *Jeopardy!* or *Who Wants to Be a Millionaire?* are responding with factual knowledge to questions that ask for information about who, what, when, and where. If these contestants were to be tested for higher-level thinking, they would be answering more challenging questions about why, how, and what if.

Remember

The focus of higher-level thinking is not just to answer questions but also to question answers.

© Rafael Ramirez Lee, 2013. Under license from Shutterstock, Inc.

As its name implies, higher-level thinking involves raising the bar and jacking up your thinking to levels that go beyond merely remembering, reproducing, or regurgitating factual information. "Education is what's left over after you've forgotten all the facts" is an old saying that carries a lot of truth. Studies show that students' memory of facts learned in college often fades with time (Pascarella & Terenzini, 1991, 2005). Memory for factual information has a short lifespan; the ability to think at a higher level is a durable, lifelong learning skill that lasts a lifetime.

Compared to high school classes, college courses focus less on memorizing information and more on thinking about issues, concepts, and principles (Conley, 2005). Remembering information in college may get a grade of "C," demonstrating comprehension of that information may get you a "B," and going beyond comprehension to demonstrate higher-level thinking will earn you an "A." In national surveys of college professors teaching freshman-through senior-level courses in various fields, more than 95 percent of them report that the most important goal of a college education is to develop students' ability to think critically (Gardiner, 2005; Milton, 1982). Similarly, college professors teaching introductory courses to freshmen and sophomores indicate that the primary educational purpose of their courses is to develop students' critical thinking skills (Higher Education Institute, 2009; Stark et al., 1990).

Simply stated, college professors are often more concerned with teaching you *how* to think than with teaching you *what* to think (i.e., what facts to remember).

Remember

Your college professors will often expect you to do more than just retain or reproduce information: they'll ask you to demonstrate higher levels of thinking with respect to what you've learned, such as analyze it, evaluate it, apply it, or connect it with other concepts that you've learned.

This is not to say that acquiring knowledge and basic comprehension are unimportant. They are important because they supply you with the raw material needed to manufacture higher-level thinking. Deep learning and a broad base of knowledge provide the stepping stones you need to climb to higher levels of thinking.

This is not to say that basic knowledge and comprehension are unimportant. Rather, they provide the foundational steps necessary for you to climb to higher levels of thinking, as illustrated in Figure 7.1.

FIGURE 7.1

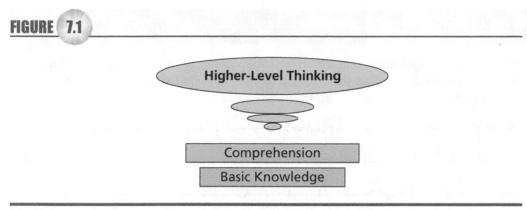

The Relationship between Knowledge, Comprehension, and Higher-Level Thinking

Defining and Describing the Major Forms of Higher-Level Thinking

When your college professors ask you to "think critically," they're usually asking you to use one or more of the eight forms of thinking listed in Snapshot Summary 7.1. As you read the description of each form of thinking, note whether or not you've heard of it before.

Snapshot Summary

7.1 Major Forms of Higher-Level Thinking

1. **Application (applied thinking).** Putting knowledge into practice to solve problems and resolve issues;
2. **Analysis (analytical thinking).** Breaking down information to identify its key parts and underlying elements;
3. **Synthesis.** Building up ideas by integrating them into a larger whole or more comprehensive system;
4. **Multidimensional thinking.** Taking multiple perspectives (i.e., viewing issues from different vantage points);

5. **Inferential reasoning.** Making arguments or judgments by inferring (stepping to) a conclusion that's supported by empirical (observable) evidence or logical consistency;
6. **Balanced thinking.** Carefully considering arguments for and against a particular position or viewpoint;
7. **Critical thinking.** Evaluating (judging the quality of) arguments, conclusions, and ideas;
8. **Creative thinking.** Generating ideas that are unique, original, or distinctively different.

Application (Applied Thinking)

When you learn something deeply, you transform information into knowledge; when you translate knowledge into action, you're engaging in a higher-level thinking process known as *application*. Applied thinking moves you beyond simply knowing something to actually doing something with the knowledge you possess: you use the knowledge you've acquired to solve a problem or resolve an issue. For example, if you use knowledge you've acquired in a human relations course to resolve an interpersonal conflict, you're engaging in application. Similarly, when you use knowledge acquired in a math course to solve a problem that you haven't seen before, you're using applied thinking. Application is a powerful form of higher-level thinking because it allows you to transfer your knowledge to new situations or contexts and put it into practice.

Look back at the eight forms of thinking described in Snapshot Summary 7.1. Which of these forms of thinking had you heard of before? Did you use any of these forms of thinking on high school exams or assignments? Explain.

Application, Analysis, Synthesis, critical and creative thinking. Yes, critical and creative in papers

Always be on the lookout for ways to apply the knowledge you acquire to your personal life experiences and current events or issues. When you use your knowledge for the practical purpose of doing something good, such as bettering yourself or others, you not only demonstrate application; you also demonstrate *wisdom* (Staudinger, 2008).

Analysis (Analytical Thinking)

The mental process of analysis is similar to the physical process of peeling an onion. When you analyze something, you take it apart or break it down and pick out its key parts, main points, or underlying elements. For example, if you were to analyze a textbook chapter, you would go beyond reading just to cover the content: you would read it to uncover the author's main ideas and distinguish them from background information and incidental details.

In an art course, you would use analysis to identify the components or elements of a painting or sculpture (e.g., its structure, texture, tone, and form). In the natural and social sciences, you would use analysis to identify underlying reasons or causes for natural (physical) phenomena and social events, which is commonly referred to as "causal analysis." For instance, causal analysis of the September 11, 2001, attack on the United States would involve identifying the factors that led to the attack or the underlying reasons for why the attack took place.

Synthesis

A form of higher-level thinking that's basically the opposite of analysis is *synthesis*. When you analyze, you break information into its parts; when you synthesize, you build it up by taking separate parts or pieces of information and connecting them to form an integrated whole (like piecing together parts of a puzzle). You engage in synthesis when you connect ideas presented in different courses: for instance, when you integrate ethical concepts learned in a philosophy course with marketing concepts learned in a business course to produce a set of ethical guidelines for marketing and advertising products.

Think About It ———————————————— *Journal Entry* **7.4**

A TV commercial for a particular brand of liquor (which shall remain nameless) once showed a young man getting out of his car in front of a house where a party is going on. The driver gets out of his car, takes out a knife, slashes his tires, and goes inside to join the party. Using the higher-level thinking skill of analysis, what would you say are the underlying or embedded messages in this commercial?

To not drink and drive -

Synthesis involves more than a summary. It goes beyond just condensing information to a higher level of thinking that involves finding and forming meaningful connections across separate pieces of information and weaving them together to form a cohesive picture. When you're synthesizing, you're thinking conceptually by converting isolated facts and separated bits of information and integrating them into a *concept*—a larger system or network of related ideas.

Although synthesis and analysis are virtually opposite thought processes, they complement each other. When you analyze, you disassemble information into its key parts. When you synthesize, you reassemble information into a whole. For instance, when writing this book, we analyzed published material in many fields (e.g., psychology, history, philosophy, and biology) and identified information from parts of these fields that were most relevant to promoting the success of beginning college students. We then synthesized or reassembled these parts to create a new whole—the textbook you're now reading.

Multidimensional Thinking

When you engage in multidimensional thinking, you view yourself and the world around you from different angles or vantage points. In particular, a multidimensional thinker is able to think from four key perspectives and determine how each of them influences, and is influenced by, the issue under discussion.

1. **Person (self).** How does this issue affect me as an individual? (The perspective of person.)
2. **Place.** What impact does this issue have on people living in different countries? (The perspective of place.)

3. **Time.** How will future generations of people be affected by this issue? (The perspective of time.)
4. **Culture.** How is this issue likely to be interpreted or experienced by groups of people who share different social customs and traditions? (The perspective of culture.)

Each of these four general perspectives has specific elements embedded within it. The four major perspectives, along with the key elements that comprise each of them, are listed and described in Snapshot Summary 7.2.

Snapshot Summary

7.2 Perspectives Associated with Multidimensional Thinking

Perspective 1: PERSON (Perspectives on different dimensions of oneself.)

Key Components

- **Intellectual (cognitive):** Knowledge, style of thinking, and self-concept
- **Emotional:** Feelings, emotional adjustment, and mental health
- **Social:** Interpersonal relationships and social interactions
- **Ethical:** Values and moral convictions
- **Physical:** Health and wellness
- **Spiritual:** Beliefs about the meaning or purpose of life and the hereafter
- **Vocational (occupational):** Means of making a living and earning an income

Perspective 2: PLACE (Perspectives beyond the self that include progressively wider social and spatial distance.)

Key Components

- **Family:** Parents, children, and other relatives
- **Community:** Local communities and neighborhoods
- **Society:** Societal institutions (e.g., schools, churches, and hospitals) and groups within society (e.g., social groups differing in age, gender, race, or socioeconomic status)
- **Nation:** One's own country or place of citizenship
- **International:** Citizens of different nations and territories
- **Global:** Planet earth (e.g., its life forms and natural resources)
- **Universe:** The galaxy that includes earth, other planets, and celestial bodies

Perspective 3: TIME (Chronological perspective.)

Key Components

- **Historical:** The past
- **Contemporary:** The present
- **Futuristic:** The future

Perspective 4: CULTURE (Perspective of particular groups of people who share the same social heritage and traditions.)

Key Components

- **Linguistic (language):** How group members communicate via spoken and written words and through nonverbal communication (body language)
- **Political:** How the group organizes societal authority and uses it to govern itself, make collective decisions, and maintain social order
- **Economic:** How the material wants and needs of the group are met through allocation of limited resources, and how wealth is distributed among its members
- **Geographical:** How the group's physical location influences the nature of social interactions and the way its members adapt to and use their environment
- **Aesthetic:** How the group appreciates and expresses artistic beauty and creativity through the arts (e.g., visual art, music, theater, literature, and dance)
- **Scientific:** How the group views, understands, and investigates natural phenomena through research (e.g., scientific tests and experiments)
- **Ecological:** How the group views its relationship to the surrounding biological world (e.g., other living creatures) and the physical environment
- **Anthropological:** How the group's culture originated, evolved, and developed over time
- **Sociological:** How the group's society is structured and organized into social subgroups and social institutions
- **Psychological:** How group members tend to think, feel, and interact with each other, and how their attitudes, opinions, or beliefs have been acquired
- **Philosophical:** The group's ideas or views on the nature of truth, goodness, wisdom, beauty, and the meaning or purpose of life
- **Theological:** Group members' ideas and beliefs about a transcendent, supreme being, and how they express their shared faith in a supreme being

Important human issues don't exist in isolation but as parts of complex, inter-connected systems that involve interplay of multiple factors and perspectives. For example, global warming is a current issue that involves the earth's atmosphere gradually thickening and trapping more heat due to a collection of greenhouse gases, which are being produced primarily by the burning of fossil fuels. It's theorized that this increase in manmade pollution is causing temperatures to rise (and sometimes fall) around the world and is contributing to natural disasters, such as droughts, wildfires, and dust storms (Joint Science Academies Statement, 2005; National Resources Defense Council, 2012). Understanding and addressing this issue involves interrelationships among a variety of perspectives, as depicted in Figure 7.2.

FIGURE 7.2

Person Global warming involves us on an individual level because our personal efforts at energy conservation in our homes and our willingness to purchase energy-efficient products can play a major role in solving this problem.

Place Global warming is an international issue that extends beyond the boundaries of one's own country to all countries in the world, and its solution will require worldwide collaboration.

Time If the current trend toward higher global temperatures caused by global warming continues, it could seriously threaten the lives of future generations of people who inhabit our planet.

Culture The problem of global warming has been caused by industries in technologically advanced cultures, yet the problem of rising global temperatures is likely to have its most negative impact on less technologically advanced cultures that lack the resources to respond to it (Joint Science Academies Statement, 2005). To prevent this from happening, technologically advanced cultures will need to use their advanced technology to devise alternative methods for generating energy that don't release heat-trapping gases into the atmosphere.

Understanding Global Warming from Four Key Perspectives

Addressing the issue of global warming also involves different components of our culture, including: (1) ecology: understanding the delicate interplay between humans and their natural environment, (2) science: need for research and development of alternative sources of energy, (3) economics: managing the cost incurred by industries to change their existing sources of energy, (4) politics: devising incentives or laws to encourage changes in industries' use of energy sources, and (5) international relations: collaboration between our nation and other nations that are currently contributing to this worldwide problem and that play pivotal roles in its future solution.

Think About It ──────────────── Journal Entry 7.5

Briefly explain how each of the perspectives of person, place, time, and culture may be involved in causing and solving one of the following problems:

1. War and terrorism

   People canstart wars & terrorism. It depends on the time and what culture.

2. Poverty and hunger

   Depends what culture and year. Happens to all people.

3. Prejudice and discrimination

   Depends on what year. It appends to all people and eny where

4. Any world issue of your choice

   Diseases- Happens to anyone, anywhere, and anytime

Inferential Reasoning

When people make arguments or arrive at conclusions, they do so by starting with a premise (a statement or an observation) and use it to infer (step to) a conclusion. The following sentence starters demonstrate the process of inferential reasoning:

> *"Because this is true, it follows that . . ."*

> *"Based on this evidence, I can conclude that . . ."*

Inferential reasoning is the primary thought process humans use to reach conclusions about themselves and the world around them. This is also the form of thinking that you will use to make arguments and reach conclusions about ideas presented in your college courses. You'll often be required to take positions and draw conclusions by supporting them with solid evidence and sound reasoning. In a sense, you'll be asked to take on the role of a courtroom lawyer trying to prove a case by supplying supporting arguments and evidence (exhibit A, exhibit B, etc.).

The following are two major ways in which you use inferential reasoning to support your points or arguments:

1. **Citing empirical (observable) evidence.** Supporting your point with specific examples, personal experiences, facts, figures, statistical data, scientific research findings, expert testimonies, supporting quotes, or statements from leading authorities in the field.
2. **Using principles of logical consistency.** Showing that your conclusion follows or flows logically from an established premise or proposition. The following are examples that demonstrate logical consistency:

   * The constitution guarantees all U.S. citizens the right to vote (established premise);
   * U.S. citizens include women and people of color; therefore,
   * Granting women and people of color the right to vote was/is logically consistent (and constitutional).

Both empirical evidence and logical consistency can be used to support the same argument. For instance, advocates for lowering the legal drinking age to 18 have argued that: (1) in other countries where drinking is allowed at age 18, statistics show that they have fewer binge-drinking and drunk-driving problems than the United States (empirical evidence), and (2) 18-year-olds in the United States are considered to be legal adults with respect to such rights and responsibilities as voting, serving on juries, joining the military, and being held responsible for committing crimes; therefore, 18-year-olds should have the right to drink.

Think About It ——————————— Journal Entry 7.6

Can you think of any arguments *against* lowering the drinking age to 18 that are based on empirical (observable) evidence or logical consistency?

Everybody drinks at 8. Less people get in trouble.

Unfortunately, errors can be made in the inferential reasoning process, often referred to as *logical fallacies*. Some of the more common logical fallacies are summarized in Snapshot Summary 7.3.

Snapshot Summary

7.3 Logical Fallacies: Inferential-Reasoning Errors

Critical thinking is a higher-level thinking skill that allows you to evaluate and detect errors in your own reasoning and in the reasoning of others. Some of the more common reasoning errors are summarized here. As you read the following list of logical errors, make a brief note in the margin of any example of these errors that you have observed or experienced.

- **Dogmatism.** Stubbornly clinging to a personally held viewpoint that's unsupported by evidence and remaining closed-minded (non-receptive) to other viewpoints that are better supported by evidence. (For instance, those who believe that America's form of capitalism is the only economic system that can work in a successful democracy, while refusing to acknowledge that there are other successful democratic countries with different types of capitalistic economies.)
- **Selective perception.** Seeing only examples and instances that support a position while overlooking or ignoring those that contradict it (e.g., those who believe in astrology who only notice and point out people whose personalities happen to fit their astrological signs, while overlooking those who don't).

"Belief can be produced in practically unlimited quantity and intensity, without observation or reasoning, and even in defiance of both by the simple desire to believe."

—George Bernard Shaw, Irish playwright and 1925 Nobel Prize winner for literature

- **Double standard.** Having two sets of standards for judgment: a higher standard for judging others and a lower standard for judging oneself. This is the classic "do as I say, not as I do" hypocrisy (e.g., critically evaluating and challenging the opinions of others but not our own).
- **Wishful thinking.** Thinking that something is true not on the basis of logic or evidence, but because the person wants it to be true. (For instance, a teenage girl who believes she will not become pregnant, even though she and her boyfriend always have sex without using any form of contraception.)
- **Hasty generalization.** Reaching a conclusion prematurely on the basis of a limited number of instances or experiences (e.g., concluding that people belonging to a group are all or nearly all "that way" on the basis of personal experiences with only one or two individuals).
- **Jumping to a conclusion.** Making a leap of logic to reach a conclusion that's based on only one reason or factor while ignoring other possible reasons and contributing factors (e.g., immediately concluding that "I must be a real loser" after being rejected for a date or a job).

- **Glittering generality.** Making a positive general statement without supplying details or evidence to back it up (e.g., writing a letter of recommendation describing someone as a "wonderful person" with a "great personality" but not providing any reasons or evidence to support these claims).
- **Straw man argument.** Distorting an opponent's argument position and then attacking it (e.g., attacking an opposing political candidate for supporting censorship and restricting civil liberties when the opponent supported only a ban on violent pornography).
- **Ad hominem argument.** Aiming an argument at the person rather than the person's argument (e.g., telling a younger person, "You're too young and inexperienced to know what you're talking about," or telling an older person, "You're too old-fashioned to understand this issue"). Literally translated, the term *ad hominem* means "to the man."
- **Red herring.** Bringing up an irrelevant issue that disguises or distracts attention from the real issue being discussed or debated (e.g., responding to criticism of former President Richard Nixon's involvement in the Watergate scandal by arguing, "He was a good president who accomplished many good things while he was in office"). The term *red herring* derives from an old practice of dragging a herring—a strong-smelling fish—across a trail to distract the scent of pursuing dogs. (In the example, Nixon's effectiveness as a president is an irrelevant issue or a red herring; the real issue being discussed is Nixon's behavior in the Watergate scandal.)
- **Smoke screen.** Intentionally disguising or covering up true reasons or motives with reasons that confuse or mislead others (e.g., opposing gun control legislation by arguing that it is a violation of the constitutional right to bear arms without revealing that the opponent of the legislation is receiving financial support from gun manufacturing companies).
- **Slippery slope.** Using fear tactics by arguing that not accepting a position will result in a "domino effect"—one bad thing happening after another, like a series of falling dominoes (e.g., "If someone experiments with marijuana, it will automatically lead to loss of motivation, harder drugs, and withdrawal from college").
- **Rhetorical deception.** Using deceptive language to conclude that something is true without providing reasons or evidence (e.g., glibly making statements such as: "Clearly this is . . ." "It is obvious that . . ." or "Any reasonable person can see . . ." without explaining why it's so clear, obvious, or reasonable).

- **Circular reasoning (a.k.a. "begging the question").** Drawing a conclusion that's merely a rewording or restatement of one's position without any supporting reasons or evidence, leaving the original question still unanswered and the issue still unsolved. This form of reasoning basically draws conclusion logically by claiming "it's true because it's true" (e.g., "Stem cell research shouldn't be legal because it shouldn't be done").
- **Appealing to authority or prestige.** Believing that if an authority figure or celebrity says it's true, then it must be true or should be done (e.g., buying product X simply because a famous actor or athlete uses it, or believing that if someone in authority, such as the U.S. president, says something should be done, then it must be the right or best thing to do).
- **Appealing to tradition or familiarity.** Concluding that if something has always been thought to be true or has always been done in a certain way, then it must be true or the best way to do it (e.g., "This is the way it's always been done, so it must be right").
- **Appealing to popularity or the majority (a.k.a. jumping on the bandwagon).** Believing that if it's popular or held by the majority of people, it must be true (e.g., "So many people believe in psychics, it has to be true; they can't all be wrong").
- **Appealing to emotion.** Believing in something based on the emotional intensity experienced when the claim is made, rather than the quality of reasoning or evidence used to support the claim (e.g., "If I feel strongly about something, it must be true"). The expressions "always trust your feelings" and "just listen to your heart" may not always lead to the most accurate conclusions and the best decisions, because they can be driven more by emotion than by reason.

Balanced Thinking

Balanced thinking involves seeking out and carefully considering evidence for and against a particular position. The process of supporting a position with evidence is technically referred to as *adduction*; when you adduce, you offer reasons *for* a position. The process of arguing against a position by presenting contradictory evidence or reasons is called *refutation*; when you refute, you provide a rebuttal by supplying evidence *against* a particular position. The opposing position's stronger arguments are acknowledged, and its weaker ones are refuted (Fairbairn & Winch, 1996).

Balanced thinking involves both adduction and refutation. The goal of a balanced thinker is not to stack up evidence for one position or the other, but to be an impartial investigator who looks at supporting and opposing evidence for both sides of an issue and attempts to reach a conclusion that's not biased or one-sided. Thus, the first step in the process of seeking truth should not be to immediately jump in and take an either-or (for or against) stance on a debatable issue. Instead, your first step should be to look at arguments for and against each position, acknowledge the strengths and weaknesses of both sides of the argument, and identify what additional information may still be needed to make a fair judgment or reach a reasonable conclusion.

Balanced thinking requires more than just adding up the number of arguments for and against a position; it also involves weighing the strength of those arguments because arguments can vary in terms of their level of importance and degree of support. When evaluating arguments, ask yourself, "How sure am I about the conclusion made by this argument?" Determine whether the evidence is:

1. **Definitive.** So strong or compelling that a definite conclusion should be reached;
2. **Suggestive.** Strong enough to suggest that a tentative conclusion may be reached; or
3. **Inconclusive.** Too weak to reach any conclusion.

"The more you know, the less sure you are."

—Voltaire, French historian, philosopher, and advocate for civil liberty

"Too often we enjoy the comfort of opinion without the discomfort of thought."

—John F. Kennedy, 35th U.S. president

Remember

A characteristic of balanced thinking is being mindful of the weight (degree of importance) you assign to different arguments and articulating how their weight has been factored into your final conclusion (e.g., in a written report or class presentation).

In some cases, after reviewing both supporting and contradictory evidence for opposing positions, balanced thinking may lead you to suspend judgment and to withhold making a firm decision that favors one position over the other. A balanced thinker may occasionally reach the following conclusions: "Right now, I can't be sure; the evidence doesn't strongly favor one position over the other" or "More information is needed before I can make a final judgment or reach a firm conclusion." This isn't being wishy-washy: it's a legitimate conclusion to draw, as long as it is an informed conclusion that's supported with sound reasons and solid evidence. In fact, it's better to hold an undecided but informed viewpoint based on balanced thinking than to hold a definite opinion that's uninformed, biased, or based on emotion, such as the opinions offered loudly and obnoxiously by people on radio and TV talk shows.

Think About It ——————————— *Journal Entry* 7.7

Consider the following positions:

1. Course requirements should be eliminated; college students should be allowed to choose the classes they want to take for their degrees.

2. Course grades should be eliminated; college students should take classes on a pass-fail basis.

Using balanced thinking, identify one or more arguments *for* and *against* each of these positions.

Pass-fail   classes—not deserving of Knowledge

Requirement — person didn't learn about anything

Remember

When you combine balanced thinking with multidimensional thinking, you become a more complex and comprehensive thinker who is capable of viewing any issue from opposing sides and different angles.

Critical Thinking

Critical thinking is a form of higher-level thinking that involves *evaluation or judgment*. The evaluation can be either positive or negative: for example, a movie critic can give a good (thumbs up) or bad (thumbs down) review of a film. However, critical thinking involves much more than simply stating, "I liked it," or "I didn't like it." Specific reasons or evidence must be supplied to support the critique; failure to do so makes the criticism unfounded—i.e., it has no foundation or basis of support.

Think About It	Journal Entry 7.8

Flash back to the journal entry at the start of this chapter. How does your response to the incomplete sentence compare with the definition of critical thinking we just provided?

Its sapost to chem arge you to think.

If you wrote that critical thinking means "being critical" or negatively criticizing something or somebody, don't feel bad. Many students think that critical thinking has this negative meaning or connotation.

Critical thinking is used to evaluate many things besides films, art, or music: it's also used to judge the quality of ideas, beliefs, choices, and decisions, whether they be your own or those of others. It's also a skill that's highly valued by professors teaching students at all stages in the college experience and all subjects in the college curriculum (Higher Education Institute, 2009; Stark et al., 1990). By working on developing these skills now, you'll significantly improve your academic performance throughout your college experience. You can start developing the mental habit of critical thinking by regularly asking yourself the following questions as criteria for evaluating any idea or argument:

1. **Validity (truthfulness).** Is it true or accurate?
2. **Morality (ethics).** Is it fair or just?
3. **Beauty (aesthetics).** Is it beautiful or artistic?
4. **Practicality (usefulness).** Can it be put to use for practical purposes?
5. **Priority (order of importance or effectiveness).** Is it the best option or alternative?

Since thinking skills are valued by professors who are teaching students at all stages of the college experience and in all subjects in the curriculum, developing these skills should be time well spent and should improve your academic performance significantly.

Creative Thinking

When you think creatively, you generate something new or different, whether that may be a novel idea, strategy, or work product. Creative thinking leads you to ask the question, "Why not?" (e.g., "Why not do it a different way?"). It could be said that when you think critically, you look "inside the box" and evaluate the quality of its content. When you think creatively, you look "outside the box" to imagine other packages containing different content.

Any time you combine two existing ideas to generate a new idea, you're engaging in creative thinking. Creative thinking can be viewed as an extension or higher form of synthesis, whereby parts of separate ideas are combined or integrated to create a final product that turns out to be different (and better) than what previously existed (Anderson & Krathwohl, 2001). Even in the arts, what's created isn't totally original or unique. Instead, artistic creativity typically involves a combination or rearrangement of previously existing elements to generate a new "whole"—a final product that is distinctive or noticeably different. For instance, hard rock was created by combining elements of blues and rock and roll, and folk rock took form when Bob Dylan combined musical elements of acoustic blues and amplified rock (Shelton et al., 2003). Robert Kearns (subject of the film *Flash of Genius*) combined preexisting mechanical parts to create the intermittent windshield wiper (Seabrook, 2008).

Creative and critical thinking are two of the most important forms of higher-level thinking, and they work well together. We use creative thinking to ask new questions and generate new ideas; we use critical thinking to evaluate or critique the ideas we create (Paul & Elder, 2004). A creative idea must not only be different or original: it must also be effective (Sternberg, 2001; Runco, 2004). If critical thinking reveals that the quality of what we've created is poor, we then shift back to creative thinking to generate something new and improved. Or, we may start by using critical thinking to evaluate an old idea or approach and come to the judgment that it's not very good. This unfavorable evaluation naturally leads to and turns on the creative thinking process, which tries to come up with a new idea or different approach that's better than the old one.

Brainstorming is a problem-solving process that effectively illustrates how creative and critical thinking complement each other. The steps or stages involved in the process of brainstorming are summarized in Do It Now! 7.1. As the brainstorming process suggests, creativity doesn't just happen suddenly or effortlessly, like the so-called stroke of genius: instead, it takes considerable mental effort (Paul & Elder, 2004; De Bono, 2007). Although creative thinking initially involves some spontaneous and intuitive leaps, it also involves careful reflection and evaluation of whether any of those leaps actually land you on a good idea.

"The principal mark of genius is not perfection but originality, the opening of new frontiers."

—Arthur Koestler, Hungarian novelist and philosopher

"The blues are the roots. Everything else are the fruits."

—Willie Dixon, blues songwriter; commenting on how all forms of contemporary American music contain elements of blues music, which originated among African American slaves

"Creativity is allowing oneself to make mistakes; art is knowing which ones to keep."

—Scott Adams, creator of the *Dilbert* comic strip and author of *The Dilbert Principle*

"Creativity isn't 'crazytivity'."

—Edward De Bono, internationally known authority on creative thinking

7.1

The Process of Brainstorming

1. List as many ideas as you can, generating them rapidly without stopping to evaluate their validity or practicality. Studies show that worrying about whether an idea is correct often blocks creativity (Basadur, Runco, & Vega, 2000). So, at this stage of the process, just let your imagination run wild; don't worry about whether the idea you generate is impractical, unrealistic, or outrageous.

2. Use the ideas on your list as a springboard to trigger additional ideas, or combine them to create new ideas.

3. After you run out of ideas, review and critically evaluate the list of ideas you've generated and eliminate those that you think are least effective.

4. From the remaining list of ideas, choose the best idea or best combination of ideas.

Note: The first two steps in the brainstorming process involve *divergent thinking*—a form of creative thinking that allows you to go off in different directions and generate diverse ideas. In contrast, the last two steps in the process involve *convergent thinking*—a form of critical thinking in which you converge (focus in) and narrow down the ideas, evaluating each of them for their effectiveness.

Author's Experience

Several years ago, I was working with a friend to come up with ideas for a grant proposal. We started out by sitting at his kitchen table, exchanging ideas while sipping coffee; then we both got up and began to pace back and forth, walking all around the room while bouncing different ideas off each other. Whenever a new idea was thrown out, one of us would jot it down (whoever was pacing closer to the kitchen table at the moment).

After we ran out of ideas, we shifted gears, slowed down, and sat down at the table again to critique each of the ideas we'd just generated during our "binge-thinking" episode. After some debate, we finally settled on an idea that we judged to be the best of all the ideas we produced, and we used this idea for the grant proposal.

Although I wasn't fully aware of it at the time, the stimulating thought process we were using was called brainstorming because it involved both of its key stages: we first engaged in creative thinking during our fast-paced walking and idea-production stage, and followed that with critical thinking during our slower-paced sitting and idea-evaluation stage.

— *Joe Cuseo*

"Imagination should give wings to our thoughts, but imagination must be checked and documented by the factual results of the experiment."

—Louis Pasteur, French microbiologist, chemist, and inventor of pasteurization (a method for preventing milk and wine from going sour)

Lastly, keep in mind that creative thinking is not restricted to the arts: it can occur in all subject areas, even in fields that seek precision and definite answers. For example, in math, creative thinking may involve using new approaches or strategies for arriving at a correct solution to a problem. In science, creative thinking takes place when a scientist first uses imaginative thinking to create a hypothesis or logical hunch ("What might happen if . . . ?"), then conducts an experiment to test whether that hypothesis proves to be true.

Strategies for Developing Higher-Level Thinking Skills and Using Them to Improve Academic Performance

Thus far, this chapter has been devoted primarily to helping you get a clear idea of what higher-level thinking is and what its major forms are. The remainder of this chapter focuses on helping you develop habits of higher-level thinking and applying (or how to apply) these habits to improve your performance in the first year of college and beyond.

1. **Cross-reference and connect any ideas you acquire in class with related ideas you acquire from your assigned reading.** When you discover information in your reading that relates to something you've learned about in class (or vice versa), make a note of it in the margin of your textbook or your class notebook. By integrating knowledge you've obtained from these two major sources, you're using synthesis—a higher-level thinking skill that you can then demonstrate on course exams and assignments to improve your course grades.

2. **When listening to lectures and completing reading assignments, pay attention not only to the content being covered, but also to the thought process that accompanies the content.** Periodically ask yourself what forms of higher-level thinking your instructors are using during major segments of a class presentation and what your textbook authors are using in different sections of a chapter. The more conscious you are of the types of higher-level thinking skills you're being exposed to, the more likely you are to acquire those thinking skills and demonstrate them on exams and assignments.

3. **Periodically pause to reflect on your own thinking process.** When working on your courses, ask yourself what type of thinking you're doing (e.g., analysis, synthesis, or evaluation) during the work process. When you think about your own thinking, you're engaging in a mental process known as *metacognition*—that is, you're aware of how you're thinking while you're thinking (Flavell, 1985; Hartman, 2001). Metacognition is a mental habit that's associated with higher-level thinking and improved problem-solving skills (Halpern, 2003; Resnick, 1986).

4. **Develop habits of higher-level thinking by asking yourself higher-level thinking questions.** One simple but powerful way to think about your thinking is through self-questioning. Since questions have the power to activate and elevate your thinking, and since thinking often involves talking silently to yourself, if you make an intentional attempt to ask yourself good questions, you can train your mind to think at a higher level. A good question can serve as a launching pad that propels you to higher levels of thinking in your quest to answer it. The higher the level of thinking called for by the questions you regularly ask yourself, the higher the level of thinking you will display in class discussions, on college exams, and in written assignments.

"To think is to talk to oneself."

—Immanuel Kant, German philosopher

"If you do not ask the right questions, you do not get the right answers."

—Edward Hodnett, British poet

Using Self-Questioning Strategies to Promote Your Critical and Creative Thinking

As we mentioned in Chapter 4, effective learners are effective self-monitors—they watch themselves while learning and monitor whether they are really understanding what they're attempting to learn (Weinstein & Underwood, 1985). Similarly, effective thinkers engage in a slightly different form of self-monitoring known as metacognition—they think about how they are thinking (Flavell, 1985).

Happy Hour, 4–6 PM
All Drinks—$2

Followed by Reflection Hour:
"What is Happiness?"
All Thoughts—Priceless

Pub
&
Grub

© Kendall Hunt

Asking yourself a good question can stimulate your higher-level thinking about almost any experience, whether it takes place inside or outside the classroom.

Think About It ——— *Journal Entry* 7.9

Critically evaluate the common practice of bars selling alcoholic drinks at reduced prices that's depicted in the preceding cartoon by answering the following questions:

1. What are the assumptions or implications of calling this practice "happy hour"?

   Thats when people come in and drink

2. What are arguments for and against this practice?

   People drink later at night.

Since questions have the power to activate and elevate your thinking, you can capitalize on their power by intentionally asking yourself good questions.

In Do It Now! 7.2, you'll find numerous questions that have been intentionally designed to promote higher-level thinking. The questions are constructed in a way that will allow you to easily fill in the blank and apply the type of thinking called for by the question to ideas or issues being discussed in any course you may take. Considerable research indicates that students can learn to use questions such as these to improve their higher-level thinking ability in various subject areas (King, 1990, 1995, 2002).

As you read each set of trigger questions, place a checkmark next to one question in the set that could be applied to a concept or issue being covered in a course you're taking this term.

7.2   DO IT NOW!

Self-Questioning Strategies for Triggering Different Forms of Higher-Level Thinking

Application (applied thinking). Putting knowledge into practice to solve problems and resolve issues.

Trigger Questions

- How can this idea be used to _____?
- How could this concept be implemented to _____?
- How can this theory be put into practice to _____?
- What could be done to prevent or reduce _____?

Analysis (analytical thinking). Breaking down information into its essential elements or parts.

Trigger Questions

- What are the main ideas contained in _____?
- What are the important aspects of _____?
- What are the issues raised by _____?
- What are the major purposes of _____?
- What assumptions or biases lie hidden within _____?
- What are the reasons behind _____?

Synthesis. Integrating separate pieces of information to form a more complete product or pattern.

Trigger Questions

- How can this idea be joined or connected with _____ to create a more complete or comprehensive understanding of _____?
- How could these different _____ be grouped together into a more general class or category?
- How could these separate _____ be reorganized or rearranged to produce a more comprehensive understanding of the big picture?

Multidimensional thinking. Thinking that involves viewing yourself and the world around you from different angles or vantage points.

Trigger Questions

- How would _____ affect different dimensions of myself (emotional, physical, etc.)?
- What broader impact would _____ have on the social and physical world around me?
- How might people living in different times (e.g., past and future) view _____?
- How would people from different cultural backgrounds interpret or react to _____?
- Have I taken into consideration all the major factors that could influence _____ or be influenced by _____?

Inferential reasoning. Making an argument or judgment by inferring (stepping to) a conclusion that's supported by empirical (observable) evidence or logical consistency.

Trigger Questions Seeking Empirical Evidence

- What examples support the argument that _____?
- What research evidence is there for _____?
- What statistical data document that this _____ is true?

Trigger Questions Seeking Logical Consistency

- Since _____ is true, why shouldn't _____ also be true?
- If people believe in _____, shouldn't they practice _____?
- To make the statement that _____, wouldn't it have to be assumed that _____?

Balanced thinking. Carefully considering reasons for and against a particular position or viewpoint.

Trigger Questions

- Have I considered both sides of _____?
- What are the strengths (advantages) and weaknesses (disadvantages) of _____?
- What evidence supports and contradicts _____?
- What are arguments for and counterarguments against _____?

Trigger Questions for Adduction (arguing for a particular idea or position by supplying supporting evidence)

- What proof is there for _____?
- What are logical arguments for _____?
- What research evidence supports _____?

Trigger Questions for Refutation (arguing against a particular idea or position by supplying contradictory evidence)

- What proof is there against _____?
- What logical arguments indicate that _____ is false?
- What research evidence contradicts _____?
- What counterarguments would provide an effective rebuttal to _____?

Critical thinking. Making well-informed evaluations or judgments.

Trigger Questions for Evaluating Validity (truthfulness)

- Is _____ true or accurate?
- Is there sufficient evidence to support the conclusion that _____?
- Is the reasoning behind _____ strong or weak?

Trigger Questions for Evaluating Morality (ethics)

- Is _____ fair?
- Is _____ just?
- Is this action consistent with the professed or stated values of _____?

Trigger Questions for Evaluating Beauty (aesthetics)

- What is the artistic merit of _____?
- Does _____ have any aesthetic value?
- Does _____ contribute to the beauty of _____?

Trigger Questions for Evaluating Practicality (usefulness)

- Will _____ work?
- How can _____ be put to good use?
- What practical benefit would result from _____?

Trigger Questions for Evaluating Priority (order of importance or effectiveness)

- Which one of these _____ is the most important?
- Is this _____ the best option or choice available?
- How should these _____ be ranked from first to last (best to worst) in terms of their effectiveness?

Creative thinking. Generating ideas that are unique, original, or distinctively different.

Trigger Questions

- What could be invented to _____?
- Imagine what would happen if _____?
- What might be a different way to _____?
- How would this change if _____?
- What would be an ingenious way to _____?

Note: Save these higher-level thinking questions so that you can use them when completing different academic tasks required by your courses (e.g., preparing for exams, writing papers or reports, and participating in class discussions or study-group sessions). Try to get into the habit of periodically stepping back to reflect on your thinking process. Ask yourself what type of thinking you are doing (such as analysis, synthesis, or evaluation) and record your personal reflections in writing. You could even keep a "thinking log" or "thinking journal" to increase self-awareness of the thinking strategies you develop across time, or how your thinking strategies may vary across different courses and academic fields. This strategy will not only help you acquire higher-level thinking skills, but will also help you describe the thinking skills you have acquired during job interviews and in letters of application for career positions.

5. **To stimulate creative thinking, use the following strategies:**

- **Be flexible.** Think about ideas and objects in unusual or unconventional ways. The power of flexible and unconventional thinking is well illustrated in the movie *Apollo 13*, which is based on the real story of an astronaut saving his life by creatively using duct tape as an air filter. The inventor of the printing press (Johannes Gutenberg) made his groundbreaking discovery while watching a machine being used to crush grapes at a wine harvest. He thought that the same type of machine could be used to press letters onto paper (Dorfman, Shames, & Kihlstrom, 1996).

- **Be experimental.** Play with ideas, trying them out to see whether they'll work and work better than the status quo. Studies show that creative people tend to be mental risk-takers who experiment with ideas and techniques (Sternberg, 2001). Consciously resist the temptation to settle for the security of familiarity. Doing things the way they've always been done doesn't mean you're doing them the best way possible. It may mean that it's just the most habitual (and mindless) way to do them. When people cling rigidly or stubbornly to what's conventional or traditional, what they're doing is clinging to the comfort or security of what's most familiar and predictable, which blocks originality, ingenuity, and openness to change.

- **Get mobile.** Get up and move around. Studies show that when we stand up, the brain gets approximately 10 percent more oxygen than it does when we're sitting down (Sousa, 2006). Since oxygen provides fuel for the brain, our ability to think creatively is stimulated when we think on our feet and move around, rather than sitting on our butts for extended periods of time.

- **Get it down.** Carry a pen and a small notepad or packet of sticky notes (or a portable electronic recording device) with you at all times to record creative ideas, because these ideas often come to mind at the most unexpected times. The process of creative ideas suddenly popping into your mind is sometimes referred to as *incubation*—just like incubated eggs can hatch at any time, ideas can suddenly hatch and pop into consciousness after you've sat on them for a while. Unfortunately, however, just as an idea can suddenly come into mind, it can just as suddenly slip out of mind when you start thinking about something else. You can prevent this from happening by having the right equipment on hand to record your creative ideas as soon as you have them.

- **Get diverse.** Seek ideas from diverse social and informational sources. Bouncing your ideas off of different people and getting their ideas about your idea is a good way to generate energy, synergy, and serendipity (accidental discoveries). Studies show that creative people venture well beyond the boundaries of their particular areas of training or specialization (Baer, 1993; Kaufman & Baer, 2002). They have wide-ranging interests and knowledge, which they draw upon and combine to generate new ideas (Riquelme, 2002). Be on the lookout to combine the knowledge and skills you acquire from different subject areas and different people to create bridges to new ideas.

- **Take a break.** When working on a problem that you can't seem to solve, stop working on it for a while and come back to it later. Creative solutions often come to mind after you stop thinking about the problem. When you're trying so hard and working so intensely on a problem or challenging task, your attention may become mentally set or rigidly fixed on one aspect of it (German & Barrett, 2005; Maier, 1970). Taking your mind off of it and returning to it at a later point allows the problem to incubate in your mind at a lower level of consciousness and stress. This can sometimes give birth to a sudden solution. Furthermore, when you come back to the task later, your focus of attention is likely to shift to a different feature or aspect of the problem. This new focus may enable you to view the problem from a different angle or vantage point, which can lead to a breakthrough idea that was blocked by your previous perspective (Anderson, 2000).

"I make progress by having people around who are smarter than I am—and listening to them. And I assume that everyone is smarter about something than I am."

—Henry Kaiser, successful industrialist, known as the father of American shipbuilding

"*Eureka!*" (Literally translated, "I have found it!")

—Attributed to Archimedes, ancient Greek mathematician and inventor, when he suddenly discovered (while sitting in a bathtub) how to measure the purity of gold

- **Reorganize the problem.** When you're stuck on a problem, try rearranging its parts or pieces. Rearrangement can transform the problem into a different pattern that provides you with a new perspective. The new perspective may position you to suddenly see a solution that was previously overlooked, much like changing the order of letters in a word jumble can suddenly enable you to see the hidden, scrambled word. By changing the wording of any problem you're working on, or by recording ideas on index cards (or sticky notes) and laying them out in different orders and arrangements, you may suddenly see a solution.

- If you're having trouble solving problems that involve a sequence of steps (e.g., math problems), try reversing the sequence and start by working from the end or middle. The new sequence changes your approach to the problem by forcing you to come at it from a different direction, which can sometimes provide you with an alternative path to its solution.

- **Be persistent.** Studies show that creativity takes time, dedication, and hard work (Ericsson, 2006; Ericsson & Charness, 1994). Creative thoughts often do not emerge in one sudden stroke of genius, but evolve gradually after repeated reflection and persistent effort.

> "Creativity consists largely of re-arranging what we know in order to find out what we do not know."
>
> —George Keller, prolific American architect and originator of the Union Station design for elevated train stations

> "Genius is 1% inspiration and 99% perspiration."
>
> —Thomas Edison, scientist and creator of more than 1,000 inventions, including the light bulb, phonograph, and motion picture camera

Think About It ———————————————— Journal Entry 7.10

Look back at the forms of thinking described in Do It Now! 7.2. Identify one question listed under each set of trigger questions and fill in the blank with an idea or issue being covered in a course you're taking this term.

What could be invented to make people happy.

Think About It ————————————————————— *Journal Entry* **7.11**

The popularity of sticky notes is no doubt due to their versatility—you can post them on almost anything, remove them from where they were stuck (without a mess), and re-stick them somewhere else.

Think creatively for a minute. In what ways could college students use sticky notes to help complete the academic tasks they face in college? Think of as many ways as possible.

To mark as important
Bookmark it.
Study sections
Questions
Vocab
Reminders

Summary and Conclusion

Since higher-level thinking is the number one educational goal of college professors, developing this skill is crucial for achieving academic excellence. In addition to improving academic performance in college, developing higher-level thinking skills has three other critical benefits.

1. **Higher-level thinking is essential in today's "information age" in which new information is being generated at faster rates than at any other time in human history.** The majority of new workers in the information age will no longer work with their hands but will instead work with their heads (Miller, 2003), and, as discussed in Chapter 10, employers will value college graduates who have inquiring minds and possess higher-level thinking skills (Harvey, Moon, Geall, & Bower, 1997; Peter D. Hart Research Associates, 2006).

2. **Higher-level thinking skills are vital for citizens in a democracy.** Authoritarian political systems, such as dictatorships and fascist regimes, suppress critical thought and demand submissive obedience to authority. In contrast, citizens living in a democracy are expected to control their political destiny by choosing (electing) their political leaders; thus, judging and choosing wisely are crucial civic responsibilities in a democratic nation. Citizens living and voting in a democracy must use higher-level reasoning skills, such as balanced and critical thinking, to make wise political choices.

3. **Higher-level thinking is an important safeguard against prejudice, discrimination, and hostility.** Racial, ethnic, and national prejudices often stem from narrow, self-centered, or group-centered thinking (Paul & Elder, 2002). Prejudice often results from oversimplified, dualistic thinking that can lead individuals to categorize other people into either "in" groups (us) or "out" groups (them). This type of dualistic thinking can lead, in turn, to ethnocentrism—the tendency to view one's own racial or ethnic group as the superior "in" group and see other

groups as inferior "out" groups. Development of higher-level thinking skills, such as taking multiple perspectives and using balanced thinking, counteracts the type of dualistic, ethnocentric thinking that leads to prejudice, discrimination, and hate crimes.

Learning More through the World Wide Web
Internet-Based Resources for Further Information on Higher-Level Thinking

For additional information related to the ideas discussed in this chapter, we recommend the following Web sites:

Critical Thinking:

www.criticalthinking.org

Creative Thinking:

www.amcreativityassoc.org

Higher-Level Thinking Skills:

www.wcu.edu/ceap/houghton/Learner/think/thinkhigherorder.html

7.1 Self-Assessment of Higher-Level Thinking Characteristics

Listed here are four general characteristics of higher-level thinkers accompanied by a set of traits related to each characteristic. When you read the traits listed beneath each of the general characteristics, place a checkmark next to any trait that you think is true of you.

Characteristics of a Higher-Level Thinker

1. **Tolerant and Accepting**
   - Keep emotions under control when someone criticizes their viewpoint
   - Do not tune out ideas that conflict with their own
   - Feel comfortable with disagreement
   - Are receptive to hearing different points of view ✓

2. **Inquisitive and Open-Minded**
   - Are eager to continue learning new things from different people and different experiences ✓
   - Have an inquiring mind that's genuinely curious, inquisitive, and ready to explore new ideas ✓
   - Find differences of opinion and opposing viewpoints interesting and stimulating ✓
   - Attempt to understand why people hold different viewpoints and try to find common ground between them

3. **Reflective and Tentative**
   - Suspend judgment until all the evidence is in, rather than making snap judgments before knowing the whole story
   - Acknowledge the complexity, ambiguity, and uncertainty associated with certain issues, and are willing to perhaps say, "I need to give this more thought," or "I need more evidence before I can draw a conclusion" ✓
   - Take time to think things through before drawing conclusions, making choices, and reaching decisions
   - Periodically reexamine personal viewpoints to see whether they should be maintained or changed as a result of new experiences and evidence ✓

4. **Honest and Courageous**
   - Give fair consideration to ideas that others may instantly disapprove of or find distasteful ✓
   - Are willing to express personal viewpoints that may not conform to those of the majority ✓
   - Are willing to change old opinions or beliefs when they are contradicted by new evidence ✓
   - Are willing to acknowledge the limitations or weaknesses of their attitudes and beliefs

Look back at the list and count the number of checkmarks you placed in each of the four general areas:

1. Tolerant and Accepting = _1_
2. Inquisitive and Open-Minded = _3_
3. Reflective and Tentative = _2_
4. Honest and Courageous = _3_

For which characteristic did you have: (a) the *most* checkmarks, (b) the *least* checkmarks? ● Inquisitive/open minded
● honest/conscious
What do you think accounts for this difference? Tolerant and Acceptim

Trick or Treat: Confusing or Challenging Test?

Students in Professor Plato's philosophy course just got their first exam back and they're going over the test together in class. Some students are angry because they feel that Professor Plato deliberately included "trick questions" to confuse them. Professor Plato responds by saying that his test questions were not designed to trick the class but to "challenge them to think."

Discussion Questions

1. Why do you think that some students thought that Professor Plato was trying to trick or confuse them?

2. What do you think the professor meant when he told his students that his test questions were designed to "challenge them to think"?

3. On future tests, what might the students do to reduce the likelihood that they will feel tricked again?

4. On future tests, what might Professor Plato do to reduce the likelihood that students will complain about being asked "trick questions"?

Chapter 7 Reflection

How can you use critical thinking to be a more successful student? Explain. List three action steps you can do to make this happen.

How can you use critical thinking to improve your personal life? Explain.

How can you use creative thinking to be a more successful student? Explain. List three action steps you can do to make this happen.

How can you use creative thinking to improve your personal life? Explain.

Welcome to Macomb Community College.

My name is Cassandra Spieles. I am the Collections and Resources Librarian at Macomb Community College and I coordinate and facilitate many events every year that center on topics of diversity, book discussions, films, poetry readings, and ideas from incredible speakers. I am a published novelist, BMI songwriter, and awardee of six degrees and certificates. I love to read, especially true stories. This is my true story.

My mother died very young. My father, a three-time convicted felon, was imprisoned or on the run nearly all of my childhood. Three out of the four grandparents I had were also deceased quite young and the only other relatives I had wanted a different life, so they went their own way when I was a toddler, and they never came back. I had two very essential things, however: my grandfather, and the unbreakable will to end up somewhere different than what I was born into.

Between living with various people (relatives, foster care, at times—alone, even as a minor), I didn't know which way was up. I remember one day in third grade asking someone, "what city is this?", because I had no clue where I even was, at that point. I was moved all around the country, and we had maybe a few meals per week outside of eating at school (I loved school lunches!). No medical care, no dentists, no new clothes, no video games, no toys, and, unfortunately from moving so often, no friends. I did have two siblings and they were my closest friends, and while I wish I could tell you they turned out the same way I have, they didn't. I attribute this difference to one simple question.

When I was nearly 8, I was able to stay with my grandfather for an entire month (a huge treat!). I asked him the most important question of my life.

"Papa, what do I need to do to not end up like *this*?" He knew exactly what I meant by *this*: poor, alone, abused when in the company of the wrong people, hungry, sad. I witnessed unspeakable things, terrible crimes. But I'll never forget what he said: "Baby doll, go to college." You see, no matter what was happening in my chaotic life, my grandfather was always in touch with me and even halfway across the country he would talk to me about one thing: school. And, boy, did I ever love school! It was consistent, stimulating, the teachers paid attention to me, and someone always gave me a meal, cold medicine, or a treat.

I wholeheartedly believed that doing well in school would change everything. By my senior year in high school I had a 4.1 GPA. Schoolmates would invite me to functions and I would tell them, "I have no time. I need to work, make myself dinner, do homework. I'm getting out of here." *I am getting out of here.* That thought consumed me.

To make a long story short, I did graduate salutatorian in my class, and I was accepted into every university to which I applied: Harvard, Hofstra, University of Michigan, University of Colorado, Michigan State University, and so on. But there was a problem. I was ineligible for federal aid due to the pending felony against my father at that time. So I could only attend with scholarship money, and while I did receive some, I didn't have so much as a dollar to come up with the rest. I was devastated. I had nowhere to go.

I visited my high school English teacher and she told me, "Go to Macomb, it's great! You'll like it!" I worked that summer and spent most of the money paying for basic needs. I lived with a woman from my church and she told me to save for school. I wasn't able to come up with even half of the tuition and book fees. I went back to my high school, East Detroit, and two English teachers handed the money to me on the spot.

The day before classes began at Macomb, I went to walk around South Campus. I met several faculty who were there prepping. I told a few of them small details of my story and they all said, "I will help you," or "If you need anything, let me know." Professor Art Ritas, now retired, asked me what I was interested in. I told him I was the editor of my high school paper, I loved to write interviews, stories, songs, plays. From that point forward he found outlets for me and endlessly encouraged me. Many instructors did. And when I couldn't afford the next semester . . . or the semester after that, they found a way. Professor Ritas even did me another favor! One day he told me to stay after my English class and he then walked me over to the library. He said, "you're working here now, not at that restaurant until midnight anymore." That was nearly 18 years ago. Seven positions later, I'm still working in the library!

After Macomb I transferred to Wayne State and studied English and Geography as an undergraduate, and then American Literature as a graduate student. I worked three part-time jobs and went to school full time; always with straight A's, because I valued every moment of school. It was my escape.

I had another escape too . . . reading. I loved to read. The books would transform me; especially the authors, who would take their own stories and tribulations and vaguely disguise these experiences in fiction books. Right as I was beginning another graduate program in Academic Library Science at Texas Women's University, Professor Russ Pudaloff at Wayne State introduced me to the works of Thomas Wolfe. If you've never heard of Thomas Wolfe, it's okay, not many people have! Who enjoys 700-page novels about family issues in the South? Well, I do. I read *Look Homeward, Angel*, in which he shares the "truth" about his own upbringing. His honesty stirred my emotions. But there was no happy ending. His other books told about the aftermath of being that truthful. The title of his novel, *You Can't Go Home Again*, says it all.

I knew I had a choice. Keep pursuing my studies, working hard, and writing my own truth . . . knowing I may never be accepted back to the family I was exposing in my words. Or keep it all inside, a secret. I chose to write.

After earning my Master's I received a full-time faculty position at Macomb in the library. It was as though my life came full circle. I was determined from that point forward to reach out to students like you, reading this letter. I wanted to tell you that you can do anything with determination, a work ethic, and help like I had from teachers throughout my life. I saved my money and immediately pursued a doctorate degree. I decided to study systematic theology, for, as I told my grandfather over the phone, "I already found my profession: I'm a writer and a librarian. If I'm going to earn a doctorate, I'm choosing the most challenging subject . . . religion." In 2008, I earned my doctorate. Then, I saved my money again.

That 17-year-old girl, so eager to prove she could come from nothing but misery, and yet, reach for Ivy League studies was calling out to me. So I contacted a Harvard Professor in American Protest Literature, John Stauffer, and said, "I'll do anything. I want a chance to study something at Harvard." I did my coursework online. Then, I spent nearly two days driving to the Harvard Coop to present on my topic. It was the ultimate self-fulfillment. But I wasn't done there. I published a novel, traveled to different states to host discussions on it, published a poetry book, and traveled again.

Now, I am working with an agent in New York on a play I wrote, I've sold two songs to Honda and NBC, and I'm studying Information Architecture at the University of Michigan.

I'm writing this letter not to impress you, but to inspire you. And, more than anything else, I want to convince you of two things. One, you can do it! Two, education is the answer. I am living proof.

I am Cassandra Spieles and I am Macomb.

Strategic Learning and Studying
Learning Deeply and Remembering Longer

8

LEARNING GOAL

To develop a set of effective strategies for studying smarter, learning deeply, and retaining what you learn longer.

What do you think is the key difference between learning and memorizing?

Learning you just listen and memorizing you have to do more work like studying, repeating, etc.

Stages in the Learning and Memory Process

Learning deeply, and remembering what you've learned, is a process that involves three key stages:

1. **Sensory input (perception).** Taking information into your brain; *— Listening, reading, hands on things, smelling*
2. **Memory formation (storage).** Saving that information in your brain; and
3. **Memory recall (retrieval).** Bringing information back to mind when you need it.

These three stages in the learning-memory process are summarized visually in Figure 8.1.

You can consider these stages of the learning and memory process to be similar to the way information is processed by a computer: (1) information is typed onto the screen (input), (2) the information is saved in a file (storage), and (3) the saved information is recalled and used when it's needed (retrieval). This three-stage process can be used to create a systematic set of strategies for effectively using the two major routes through which you acquire information and knowledge in college: taking notes as you listen to lectures, and reading textbooks.

FIGURE 8.1

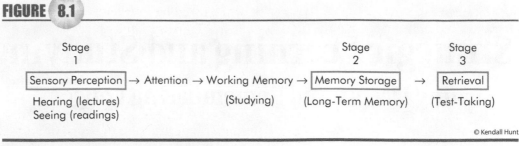

Key Stages in the Learning and Memory Process

Effective Lecture-Listening and Note-Taking Strategies

The importance of effective listening skills in the college classroom is highlighted by a study of more than 400 first-year students who were given a listening test at the start of their first term in college. At the end of their first year in college, 49 percent of those students who scored low on the listening test were on academic probation, compared to only 4.4 percent of students who scored high on the listening test. On the other hand, 68.5 percent of students who scored high on the listening test were eligible for the honors program at the end of their first year—compared to only 4.17 percent of those students who had low listening test scores (Conaway, 1982).

| Think About It | Journal Entry 8.2 |

Do you think writing notes in class helps or hinders your ability to pay attention and learn from your instructors' lectures?

Why?

In some cases it can help you but in other cases it can distract you from learning

Studies show that information delivered during lectures is the number one source of test questions (and answers) on college exams (Brown, 1988; Kuhn, 1988). **When lecture information appears on a test that hasn't been recorded in the student's notes, it has only a 5 percent chance of being recalled** (Kiewra et al., 2000). Students who write notes during lectures achieve higher course grades than students who just listen to lectures (Kiewra, 1985, 2005), and students with a more complete set of notes are more likely to demonstrate higher levels of overall academic achievement (Johnstone & Su, 1994; Kiewra & DuBois, 1998; Kiewra & Fletcher, 1984).

Contrary to popular belief that writing while listening interferes with the ability to listen, students report that taking notes actually increases their attention and concentration in class (Hartley, 1998; Hartley & Marshall, 1974). Studies also show that when students write down information that's presented to them, rather than just sitting and listening to it, they're more likely to remember the most important aspects of that information when tested later (Bligh, 2000; Kiewra et al., 1991). One study discovered that students with grade point averages (GPAs) of 2.53 or higher record more information in their notes and retain a larger percentage of the most important information than do students with GPAs of less than 2.53 (Einstein, Morris, & Smith, 1985). These findings are not surprising when you consider that *hearing* information, *writing* it, and then *seeing* it after you've written it produces three different memory traces (tracks) in the brain, which combine to multiply your chances of remembering it. Furthermore, students with a good set of notes have a written record of that information that can be reread and studied later.

These research findings suggest that you should view each lecture as if it were a test-review session during which your instructor is giving out test answers and you're given the opportunity to write all those answers in your notes. Come to class with the attitude that your instructors are dispensing answers to test questions as they speak, and your job is to pick out and pick up these answers.

Remember

If important points your professor makes in class make it into your notes, they can become points learned; these learned points, in turn, will turn into earned points on your exams (and higher grades in the course).

The next sections give strategies for getting the most out of lectures at three stages in the learning process: *before*, *during*, and *after* lectures.

Pre-Lecture Strategies: What to Do before Lectures

1. **Check your syllabus to see where you are in the course and determine how the upcoming class fits into the total course picture.** Checking your syllabus before individual class sessions strengthens learning because you will see how each part (individual class session) relates to the whole (the entire course). This strategy also capitalizes on the brain's natural tendency to seek larger patterns and see the "big picture." Rather than seeing things in separate parts, the brain is naturally inclined to connect parts into a meaningful whole (Caine & Caine, 1991). In other words, the brain looks for meaningful patterns and connections rather than isolated bits and pieces of information (Jensen, 2000). In Figure 8.2, notice how your brain naturally ties together and fills in the missing information to perceive a meaningful whole pattern.

2. **Get to class early so that you can look over your notes from the previous class session and from any reading assignment that relates to the day's lecture topic.** Research indicates that when students preview information related to an upcoming lecture topic, it improves their ability to take more accurate and complete lecture notes (Kiewra, 2005; Ladas, 1980). Thus, a good strategy to help you learn from lectures is to review your notes from the previous class session and read textbook information related to an upcoming lecture topic *before* hearing the lecture. This strategy will help you better understand and take more detailed notes on the lecture. Reviewing previously learned information also activates your previous knowledge, enabling you to build a mental bridge from one class

FIGURE 8.2

You perceive a white triangle in the middle of this figure. However, if you use three fingers to cover up the three corners of the white triangle that fall outside the other (background) triangle, the white triangle suddenly disappears. What your brain does is take these corners as starting points and fill in the rest of the information on its own to create a complete or whole pattern that has meaning to you. (Also, notice how you perceive the background triangle as a complete triangle, even though parts of its left and right sides are missing.)

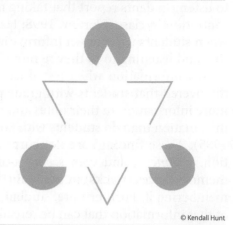

© Kendall Hunt

Triangle Illusion

session to the next, connecting new information to what you already know—a key to deep learning (Bruner, 1990; Piaget, 1978; Vygotsky, 1978). Acquiring knowledge isn't a matter of simply pouring information into the brain as if it were an empty jar. It's a matter of attaching or connecting new ideas to ideas that are already stored in the brain. When you learn deeply, a physical connection is actually made between nerve cells in your brain (Alkon, 1992), as illustrated in Figure 8.3.

Listening and Note-Taking Strategies: What to Do during Lectures

1. **Take your own notes in class.** Don't rely on someone else to take notes for you. Taking your own notes in your own words focuses your attention and ensures that you're taking notes that make sense to you. Research shows that students who record and review their own notes earn higher scores on memory tests for that information than do students who review the notes of others (Fisher, Harris, & Harris, 1973; Kiewra, 2005). These findings point to the importance of taking

FIGURE 8.3

© Jurgen Ziewe, 2013. Under license from Shutterstock, Inc.

When something is learned, it's stored in the brain as a link in an interconnected network of brain cells. Thus, deep learning involves making connections between what you're trying to learn and what you already know.

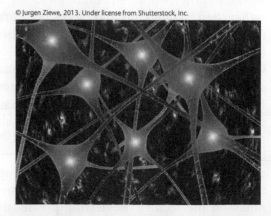

Network of Brain Cells

and studying your own notes because they will be most meaningful to you. You can collaborate with classmates to compare notes for completeness and accuracy or to pick up points you may have missed. However, don't routinely rely on someone else to take notes for you.

Students who take notes during lectures have been found to achieve higher class grades than those who just listen.

2. **Focus full attention on the most important information.** Attention is the critical first step to successful learning and memory. Since the human attention span is limited, it's impossible to attend to and make note of (or take notes on) everything. Thus, you need to use your attention *selectively* to focus on, detect, and select information that matters most. Here are some strategies for attending to and recording the most important information delivered by professors in the college classroom:

   - Pay attention to information your instructors put *in print*—on the board, on a slide, or in a handout. If your instructor takes the time and energy to write it out or type it out, that's usually a good clue that the information is important and you're likely to see it again—on an exam.

   - Pay attention to information presented during the first and last few minutes of class. Instructors are more likely to provide valuable reminders, reviews, and previews at these two points in time.

   - Use your instructor's *verbal and nonverbal cues* to detect important information. Don't just tune in when the instructor is writing something down and tune out at other times. It's been found that students record almost 90 percent of information written on the board, but less than 50 percent of important ideas that professors state but don't write on the board (Johnstone & Su, 1994; Locke, 1977; Titsworth & Kiewra, 2004). Don't fall into the reflexive routine of just writing something in your notes when you see your instructor writing on the board. Listen actively to receive and record important ideas in your notes that you *hear* your instructor saying. In Do It Now! 8.1, you'll find strategies for detecting clues to important information that professors deliver during lectures.

3. **Take organized notes.** Keep taking notes in the same paragraph if the instructor is continuing on the same point or idea. When the instructor shifts to a new idea, skip a few lines and shift to a new paragraph. Be alert to phrases that your instructor may use to signal a shift to a new or different idea (e.g., "Let's turn to . . ." or "In addition to . . ."). Use these phrases as cues for taking notes in paragraph form. By recording different ideas in different paragraphs, you improve the organizational quality of your notes, which will improve your comprehension and retention of them. Also, be sure to leave extra space between paragraphs (ideas) to give yourself room to add information later that you may have initially missed, or to translate the professor's words into your own words that are more meaningful to you. If your instructor provides notes (in handout form, PowerPoints, etc.), it is helpful to take your notes directly on the material provided.

8.1 ・ DO IT NOW

Detecting When Instructors Are Delivering Important Information during Class Lectures

1. **Verbal cues**
   - Phrases signal important information (e.g., "The point here is . . ." or "What's most significant about this is . . .").
   - Information is repeated or rephrased in a different way (e.g., "In other words . . .").
   - Stated information is followed with a question to check understanding (e.g., "Is that clear?" "Do you follow that?" "Does that make sense?" or "Are you with me?").

2. **Vocal (tone of voice) cues**
   - Information is delivered in a louder tone or at a higher pitch than usual, which may indicate excitement or emphasis.

   - Information is delivered at a slower rate or with more pauses than usual, which may be your instructor's way of giving you more time to write down these important ideas.

3. **Nonverbal cues**
   - Information is delivered by the instructor with more than the usual:
     a. facial expressiveness (e.g., raised or furrowed eyebrows);
     b. body movement (e.g., more gesturing and animation); or
     c. eye contact (e.g., looking more directly and intently at the faces of students to see whether they are following or understanding what's being said).
   - The instructor moves closer to the students (e.g., moving away from the podium or blackboard).
   - The instructor's body is oriented directly toward the class (i.e., both shoulders directly or squarely face the class).

Another popular strategy for taking organized notes, the Cornell Note-Taking System, is summarized in Do It Now! 8.2.

4. **Keep taking notes even if you don't immediately understand what your instructor is saying.** If you are uncertain or confused about what your instructor is saying, don't stop writing—your notes will at least leave you with a record of the information to review later when you have more time to think about and grasp their meaning. If you still don't understand it after taking time to review it, check it out in your textbook, with your instructor, or with a classmate.

Remember

Your primary goal during lectures is to get important information into your brain long enough to note it mentally and then physically in your notes. Making sense of that information often has to come later, when you have time to reflect on the notes you took in class.

Post-Lecture Strategies: What to Do after Lectures

1. **As soon as class ends, quickly check your notes for missing information or incomplete thoughts.** Since the information is likely to be fresh in your mind immediately after class, a quick check of your notes at this time will allow you to take advantage of your short-term memory. By reviewing and reflecting on it, you can help move the information into long-term memory before forgetting takes place. This quick review can be done alone or, better yet, with a motivated classmate. If you both have gaps in your notes, check them out with your instructor before he or she leaves the classroom. Even though it may be weeks be-

fore you will be tested on the material, the quicker you address missed points and clear up sources of confusion, the better, because you'll be able to use your knowledge to help you understand and learn upcoming material. Catching confusion early in the game also enables you to avoid the mad last-minute rush of students seeking help from the instructor just before test time. You want to reserve the critical time just before exams for studying a set of notes that you know are complete and accurate, rather than rushing around trying to find missing information and getting cheap fast-food help on concepts that were presented weeks ago.

Think About It ———————————————— *Journal Entry* **8.2**

1. What do you tend to do immediately after a class session ends?

   go home or eat.

2. Why? What could you do immediately after class to be a more successful student?

   Because I am tired and can go home and do my homework right away.

2. **Before the next class session meets, reflect on and review your notes to make sense of them.** Your professors will often lecture on information that you may have little prior knowledge about, so it is unrealistic to expect that you will understand everything that's being said the first time you hear it. Instead, you'll need to set aside time for making notes or taking notes on your own notes (i.e., rewriting them in your own words so that they make sense to you).

   During this reflect-and-rewrite process, we recommend that you take notes on your notes by:

   - Translating technical information into your own words to make it more meaningful to you; and
   - Reorganizing your notes to get ideas related to the same point in the same place.

8.2

The Cornell Note-Taking System

1. On the page on which you're taking notes, draw a horizontal line about 2 inches from the bottom edge of the paper.
2. If there's no vertical line on the left side of the page, draw one line about 2½ inches from the left edge of the paper (as shown in the scaled-down illustration here).
3. When your instructor is lecturing, use the large space to the right of the vertical line (area A) to record your notes.
4. After a lecture, use the space at the bottom of the page (area B) to summarize the main points you recorded on that page.
5. Use the column of space on the left side of the page (area C) to write questions that are answered in the notes on the right.
6. Quiz yourself by looking at the questions listed in the left margin while covering the answers to them that are found in your class notes on the right.

Note: You can use this note-taking and note-review method on your own, or you could team up with two or more students and do it collaboratively.

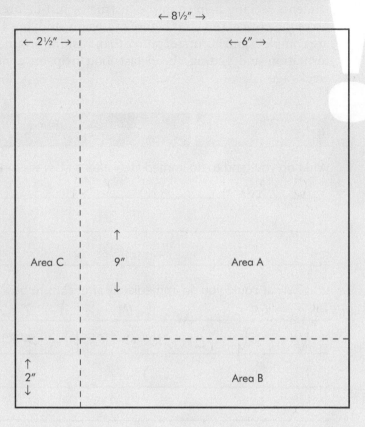

Studies show that when students organize lecture information into meaningful categories, they demonstrate greater recall for that information on a delayed memory test than do students who simply review their notes without organizing them into categories (Howe, 1970; Kiewra, 2005).

Remember

Look at note taking as a two-stage process: Stage 1 involves actively taking notes in class, and Stage 2 takes place later, when you have time to reflect on your notes and process them more deeply.

Author's Experience   My first year in college was mainly spent trying to manipulate my schedule to find some free time. I took all of my classes in a row without a break to save some time at the end of the day for relaxation and hanging out with friends before I went to work. Seldom did I look over my notes and read the material that I was assigned on the day I took the lecture notes and received the assignment. Thus, on the day before the test I was in a panic trying to cram the lecture notes into my head for the upcoming test. Needless to say, I did not perform well on many of these tests. Finally, I had a professor who told me that if I spent time each day after a couple of my classes catching up on reading and rewriting my notes, I would retain the material longer, increase my grades, and decrease my stress at test time. I employed this system, and it worked wonderfully.

Aaron Thompson

Reading Strategically to Comprehend and Retain Textbook Information

Second only to lecture notes as a source of test questions on college exams is information found in assigned readings (Brown, 1988). You're likely to find exam questions on information contained in your assigned reading that your professors didn't talk about specifically in class (or even mention in class). College professors often expect you to relate or connect what they lecture about in class with material that you've been assigned to read. Furthermore, they often deliver class lectures with the assumption that you have done the assigned reading, so if you haven't done it, you're likely to have more difficulty following what your instructor is talking about in class.

Remember

Do the assigned reading and do it according to the schedule your instructor has established. It will help you better understand class lectures, improve the quality of your participation in class, and raise your overall course grade.

Think About It ———————————— *Journal Entry* 8.3

Rate yourself in terms of how frequently you use these note-taking strategies according to the following scale:

4 = always, 3 = sometimes, 2 = rarely, 1 = never

1. I take notes aggressively in class.   4 3 2 1
2. I sit near the front of the room during class.   4 3 2 1
3. I sit upright and lean forward while in class.   4 3 2 1
4. I take notes on what my instructors say, not just what
   they write on the board.   4 3 2 1
5. I pay special attention to information presented at the
   start and end of class.   4 3 2 1
6. I take notes in paragraph form.   4 3 2 1
7. I review my notes immediately after class to check
   that they are complete and accurate.   4 3 2 1

What areas do you need to improve in? How can you improve in theses areas?

6 & 7 I will learn more if I look at them and read them more after class

When completing your reading assignments, use effective reading strategies that are based on sound principles of human learning and memory, such as those listed here.

What follows is a series of research-based strategies for effective reading at three key stages in the learning process: before, during, and after reading.

Pre-Reading Strategies: What to Do before Reading

1. **Before jumping into your assigned reading, look at how it fits into the overall organizational structure of the book and course.** You can do this efficiently by taking a quick look at the book's table of contents to see where the chapter you're about to read is placed in the overall sequence of chapters, especially its relation to chapters that immediately precede and follow it. Using this strategy will give you a sense of how the particular part you're focusing on connects with the bigger picture. Research shows that if learners gain access to advanced knowledge of how information they're about to learn is organized—if they see how its parts relate to the whole—*before* they attempt to start learning the specific parts, they're better able to comprehend and retain the material (Ausubel, Novak, & Hanesian, 1978; Mayer, 2003). Thus, the first step toward improving reading comprehension and retention of a book chapter is to see how it relates to the whole book before you begin to examine the chapter part by part.

Think About It ———————————————————— *Journal Entry* **8.4**

When you open a textbook to read a chapter, how do you start the reading process? That is, what's the first thing you do? Why do you do this?

I just open and start reading,
but look at the pages first.

---

2. **Preview the chapter you're about to read by reading its boldface headings and any chapter outline, objectives, summary, or end-of-chapter questions that may be included.** Before jumping right into the content, get in the habit of previewing what's in a chapter to gain an overall sense of its organization and what it's about. If you dive into the specific details first, you lose sight of how the smaller details relate to the larger picture. The brain's natural tendency is to perceive and comprehend whole patterns rather than isolated bits of information. Start by seeing how the parts of the chapter are integrated into the whole. This will enable you to better connect the separate pieces of information you encounter while you read, similar to seeing the whole picture of a completed jigsaw puzzle before you start assembling its pieces.

3. **Take a moment to think about how what you already know relates to the material in the chapter you're about to read.** By thinking about knowledge you possess about the topic you're about to read, you activate the areas of your brain where that knowledge is stored, thereby preparing it to make meaningful connections with the material you're about to read.

Strategies to Use while Reading

1. **Read selectively to locate the most important information.** Rather than jumping into reading and randomly highlighting, effective reading begins with a plan or goal for identifying what should be noted and remembered. Here are three strategies to use while reading to help you determine what information should be noted and retained.

   - **Use boldface or dark-print headings and subheadings as cues for identifying important information.** These headings organize the chapter's major points; thus, you can use them as "traffic" signs to direct you to the most important information in the chapter. Better yet, turn the headings into questions and then read to find answers to these questions. This question-and-answer strategy will ensure that you read actively and with a purpose. (You can set up this strategy when you preview the chapter by placing a question mark after each heading contained in the chapter.) Creating and answering questions while you read also keeps you motivated; the questions help stimulate your curiosity and finding answers to them serves to reward or reinforce your reading (Walter, Knudsbig, & Smith, 2003). Lastly, answering questions about what you're reading is an effective way to prepare for tests because you're practicing exactly what you'll be expected to do on exams—answering questions. You can quickly write the heading questions on separate index cards and use them as flash cards to review for exams. Use the question on the flash card as a way to flash back and trigger your recall of information from the text that answers the question.

   - **Pay special attention to words that are *italicized, <u>underlined</u>, or in boldface print.*** These are usually signs for building-block terms that must be understood and built on before you can proceed to understand higher-level concepts covered later in the reading. Don't simply highlight these words because their special appearance suggests they are important. Read these terms carefully and be sure you understand their meaning before you continue reading.

   - **Pay special attention to the first and last sentences in each paragraph.** These sentences contain an important introduction and conclusion to the ideas covered in the paragraph. It's a good idea to reread the first and last sentences of each paragraph before you move on to the next paragraph, particularly when reading sequential or cumulative material (e.g., science or math) that requires full comprehension of what was previously covered to understand what will be covered next.

Reread your chapter notes and highlights after you've listened to your instructor lecture on the material contained in the chapter. You can use your lecture notes as a guide to help you focus on what information in the chapter your instructor feels is most important. If you adopt this strategy, your reading before lectures will help you understand the lecture and take better class notes, and your reading after lectures will help you locate and learn information in the textbook that your instructor is emphasizing in class—which is likely to be the information your instructor thinks is most important and is most likely to show up on your exams. Thus, it's a good idea to have your class notes nearby when you're completing your reading assignments to help you identify what you should pay special attention to while reading.

. Remember

Your goal when reading is not merely to cover the assigned pages, but to uncover the most important information and ideas contained on those pages.

2. **Take written notes on what you're reading.** Just as you should take notes in class, you should take notes in response to the author's words in the text. Writing requires more active thinking than highlighting because you're creating your own words rather than passively highlighting words written by somebody else. Don't get into the habit of using your textbook as a coloring book in which the artistic process of highlighting what you're reading with spectacular kaleidoscopic colors distracts you from the more important process of learning actively and thinking deeply.

> "I would advise you to read with a pen in your hand, and enter in a little book of short hints of what you find that is curious, or that might be useful; for this will be the best method of imprinting such particulars in your memory, where they will be ready."
>
> —Benjamin Franklin, 18th-century inventor, newspaper writer, and signer of the *Declaration of Independence*

Highlighting textbooks in spectacular colors is a very popular reading strategy among college students, but it's a less effective strategy for producing deep learning than taking written notes on what you read.

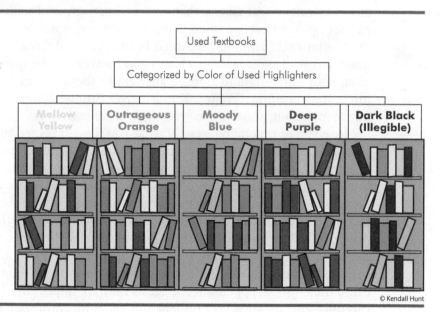

© Kendall Hunt

> "I had the worst study habits and the lowest grades. Then I found out what I was doing wrong. I had been highlighting with a black magic marker."
>
> —Jeff Altman, American comedian

If you can express what someone else has written in words that make sense to you, this means that you're relating it to what you already know—a sign of deep learning (Demmert & Towner, 2003). A good time to pause and summarize what you've read in your own words is when you encounter a boldface heading, because this indicates you've just completed reading about a major concept and are about to begin a new one.

. Remember

Effective reading isn't a passive process of covering pages: it's an active process in which you uncover meaning in the pages you read.

3. **Use the visual aids included in your textbook.** Don't fall into the trap of thinking that visual aids can or should be skipped because they're merely secondary supplements to the written words in the body of the text. Visual aids, such as

charts, graphs, diagrams, and concept maps, are powerful learning and memory tools for a couple of reasons: (1) they enable you to "see" the information in addition to reading (hearing) it, and (2) they organize and connect separate pieces of information into an integrated whole.

Think About It ———————————— *Journal Entry* **8.5**

When reading a textbook, do you usually have the following tools on hand?

Highlighter:	*yes*	no
Pen or pencil:	*yes*	no
Notebook:	*yes*	no
Class notes:	yes	*no*
Dictionary:	yes	*no*
Glossary:	yes	*no*

Why or why not?

Because I am Lazy.

Furthermore, visual aids allow you to experience a different form of information input than repeatedly processing written words. This occasional change of sensory input brings variety to the reading process, which can recapture your attention and recharge your motivation.

Post-Reading Strategies: What to Do after Reading

1. **End a reading session with a short review of the information you've noted or highlighted.** Most forgetting that takes place after you receive and process information occurs immediately after you stop focusing on the information and turn your attention to another task (Baddeley, 1999; Underwood, 1983). (See Figure 8.4.) Taking a few minutes at the end of your reading time to review the most important information works to lock that information into your memory before you turn your attention to something else and forget it.

    The graph in Figure 8.4 represents the results of a classic experiment on how well information is recalled at various times after it was originally learned. As you can see on the far left of the graph, most forgetting occurs soon after information has been taken in (e.g., after 20 minutes, the participants in the study forgot more than 60 per-

FIGURE 8.4

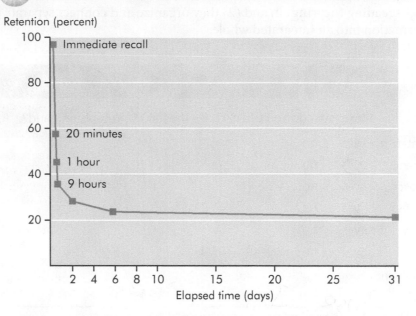

Source: Hermann Ebbinghaus, *Memory: A Contribution to Experimental Psychology*, 1885/1913.

The Forgetting Curve

cent of it). The results of this classic study, which have been confirmed multiple times (Schacter, 2001), point to the importance of reviewing information you've acquired through reading immediately after you've read it. When you do so, your memory for that information will improve dramatically because you're intercepting the forgetting curve at its steepest point of memory loss—immediately after information has been read.

2. **For difficult-to-understand concepts, seek out other information sources.** If you find you can't understand a concept explained in your text, even after re-reading and repeatedly reflecting on it, try the following strategy:

    *   **Look at how another textbook explains it.** Not all textbooks are created equally: some do a better job of explaining certain concepts than others. Check to see whether your library has other texts in the same subject as your course, or check your campus bookstore for textbooks in the same subject area as the course you're taking. A different text may be able to explain a hard-to-understand concept much better than the textbook you purchased for the course.

    *   **Seek help from your instructor.** If you read carefully and made every effort to understand a particular concept but still can't grasp it, most instructors should be willing to assist you. If your instructor is unavailable or unwilling, seek help from the professionals and peer tutors in the Learning Center or Academic Support Center on campus.

Snapshot Summary

8.1   SQ3R: A Method for Improving Reading Comprehension and Retention

A popular reading strategy for organizing and remembering information is the SQ3R method. SQ3R is an acronym for five steps you can take to increase textbook reading comprehension and retention, particularly when reading highly technical or complex material. The following sequences of steps comprise this method:

1. Survey
2. Question
3. Read
4. Recite
5. Review

S = Survey: Get a preview and overview of what you're about to read.

1. Read the title to activate your thoughts about the subject and prepare your mind to receive information related to it.
2. Read the introduction, chapter objectives, and chapter summary to become familiar with the author's purpose, goals, and most important points.
3. Note the boldface headings and subheadings to get a sense of the chapter's organization before you begin to read. This creates a mental structure or framework for making sense of the information you're about to read.
4. Take note of any graphics, such as charts, maps, and diagrams; they provide valuable visual support and reinforcement for the material you're reading.
5. Pay special attention to reading aids (e.g., italics and boldface font) that you can use to identify, understand, and remember key concepts.

Q = Question: Stay active and curious.

As you read, use the boldface headings to formulate questions you think will be answered in that particular section. When your mind is actively searching for answers to questions, it becomes more engaged in the learning process. As you read, add any questions that you have about the reading.

R = Read: Find the answer to the questions you've created.

Read one section at a time, with your questions in mind, and search for answers to these questions. Also, keep an eye out for new questions that need to be asked.

R = Recite: Rehearse your answers.

After you complete reading each section, recall the questions you asked and see whether you can answer them from memory. If not, look at the questions again and practice your answers to them until you can recall them without looking. Don't move on to the next section until you're able to answer all questions in the section you've just completed.

R = Review: Look back and get a second view of the whole picture.

Once you've finished the chapter, review all the questions you've created for different parts or sections. See whether you can still answer them without looking. If not, go back and refresh your memory.

Study Strategies for Learning Deeply and Remembering Longer

The final step in the learning process is to save that information you have in your brain and bring it back to mind at the time you need it—e.g., test time. Described here is a series of effective study strategies for acquiring knowledge, keeping that knowledge in your brain (memory storage), and accessing that information when you need it (memory retrieval).

The Importance of Undivided Attention

The human attention span has limited capacity; we have only so much of it available to us at any point in time, and we can give all or part of it to whatever task we're working on. If study time is spent engaging in other activities besides studying (e.g., listening to music, watching TV, or text messaging friends), the total amount of attention available for studying is subtracted and divided among the other activities. In other words, studying doesn't receive your undivided attention.

Studies show that when people multitask, they don't pay equal attention to all tasks at the same time. Instead, they divide their attention by shifting it back and forth between tasks (Howard, 2000), and their performance on the task that demands the most concentration or deepest thinking is the one that suffers the most (Crawford & Strapp, 1994). Furthermore, research shows that multitasking can increase boredom for the task that requires the most intense concentration. One study found that with even a low level of stimulation from another source of sensory input, such as a TV turned to a low volume in the next room, students were more likely to describe the mental task they were concentrating on as "boring" (Damrad-Frye & Laird, 1989).

Think About It ——————— *Journal Entry* 8.6

Rate yourself in terms of how frequently you use these reading strategies according to the following scale:

4 = always, 3 = sometimes, 2 = rarely, 1 = never

1. I read the chapter outlines and summaries before I start reading the chapter content.   4 3 2 (1)
2. I preview a chapter's boldface headings and subheadings before I begin to read the chapter.   4 3 2 (1)
3. I adjust my reading speed to the type of subject I am reading about.   (4) 3 2 1
4. I look up the meaning of unfamiliar words and unknown terms that I come across before I continue reading.   4 3 (2) 1
5. I take written notes on information I read.   (4) 3 2 1
6. I use the visual aids included in my textbooks.   (4) 3 2 1
7. I finish my reading sessions with a review of important information that I noted or highlighted.   4 3 (2) 1

What areas need the most improvement? How can you improve in these areas?

1 & 2: preview and look at the outlines.

When performing complex mental tasks that cannot be done automatically or mindlessly, other tasks and sources of external stimulation interfere with the quiet, internal reflection time needed for permanent connections to form between brain cells—which is what must happen if deep, long-lasting learning is to take place (Jensen, 2000).

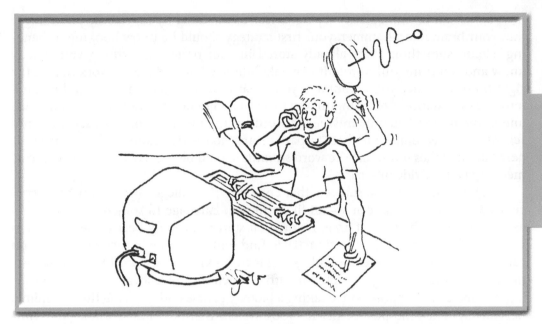

> **Studies show that doing challenging academic work while multitasking divides up attention and drives down comprehension and retention.**

Remember

Attention must happen first in order for retention to happen later.

Making Meaningful Associations

Connecting what you're trying to learn to something you already know is a powerful memory-improvement strategy because knowledge is stored in the form of a connected network of brain cells (Coward, 1990; Chaney, 2007). (See Figure 8.3 on p. 222.)

The brain's natural tendency to seek meaningful, connected patterns applies to words as well as images. This is illustrated in the following passage that once appeared anonymously on the Internet. See whether you can read it and grasp its meaning.

> *Aoccdrnig to rscheearch at Cmabridge Uinverstisy, it deos't mattaer in what order the ltteers in a word are, the only iprmoetnt thing is that the frist and lsat ltteer be at the rghit pclae. The rset can be a total mses and you can still raed it wouthit a porbelm. This is bcusae the human mind deos not raed ervey lteter by istlef, but the word as a wlohe. Amzanig huh?*

Notice how easily you found the meaning of the misspelled words by naturally transforming them into correctly spelled words—which you knew because the correctly spelled words were already stored in your brain. Thus, whenever you learn meaningfully, you do so by connecting what you're trying to understand to what you already know.

Learning by making meaningful connections is referred to as *deep learning* (Biggs & Tang, 2007; Entwistle & Ramsden, 1983). It involves moving beyond shallow memorization to deeper levels of understanding. This is a major shift from the old view that learning occurs by passively absorbing information like a sponge—for example, by receiving it from the teacher or text and studying it in the same prepackaged form as you received it. Instead, you want to adopt an approach to learning that involves actively transforming the information you receive into a form that's meaningful to you (Feldman & Paulsen, 1994; Mayer, 2002). This transforms short-term surface-level learning (memorization of information) into deep and meaningful long-term learning (acquisition of knowledge).

"The extent to which we remember a new experience has more to do with how it relates to existing memories than with how many times or how recently we have experienced it."

—Morton Hunt, *The Universe Within: A New Science Explores the Human Mind*

So, instead of immediately trying to learn something by repeatedly pounding it into your brain like a hammer, your first strategy should be to try hooking or hanging it onto something that's already stored in your brain—something you already know and is meaningful to you. It may take a little while and a little work to find the right hook, but once you've found it, you'll learn the information faster and retain it longer. For instance, a meaningful way to learn and remember how to correctly spell one of the most frequently misspelled words in the English language: *separate* (not *seperate*). By remembering that "to par" means "to divide," as in the words pa*r*ts or pa*r*tition, it makes sense that the word *separate* should be spelled *sepa*r*ate* because its meaning is "to divide into parts."

Each of the academic subjects that comprise the college curriculum has a specialized vocabulary that can sound like a foreign language to someone who has no experience with the subject area. Before you start to brutally beat these terms into your brain through sheer repetition, try to find some meaning in them. One way you can make a term more meaningful to you is by looking up its word root in the dictionary or by identifying its prefix or suffix, which may give away the term's meaning. For instance, suppose you're taking a biology course and studying the autonomic nervous system—the part of the nervous system that operates without your conscious awareness or voluntary control (e.g., your heart beating and lungs breathing). The meaning of the phrase is given away by the prefix *auto*, which means "self-controlling"—as in the word *automatic* (e.g., automatic transmission).

If looking up the term's root, prefix, or suffix doesn't give away its meaning, see if you can make it meaningful to you in some other way. For instance, suppose you looked up the root of the term *artery* and nothing about the origins of this term suggested its meaning or purpose. You could create your own meaning for this term by taking its first letter (a), and have it stand for "away"—to help you remember that arteries carry blood away from the heart. Thus, you've taken a biological term and made it personally meaningful (and memorable).

Think About It ——————————————— *Journal Entry* 8.7

Think of a key term or concept you're learning in a course this term that you could form a meaningful association to remember.

1. What is the information you're attempting to learn?

    Children Development
    _____

    _____

2. What is the meaningful association you could use to help you remember it?

    Kids growing up.
    _____

    _____

Author's Experience   When my son was about three years old, we were riding in the car together and listening to a song by the Beatles titled "Sergeant Pepper's Lonely Hearts Club Band." You may be familiar with this tune, but in case you're not, there is a part in it where the following lyrics are sung repeatedly: "Sergeant Pepper's lonely, Sergeant Pepper's lonely, Sergeant Pepper's lonely . . ."

When this part of the song was being played, I noticed that my three-year-old son was singing along. I thought that it was pretty amazing for a boy his age to be able to understand and repeat those lyrics. However, when that part of the song came on again, I noticed that he wasn't singing "Sergeant Pepper's lonely, Sergeant Pepper's lonely." Instead, he was singing "sausage pepperoni, sausage pepperoni" (which were his two favorite pizza toppings).

My son's brain was doing what all brains tend to naturally do. It took unfamiliar information (song lyrics) that didn't make any sense to him and transformed it into a form that was very meaningful to him!

— *Joe Cuseo*

Remember

The more meaningful what you're learning is to you, the deeper you'll learn it and the longer you'll remember it.

Compare and Contrast

When you're studying something new, get in the habit of asking yourself the following questions:

1. Is this idea similar or comparable to something that I've already learned? (Compare)
2. How does this idea differ from what I already know? (Contrast)

Research indicates that this simple strategy is one of the most powerful ways to promote learning of academic information (Marzano, Pickering, & Pollock, 2001). Asking yourself the question "How is this similar to and different from concepts that I already know?" makes learning more personally meaningful because you are relating what you're trying to learn to what you already know.

Integration and Organization

Integrate or connect ideas from your class notes and assigned readings that relate to the same major point by organizing them into the same category. For example, get these related ideas in the same place by recording them on the same index card under the same category heading. Index cards are a good tool for such purposes; you can use each card as a miniature file cabinet for different categories of information. The category heading on each card functions like the hub of a wheel, around which individual pieces of related information are attached like spokes. Integrating information related to the same topic in the same place and studying it at the same time divides the total material you're learning into identifiable and manageable parts. In contrast, when ideas pertaining to the same point or concept are spread all over the place, they're more likely to take that form in your mind—leaving them mentally disconnected and leaving you confused (as well as feeling stressed and overwhelmed).

Remember

Just as important as organizing course materials is organizing course concepts. Ask yourself the following questions: How can this specific concept be categorized or classified? How does this particular idea relate to or "fit into" something bigger?

Spreading out your studying into shorter sessions improves your memory by reducing loss of attention due to fatigue.

Divide and Conquer

Effective learning depends not only on *how* you learn (your method), but also on *when* you learn (your timing). Although cramming just before exams is better than not studying, it's far less effective than studying that's spread out across time. Rather than cramming all your studying into one long session, use the method of *distributed practice*—spread or "distribute" your study time over several shorter sessions. Research consistently shows that short, periodic practice sessions are more effective than a single marathon session.

Distributing study time over several shorter sessions improves your learning and memory by:

- Reducing loss of attention due to fatigue or boredom; and
- Reducing mental interference by giving your brain some downtime to cool down and lock in information it has received before it's interrupted by the need to deal with additional information (Malmberg & Murnane, 2002; Murname & Shiffrin, 1991).

If the brain's downtime is interfered with by the arrival of additional information, it gets overloaded and its capacity for handling information becomes impaired. This is what cramming does—it overloads the brain with lots of information in a limited period of time. In contrast, distributed study does just the opposite—it uses shorter sessions with downtime between sessions, thereby giving the brain the time and opportunity to retain the information that it has received and processed (studied).

Another major advantage of distributed study is that it's less stressful and more motivating than cramming. Shorter sessions provide you with an incentive to start studying because you know that you're not going to be doing it for a long stretch of time or lose any sleep over it. It's easier to maintain your interest and motivation for any task that's done for a shorter rather than a longer period. Furthermore, distributing studying makes exam preparation easier because you know that if you run into difficulty understanding anything, you'll still have plenty of time to get help with it before you're tested and graded on it.

The "Part-to-Whole" Study Method

The part-to-whole method of studying is a natural extension of the distributed practice just discussed. With the part-to-whole method, you break up the material you need to learn into smaller parts and study those parts in separate sessions in advance of the exam; then you use your last study session just before the exam to review (re-study) all the parts you previously studied in separate sessions. Thus, your last session is not a cram session or even a study session: it's a review session.

Research shows that students of all ability levels learn material in college courses more effectively when it's studied in small units and when progression to the next unit takes place only after the previous unit has been mastered or understood (Pascarella & Terenzini, 1991, 2005). This strategy has two advantages: (1) it reinforces your memory for what you previously learned, and (2) it builds on what you already know to help you learn new material. These advantages are particularly important in cumulative subjects that require memory for problem-solving procedures or steps, such as math and science. When you repeatedly practice these procedures, they become more automatic and you're able to retrieve them quicker (e.g., on a timed test). This enables you to use them efficiently without having to expend a lot of mental effort and energy (Samuels & Flor, 1997), freeing your working memory for more important tasks such as critical thinking and creative problem solving (Schneider & Chein, 2003).

| Think About It | Journal Entry 8.8 |

Are you more likely to study in advance of exams or cram just before exams? Why?

Cram because I procrastinate.

Don't buy into the myth that studying in advance is a waste of time because you'll forget it all by test time. As discussed in Chapter 6, this is a myth that procrastinators often use to rationalize their habit of putting off studying until the very last moment, which forces them to cram frantically the night before exams. Do not underestimate the power of breaking material to be learned into smaller parts and studying those parts some time before a major exam. Even if you cannot recall what you previously studied, when you start reviewing it you'll find that you will relearn it much faster than when you studied it the first time. This proves that studying in advance is not a waste of time because it takes less time to relearn the material, indicating that information studied in the earlier sessions was still retained in your brain (Kintsch, 1994).

Build Variety into the Study Process

You can increase your concentration and motivation by using the following strategies to infuse variety and a change of pace into your study routine.

Periodically vary the type of academic work you do while studying. Changing the nature of your work activities or the type of mental tasks you're performing while studying increases your level of alertness and concentration by reducing *habituation*—attention loss that occurs after repeated engagement in the same type of mental task (McGuiness & Pribram, 1980). To combat attention loss due to habituation, occasionally vary the type of study task you're performing. For instance, shift periodically among tasks that involve reading, writing, studying, and problem-solving skills (e.g., math or science problems).

Study different subjects in different places. Studying in different locations provides different environmental contexts for learning, which reduces the amount of interference that normally builds up when all information is studied in the same place (Rankin et al., 2009). In addition to spreading out your studying at different times, it's also a good idea to spread it out in different places. The great public speakers in ancient Greece and Rome used this method of changing places to remember long speeches by walking through different rooms while rehearsing their speeches, learning each major part of a speech in a different room (Higbee, 1998).

Changing the nature of the learning task and place where learning takes place provides a change of pace that infuses variety into the learning process, which, in turn, stimulates your attention, concentration, and motivation. Although it's useful to have a set time and place to study for getting you into a regular work routine, this doesn't mean that learning occurs best by habitually performing all types of academic tasks in the same place. Instead, research suggests that you should periodically change the learning tasks you perform and the environment in which you perform them to maximize attention and minimize interference (Druckman & Bjork, 1991).

Remember

Change of pace and place while studying can stimulate your attention to what you're studying as well as your interest in and motivation for studying.

Mix long study sessions with short study breaks that involve physical activity (e.g., a short jog or brisk walk). Study breaks that include physical activity not only refresh the mind by giving it a rest from studying, but also stimulate the mind by increasing blood flow to your brain, which will help you retain what you've already studied and regain concentration for what you'll study next.

Learning Styles: Identifying Your Learning Preferences

Your learning style is another important personal characteristic you should be aware of when choosing your major. Learning styles refer to individual differences in learning preferences—that is, ways in which individuals prefer to perceive information (receive or take it in) and process information (deal with it after taking it in). Individuals may differ in terms of whether they prefer to take in information by reading about it, listening to it, seeing an image or diagram of it, or physically touching and manipulating it. Individuals may also vary in terms of whether they like to receive information in a structured and orderly format or in an unstructured form that allows them the freedom to explore, play with, and restructure it in their own way. Once information has been received, individuals may also differ in terms of how they prefer to process or deal with it mentally. Some might like to think about it on their own; others may prefer to discuss it with someone else, make an outline of it, or draw a picture of it.

Author's
Experience

In my family, whenever there's something that needs to be assembled or set up (e.g., a ping-pong table or new electronic equipment), I've noticed that my wife, my son, and myself have different learning styles in terms of how we go about doing it. I like to read the manual's instructions carefully and completely before I even attempt to touch anything. My son prefers to look at the pictures or diagrams in the manual and uses them as models to find parts; then he begins to assemble those parts. My wife seems to prefer not to look at the manual. Instead, she likes to figure things out as she goes along by grabbing different parts from the box and trying to assemble those parts that look like they should fit together—piecing them together as if she were completing a jigsaw puzzle.

Joe Cuseo

You can take specially designed tests to assess your particular learning style and how it compares with others. There are many of them and most cost money to take. *My Power Learning* is just one example of the many tests you can take. VARK (www.vark-learn.com) is another example. Edutopia (www.edutopia.org/mi-quiz) is another.

Probably the most frequently used learning styles test is the Myers-Briggs Type Indicator (MBTI; Myers, 1976; Myers & McCaulley, 1985), which is based on the personality theory of psychologist Carl Jung. The test consists of four pairs of opposing traits and assesses how people vary on a scale (low to high) for each of these four sets of traits.

Learning styles are no more or no less common ways that people learn. We all have a mix of multiple learning styles, thus we have different and multiple ways of learning. Many students may find that they have a dominant learning style but using other styles that are less dominant. In many cases, you might use different styles for different learning circumstances. No style is set in concrete. They can change and there is no perfect mix for greater learning. You have the ability to increase your lesser used methods to make them more dominant while strengthening your dominant one. Since students have different learning styles and academic fields emphasize different styles of learning, it's important to consider how your learning style meshes with the style of learning emphasized by the field you're considering as a major. If the match seems to be close or compatible, then the marriage between you and that major could be one that leads to a satisfying and successful learning experience.

Although there are many (multiple) learning styles, the three that are considered most common are:

- Visual-Spatial Learning (learning by seeing),
- Auditory-Sequential Learning (learning by hearing),
- Kinesthetic Learning (learning by doing).

In addition to taking formal tests to assess which or how many of these are your learning style(s), you can gain awareness of your learning styles through some simple introspection or self-examination. Take a moment to complete the following sentences that are designed to stimulate personal reflection on your learning style:

I learn best if . . .
I learn most from . . .
I enjoy learning when . . .

Knowing your preferred learning style can make studying easier for you. Once you discover your dominant learning style, research some ways you can incorporate your learning style into your study routine (i.e., if your learning style is visual, read over notes or use flashcards; if you are an auditory learner, read your notes out loud to yourself; if you are a kinesthetic learner, rewrite your notes).

To sum up, the most important factor to consider when reaching decisions about a major is whether it is compatible with four characteristics of yourself: (1) your learning style, (2) your abilities, (3) your personal interests, and (4) your values. These four pillars provide the foundation for effective decisions about a college major.

Learn with all of your senses. When studying, try to use as many sensory channels as possible. Research shows that information perceived through multiple sensory modalities is remembered better because it creates multiple interconnections in long-term memory areas of the brain (Bjork, 1994; Shams & Seitz, 2011; Zull, 2002). When a memory is formed in the brain, different sensory aspects of it are stored in different areas. For example, when your brain receives visual, auditory (hearing), and motor (movement) input while learning, each of these forms of sensory input is stored as a memory trace in a different part of the brain. Figure 8.5 shows a map of the outer surface of the human brain; you can see how different parts of the brain are specialized to receive input from different sensory modalities. When you use all of these sensory modalities while learning, multiple memory traces of what you're studying are recorded in different parts of your brain, which leads to deeper learning and stronger memory for what you have learned (Education Commission of the States, 1996).

FIGURE 8.5

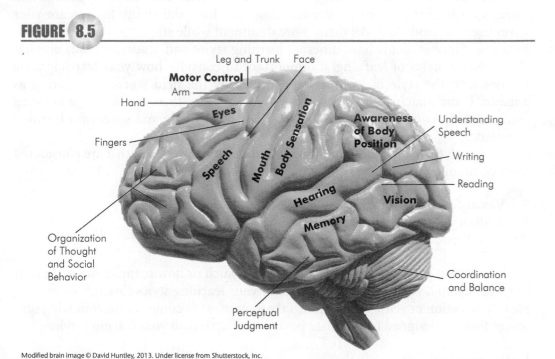

Modified brain image © David Huntley, 2013. Under license from Shutterstock, Inc.

A Map of the Functions Performed by the Outer Surface of the Human Brain

Learn visually. The human brain consists of two hemispheres (half spheres): the left and the right (see Figure 8.6). Each hemisphere of the brain specializes in a different type of learning. In most people, the left hemisphere specializes in verbal learning, dealing primarily with words. In contrast, the right hemisphere specializes in visual-spatial learning, dealing primarily with perceiving images and objects that occupy physical space. If you use both hemispheres while studying, you lay down two different memory traces in your brain: one in the left hemisphere where words are stored, and one in the right hemisphere where images are stored. This process of laying down a double memory trace (verbal and visual) is referred to as *dual coding* (Paivio, 1990). When this happens, memory for what you're learning is substantially strengthened, primarily because two memory traces are better than one.

FIGURE 8.6

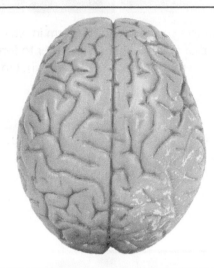

The human brain consists of the left hemisphere, which processes words, and the right hemisphere, which processes images.

© JupiterImages Corporation.

To capitalize on the advantage of dual coding, be sure to use any visual aids that are available to you, including those provided in your textbook and by your instructor in class. You can also create your own visual aids by drawing pictures, symbols, and concept maps, such as flowcharts, Venn diagrams, spiderwebs, wheels with spokes, or branching tree diagrams. (For example, see Figure 8.7 for a tree diagram that could be used to help you remember the parts and functions of the human nervous system.)

Remember

Drawing and other forms of visual illustration are not just artistic exercises: they can also be powerful learning tools—you can draw to learn! Drawing keeps you actively involved in the process of learning, and by representing what you're learning in visual form, you're able to dual-code the information you're studying, which doubles the number of memory traces recorded in your brain. As the old saying goes, "A picture is worth a thousand words."

FIGURE 8.7

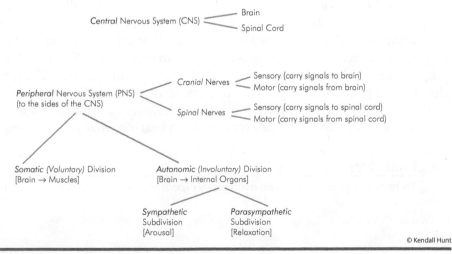

ORGANIZATION OF THE HUMAN NERVOUS SYSTEM

© Kendall Hunt

Concept Map for the Human Nervous System

Think About It ——————————————— *Journal Entry* 8.9

Think of a course you're taking this term in which you're learning related pieces of information that could be joined together to form a concept map. In the space that follows, make a rough sketch of this map that includes the information you need to remember.

Learn by moving or using motor learning (a.k.a. muscle memory). In addition to hearing and seeing, movement is a sensory channel. When you move, your brain receives kinesthetic stimulation—the sensations generated by your muscles. Research shows that memory traces for movement are commonly stored in an area of your brain that plays a major role in all types of learning (Middleton & Strick, 1994). Thus, associating movement with what you're learning can improve your ability to retain it because you add a muscle memory trace in the motor control area of your brain (see Figure 8.5).

Author's Experience

I was talking about memory in class one day and mentioned that when I temporarily forget how to spell a word, its correct spelling comes back to me once I start to write it. One of my students raised her hand and said the same thing happens to her when she forgets a phone number—it comes back to her when she starts dialing it. Both of these experiences illustrate how motor memory brings information back to mind that was temporarily forgotten, pointing to the power of movement for promoting learning and memory.

— *Joe Cuseo*

You can use movement to help you learn and retain academic information by using your body to act out what you're studying or to symbolize it with your hands (Kagan & Kagan, 1998). For example, if you're trying to remember five points about something (e.g., five consequences of the Civil War), when you're studying these points, count them on your fingers as you try to recall each of them. Also, remember that talking involves muscle movement of your lips and tongue. Thus, if you speak aloud when you're studying, either to a friend or to yourself, your memory of what you're studying may be improved by adding kinesthetic stimulation to the auditory or sound stimulation your brain receives from hearing what you're saying.

Student Perspective

"When I have to remember something, it's better for me to do something with my hands so I could physically see it happening."

—First-year college student

Remember

Try to make the learning process a total body experience—hear it, see it, say it, and move it.

Learn with emotion. Information reaches the brain through your senses and is stored in the brain as a memory trace; the same is true of emotions. Numerous connections occur between brain cells in the emotional and memory centers (Zull, 1998). For instance, when you're experiencing emotional excitement about what you're learning, adrenaline is released and is carried through the bloodstream to the brain. Once adrenaline reaches the brain, it increases blood flow and glucose production, which stimulates learning and strengthens memory (LeDoux, 1998; Rosenfield, 1988). In fact, emotionally intense experiences can release such a substantial amount of adrenaline into the bloodstream that memories of them can be immediately stored in long-term memory and last an entire lifetime. For instance, most people remember exactly what they were doing at the time they experienced such emotionally intense events as the September 11 terrorist attack on the United States, their first kiss, or their favorite team winning a world championship.

What does this emotion-memory link have to do with helping you remember academic information while studying? Research indicates that emotional intensity, excitement, and enthusiasm strengthen memories of academic information just as they do for memories of life events and personal experiences. If you get psyched up about what you're learning, you have a much better chance of learning and remembering it. If you're passionate or intense about what you're learning and convince yourself that it's really important to know, you're more likely to remember it (Howard, 2000; Minninger, 1984). So, keep in mind the importance or significance of what you're learning. For instance, if you're learning about photosynthesis, remind yourself that you're not just learning about a chemical reaction—you're learning about the driving force that underlies all plant life on the planet! If you aren't aware of the importance or significance of a particular concept you're studying, ask your instructor or a student majoring in the field. Enthusiasm can be contagious; you may catch it and become more passionate about learning the concept.

Remember

You learn most effectively when you actively involve all your senses (including bodily movement) and when you learn with passion and enthusiasm. In other words, learning grows deeper and lasts longer when you put your whole self into it—your heart, your mind, and your body.

Learn by collaborating with others. Research indicates that college students who work regularly in small groups of four to six become more actively involved in the learning process and learn more (Light, 2001). To maximize the power of study groups, each member should study individually *before* studying in a group and should come prepared with specific information or answers to share with teammates, as well as questions or points of confusion that the team can attempt to help answer or clarify. (For specific team-learning strategies, see Chapter 4, pp. 120–123.)

Student Perspective

"I would suggest students get to know [each] other and get together in groups to study or at least review class material. I find it is easier to ask your friends or classmates with whom you are comfortable 'dumb' questions."

—Advice to first-year students from a college sophomore (Walsh, 2005)

When I was in my senior year of college, I had to take a theory course by independent study because the course would not be offered again until after I planned to graduate. Another senior found himself in the same situation. The instructor allowed both of us to take this course together and agreed to meet with us every two weeks. My fellow classmate and I studied independently for the first two weeks.

I prepared for the biweekly meetings by reading thoroughly, yet I had little understanding of what I had read. After our first meeting, I left with a strong desire to drop the course but decided to stick with it. Over the next two weeks, I spent many sleepless nights trying to prepare for our next meeting and was feeling pretty low about not being the brightest student in my class of two. During the next meeting with the instructor, I found out that the other student was also having difficulty. Not only did I notice, so did the instructor. After that meeting, the instructor gave us study questions and asked us to read separately and then get together to discuss the questions. During the next two weeks, my classmate and I met several times to discuss what we were learning (or attempting to learn). By being able to communicate with each other about the issues we were studying, we both ended up gaining greater understanding. Our instructor was delighted to see that he was able to suggest a collaborative learning strategy that worked for both of us.

— Aaron Thompson

Self-Monitor Your Learning

Successful learners don't just put in study time: they reflect and check on themselves to see if they're putting in quality time and really understanding what they're attempting to learn. They monitor their comprehension as they go along by asking themselves questions such as "Am I following this?" "Do I really understand it?" and "Do I know it for sure?"

How do you know if you really know it? Probably the best answer to this question is "I find *meaning* in it—that is, I can relate to it personally or put it in terms that make sense to me" (Ramsden, 2003).

Discussed below are some strategies for checking whether you truly understand what you're trying to learn. They help you answer the question "How do I know if I really know it?" These strategies can be used as indicators or checkpoints for determining whether you're just memorizing or learning at a deeper level.

- **Can you paraphrase (restate or translate) what you're learning into your own words?** When you can paraphrase what you're learning, you're able to complete the following sentence: "In other words . . ." If you can complete that sentence in your own words, this is a good indication that you've moved beyond memorization to comprehension, because you've transformed what you're learning into words that are meaningful to you. You know you know it if you're not stating it the same way your instructor or textbook stated it, but restating it in words that are your own.

- **Can you explain what you're learning to someone who is unfamiliar with it?** Simply put, if you can't explain it to someone else, you probably don't really understand it yourself. If you can explain to a friend what you've learned, this is a good sign that you've moved beyond memorization to comprehension, because you're able to translate it into language that's understandable to anyone. Studies show that students gain deeper levels of understanding for what they're learning when they're asked to explain it to someone else (Chi, De Leeuw, Chiu, & La-Vancher, 1994). Sometimes, we only become aware of how well we know or don't know something when we have to explain it to someone who's never heard it before (just ask any teacher). If you cannot find someone else to explain it to, then explain it aloud as if you were talking to an imaginary friend.

"When you know a thing, to recognize that you know it; and when you do not, to know that you do not know; that is knowledge."

—Confucius, influential Chinese thinker and educator

"Most things used to be external to me—out of a lecture or textbook. It makes learning a lot more interesting and memorable when you can bring your experiences into it. It makes you want to learn."

—Returning adult student

"You do not really understand something unless you can explain it to your grandmother."

—Albert Einstein, considered the "father of modern physics" and named "Person of the (20th) Century" by *Time Magazine*

- **Can you think of an example of what you've learned?** If you can come up with an instance or illustration of what you're learning that's your own—not one given by your instructor or textbook—this is a good sign that you truly understand it. It shows you're able to take a general, abstract concept and apply it to a specific, real-life experience (Bligh, 2000). Furthermore, a personal example is a powerful memory tool. Studies show that when people retrieve a concept from memory, they first recall an example of it. The example then serves a memory-retrieval cue to trigger their memory of other details about the concept, such as its definition and relationship to other concepts (Norman, 1982; Okimoto & Norman, 2010; Park, 1984).

- **Can you represent or describe what you've learned in terms of an analogy or metaphor that compares it to something with similar meaning, or which works in a similar way?** Analogies and metaphors are basically ways of learning something new by understanding it in terms of its similarity to something you already understand. For instance, the computer can be used as a metaphor for the human brain to get a better understanding of learning and memory as a three-stage process in which information is: (1) inputted—perceived or received (through lectures and readings), (2) stored or saved—by studying, and (3) retrieved—recalled from storage at test time. If you can use an analogy or metaphor to represent what you're learning, you're grasping it at a deep level because you're building a mental bridge that connects it to what you already know (Cameron, 2003).

- **Can you apply what you're learning to solve a new problem that you haven't previously seen?** The ability to use knowledge by applying it in a different situation is a good indicator of deep learning (Erickson & Strommer, 2005). Learning specialists refer to this mental process as *decontextualization*—taking what you learned in one context (situation) and applying it to another (Bransford, Brown, & Cocking, 1999). For instance, you know that you've learned a mathematical concept deeply when you can use that concept to solve math problems that are different from the ones used by your instructor or your textbook. This is why your math instructors rarely include on exams the exact problems they solved in class or were solved in your textbook. They're not trying to "trick" you at test time: they're trying to see whether you've learned the concept or principle deeply.

Think About It —————————————— *Journal Entry* **8.10**

Rate yourself in terms of how frequently you use these study strategies according to the following scale:

4 = always, 3 = sometimes, 2 = rarely, 1 = never

1. I block out all distracting sources of outside stimulation when I study.   4 ③ 2 1

2. I try to find meaning in technical terms by looking at their prefixes or suffixes or by looking up their word roots in the dictionary.   4 ③ 2 1

3. I compare and contrast what I'm currently studying with what I've already learned.   4 3 ② 1

4. I organize the information I'm studying into categories or classes.   4 3 ② 1

(continued)

5. I integrate or pull together information from my class notes and readings that relates to the same concept or general category.   ④ 3 2 1

6. I distribute or spread out my study time over several short sessions in advance of the exam, and I use my last study session before the test to review the information I previously studied.   ④ 3 2 1

7. I participate in study groups with my classmates.   ④ 3 2 1

Which of these areas needs improvement? How can you improve in these areas?

3 & 4. I need to compare and contrast and be more organized

Summary and Conclusion

Information delivered during lectures is most likely to form questions and answers on college tests. Students who do not record information presented during lectures in their notes have a slim chance of recalling the information at test time. Thus, effective note taking is critical to successful academic performance in college.

Information from reading assignments is the next most common source of test questions on college exams. Professors often don't discuss information contained in assigned reading during class lectures. Thus, doing the assigned reading, and doing it in a way that's most effective for promoting comprehension and retention, plays an important role in your academic success.

The most effective strategies for promoting effective classroom listening, textbook reading, and studying are those that reflect three of the college-success principles discussed in Chapter 3: (1) active involvement, (2) collaboration, and (3) self-awareness.

Active involvement is critical for learning from lectures (e.g., actively taking notes while listening to lectures) and learning from reading (e.g., actively taking notes while reading). While active involvement is necessary for learning because it engages your attention and enables information to enter the brain, personal reflection is also necessary for deep learning because it keeps that information in the brain by locking it into long-term memory. Reflection also encourages deep learning by promoting self-awareness. Periodically pausing to reflect on whether you're truly understanding what you're studying will make you a more self-aware learner and a more successful student.

Learning is also deepened when it's a multisensory experience—when you engage as many senses as possible in the learning process, particularly the sense of vision. Lastly, learning is strengthened when it's done collaboratively. You can collaborate with peers to take better notes in class, to identify what's most important in your assigned reading, and to study lecture and reading notes in preparation for course exams.

Learning More through the World Wide Web

Internet-Based Resources for Further Information on Strategic Learning and Memory Improvement

For additional information related to the ideas discussed in this chapter, we recommend the following Web sites:

Strategic Learning and Study Strategies:

www.dartmouth.edu/~acskills/success/index.html

www.muskingum.edu/~cal/database/general/

Learning Math and Overcoming Math Anxiety:

www.mathacademy.com/pr/minitext/anxiety

www.onlinemathlearning.com/math-mnemonics.html

Chapter 8 Exercises

8.1 Self-Assessment of Note-Taking and Reading Habits

Look back at the ratings you gave yourself for effective note-taking (p. 220), reading (p. 227), and studying (p. 233) strategies. Add up your total score for these three sets of learning strategies (the maximum score for each set is 28):

Note Taking = 4

Reading = 8

Studying = 3

Total Learning Strategy Score = 15

Self-Assessment Questions

1. In which learning strategy area did you score lowest? *Studying*

2. Do you think that the strategy area in which you scored lowest has anything to do with your lowest course grade at this point in the term? Explain. *Yes, if I study better I get better grades*

3. Of the seven strategies listed within the area in which you scored lowest, which ones could you immediately put into practice to improve your lowest course grade this term? *Studying*

4. What is the likelihood that you will put the preceding strategies into practice this term? How can you do this? *Start the ones you struggle with the most.*

8.2 Consulting with a Learning Center or Academic Development Specialist

Make an appointment to visit your Learning Center or Academic Support Center on campus to discuss the results of your note-taking, reading, and studying self-assessment in Exercise 8.1 (or any other learning self-assessment you may have taken). Ask for recommendations about how you can improve your learning habits in your lowest-scoring area. Following your visit, answer the following questions.

Learning Resource Center Reflection

1. Whom did you meet with in the Learning Center? *Kate*

2. Was your appointment useful (e.g., did you gain any insights or acquire any new learning or test-taking strategies)? *Yes.*

3. What steps were recommended to you for improving your academic performance? *Grammar stuff*

4. How likely is it that you will take the steps mentioned in the previous question: (a) definitely, (b) probably, (c) possibly, or (d) unlikely? Why? *Probably I will need the step.*

5. Do you plan to visit the Learning Center again? If yes, why? If no, why not? *Yes, its free and helpfull.*

Too Fast, Too Frustrating: A Note-Taking Nightmare

Susan Scribe is a first-year student who is majoring in journalism, and she's enrolled in an introductory course that is required for her major (Introduction to Mass Media). Her instructor for this course lectures at a rapid rate and uses vocabulary words that go right over her head. Since she cannot get all her instructor's words down on paper and cannot understand half the words she does manage to write down, she becomes frustrated and stops taking notes. She wants to do well in this course because it's the first course in her major, but she's afraid she will fail it because her class notes are so pitiful.

Discussion Questions

1. Can you relate to this case personally, or do you know any students who are in the same boat as Susan? Explain.

2. What would you recommend that Susan do at this point?

3. Why did you make the preceding recommendation?

Chapter 8 Reflection

List and describe at least five principles discussed in this chapter that can help you take better notes in class and improve your reading comprehension.

1.

2.

3.

4.

5.

Now explain how you can put these principles into practice.

Welcome to Macomb Community College!

My name is Tanya Balcom, and I am a Professor of Business Management here at Macomb. I teach most of the courses in the Business Management program and also coordinate the Hospitality Management program. Just like you, I started my college education at Macomb. I came here right out of high school and to be completely honest with you, I wasn't thrilled about it. I had aspirations to attend a major university, live in dorms, and get what I thought was a "real" education that would help me become an executive. I underestimated Macomb and all that it had to offer until a couple of semesters in. I was working full time to put myself through college and didn't appreciate my education. Then I met her . . . my Business Communications instructor, Mrs. Sypniewski.

I was a shy student and didn't say much in any of my classes. This was the first night class that I took, and I wasn't sure what to expect. She walked in and said excitedly "I am so happy to be here! We are going to have a wonderful semester and you are going to learn a lot that will stick with you the rest of your lives . . . I promise." I found out that she used to be an administrator at the college, and missed teaching and the frequent interaction with the students so much, she left her Dean position to teach. As a business major, this piqued my curiosity, as I couldn't fathom why someone would leave an executive level, 9–5 position to teach, and at night nonetheless. I soon found out through the passion she showed every minute of class and the genuine concern for each individual's learning was what was important to her. I worked and studied as hard as I ever did for her class; I didn't want to let her down. I realized that meeting her expectations and standards would make me a better person, personally and professionally. Most of all, I decided I wanted to be like her. That semester, I earned Dean's list honors for the first time. I walked out of that class wanting to become a community college professor.

After her class, I continued to take as many credits in marketing and management as possible. I came across more teachers that loved to teach and cared about the students. I told them I would be back one day to teach, and they assured me they would remember me. I earned two degrees at Macomb and transferred my credits to Walsh College, where I earned Bachelor's and Master's degrees. I worked in management the entire time, and when I was finished with college, I applied at Macomb to teach part time. I wasn't hired and was absolutely devastated. One evening, over a year later, the call came from one of my favorite former professors. He said "Hi Tanya, this is Paul Thacker . . . do you remember me?" Absolutely, I did, and was flattered he remembered me. He offered me a job teaching one class part time, and ten years later I became full time. I now get to teach side-by-side with these influential instructors. What more could I ask for?

I look back at my college experience and am so happy I chose to come here. You are about to learn some very important test taking skills in this chapter. Please make the time to study hard for those tests, whether individually or as a group, and treat yourself to the extra help in the learning center if you need it. I always found that relating the material to a specific example personally helped me remember it better; therefore, I had to study that specific material less. I kept my study materials close by and would review them in shorter periods of time but more frequently. Learn as much from each teacher as you can, and don't let a question go without asking it. If you are hesitant or shy like I was to ask in front of everyone, then wait until after class to ask, or send an e-mail, but don't short yourself of any knowledge you deserve. Lastly, I allowed myself to make a mistake on a test without dwelling on it and letting it hold me back the next time. After all, nobody's perfect!

I urge you to take advantage of all we have to offer. Never give up, even if you feel frustrated. We will be there clapping when you proudly walk across the stage to accept your degree. Follow your dreams—you deserve it!

I am Tanya Balcom and I am Macomb.

Test-Taking Skills and Strategies

What to Do before, during, and after Exams

THOUGHT STARTER | *Journal Entry* **9.1** | **LEARNING GOAL**

To strengthen your performance on college exams and professional tests.

1. On which of the following types of activities do you tend to perform best? (Circle one.) On which do you perform worst? (Circle one.)

   ~~Taking multiple-choice tests~~ B

   ~~Taking essay tests~~ W

   Writing papers

   Making oral presentations

2. What do you think accounts for the fact that you perform better on one than the other?

   I can rember if the answer is there.

Test-Taking Strategies

Academic learning in college involves three stages: acquiring information from lectures and readings, studying that information and storing it in your brain as knowledge, and demonstrating that knowledge on exams. What follows is a series of strategies related to stage three of this process: test taking. The strategies are divided into three categories:

- Strategies to use in advance of the test,
- Strategies to use during the test, and
- Strategies to use after test results are returned.

263

Pre-Test Strategies: What to Do in Advance of the Test

Your ability to remember what you've studied depends not only on how much and how well you studied, but also on how you will be tested (Stein, 1978). You may be able to remember what you've studied if you are tested in one format (e.g., multiple-choice questions), but may not remember the material as well if the test is in a different format (e.g., essay questions). You need to be aware of the type of test you'll be taking and adjust your study strategies accordingly.

College test questions fall into two major categories: (1) recognition questions, and (2) recall questions. Each of these types of questions requires a different type of memory and a different study strategy.

1. **Recognition test questions.** Recognition questions ask you to select or choose the correct answer from choices that are provided for you. Falling into this category are multiple-choice, true-false, and matching questions. These test questions don't require you to supply or produce the correct answer on your own; instead, you're asked to recognize or pick out the correct answer, similar to identifying the correct criminal in a lineup of suspects.

2. **Recall test questions.** Recall questions require you to retrieve information you've studied and reproduce it on your own at test time. As the word *recall* implies, you have to call back to mind the information you need and supply it yourself, rather than selecting it or picking it out from information that's supplied for you. Recall test questions include essay, fill-in-the-blank, and short-answer questions, which require a written response.

Since recognition test questions ask you to recognize or identify the correct answer from among answers that are provided for you, repeatedly reading over your class and textbook notes to identify important concepts may be an effective study strategy for multiple-choice and true-false test questions. Doing so matches the type of mental activity you'll be asked to perform on the exam—read over and identify correct answers.

On the other hand, recall test questions, such as essay questions, require you to retrieve information and generate answers on your own. Studying for essay tests by looking over your class notes and highlighted reading will not prepare you to recall information because it does not simulate what you'll be doing on the test itself. However, when you study for essay tests, if you retrieve information without looking at it and write out your answers to questions, you ensure that your practice (study) sessions match your performance (test) situation because you are rehearsing what you'll be expected to do on the test—write essays.

Two strategies that are particularly effective for practicing the type of memory retrieval you will need to perform on essay tests are recitation and creation of retrieval cues. Each of these strategies is described below.

Recitation

Recitation involves saying the information you need to recall without looking at it. Research indicates that memory for information is significantly strengthened when students study by trying to generate that information on their own, rather than simply looking it over or rereading it (Roediger & Karpicke, 2006). Reciting strengthens recall memory in three ways:

1. Recitation forces you to actively retrieve information, which is what you will have to do on the test, instead of passively reviewing information that's in front of you and in full view, which is not what you will do on the test.
2. Recitation gives you clear feedback on whether you can recall the information you're studying. If you can't retrieve and recite it without looking at it, you know for sure that you won't be able to recall it at test time and that you need to study it further. One way to provide yourself with this feedback is to put the question on one side of an index card and the answer on the flip side. If you find yourself flipping over the index card to look at the answer in order to remember it, you clearly cannot retrieve the information on your own and need to study it further.
3. Recitation encourages you to use your own words; this gives you feedback on whether you can paraphrase the information. If you can paraphrase it (rephrase it in your own words), it's a good indication you really understand it, and if you really understand it, you're more likely to recall it at test time.

Recitation can be done silently, by speaking aloud, or by writing out what you're saying. We recommend speaking aloud or writing out what you're reciting because these strategies involve physical action, which keeps you actively involved in the learning process.

Creation of Retrieval Cues

Suppose you're trying to remember the name of a person you know but just cannot recall it. If a friend gives you a clue (e.g., the first letter of the person's name or a name that rhymes with it), it's likely to suddenly trigger your memory of that person's name. What your friend did was provide you with a retrieval cue. A *retrieval cue* is a type of memory reminder (like a string tied around your finger) that brings back to your mind what you've temporarily forgotten. Since human memories are stored as parts in an interconnected network, if you're able to recall one piece or segment of the network (the retrieval cue), it can trigger recall of the other pieces of information linked to it in the same organizational network (Willingham, 2001).

Think About It —————————— *Journal Entry* **9.2**

1. Think of material in a course you're taking this term that could be easily grouped into categories to help you remember that material. What is the course?

_____ Babys _____

2. What categories could you use to organize information that's been covered in the course?

_____ Nar- Cards, notes, reading, _____
etc

Studies show that students who can't remember previously studied information are better able to recall that information if they are given a retrieval cue. In one study, students studied a long list of items that included different animals (e.g., giraffe, coyote, and turkey). When given a blank sheet of paper to write down the names of those animals, they weren't able to recall all of them. However, when the word *animals* was written on top of the answer sheet to provide a retrieval cue, the students were often able to recall many animals they couldn't name without the retrieval cue (Tulving, 1983). Research findings such as these suggest that category names can serve as powerful retrieval cues. If you take information that you need to recall on an essay test and organize it into categories, you can use these category names as retrieval cues at test time.

Another strategy for creating retrieval cues is to come up with your own catchwords or catchphrases that you can use to "catch" or batch together all related ideas you're trying to remember. For instance, an acronym can serve as a catchword, with each letter acting as a retrieval cue for a batch of related ideas. Suppose you're studying for an essay test in abnormal psychology that will include questions testing your knowledge of different forms of mental illness. You could create the acronym SCOT as a retrieval cue to help you remember to include each of the following elements of mental illness in your essay answers: symptoms (S), causes (C), outcomes (O), and therapies (T). See Do It Now! 9.1 for ideas on how to create your own memory retrieval cues.

9.1   DO IT NOW

Key Questions to Guide Creation of Your Own Retrieval Cues

1. Can you relate or associate what you're trying to remember with something you already know, or can you create a short meaningful story out of it? (Meaningful Association)
2. Can you remember it by visualizing an image of it, or by visually associating the pieces of information you want to recall with familiar places or sites? (Visualization)
3. Can you represent each piece of information you're trying to recall as a letter and string the letters together to form a single word or short phrase? (Acronym)
4. Can you rhyme what you're trying to remember with a word or expression you know well, or can you create a little poem, jingle, or melody out of it that contains the information? (Rhythm and Rhyme)

Remember

On multiple-choice questions, you're given a list of answers and you pick out the right one. On essay questions, you have a blank sheet of paper and you have to dig out the answer on your own, which means you have to recite (rehearse) your answers before the test and use memory retrieval cues during the test to dig up the information you need to remember.

Strategies to Use Immediately before a Test

1. **Before the exam, try to take a brisk walk.** Physical activity increases mental alertness by increasing oxygen flow to the brain; it will also decrease tension by increasing the brain's production of emotionally "mellowing" brain chemicals (e.g., serotonin and endorphins).

2. **Come fully armed with all the test-taking tools you need.** In addition to the required supplies (e.g., No. 2 pencil, pen, blue book, Scantron, calculator, etc.), bring backup equipment in case you experience equipment failure (e.g., an extra pen in case your first one runs out of ink or extra pencils in case your original one breaks).

3. **Try to get to the classroom a few minutes early.** Arriving at the test ahead of time gives you a chance to review any formulas and equations you may have struggled to remember and any memory retrieval cues you've created (e.g., acronyms). You want to be sure that you have this information in your working memory when you receive the exam so that you can get it down on paper before you forget it. Arriving early also allows you to take a few minutes to get into a relaxed pre-test state of mind by thinking positive thoughts, taking slow, deep breaths, and stretching your muscles. Also, avoid last-second discussions with unprepared classmates about the test just before the test is to be handed out; their hurried and harried questions can often cause confusion and elevate your level of test anxiety.

4. **Sit in the same seat that you normally occupy in class.** Research indicates that memory is improved when information is recalled in the same place where it was originally received or reviewed (Sprenger, 1999). Thus, taking the test in the same seat you normally occupy during lectures should improve your test performance because it puts you in the same place where you originally heard much of the information that is going to appear on the test. Studies show that when students take a test in the same environment that they studied in, they tend to remember more of that information at test time than do students who study in one place and take the test in a different place (Smith, Glenberg, & Bjork, 1978). While it is unlikely that you'll be able to do all your studying in the same room that you will take your test in, it may be possible to do your final review in your classroom or in an empty classroom with similar features. This could strengthen your memory for the information you studied because the features of the room may become associated with the information, and seeing these features again at test time may help trigger memory of it (Tulving, 1983).

A classic and intriguing study supporting this hypothesis was conducted on a group of deep-sea divers who learned a list of words on a beach or underwater and were later tested for their memory of the words. Half of the divers who learned the words on the beach remained there to take the test while the other half were tested underwater; and half of the group who studied the words underwater took the test there while the other half took the test on the beach. The results showed that the divers who took the test in the same place where they learned recalled 40 percent more than the divers who did their learning and testing in different places (Godden & Baddeley, 1975). This finding strongly suggests that the retrieval of information is improved if it takes place in the same place where learning occurs.

Other studies have shown that if students are exposed to a distinctive or unique aroma while they are studying (e.g., the smell of chocolate) and are exposed to that same smell again during a later memory test, they display better memory for the information they studied than do students who didn't study and take the test with the same aroma present (Schab, 1990). Perhaps one practical application of this finding is to wear a distinctive-smelling cologne or perfume while studying and use it again on the day of the test. This might improve your memory for the information you studied by matching the scent of your study environment with the scent of your test environment. Although this strategy may seem silly, keep in mind that the area of the human brain where smell is perceived has connections with the brain's memory pathways (Jensen, 1998). This may account for why people commonly report that certain smells can trigger memories of past experiences (e.g., the smell of a summer breeze triggering memories of summer games played during childhood). Thus, don't underestimate the sense of smell's potential for promoting memory.

9.2   DO IT **NOW**!

Nutritional Strategies for Strengthening Your Academic Performance

There is evidence that the following nutritional strategies can improve mental performance on days when our knowledge is tested:

1. **Eat breakfast on the day of the exam.** Numerous studies show that students who eat a nutritious breakfast on the day they are tested are more likely to achieve higher test scores than students who do not. Breakfast on the day of an exam should include grains, such as whole-wheat toast, whole-grain cereal, oatmeal, or bran, because those foods contain complex carbo-hydrates that will deliver a steady stream of energy to the body throughout the day; this should help sustain your test-taking endur-ance or stamina. Also, these complex carbohydrates should help your brain generate a steady stream of serotonin, which may reduce your level of nervous-ness or tension on test days.

   > "No man can be wise on an empty stomach."
   > —George Eliot, 19th-century English novelist

2. **Make the meal you eat before an exam a light meal.** You don't want to take tests while feeling hungry, but the meal you consume nearest test time should not be a large one. We tend to get sleepy after consuming a large meal because it elevates our blood sugar to such a high level that large amounts of insulin are released into the bloodstream in order to reduce our blood sugar level. This draws blood sugar away from the brain, which results in a feeling of mental fatigue.

3. **If you feel you need an energy boost immediately before an exam, eat a piece of fruit rather than a candy bar.** Candy bars are processed sweets that can offer a short burst of energy provided by synthetic sugar. Unfortunately, this short-term rise in blood sugar and quick jolt of energy are typically accom-panied by increased bodily tension followed by a sudden drop in energy and a feeling of sluggishness (Haas, 1994). The key is to find a food that can produce a state of elevated energy without elevating tension (Thayer, 1996) and maintains that state of energy at an even level. The best nutritional option for producing a sustained, steady state of energy is the natural sugar contained in a piece of fruit, not processed sugar that's artificially slipped into a candy bar.

4. **Avoid consuming caffeine before an exam.** Even though caffeine is a stimulant that increases alert-ness, it also qualifies as a legal drug that can signifi-cantly increase bodily tension and nervousness; these are feelings you don't want to experience during a test, particularly if you're prone to test anxiety. Also, caffeine is a diuretic, which means it will increase your urge to urinate. This is a distracting urge you certainly want to avoid during an exam when you're confined to a classroom for an extended period of time, sitting on your butt (and bladder).

Consuming large doses of caffeine or other stimulants before exams may increase your alert-ness, but may also increase your level of stress and test anxiety.

Strategies to Use during a Test

1. **Read the directions completely and look over the entire test.** It is important to read the instructions and understand what is being asked of you on the test. You should also look over the test in its entirety so you know what type of questions are being asked, how many questions there are, and approximately how much time you will need to complete the test.

2. **As soon as you receive a copy of the test, write down key information you need to remember.** In particular, write down any hard-to-remember terms, formulas, and equations and any memory retrieval cues you may have created as soon as you start the exam to ensure that you don't forget this information once you begin getting involved with answering specific test questions.

3. **Answer the easier test questions first.** As soon as you receive the test, before launching into answering the first question listed, check out the layout of the test. Note the questions that are worth the most points and the questions that you know well. You can do this by first surveying the test and putting a checkmark next to questions whose answers you're unsure of; come back to these questions later after you've answered the questions you're sure of, to ensure all their points are added into your final test score.

Think About It ——————————————— *Journal Entry* **9.3**

1. During tests, if I experience memory block, I usually . . .

    look at past questions, so on,
    and come back.

2. I am most likely to experience memory block in the following subject areas:

    Everything but common
    sense

---

4. **Prevent "memory block" from setting in.** If you tend to experience memory block for information that you know is stored in your brain, use the following strategies:

    - Mentally put yourself back in the environment or situation where you studied the information. Recreate the steps in which you learned the information that you've temporarily forgotten by mentally picturing the place where you first heard or saw it and where you studied it, including sights, sounds, smells, and time of day. This memory-improvement strategy is referred to as *guided retrieval*, and research supports its effectiveness for recalling information, including information recalled by eyewitnesses to a crime (Glenberg, 1997; Glenberg, Bradley, Kraus, & Renzaglia, 1983).

- Think of any idea or piece of information that may be related to the information you can't remember. Studies show that when students experience temporary forgetting, they're more likely to suddenly recall that information if they first recall a piece or portion of information that relates to it in some way (Reed, 1996). This related piece of information can trigger your memory for the forgotten information because related pieces of information are typically stored within the same neural network of cells in the brain.
- Take your mind off the question and turn to another question. This may allow your subconscious to focus on the forgotten information, which may trigger your conscious memory of it. Also, you may find some information included in the other questions that can help you remember an answer to a previous test question.
- Before turning in your test, carefully review and double-check your answers. This is the critical last step in the process of effective test taking. Sometimes the rush and anxiety of taking a test can cause test takers to overlook details, misread instructions, unintentionally skip questions, or make absentminded mistakes. When you're done, take time to look over your answers to be sure you didn't make any mindless mistakes. Avoid the temptation to immediately cut out because you're pooped out, or to take off on an ego trip by being among the first and fastest students in class to finish the test. Instead, take the full amount of test time available to you. When you think about the amount of time and effort you put into preparing for the exam, it's foolish not to take a little more time on the exam itself.

Strategies to Answer Multiple-Choice Questions

Multiple-choice questions are commonly used on college tests, on certification or licensing exams to practice in particular professions (e.g., nursing and teaching), and on admissions tests for graduate school (e.g., master's and doctoral degree programs) or professional school (e.g., law school and medical school). Since you're likely to encounter multiple-choice tests frequently in college and beyond, this section of the text is devoted to a detailed discussion of strategies for answering such test questions. These strategies are also applicable to true-false tests, which are really multiple-choice tests that involve two choices (true or false).

Think About It ——————————— Journal Entry 9.4

1. How would you rate your general level of test anxiety during most exams? (Circle one.)

    (high)   moderate   low

    Explain. _I need to pass it but I freak out_

2. What types of tests or subjects tend to produce the most test stress or test anxiety for you?

The really important ones.

Why?

High stakes. high price.

---

1. **Read the question and think of the answer in your head before looking at the answers.** If you do this and your answer is one of the options, there is a good chance that it is the correct answer.

2. **Read all choices listed and use a process-of-elimination approach.** You can find an answer by eliminating choices that are clearly wrong and continue to do so until you're left with one answer that is the most accurate option. Keep in mind that the correct answer is often the one that has the highest probability or likelihood of being true; it doesn't have to be absolutely true—just truer than the other choices listed.

3. **Use *test-wise* strategies when you don't know the correct answer.** Your first strategy on any multiple-choice question should be to choose an answer based on your knowledge of the material, rather than trying to outsmart the test or the test maker by guessing the correct answer based on how the question is worded. However, if you've relied on your knowledge and used the process-of-elimination strategy to eliminate clearly wrong choices but you're still left with two or more answers that appear to be correct, then you should turn to being *test wise*, which refers to your ability to use the characteristics of the test question itself (such as its wording or format) to increase your chances of selecting the correct answer (Flippo & Caverly, 2009). Listed here are three test-wise strategies for multiple-choice questions whose answers you don't know or can't remember:

   - **Pick an answer that contains qualifying words.** Look for words such as *usually, probably, likely, sometimes, perhaps,* or *may.* Knowledge often doesn't come neatly wrapped in the form of absolute truths, so choices that are stated as broad generalizations are more likely to be false. For example, answers containing words such as *always, never, only, must,* and *completely* are more likely to be false than true.

   - **Pick the longest answer.** True statements often require more words to make them true.

A *process-of-elimination* approach is an effective test-taking strategy to use when answering difficult multiple-choice questions.

- **Pick a middle answer rather than the first or last answer.** For example, on a question with four choices, if you've narrowed down the correct answer to a "b" or "c" versus an "a" or "d" choice, go with the "b" or "c" choice. Studies show that instructors have a tendency to place correct answers as middle choices rather than as the first or last choice (Linn & Gronlund, 1995), perhaps because they think the correct answer will be too obvious or stand out if it's listed at the beginning or end.

4. **Check to be sure that your answers are aligned with the right questions.** When looking over your test before turning it in, search carefully for questions you may have skipped and intended to go back to later. Sometimes you may skip a test question on a multiple-choice test and forget to skip the number of that question on the answer form, which will throw off all your other answers by one space or line. On a computer-scored test, this means that you may get multiple items marked wrong because your answers are misaligned, resulting in a "domino effect" of wrong answers, which can do major damage to your test score. As a damage-prevention measure, check all of your answers to be sure there are no blank lines or spaces on your answer sheet to set off this damaging domino effect.

5. **Don't feel that you must remain locked in to your first answer.** When checking your answers on multiple-choice and true-false tests, don't be afraid to change an answer after you've given it more thought. There have been numerous studies on the topic of changing answers on multiple-choice and true-false tests dating back to 1928 (Kuhn, 1988). These studies consistently show that most changed test answers go from being incorrect to correct, resulting in improved test scores (Bauer, Kopp, & Fischer, 2007; Benjamin, Cavell, & Shallenberger, 1984; Prinsell, Ramsey, & Ramsey, 1994). In one study of more than 1,500 students' midterm exams in an introductory psychology course, it was found that students who changed answers went from incorrect to correct 75 percent of the time (Kruger, Wirtz, & Miller, 2005). These findings probably reflect the fact that students often catch mistakes when they read the question again or when they find some information later in the test that causes them to reconsider their first answer.

Don't buy into the common belief that your first answer is always your best answer. If you have good reason to think a change should be made, don't be afraid to make it. The only exception to this general rule is when you find yourself changing many of your original answers; this is an indication that you were not well prepared for the exam and are just doing a lot of random second-guessing.

Think About It ——————————— *Journal Entry* 9.5

1. On exams, do you ever change your original answers?

    Yes. All the time.

2. If you do change answers, what's the usual reason you make changes?

    doubt.

Strategies for Answering Essay Questions

Along with multiple-choice questions, essay questions are among the most commonly used forms of questions on college exams. Listed below are strategies that will help you achieve peak levels of performance on essay questions.

1. **Focus on main ideas first.** Before you begin answering the question by writing full sentences, make a brief outline or list of bullet points to represent the main ideas you will include in your answers. Outlines are effective for several reasons:

    - **An outline helps you remember the major points.** It prevents you from becoming so wrapped up in the details of constructing sentences and choosing words for your answers that you lose the big picture and forget the most important points you need to make.
    - **An outline improves your answer's organization.** In addition to reminding you of the points you intend to make, an outline gives you a plan for sequencing your ideas in an order that ensures they flow smoothly. One factor that instructors consider when awarding points for an answer to an essay question is how well that answer is organized. An outline makes your answer's organization clearer by calling your attention to its major categories and subcategories.
    - **Having an advanced idea of what you will write reduces your test anxiety.** An outline takes care of the answer's organization beforehand so you don't have the added stress of worrying about how to organize your answer at the same time you're writing and explaining your answer.

- **An outline can add points to an incomplete answer's score.** If you run out of test time before writing out your full answer to an essay question, an outline allows your instructor to see what you planned to include in your written answer. Your outline itself is likely to earn you points because it demonstrates your knowledge of the major points called for by the question. In contrast, if you skip an outline and just start writing answers to test questions one at a time, you run the risk of not getting to questions you know well before your time is up; you'll then have nothing on your test to show what you know about those unfinished questions.

Exhibit 1

Identical twins

Parents/family tree

Adoption
6/6

No freewill

No afterlife

6/6

1. There are several different studies that scientists conduct, but one study that they conduct is to find out how genetics can influence human behavior in <u>identical twins</u>. Since they are identical, they will most likely end up very similar in behavior because of their identical genetic makeup. Although environment has some impact, genetics are still a huge factor and they will, more likely than not, behave similarly. Another type of study is with <u>parents and their family trees</u>. Looking at a subject's family tree will explain why a certain person is bipolar or depressed. It is most likely caused by a gene in the family tree, even if it was last seen decades ago. Lastly, another study is with adopted children. If an <u>adopted child</u> acts a certain way that is unique to that child, and researchers find the parents' family tree, they will most likely see similar behavior in the parents and siblings as well.

2. The monistic view of the mind-brain relationship is so strongly opposed and criticized because there is a belief or assumption that <u>free will</u> is taken away from people. For example, if a person commits a horrendous crime, it can be argued "monistically" that the chemicals in the brain were the reason, and that a person cannot think for themselves to act otherwise. This view limits responsibility.

Another reason that this view is opposed is because it has been said that <u>there is no afterlife</u>. If the mind and brain are one and the same, and there is <u>NO</u> difference, then once the brain is dead and is no longer functioning, so is the mind. Thus, it cannot continue to live beyond what we know today as life. <u>And</u> this goes against many religions, which is why this reason, in particular, is heavily opposed.

Written answers to two short essay questions given by a college sophomore, which demonstrate effective use of bulleted lists or short outlines (in the side margin) to ensure recall of most important points.

---

2. **Get directly to the point on each essay question.** Avoid elaborate introductions that take up your test time (and your instructor's grading time) but don't earn you any points. For example, an answer that begins with the statement "This is an interesting question that we had a great discussion on in class . . ." is pointless because it will not add points to your test score. The time available to you on essay tests is often limited, so you can't afford flowery introductions that waste valuable test time and don't contribute anything to the overall test score.

One effective way to get directly to the point on essay questions is to include part of the question in the first sentence of your answer. For example, suppose the test question asks you to "Argue for or against capital punishment by explaining how it will or will not reduce the nation's murder rate." Your first sentence could be "Capital punishment will not reduce the murder rate for the following reasons . . ." Thus, your first sentence becomes your thesis statement, which immediately points you directly to the major points you're going to make in your answer and earns immediate points for your answer.

3. **Answer all essay questions with as much detail as possible.** Don't assume that your instructor already knows what you're talking about or will be bored by details. Instead, take the approach that you're writing to someone who knows little or nothing about the subject—as if you're an expert teacher and the reader is a clueless student.

> **Remember**
> As a rule, it's better to over explain than under explain your answers to essay questions.

4. **Support your points with evidence—facts, statistics, quotes, or examples.** When taking essay tests, take on the role of a lawyer making a case by presenting concrete evidence (exhibit A, exhibit B, etc.). Since timed essay tests can often press you for time, be sure to prioritize and cite your most powerful points and persuasive evidence. If you have time later, you can return to add other points worth mentioning.

Do It Now! 9.3 contains thinking verbs that you're likely to see in college writing assignments and the types of mental action typically called for by each of these verbs. As you read the following list, make a short note after each mental action, indicating whether or not you've been asked to use such thinking on any assignments you completed before college.

9.3 DO IT NOW!

Ten Mental-Action Verbs Commonly Found in Essay-Test Questions

1. **Analyze.** Break the topic down into its key parts and evaluate the parts in terms of their accuracy, strengths, and weaknesses.
2. **Compare.** Identify the similarities and differences between major ideas.
3. **Contrast.** Identify the differences between ideas, particularly sharp differences and opposing viewpoints.
4. **Describe.** Provide details (e.g., who, what, where, and when).
5. **Discuss.** Analyze (break apart) and evaluate the parts (e.g., strengths and weaknesses).
6. **Document.** Support your judgment and conclusions with references or information sources.
7. **Explain.** Provide reasons that answer the questions "Why?" and "How?"
8. **Illustrate.** Supply concrete examples or specific instances.
9. **Interpret.** Draw your own conclusion about something, and explain why you came to that conclusion.
10. **Support.** Back up your ideas with research findings, factual evidence, or logical arguments.

"I keep six honest serving men. They taught me all I knew. Their names are what and why and how and when and where and who."

—Rudyard Kipling, "The Elephant's Child," *Just So Stories*

Think About It ———————————— *Journal Entry* **9.6**

1. Which of the mental actions in the list in Do It Now! 9.3 were most often required on your high school writing assignments?

   Contrast was the most required

2. Which were least often (or never) required?

   Document, interpret, illustrate.

5. **Leave space between your answers to essay questions.** This strategy will enable you to easily add information to your original answers if you have time or if you recall something later in the test that you forgot initially.

6. **Proofread your essay for spelling and grammar.** Before turning in your test, proofread what you've written and correct any obvious spelling or grammatical errors you find. Eliminating them is likely to improve your test score. Even if your instructor doesn't explicitly state that grammar and spelling will count in determining your grade, these mechanical mistakes are still likely to influence your professor's overall evaluation of your written work.

7. **Neatness counts.** Many years of research indicates that neatly written essays tend to be scored higher than sloppy ones, even if the answers are essentially the same (Huck & Bounds, 1972; Klein & Hart, 1968; Hughes et al., 1983; Pai et al., 2010). These findings are understandable when you consider that grading essay answers is a time-consuming task that requires your instructor to plod through multiple styles of handwriting whose readability may range from crystal-clear to cryptic. Make an earnest attempt to write as clearly as possible, and if you finish the test with time to spare, clean up your work by rewriting any sloppily written words or sentences.

Think About It ———————————— *Journal Entry* **9.7**

Rate yourself in terms of how frequently you use these test-taking strategies according to the following scale:

4 = always   3 = sometimes   2 = rarely   1 = never

1. I take tests in the same seat that I usually sit in to take class notes.	4	③ 2	1
2. I answer easier test questions first.	4	3	② 1

3. I use a process-of-elimination approach on multiple-choice tests to eliminate choices until I find one that is correct or appears to be the most accurate option. 4 ③ 2 1

4. On essay questions, I outline or map out my ideas before I begin to write the answer. 4 3 2 ①

5. I look for information included on the test that may help me answer difficult questions or that may help me remember information I've forgotten. ④ 3 2 1

6. I leave extra space between my answers to essay questions in case I want to come back and add more information later. 4 3 ② 1

7. I carefully review my work, double-checking for errors and skipped questions before turning in my tests. 4 ③ 2 1

How can you improve in the areas you scored the lowest?

By working onther. Make Buble Leave extra space, etc.

Strategies for Online Tests

More instructors are using technology to enhance their courses. It is very possible that you could have to take an online test even when you are not taking an online course. When taking a test online, you should always read the instructions carefully. Below are some things you should consider when taking online tests.

1. **Online tests are often timed.** Because you are taking these tests outside of class, you are able to use your notes and books. For this reason, many instructors will place a time limit on the test. If you do not complete the test in time, it will shut off when your time is up and you won't be able to do the rest of the test. Be sure to study for online timed tests. You will not have enough time to look up all of the answers, and if you don't study, you won't do well.
2. **Backtracking might be prohibited.** Sometimes you have to answer a question before you can move on to the next question, and once you move on, you cannot go back and change an answer. If this is a timed test, be sure to use your time wisely and don't spend too much time on any one question.

When taking online tests, be sure you are using a reliable computer and you are free from anything that could take your focus away from the test (i.e., cell phone, children, etc.). If something does go wrong during the test, be sure to contact your instructor immediately.

Post-Test Strategies: What to Do after Receiving Test Results

1. **Use your test results as feedback to improve your future performance.** Your test score is not just an end result: it can be used as a means to an end—a higher score on your next test performances and a higher course grade. When you get tests back, examine them carefully and be sure to note any written comments your instructor may have made. If your test results are disappointing, don't get bitter, get better. Use the results as feedback to diagnose where you went wrong so that you can avoid making the same mistakes again. If your test results were positive, see where you went right so you can do it right again.

2. **Seek additional feedback.** In addition to using your own test results as a source of feedback, ask for feedback from others whose judgment you trust and value. Three social resources you can use to obtain feedback on how to improve your performance are your instructors, professionals in your Learning or Academic Support Center, and your peers.

Make appointments with your instructors to visit them during office hours and get their feedback on how you might be able to improve your test performance. You'll likely find it easier to see your instructors after a test than before it, because most students don't realize that it's just as valuable to seek feedback from instructors following an exam as it is to get last-minute help before an exam.

Tutors and other learning support professionals on your campus can be excellent sources of feedback about what adjustments to make in your study habits or test-taking strategies to improve your future performance. Also, be alert and open to receiving feedback from trusted peers. While feedback from experienced professionals is valuable, don't overlook your peers as another source of information on how to improve your performance. You can review your test with other students in class, particularly with students who did exceptionally well. Their tests can provide you with models of what type of work your instructor expects on exams. You might also consider asking successful students what they did to be successful—for example, what they did to prepare for the test and what they did during the test.

Whatever you do, don't let a bad test grade get you mad, sad, or down, particularly if it occurs early in the course when you're still learning the rules of the game. Look at mistakes in terms of what they can do *for* you, rather than to you. A poor test performance can be turned into a valuable learning experience by using test results as a source of feedback and as an error detector to pinpoint the source of your mistakes. Look back at your mistakes so you can move forward and progress toward future success.

"When you make a mistake, there are only three things you should do about it: admit it; learn from it; and don't repeat it."

—Paul "Bear" Bryant, legendary college football coach

"Failure is not fatal, but failure to change might be."

—John Wooden, legendary college basketball coach

Remember

Your past mistakes should be neither ignored nor neglected: they should be detected and corrected so that you don't replay them on future tests.

Snapshot Summary

9.1   Key Features of Performance-Enhancing Feedback

When asking for feedback from others on your academic performance, seek feedback that is likely to improve your future performance. Effective performance-enhancing feedback has the following features:

- **Performance-enhancing feedback is** *specific*. It precisely identifies what you should do to improve your performance and how you should go about doing it. For example, after a test, seek feedback from your instructors that provides you with more than just information about what your grade is or why you lost points: seek specific information about what you could do to improve your performance next time.

- **Performance-enhancing feedback is** *prompt*. It comes soon after completing a task, because this is the time when you are most motivated to receive it and most likely to retain it. For example, as soon as possible after completing tests or assignments, review your performance with classmates or your professor.

- **Performance-enhancing feedback is** *proactive*. It comes early in the learning process when you still have plenty of time to use it to improve your performance. For example, seek feedback from instructors early in the term, so you have more time to use that feedback to improve your course performance and course grade.

Remember

Just as you learn before tests by preparing for your performance, you can learn after tests by reviewing your performance.

Strategies for Pinpointing the Source of Lost Points on Exams

On test questions where you lost points, identify the stage in the learning process where the breakdown occurred by asking yourself the following questions:

1. **Did you have the information you needed to answer the question correctly?** If you didn't have the information, what was the source of the missing information? Was it information presented in class that didn't get into your notes? If so, look at our strategies for improving listening and note-taking habits (see p. 222). If the missing information was contained in your assigned reading, check whether you're using effective reading strategies (see p. 227).

2. **Did you have the information but not study it because you didn't think it was important?** If you didn't realize the information would be on the test, review the study strategies for finding and focusing on the most important information in class lectures and reading assignments (see p. 224).

3. **Did you study it, but not retain it?** Not remembering information you studied may mean one of three things:

   - You didn't store the information adequately in your brain, so your memory trace wasn't strong enough to recall. This suggests that more study time needs to be spent on recitation or rehearsal (see p. 256).

   - You may have tried to cram in too much information in too little time just before the exam and may have not given your brain time enough to "digest" (consolidate) it and store it in long-term memory. The solution would be to distribute your study time more evenly in advance of the next exam and take advantage of the part-to-whole study method (see p. 238).

   - You put in enough study time and you didn't cram, but you didn't study effectively or strategically. For example, you may have studied for essay questions by just reading over your class notes and reading highlights rather than rehearsing and reciting them. The solution would be to adjust your study strategy so that it better matches or aligns with the type of test you're taking (see p. 256).

4. **Did you study the material but not really understand it or learn it deeply?** This suggests you may need to self-monitor your comprehension more carefully while studying to track whether you truly understand the material at a deeper level (see p. 246).

5. **Did you know the information but find yourself unable to retrieve it during the exam?** If you had the information on the "tip of your tongue" during the exam, this indicates that you did retain it and it was stored (saved) in your brain, but you couldn't get at it and get it out (retrieve it) when you needed it. This error may be corrected by making better use of memory retrieval cues (see p. 257).

6. **Did you know the answer but just make a careless test-taking mistake?** If your mistake was careless, the solution may be simply to take more time to review your test once you've completed it and check for absentminded errors before turning it in (see p. 264). Or, your careless errors may be the result of test anxiety that's interfering with your ability to concentrate during exams.

Strategies for Reducing Test Anxiety

1. **Understand what test anxiety is and what it's not.** Don't confuse anxiety with stress. Stress is a physical reaction that prepares your body for action by arousing and energizing it; this heightened arousal and energy can be used productively to strengthen your performance. In fact, if you're totally stress-free during an exam, it may mean that you're too "laid back" and couldn't care less about how well you're doing. Stress is something that cannot and should not be completely eliminated when you're trying to reach peak levels of performance, whether academic or athletic. Instead of trying to block out stress altogether, your goal should be to control it, contain it, and maintain it at a level that maximizes the quality of your performance. The key is to keep stress at a moderate level, thereby capitalizing on its capacity to help you get psyched up or pumped up, but preventing it from reaching such a high level that you become psyched out or stressed out.

   If you experience the following symptoms during tests, your stress level may be high enough to be accurately called test anxiety:

   - You feel physical symptoms of tension during the test, such as pounding heartbeat, rapid pulse, muscle tension, sweating, or an upset stomach.
   - Negative thoughts and feelings rush through your head—for example, fear of failure or self-defeating putdowns such as "I always mess up on exams."
   - You rush through the test just to get it over with (probably because you want to get rid of the anxiety you're experiencing).
   - You have difficulty concentrating or focusing your attention while answering test questions.
   - Even though you studied and know the material, you go blank during the exam and forget what you studied. (However, you're able to remember the information after you turn in your test and leave the test situation.)

To minimize test anxiety, consider the following practices and strategies:

2. **Avoid cramming for exams.** Research indicates that college students who display greater amounts of procrastination experience higher levels of test anxiety (Rothblum, Solomon, & Murakami, 1986). High levels of pre-test tension associated with rushing and late-night cramming are likely to carry over to the test itself, resulting in higher levels of test-taking tension. Furthermore, loss of sleep caused by previous-night cramming results in lost dream (REM) sleep, which, in turn, elevates anxiety levels the following day—test day.

3. **Use effective test-preparation strategies prior to the exam.** Test-anxiety research indicates that college students who prepare well for exams not only achieve higher test scores, but also experience lower levels of test anxiety (Zohar, 1998). Other research findings demonstrate that using effective study strategies prior to the exam, such as those discussed in Chapter 8, reduces test anxiety during the exam (Benjamin, McKeachie, Lin, & Holinger, 1981; Jones & Petruzzi, 1995; Zeidner, 1995)

4. **During the exam, concentrate on the here and now.** Devote your attention fully to answering the test question that you're currently working on; don't spend time thinking (and worrying) about the test's outcome and what your grade will be.

5. **Stay focused on the test in front of you, not the students around you.** Don't spend valuable test time looking at what others are doing and wondering whether they're doing better than you are. If you came to the test well prepared and still find the test difficult, it's very likely that other students are finding it difficult too. If you happen to notice that other students are finishing before you do, don't assume that they breezed through the test or that they're smarter than you. Their faster finish may simply reflect the fact that they didn't know many of the answers and decided to give up and get out, rather than prolong the agony.

6. **Don't spend a lot of time focusing on the amount of time left in the exam.** Repeatedly checking the time during the test can disrupt the flow of your thought process and increase your stress level. Although it's important that you remain aware of how much time remains to complete the exam, only check the time periodically, and do your time-checking after you've completed answering a question so you don't disrupt or derail your train of thought.

7. **Control your thoughts by focusing on what you're getting right, rather than worrying about what answers you don't know and how many points you're losing.** Our thoughts influence our emotions (Ellis, 1995), and positive emotions, such as those associated with optimism and a sense of accomplishment, can improve mental performance by enhancing the brain's ability to process, store, and retrieve information (Rosenfield, 1988). Keep in mind that college exams are often designed to be more difficult than high school tests, so it's less likely that students will get 90 to 100 percent of the total points. You can still achieve a good grade on a college test without having to achieve a near-perfect test score.

8. **Remember that if you're experiencing a *moderate* amount of stress during the exam, this isn't abnormal or an indication that you're suffering from test anxiety.** If you're experiencing moderate levels of tension, it indicates that you're motivated and want to do well. In fact, research shows that experiencing *moderate* levels of tension during tests and other performance-evaluation situations serves to maximize alertness, concentration, and memory (Sapolsky, 2004).

9. **Don't forget that it's just a test: it's not a measure of your ability or character.** An exam is not a measure of your overall intelligence, your overall academic ability, or your quality as a person. In fact, a test grade may be less of an indication of your effort or ability than the level of complexity of the particular content covered by the test material or the nature of the test itself. Furthermore, one low grade on one particular test doesn't mean you're not capable of doing good work and are going to end up with a poor grade in the course, particularly if you use the results as feedback to improve your next test performance (see pp. 270–271).

One final note on the topic of test anxiety: if you continue to experience test anxiety after implementing the above strategies, don't hesitate to seek assistance from a professional in your Learning (Academic Support) Center or Personal Counseling Office.

Summary and Conclusion

Improving performance on college exams involves strategies used in advance of the test, during the test, and after test results are returned. Good test performance begins with good test preparation and adjustment of your study strategy to the type of test you'll be taking (e.g., multiple-choice or essay test).

You can learn and improve your grades not only by preparing for tests but also by reviewing your tests and using them as feedback to apply as you continue in the course. Past mistakes shouldn't be ignored or neglected; they should be detected and corrected so that they're not replayed on future tests.

Learning More through the World Wide Web
Internet-Based Resources for Further Information on Test-Taking Skills

For additional information related to ideas discussed in this chapter, we recommend the following Web sites:

Test-Taking Strategies:

www.muskingum.edu/~cal/database/general/testtaking.html

web.mit.edu/arc/learning/modules/test/testtypes.html

Overcoming Test Anxiety:

www.studygs.net/tstprp8.htm

www.swccd.edu/~asc/lrnglinks/test_anxiety.html

9.1 Midterm Self-Evaluation

Since you are near the midpoint of this textbook, you may be near the midpoint of your first term in college. At this time of the term you are likely to experience the midterm crunch—a wave of midterm exams and due dates for certain papers and projects. This may be a good time to step back and assess your academic progress thus far.

Use the form that follows to list the courses you're taking this term and the grades you are currently receiving in each of these courses. If you do not know what your grade is, take a few minutes to check your syllabus for your instructor's grading policy and add up your scores on completed tests and assignments; this should give you at least a rough idea of where you stand in your courses. If you're having difficulty determining your grade in any course, even after checking your course syllabus and returned tests or assignments, then ask your instructor how you could estimate your current grade.

Course No.	Course Title	Instructor	Grade
1.	College Success	Jeffers	A
2.	English	Shauman	C
3.	Child development	?	B
4.			
5.			

Self-Assessment Questions

1. Were these the grades you were hoping for? Are you pleased or disappointed by them? All A's and no.

2. Were these the grades you expected to get? If not, were they better or worse than expected? Not that Bad.

3. Do you see any patterns in your performance that suggest things you are doing well or things that you need to improve? Yes.

4. If you had to pinpoint one action you could immediately take to improve your lowest course grades, what would it be? Study harder.

9.2 Calculating Your Midterm Grade Point Average

Use the information in Snapshot Summary 9.2 to calculate what your grade point average (GPA) will be if these grades turn out to be your final course grades for the term.

9.2 How to Compute Your Grade Point Average (GPA)

Most colleges and universities use a grading scale that ranges from 0 to 4.0 to calculate a student's grade point average (GPA) or quality point average (QPA). Some schools use letter grades only, while other institutions use letter grades with pluses and minuses.

Grading System Using Letters Only

Grade = Point value

A = 4
B = 3
C = 2
D = 1
F = 0

GRADE POINTS Earned Per Course = Course Grade Multiplied by the Number of Course Credits (Units)

$$\text{GRADE POINT AVERAGE (GPA)} = \frac{\text{Total Number of Grade Points for All Courses}}{\text{Divided by Total Number of Course Units}}$$

SAMPLE/EXAMPLE

Course	Units	×	Grade	=	Grade Points
Roots of Rock 'n' Roll	3	×	C (2)	=	6
Daydreaming Analysis	3	×	A (4)	=	12
Surfing Strategies	1	×	A (4)	=	4
Wilderness Survival	4	×	B (3)	=	12
Sitcom Analysis	2	×	D (1)	=	2
Love and Romance	3	×	A (4)	=	12
	16				**48**

$$\text{GPA} = \frac{48}{16} = 3.0$$

1. What is your overall GPA at this point in the term?

2. At the start of this term, what GPA were you hoping to attain?

3. Do you think your actual GPA at the end of the term will be higher or lower than it is now? Why?

Notes: It's normal for GPAs to be lower in college than they were in high school, particularly during the first year of college. Here are the results of one study that compared students' high school GPAs with the GPAs after their first year of college:

- 29 percent of beginning college students had GPAs of 3.75 or higher in high school, but only 17 percent had GPAs that high at the end of their first year of college.
- 46 percent had high school GPAs between 3.25 and 3.74, but only 32 percent had GPAs that high after the first year of college (National Resource Center for the First-Year Experience and Students in Transition, 2004).

9.3 Preparing an Oral Presentation on Student Success

1. Scan this textbook and identify a chapter topic or chapter section that you find most interesting or think is most important to you.

2. Create an introduction for a class presentation on this topic that:
    a. provides an overview or sneak preview of what you will cover in your presentation;
    b. grabs the attention of your audience (your classmates); and
    c. demonstrates the topic's relevance or importance for your audience.

3. Create a conclusion to your presentation that:
    a. relates back to your introduction;
    b. highlights your most important point or points; and
    c. leaves a memorable last impression.

Bad Feedback: Shocking Midterm Grades

Joe Frosh has enjoyed his first weeks on campus. He has met lots of interesting people and feels that he fits in socially. He's also very pleased to discover that his college schedule doesn't require him to be in class for five to six hours per day, like it did in high school. This is the good news. The bad news is that unlike high school, where his grades were all As and Bs, his first midterm grades in college are three Cs, one D, and one F. He's stunned and a bit depressed by his midterm grades because he thought he was doing well. Since he never received grades this low in high school, he's beginning to think that he's not college material and may flunk out.

Discussion Questions

1. What factors may have caused or contributed to Joe's bad start?

    Talking to so that people and having extra time.

2. What are Joe's options at this point?

    Try harder.

3. What do you recommend Joe do right now to get his grades up and avoid being placed on academic probation?

    Focus on school.

4. What might Joe do in the future to prevent this midterm setback from happening again?

    Focus on school then his life.

Chapter 9 Reflection

What are some ways that you currently prepare for tests that do not seem to be working? Why do you think these methods of preparing for tests do not work?

Note cards. I do better without them.

List and explain three ways you can change your current methods of preparing for tests that you believe will help you perform better on tests.

1. Notes

2. Study over and over

3. talk outcaud

What are two things you can do during the test that will help you perform better?

1. talk out loud

2. thinking back

What are two things you can do after you get your test back that can help you perform better on future tests?

1. Look over the low points

2. try a new learning way.

Welcome to Macomb Community College!

My name is Carl Seitz. I serve as the Director of the Public Service Institute, where I am responsible for all education and training in the area of law enforcement, fire-fighting, EMS, and Homeland Security. I came to work at Macomb after a 31 year fire service career that eventually led to becoming chief of my department. The field of public safety is a career that I have absolutely loved, and it all began many years ago right here at Macomb Community College.

As has been the case for many public safety professionals, Macomb prepared me well for my career field. It is where I attended the academy and where I received my first degree. It is where I learned to think critically and to develop the problem solving skills that would serve me for many years to come, While I did not fully realize it at the time, my success at Macomb was the result of an entire community of people who wanted to see me succeed. Some of them were the instructors and professors who taught the classes that I attended; but, many were support staff who were always willing to help. I remember the librarian who spent countless hours teaching me the value of good solid research, the tutor who took the time to discover my learning style, and the counselor who put me at ease when I decided to transfer to a university for another degree. Like any journey worth taking, there are stumbling blocks along the way. There are, however, always resources that are available to help overcome difficulties if you just take the time to ask.

None of us are capable of succeeding on our own. There is an entire community of people here for you as well, and we all want to see you succeed. What endeared me to the field of public safety was the ability to make a difference in the lives of people. It is this same privilege that has endeared me to Macomb Community College. As T. S. Eliot once wrote, "... *and the end of all our exploring will be to arrive where we started and know the place for the first time.*"

I am Carl Seitz and I am Macomb!

Courtesy of Carl Seitz

Educational and Career Planning and Decision Making

10

Making Wise Choices about Your Courses, Major, Degree, and Career Plans

LEARNING GOAL

To develop strategies for exploring different academic fields and for choosing an educational path that will enable you to achieve your personal and career goals.

1. Are you decided or undecided about a college major?

   Undecided

2. If you are undecided, list any subjects that might be possibilities:

   Cosmotology
   Hair

3. If you are decided, what is your choice and why did you choose this major?

   Because I love it

4. Indicate how sure you are about that choice by circling one of the following options:

   absolutely sure   fairly sure   not too sure   likely to change

   Why?

   I have known for awhile

The Importance of Long-Range Educational Planning

College will allow you many choices about what courses to enroll in and what field to specialize in. By looking ahead and developing a tentative plan for your courses beyond the first term of college, you will position yourself to view your college experience as a full-length movie and get a sneak preview of the total picture. In contrast, scheduling your classes one term at a time just before each registration period (when everyone else is making a mad rush to get their advisor's signature for the following term's classes) forces you to view your academic experience as a series of short, separate snapshots that lack connection or direction.

Long-range educational planning also enables you to take a proactive approach to your future. Being proactive means you are taking early, preventative action that anticipates events before they sneak up on you and force you to react without time to

"When you have to make a choice and don't make it, that is in itself a choice."

—William James, philosopher and one of the founders of American psychology

"Education is our passport to the future; for tomorrow belongs to the people who prepare for it today."

—Malcolm X, African American civil rights leader

Don't take the denial and avoidance approach to planning your educational future.

plan your best strategy. As the old saying goes, "If you fail to plan, you plan to fail." Through advanced planning, you can actively take charge of your academic future and make it happen *for* you, rather than waiting and passively letting it happen *to* you.

Remember

Any long-range plan you develop is not set in stone: it can change depending on changes in your academic interests and future plans. The purpose of long-range planning is not to lock you into a particular plan but to free you from shortsightedness, procrastination, or denial about choosing to take charge of your life.

Think About It ——————————   *Journal Entry* **10.2**

Choosing a major is a life-changing decision because it will determine what you do for the rest of your life. Would you agree or disagree with this statement? Why?

No because you can always change it.

One important element of long-range educational planning is deciding whether you're going to continue your education beyond your community college experience by transferring to a four-year college or university and when you plan to make that transition. Some community college students plan to transfer to a four-year college before completing their associate degree at their community college. However, we strongly recommend that you complete your general education program before attempting to transfer, because multiple advantages are associated with completing 60 or more units at a two-year college and attaining an associate degree. These advantages are listed in the next section.

Advantages of Completing an Associate Degree before Transferring to a Four-Year College or University

1. **You will acquire a college degree before completing a bachelor's degree.** Regardless of whether you receive academic or cocurricular distinctions and awards, completion of an associate degree is an achievement in itself for two reasons:

   - It indicates that you have survived the two most critical years of the college experience. Research shows that almost 75 percent of those students who withdraw from college do so during the freshman and sophomore years (American College Testing, 2009). The associate degree is evidence to four-year colleges and future employers that you have persisted through, and completed, these two critical years.
   - The associate degree signifies that you have successfully completed the general education component of the college experience. In some ways, this is the most important component of the college experience because it represents the acquisition of breadth of knowledge and the development of essential learning skills (e.g., written and oral communication). Surveys indicate that employers look for and value these skills the most in their employees (National Association of Colleges & Employers, 2003).

   Having your associate degree after your sophomore year will also improve your job prospects during your junior and senior years of college (e.g., your chances of obtaining an internship, part-time employment during the academic year, or full-time employment during the summers between your sophomore and your junior years and between your junior and your senior years). In addition, those with an associate degree, on average, earn more than $13,000 more per year than individuals with a high school diploma (College Board, 2008). Thus, the two-year degree should not only increase your chances of being hired, but also increase the amount of pay you receive. Furthermore, this vocational advantage of earning an associate degree will be particularly important if, for some reason, you're unable to complete the bachelor's (or baccalaureate) degree or if you have to postpone its completion.

2. **You will complete general education requirements, basic skills courses, and premajor requirements before transferring.** Completing an associate degree will enable you to finish up general education requirements and skill-building courses (e.g., writing and math) in smaller classes where you are likely to receive more individual attention and more personalized feedback and academic support from instructors. Thus, you will have a broader base of knowledge and a more highly developed set of academic skills before transferring. Studies show that students who transfer to four-year institutions after completing just one year at a two-year college have a greater "dip" or drop in grade point average (GPA) than students who transfer after two years (Cuseo, 2003a; Diaz, 1992). The bigger drop in GPA for early transfers may also be due to greater culture shock ex-

perienced by students who transfer after one year because they enter four-year institutions neither as freshmen nor as juniors—the two years when most other students enter four-year colleges. Sophomore-year transfers begin their four-year college experience as interlopers or "betweeners." This can make it difficult for sophomore transfers to fit into the student culture because they have fewer peers entering with them and because orientation activities are more likely to be geared toward entering freshmen and junior transfers.

3. **You will have extra time and advisement for deciding on an academic major and a four-year college.** For students who are not sure about what their particular major will be or what particular four-year institution they should transfer to, returning to their community college for the sophomore year will provide an additional year of time and advisor contact that can be used to reach both of these important decisions. Making these two decisions is a complex and interrelated process. What major you eventually decide on may influence what college you should attend. Some academic majors may not be offered at all colleges, and the nature and quality of the same major may vary from one college to another. For example, the psychology major at College X may require different courses and have a different career-preparation emphasis than the psychology major at college Y. Also, transfer students may report different levels of satisfaction with the psychology program and the professors in the psychology department at College X than they do at College Y.

Since so many of the courses you will be taking during your last two years of college will be courses in your major, when you choose a four-year college for transfer, you're also choosing the particular department within the college that houses your particular major. Your second year at a community college can supply you with the time needed to finalize your decision about what major to declare and to consult with a network of advisors concerning what four-year colleges would be best for your particular major and your future career goals.

4. **You may have a higher college GPA at the end of your sophomore year.** It's likely that your GPA will be higher after your sophomore year at your community college than it is after your freshman year because you've made the critical first-year adjustment and have gained greater experience with the system. A higher GPA when you transfer will increase the likelihood that you will be accepted, particularly if you're applying for admission into "impacted" majors (i.e., majors that are competitive and hard to get into because they are overcrowded). It also increases your likelihood of getting a transfer scholarship when you transfer to your four-year institution.

5. **There will be less emphasis on high school grades and SAT or ACT scores by four-year colleges.** Four-year colleges and universities are less likely to place less emphasis on high school grades and SAT or ACT scores when reviewing the applications of students who've completed two full years of college than they are for students who are attempt to transfer earlier. Some four-year campuses require SAT or ACT scores for high school seniors and for students attempting to transfer after one year of college, but will not require SAT or ACT scores from transfer students who have completed two full years of college and hold an associate degree.

6. **You will have more opportunity to receive academic recognition and awards before transferring.** If you're doing well academically during your first year at your community college, returning for the sophomore year will enable you to enter the community college's honors program, take honors courses, and become

a member of the National Collegiate Honors Council and Phi Theta Kappa—an international honor society for two-year college students. If you then complete your associate degree at a community college, you become eligible for academic honors at graduation, such as graduating magna cum laude (with high distinction) or summa cum laude (with highest distinction). These awards can increase your prospects for acceptance at four-year colleges, as well as your chances for scholarships and other types of merit-based financial aid that are earmarked for junior-transfer students. These academic achievements will be listed on your transcript and will provide you with a distinctive advantage for acceptance at four-year schools, as well as increase your eligibility for entry into their honors programs. Furthermore, these accomplishments will remain on your permanent college record after you graduate with a four-year (bachelor's) degree, which should increase your job prospects after graduation and your chances for acceptance at graduate schools (e.g., to pursue a master's or doctoral degree) and professional schools (e.g., to pursue a law or medical degree).

7. **You will have opportunities and recognition for leadership activities before transferring.** If you are a first-year college student with leadership potential, or if you are committed to developing your leadership skills, you may become eligible for various resume- and character-building leadership opportunities during your sophomore year at a community college (e.g., peer tutoring or peer mentoring). At four-year colleges, sophomores are often unable to assume these leadership positions because they may be reserved for more experienced upper-division students (juniors and seniors). At your community college, you can get these experiences as a sophomore and use them to: (1) increase your chances of acceptance at four-year colleges, (2) qualify for similar leadership positions at the four-year college to which you transfer, and (3) enhance your job prospects during your last two years of college and after you complete your bachelor's degree.

8. **You will have a chance to participate in a graduation ceremony after completing the associate degree program.** Completion of an associate degree will also enable you to participate in your community college's graduation ceremony. The significance of this celebratory event should not be underestimated. This is an opportunity for you to be recognized publicly, in front of family, friends, faculty, and fellow students, for your completion of general education and for any academic and cocurricular awards you achieved along the way.

Research indicates that student involvement in college rituals or ceremonial events (such as graduation) reinforces students' motivation and commitment to continue their education and promotes their ability to persist or persevere until achieving their final degree objective (Kuh et al., 1991, 2005). Thus, participation in your community college's graduation ceremony may not only celebrate your attainment of the associate degree, but also strengthen or stimulate your drive to achieve a bachelor's degree.

Proof of the power of the graduation experience is illustrated in the following excerpt of a letter written by a student who graduated from a two-year college and transferred to a four-year campus to complete her bachelor's degree.

> *I graduated with my associate degree [several years ago] and I just wanted to get in touch and let you know how I am doing. I successfully graduated from USF [University of San Francisco] in 4 years (including the 2 before I transferred). During the graduation ceremony after my sophomore year, I saw some fellow students wearing the yellow shawl that represented walking with honors. I thought to myself, "I am going to walk with honors when I get my B.A." And that I did!*

Who would have ever thought? [Now] I have decided that I want to go to graduate school.

—*Letter from a two-year college graduate received by Joe Cuseo*

Snapshot Summary

10.1 Tips for Students Transferring to Four-Year Colleges and Universities

The following criteria are those that most likely will be used by four-year colleges to evaluate your application and decide on your acceptance:

- **Academic record.** Colleges will look at your overall GPA and grades for courses in your chosen major.
- **Out-of-class experiences.** For example, your involvement in leadership activities and volunteer experience in the community or on campus can play a role in your acceptance to a four-year college.
- **Letters of recommendation.** Letters can come, for example, from course instructors and academic advisors. Provide the following courtesies for those you ask to write letters of recommendation for you:
  - A *fact sheet* about yourself that will enable them to cite concrete examples or evidence of your achievements and contributions (which will make the letter more powerful)
  - Give the person at least two weeks' notice.
  - A *stamped, addressed* envelope (a personal courtesy that makes the job a little easier for your reference)
  - A *thank-you note* close to the date that the letter is due (not only a nice thing to do but also a reminder in case the person has forgotten about your letter or has not yet set aside time to write it)
- **Personal statement.** In your letter of application for admission, which you write

when applying to a school, try to demonstrate your knowledge of:

- *yourself* (e.g., your personal interests, abilities, and values);
- your intended *major* (e.g., why you're interested in it and what you might do with it after graduation); and
- the *college* to which you're applying by showing that you know something specific about the school (e.g., its mission, philosophy, and programs—especially the particular program to which you're applying).

To maximize your success at four-year colleges and universities, take the initiative to connect with people who can contribute to your success, including the following:

- **Faculty.** Make sure they know who you are (e.g., sit in front of class, come up to speak with them after class, visit them in their offices, or volunteer to help them with research they're doing that you find interesting or relevant to your career interests).
- **Students in your major.** Connect with them in study groups and major clubs (psychology club, history club, etc.).
- **Career development specialists.** Connect with these professionals on strategies for enhancing your marketability after graduation. Ask them about what graduates (alumni) with your major have gone on to do and whether they can connect you with an alum in a career that you intend to pursue.

To Be or Not to Be Decided about a College Major: What the Research Shows

Studies of student decisions about a college major show that:

- Less than 10 percent of new college students feel they know a great deal about the fields that they intend to major in.
- As students proceed through the first year of college, they grow more uncertain about the majors they chose when they began college.
- More than two-thirds of new students change their minds about their majors during the first year of college.

Snapshot Summary

10.2 A Checklist of Course-Registration Reminders for Community College Students

Achieving your educational goals requires both long- and short-range planning. Your long-range plan involves completing your degree, and your short-range plan involves continuing your enrollment in college from term to term. When planning to register for the next academic term, keep the following list of reminders handy to ensure that your term-to-term transition proceeds smoothly.

- Check the registration dates and be prepared to register at the earliest date that's available to you.
- Check with an academic advisor to be sure that you're planning to take the right classes for your program, major, and any four-year school you plan to transfer to.
- Let your advisor know what your educational goals are and if you've changed your goals since the last time you registered.
- Let your advisor know the total number of hours per week you plan to work so that you create a schedule that will allow you to successfully balance schoolwork and for-pay work.

- If you're receiving financial aid, meet with a financial aid counselor or advisor to be sure that you have adequate funds to cover next term's tuition, book costs, and parking fees.
- Once you've registered, periodically check the status of your courses because last-minute changes can occur in the time and day when courses meet and it's possible that one of your courses might be canceled (e.g., due to insufficient enrollment).

Remember

Unlike in high school, summer school in college isn't something you do to make up for courses that were failed or should have been taken during the "regular" school year (fall and spring terms). Instead, it's an additional term that you can use to make further progress toward your college degree and reduce the total time it takes to complete your degree.

- Only one in three college seniors eventually major in the same fields that they chose during their first year of college (Cuseo, 2005).

These findings demonstrate that the vast majority of students entering college are not certain about their college majors. Many students don't reach their final decision about a major *before* starting their college experience; instead, they make that decision *during* their college experience. Being uncertain about a major is nothing to be embarrassed about. Being "undecided" or "undeclared" doesn't mean that you're irresponsible, clueless, or lost. Beginning college students may be undecided for very good reasons. For instance, you may be undecided simply because you have interests in various subjects; this is a healthy form of indecision because it shows that you have a range of interests and a high level of motivation to learn about different subjects. You may also be undecided simply because you're a careful, reflective thinker whose decision-making style is to gather more information before making a firm and final commitment.

In one study of students who were undecided about a major at the start of college, 43 percent had several ideas in mind but were not yet ready to commit to one of them (Gordon & Steele, 2003). These students were not clueless or lacking direction; they had some ideas but still wanted to explore them and keep their options open, which is an effective way to go about making decisions.

As a first-year student, it's only natural to be at least somewhat uncertain about your educational goals because you haven't yet experienced the variety of subjects and academic programs that make up the college curriculum, some of which you didn't know existed. In fact, one purpose of general education courses is to help new

"Not all who wander are lost."

—J. R. R. Tolkien, *The Lord of the Rings*

students develop the critical thinking skills needed to make wise choices and well-informed decisions, such as their choice of a college major.

Similarly, changing your original educational plans is not necessarily a bad thing. It may mean that you have discovered another field that's more interesting to you or that's more compatible with your personal interests and talents. It's OK to start off not knowing what your major will be or whether you want to pursue a four-year degree or a shorter-range educational goal, such as an associate degree or vocational-technical certificate. You still have time to make up your mind and to change your mind. Don't think that you must lock yourself into a particular plan and must either stick with it or drop out of college if your plans change. You can take courses that will count toward graduation, regardless of what major or educational track you end up taking.

Changing your educational plan has one downside: if you make that change late in your college experience, it can result in more time to graduation (and more tuition) because you may need to complete additional courses required for your newly chosen field.

"When you get to a fork in the road, take it."

—Yogi Berra, Hall of Fame baseball player

> I've decided to change my major.
>
> HAHAH HAH HA

Remember

As a rule, you should reach a fairly firm decision about your major during your second (sophomore) year in college. However, to reach a good decision within this time frame, the process of exploring and planning should begin now—during your first term in college.

Think About It ———   *Journal Entry* **10.3**

If you've already chosen a major or specialized program, what led you to this choice?

My Dad made me.

_____

_____

_____

_____

Myths about the Relationship between Majors and Careers

Good decisions are based not on misconceptions or myths, but on accurate information. Effective planning for a college major requires accurate information about the relationship between majors and careers. Unfortunately, several popular myths about the relationship between majors and careers can lead to uninformed or unrealistic choices of a college major.

Myth 1. When you choose your major, you're choosing your career. While some majors lead directly to a particular career, most do not. Majors leading directly to specific careers are called preprofessional or prevocational majors, and they include such fields as accounting, engineering, and nursing. However, most college majors don't channel you directly down one particular career path: they leave you with various career options. All physics majors don't become physicists, all philosophy majors don't become philosophers, all history majors do not become historians, and all English majors do not become Englishmen (or Englishwomen). The career paths of most college graduates are not straight lines that run directly from their majors to their careers. The trip from college to career or careers is more like climbing a tree. As illustrated in Figure 10.1, you begin with the tree's trunk—the foundation of general education (courses required of all college students, whatever their major may be)—which grows into separate limbs (different college majors) that, in turn, lead to different branches (different career paths or options).

FIGURE 10.1

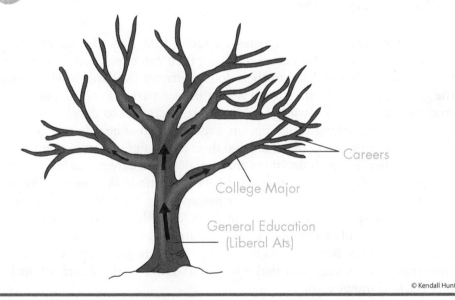

© Kendall Hunt

The Relationship between General Education (Liberal Arts), College Majors, and Careers

Note that the career branches grow from the same limb. Likewise, the same major leads to a "family" of related careers. For example, an English major often leads to careers that involve use of the written language (e.g., editing, journalism, and publishing), while a major in art leads to careers that involve use of visual media (e.g., illustration, graphic design, and art therapy). (Note that the Web site www.mymajors.com provides useful and free information on groups or families of jobs that tend to be related to different majors.)

Also, different majors can lead to the same career. For instance, many majors can lead a student to law school and to an eventual career as a lawyer; there is no undergraduate major in law or prelaw. Similarly, premed isn't a major. Although most students interested in going to medical school after college major in some field in the natural sciences (e.g., biology or chemistry), it's possible for students to go to medical school with majors in other fields, particularly if they take and do well in certain science courses that are emphasized in medical school (e.g., general biology, general chemistry, and organic and inorganic chemistry).

Thus, don't presume that your major is your career or that your major automatically turns into your career. This is one reason some students procrastinate about choosing a major; they think they are making a lifelong decision and fear that if they make the "wrong" choice they'll be stuck doing something they hate for the rest of their lives. The belief that your major becomes your career may also account for 58 percent of college graduates choosing to major in a preprofessional or prevocational field such as nursing, accounting, or engineering (Association of American Colleges & Universities, 2007). These majors have careers obviously connected to them, which reassures students (and their family members) that they will have jobs after graduation. However, although students in prevocational majors may be more likely to be hired immediately after graduation, tracking college graduates with other college majors has shown that six months after graduation they too have jobs; thus, they are not more likely to be unemployed (Pascarella & Terenzini, 2005).

Remember

Don't assume that choosing your college major means you're choosing what you'll be doing for as long as you'll be living.

Research on college graduates indicates that they change careers numerous times, and the further they continue along their career paths, the more likely they are to work in fields unrelated to their college majors (Millard, 2004). Remember that the general education curriculum is a significant part of a college education. It allows students to acquire knowledge in diverse subjects and to develop durable, transferable skills (e.g., writing, speaking, and organizing) that qualify college graduates for a diversity of careers, regardless of what their particular majors happened to be.

The order in which decisions about majors and careers are covered in this book reflects the order in which they are likely to be made in your life. For most college majors, students first decide on their majors; later, they decide on their careers. Although it is important to think about the relationship between your choice of major and your choice of career or careers, these are different choices that are usually made at different times. Both choices relate to your future goals, but they involve different time frames: choosing your major is a short-range goal, whereas choosing your career is a long-range goal.

Remember

Choosing a major and choosing a career are not always the same decision: they are often separate decisions that don't have to be made at the same time.

Myth 2. After a bachelor's degree, any further education must be in the same field as your college major. After college graduation, you have two main options or alternative paths available to you:

1. You can enter a career immediately.
2. You can continue your education in graduate school or professional school. (See Figure 10.2 for a visual map of the signposts or stages in the college experience and the basic paths available to you after college graduation.)

FIGURE **10.2**

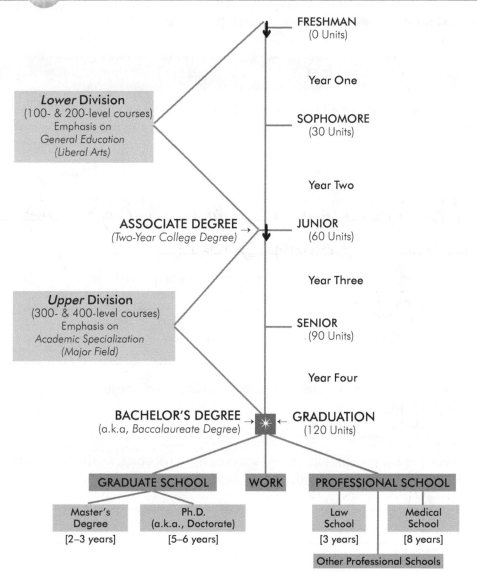

Notes

1. The total number of *general education* units and the total number of units needed to **graduate** with a bachelor's degree may vary somewhat from school to school. Also, the total number of units required for a *major* will vary somewhat from major to major and from school to school.

2. It often takes college students longer than four years to graduate due to a variety of reasons, such as working part-time and taking fewer courses per term, needing to repeat courses that were failed or dropped, or making a late change to a different major and needing to fulfill additional requirements for the new major.

3. *Graduate* and *professional* schools are options for continuing to higher levels of education after completion of an undergraduate (college) education.

4. Compared to graduate school, *professional* school involves advanced education in more "applied" professions (e.g., pharmacy or public administration).

© Kendall Hunt

Timeline to the Future: A Snapshot of the College Experience and Beyond

Once you complete a bachelor's degree, it's possible to continue your education in a field that's not directly related to your college major. This is particularly true for students who are majoring in preprofessional careers that funnel them directly into a particular career after graduation (Pascarella & Terenzini, 2005). For example, if you major in English, you can still go to graduate school in a subject other than English; you could go to law school or get a master's degree in business administration. It's common to find graduate students in masters of business administration programs who were not business majors in college (Dupuy & Vance, 1996).

| Think About It | Journal Entry 10.4 |

Reflect back on the preceding timeline and Figure 10.2, which suggests that it will take you two years to complete an associate degree and four years to complete a bachelor's degree.

1. Do you see yourself completing an associate degree in two years? A bachelor's degree in four years? Why or why not?

   No. Just trying to get though this to go to beauty school.

2. Do you plan to transfer after completing an associate degree?

   _No._

   If yes, to what college or university?

   _____

   If no, do you ever see yourself eventually returning to college to complete your bachelor's degree?

   _No._

3. Do you see any possible interfering factors or potential obstacles that might prolong the time you need to reach your educational goals?

   My Dad.

   _____

   _____

Myth 3. You should major in business because most college graduates work in business settings. Studies show that college graduates with various majors end up working in business settings. For instance, engineering majors are likely to work in accounting, production, and finance. Liberal arts majors are likely to move on to positions in business settings that involve marketing, human resources, or public affairs (Bok, 2006; Useem, 1989). Research also reveals that the career mobility and career advancement of nonbusiness majors in the business world are equal to those attained by business majors (Pascarella & Terenzini, 1991, 2005).

Author's Experience My undergraduate degree was in political science and sociology. When I graduated from college, I spent the first eight years of my professional life becoming a corporate manager. I did not major in business, but found that my liberal arts background gave me the problem-solving and communication skills that were crucial in working with a variety of people in my profession. You do not need to major in business to be a successful business person. Indeed, employers are telling us that they are looking for those who can problem solve, critically think, write and speak well, and work with a diversity of people and thought.

Aaron Thompson

"Employers are far more interested in the prospect's ability to think and to think clearly, to write and speak well, and how (s)he works with others than in his major or the name of the school (s)he went to. Several college investigating teams found that these were the qualities on which all kinds of employers, government and private, base their decisions."

—Lauren Pope, *Looking beyond the Ivy League* (1990)

Don't restrict your choices of a major to business by believing in the myth that you must major in business to work for a business after graduation.

Myth 4. If you major in a liberal arts field, the only career available is teaching. Liberal arts majors are not restricted to teaching careers. Many college graduates with majors in liberal arts fields have proceeded to, and succeeded in, careers other than teaching. Among these graduates are such notable people as:

- Jill Barad (English major), CEO, Mattel Toys;
- Steve Case (political science major), CEO, America Online;
- Brian Lamb (speech major), CEO, C-Span; and
- Willie Brown (liberal studies major), mayor, San Francisco.

Source: Indiana University (2004).

Student Perspective

"They asked me during my interview why I was right for the job and I told them because I can read well, write well and I can think. They really liked that because those were the skills they were looking for."

—English major hired by a public relations firm (*Los Angeles Times*, April 4, 2004)

Studies show that college graduates in liberal arts majors are just as likely to advance to the highest levels of corporate leadership as graduates majoring in preprofessional fields, such as business and engineering (Pascarella & Terenzini, 2005). If you are considering a major in a liberal arts field, you should not be dismayed or discouraged by those who may question your choice by asking, "What are you going to do with a degree in *that* major?"

Note: A good career-information Web site for liberal arts majors can be found at www.eace.org/networks/liberalarts.html.

Myth 5. Specialized skills are more important for career success than general skills. You may find that general education (liberal arts) courses are sometimes viewed by students as unnecessary requirements that they have to "get out of the way" before they can "get into what's really important"—their major or academic specialization. However, general education courses develop practical, durable, and transferable skills that supply a strong foundation for success in any career.

Also, don't forget that the general skills and qualities developed by the liberal arts increase career advancement (your ability to move up the career ladder) and career mobility (your ability to move into different career paths). Specific technical skills may be important for getting into a career, but general educational skills are more important for moving up the career ladder. The courses you take as part of your general education will prepare you for your advanced career positions, not just your first one (Boyer, 1987; Miller, 2003). Furthermore, general professional skills are growing even more important for college graduates entering the workforce in the 21st century because the demand for upper-level positions in management and leadership will exceed the supply of workers available to fill these positions (Herman, 2000).

Think About It ——————————— *Journal Entry* **10.5**

In what ways do you think your general education courses will improve your work performance in the career field you may pursue?

I will have a back up job.

Factors to Consider When Choosing Your Major or Field of Study

Gaining self-awareness is the critical first step in making decisions about a college major, or any other important decision. You must know yourself before you can know what choice is best for you. While this may seem obvious, self-awareness and self-discovery are often overlooked aspects of the decision-making process. In particular, you need awareness of:

- Your *interests*, what you like doing;
- Your *abilities*, what you're good at doing; and
- Your *values*, what you feel good about doing.

Research indicates that students are more likely to continue in college and graduate when they choose majors that reflect their personal interests and talents (Leuwerke et al., 2004).

"I try to do more to please myself, and making good grades and doing well in school helps my ego. It gives me confidence, and I like that feeling."

—First-year student (Franklin, 2002)

Think About It ——————————— *Journal Entry* **10.6**

In Chapter 5 (pp. 138–139), you answered self-awareness questions related to three elements of "self": interests, abilities (talents), and values. Review your answers to these questions. Do you notice any patterns across your answers suggesting that a certain major would provide a nice "fit" or "match" with your personal interests, abilities, and values?

Yes, Its what I want to do as well with my interests

Multiple Intelligences: Identifying Personal Abilities and Talents

One element of the self that you should be aware of when choosing a major is your mental strengths, abilities, or talents. Intelligence was once considered to be one general trait that could be detected and measured by a single intelligence test score. The singular word *intelligence* has now been replaced by the plural word *intelligences* to reflect the fact that humans can display intelligence (mental ability) in many forms other than performance on an IQ test.

Listed in Snapshot Summary 10.3 are forms of intelligence identified by Howard Gardner (1999, 2006) based on studies of gifted and talented individuals, experts in different lines of work, and various other sources. As you read through the types of intelligence, place a checkmark next to the type that you think represents your strongest ability or talent. (You can possess more than one type.) Keep your type(s) of intelligence in mind when you're choosing a college major because different majors emphasize different thinking skills. Ideally, you want to select an academic field that allows you to utilize your strongest skills and talents. Choosing a major that's compatible with your abilities should enable you to master the concepts and skills required by your major more easily and more deeply. If you follow your academic talents, you're also more likely to succeed or excel in what you do, which will bolster your academic self-confidence and motivation.

Snapshot Summary

10.3 Multiple Forms of Intelligence

- **Linguistic intelligence.** Ability to communicate through language—e.g., verbal skills in the areas of speaking, writing, listening, and reading.
- **Logical-mathematical intelligence.** Ability to reason logically and succeed in tasks that involve mathematical problem solving—e.g., making logical arguments and following logical reasoning, or ability to work well with numbers and make quantitative calculations.
- **Spatial intelligence.** Ability to visualize relationships among objects arranged in different spatial positions and the ability to perceive or create visual images—e.g., forming mental images of three-dimensional objects; detecting detail in objects or drawings; artistic talent for drawing, painting, sculpting, and graphic design; and skills related to sense of direction and navigation.
- **Musical intelligence.** Ability to appreciate or create rhythmical and melodic sounds—e.g., playing, writing, and arranging music.
- **Interpersonal (social) intelligence.** Ability to relate to others, to accurately identify others' needs, feelings, or emotional states of mind, and to effectively express emotions and feelings to others—e.g., interpersonal communication skills, ability to accurately "read" the feelings of others, and ability to meet their emotional needs.
- **Intrapersonal (self) intelligence.** Ability to introspect and understand one's own thoughts, feelings, and behavior—e.g., capacity for personal reflection, emotional self-awareness, and self-insight.

- **Bodily-kinesthetic (psychomotor) intelligence.** Ability to use one's own body skillfully and learn through bodily sensations or movements—e.g., skilled at tasks involving physical coordination, ability to work well with hands, mechanical skills, talent for building models, assembling things, and using technology.

Student Perspective

> "I used to operate a printing press. In about two weeks I knew how to run it and soon after I could take the machine apart in my head and analyze what each part does, how it functioned, and why it was shaped that way."
>
> —Response of college sophomore to the questions "What are you really good at? What comes easily or naturally to you?"

- **Naturalist intelligence.** Ability to carefully observe and appreciate features of the natural environment—e.g., keen awareness of nature or natural surroundings, and ability to understand causes and consequences of events occurring in the natural world.
- **Existential.** Ability to conceptualize phenomena and experiences that require one to go beyond sensory or physical evidence, such as questions and issues involving the origin of the universe and human life, and the purpose of human existence.

Source: Gardner (1993, 1999, 2006).

Think About It —————————— Journal Entry 10.7

Which types of intelligence listed in Snapshot Summary 10.3 are your strongest areas? Which majors or fields of study do you think may be the best match for your natural talents?

Linguistic intellegence

intrapersonal intelligence

Bodily Kinestic

Author's Experience   I first noticed that students in different academic fields may have different learning styles when I was teaching a psychology course that was required for students majoring in nursing and social work. I noticed that some students in class seemed to lose interest (and patience) when we got involved in lengthy class discussions about controversial issues or theories, while others seemed to love it. On the other hand, whenever I lectured or delivered information for an extended period, some students seemed to lose interest (and attention), while others seemed to get into it and took great notes. After one class period that involved quite a bit of class discussion, I began thinking about which students seemed most involved in the discussion and which seemed to drift off or lose interest. I suddenly realized that the students who did most of the talking and seemed most enthused during the class discussion were the students majoring in social work. On the other hand, most of the students who appeared disinterested or a bit frustrated were the nursing majors.

When I began to think about why this happened, it dawned on me that the nursing students were accustomed to gathering factual information and learning practical skills in their major courses and were expecting to use that learning style in my psychology course. The nursing majors felt more comfortable with structured class sessions in which they received lots of factual, practical information from the professor. On the other hand, the social work majors were more comfortable with unstructured class discussions because courses in their major often emphasized debating social issues and hearing viewpoints or perspectives.

As I left class that day, I asked myself: Did the nursing students and social work students select or gravitate toward their major because the type of learning emphasized in the field tended to match their preferred style of learning?

Joe Cuseo

To sum up, the most important factor to consider when reaching decisions about a major is whether it is compatible with four characteristics of your self: (1) your learning style, (2) your abilities, (3) your personal interests, and (4) your values (see Figure 10.3). These four pillars provide the foundation for effective decisions about a college major.

Strategies for Discovering a Major Compatible with Your Interests, Talents, and Values

If you're undecided about a major, there's no need to feel anxious or guilty. You're at an early stage in your college experience. Although you've decided to postpone your decision about a major, this doesn't mean you're a clueless procrastinator as long as you have a plan for exploring and narrowing down your options. Just be sure that you don't put all thoughts about your major on the back burner and simply drift along until you have no choice but to make a choice. Start exploring and developing a game plan now that will lead you to a wise decision about your major.

Similarly, if you've already chosen a major, this doesn't mean that you'll never have to give any more thought to that decision or that you can just shift into cruise control and motor along a mindless ride in the major you've selected. Instead, you should continue the exploration process by carefully testing your first choice, making sure it's a choice that is compatible with your abilities, interests, and values. In other words, take the approach that it's your *current* choice; whether it becomes your firm and *final* choice will depend on how well you perform, and how interested you are, in the first courses you take in the field.

To explore and identify majors that are compatible with your personal strengths and interests, use the following strategies:

1. **Use past experience to help you choose a major.** Think about the subjects that you experienced during high school and your early time in college. As the old saying goes, "Nothing succeeds like success itself." If you have done well and continue to do well in a certain field of study, this may indicate that your natural abilities and learning style correspond well with the academic skills required by that particular field. This could translate into future success and satisfaction in the field if you decide to pursue it as a college major.

   You can enter information about your academic performance in high school courses at the Web site mymajors.com, which will analyze it and provide you with college majors that may be a good match for you (based on your academic experiences in high school).

2. **Use your elective courses to test your interests and abilities in subjects that you might consider as majors.** As the name implies, "elective" courses are those that you elect or choose to take. Your college electives come in two forms: free electives and restricted electives. *Free electives* are courses that you may elect (choose) to enroll in; they count toward your college degree but are not required for general education or your major. *Restricted electives* are courses that you must take, but you choose them from a restricted list of possible courses that have been specified by your college as fulfilling a requirement in general education or your major. For example, your campus may have a general education requirement in social or behavioral sciences that requires you to take two courses in this field, but you're allowed to choose what those two courses are from a menu of options in the field, such as anthropology, economics, political science, psychology, or sociology. If you're considering one of these subjects as a possible major, you can take an introductory course in that subject to test your interest in it while simultaneously fulfilling a general education requirement needed for graduation. This strategy will allow you to use general education as the main highway for travel toward your final destination (a college degree) while using your electives to explore side roads (potential majors) along the way. If you find one that's compatible with your talents and interests, you may have found yourself a major.

3. **Be sure you know the courses that are required for the major you're considering.** In college, it's expected that students may know the requirements for the major they've chosen. These requirements vary considerably from one major to another. Be sure to review your college catalog carefully to determine what courses are required for the major you're considering. If you have trouble tracking down the requirements in your college catalog, don't become frustrated. These catalogs are often written in a technical manner that can sometimes be hard to interpret. If you need help identifying and understanding the requirements for a major that you are considering, don't be embarrassed about seeking assistance from a professional in your school's Academic Advisement Center.

Author's Experience

As an academic advisor, I often see students who are confused about what they want to major in, especially traditionally aged (18 to 24 years old) students. I can relate to these students because I changed my major multiple times before I reached a final decision. The first piece of advice I give students about choosing majors is to use their resources (e.g., academic advisement) and to do some research on the courses required for the majors they're considering. Over the last few years, I've seen many students who want to major in forensic science—largely due to the popularity of the *CSI* shows. I then ask them how they feel about science and math, and many of these students tell me they hate those subjects. When I inform them that becoming a forensic scientist often involves a minimum of a master's in chemistry, they decide to look at other majors. Fewer surprises like this would occur if students did at least some research on what courses are required for the majors and careers they're considering.

Julie McLaughlin

Keep in mind that college majors often require courses in fields outside of the major. Such courses are designed to support the major. For instance, psychology majors are often required to take at least one course in biology, and business majors are often required to take calculus. If you are interested in majoring in a particular subject area, be sure you are fully aware of such outside requirements and are comfortable with them.

Once you've accurately identified all courses required for the major you're considering, ask yourself the following two questions:

- Do the course titles and descriptions appeal to my interests and values?
- Do I have the abilities or skills needed to do well in these courses?

You don't want to be surprised by unexpected requirements after you have already committed to a major, particularly if these unanticipated requirements do not match your personal abilities, interests, or learning styles.

4. **Talk with students majoring in the field you are considering and ask them about their experiences.** Try to speak with several students in the field so that you get a balanced perspective that goes beyond the opinion of one individual. A good way to find students in the major you're considering is to visit student clubs on campus related to the major (e.g., psychology club or history club). The following questions may be good ones to ask students in a major that you're considering:

- What first attracted you to this major?
- What would you say are the advantages and disadvantages of majoring in this field?
- Knowing what you know now, would you choose the same major again?

Also, ask students about the quality of teaching and advising in the department. Studies show that different departments within the same college or university can vary greatly in terms of the quality of teaching, as well as their educational philosophy and attitude toward students (Pascarella & Terenzini, 1991).

5. **Sit in on some classes in the field you are considering as a major.** If the class you want to visit is large, you probably could just slip into the back row and listen. However, if the class is small, you should ask the instructor's permission. When visiting a class, focus on the content or ideas being covered in class rather than the instructor's personality or teaching style. (Keep in mind that you're trying to decide whether you will major in the subject, not in the teacher.)

6. **Discuss the major you're considering with an academic advisor.** It's probably best to speak with an academic advisor who advises students in various majors rather than to someone who advises only students in their particular academic department or field. You want to be sure to discuss the major with an advisor who is neutral and will give you unbiased feedback about the pros and cons of majoring in that field.

7. **Speak with some faculty members in the department that you're considering as a major.** Consider asking them the following questions:

   - What academic skills or qualities are needed for a student to be successful in your field?
   - What are the greatest challenges faced by students majoring in your field?
   - What do students seem to like most and least about majoring in your field?
   - What can students do with a major in your field after college graduation?
   - What types of graduate programs or professional schools would a student in your major be well prepared to enter?

8. **Visit your Career Development Center.** See whether information is available on college graduates who've majored in the field you're considering and what they've gone on to do with that major after graduation. This will give you an idea about the types of careers the major can lead to or what graduate and professional school programs students often enter after completing a major in the field that you're considering.

9. **Surf the Web site of the professional organization associated with the field that you're considering as a major.** For example, if you're thinking about becoming an anthropology major, check out the Web site of the American Anthropological Association. If you're considering history as a major, look at the Web site of the American Historical Association. The Web site of a professional organization often contains useful information for students who are considering that field as a major. For example, the Web site of the American Philosophical Association contains information about nonacademic careers for philosophy majors, and the American Sociological Association's Web site identifies various careers that sociology majors are qualified to pursue after college graduation. To locate the professional Web site of the field that you might want to explore as a possible major, ask a faculty member in that field or complete a search on the Web by simply entering the name of the field followed by the word *association*.

10. **Be sure you know what academic standards must be met for you to be accepted for entry into a major.** Because of their popularity, certain college majors may be impacted or oversubscribed, which means that more students are interested in majoring in these fields than there are openings for them. Preprofessional majors that lead directly to a particular career are often the ones that become oversubscribed (e.g., accounting, education, engineering, premed, nursing, or physical therapy). On some campuses, these majors are called restricted majors, meaning that departments control their enrollment by limiting the number of students they let into the major. For example, departments may restrict entry to their major by admitting only students who have achieved an overall GPA of 3.0 or higher in certain introductory courses required by the majors, or they may

take all students who apply for the major, rank them by their GPA, and then count down until they have filled their maximum number of available spaces (Strommer, 1993).

Be sure you know whether the major you're considering is impacted or oversubscribed and whether it requires you to meet certain academic standards before you can be admitted. As you complete courses and receive grades, check to see whether you are meeting these standards. If you find yourself failing to meet these standards, you may need to increase the amount of time and effort you devote to your studies and seek assistance from your campus Learning Center. If you're working at your maximum level of effort and are regularly using the learning assistance services available on your campus but are still not meeting the academic standards of your intended major, consult with an academic advisor to help you identify an alternative field that may be closely related to the restricted major you were hoping to enter.

| Think About It | Journal Entry 10.8 |

Do you think that the major you're considering is likely to be oversubscribed (i.e., there are more students wanting to major in the field than there are openings in the courses)? Explain.

yes, But there are Millions of kids

11. **Consider the possibility of a college minor in a field that complements your major.** A college minor usually requires about one-half the number of credits (units) required for a major. Most campuses allow you the option of completing a minor with your major. Check with your academic advisor or the course catalog of the school you're considering transferring to; if the school offers a minor that interests you, find out what courses are required to complete it.

If you have strong interests in two different fields, a minor will allow you to major in one of these fields while minoring in the other. Thus, you can pursue two fields that interest you without having to sacrifice one for the other. Furthermore, a minor can be completed at the same time as most college majors without delaying your time to graduation. (In contrast, a double major will typically lengthen your time to graduation because you must complete the separate requirements of two different majors.) You can also pursue a second field of study alongside your major without increasing your time to graduation by completing a cognate area—a specialization that requires fewer courses to complete than a minor (e.g., four to five courses instead of seven to eight courses). A concentration area may have even fewer requirements (only two to three courses).

Taking a cluster of courses in a field outside your major can be an effective way to strengthen your resume and increase your employment prospects because it demonstrates your versatility and allows you to gain experience in areas that may be missing or underemphasized in your major. For example, students majoring in the fine arts (e.g., music or theater) or humanities (e.g., English or history) may take courses in the fields of mathematics (e.g., statistics), technology (e.g., computer science), and business (e.g., economics)—none of which are emphasized by their majors.

12. **Join a professional organization as a student.** Many professional organizations offer discounted rates for students. These organizations offer opportunities for networking with those already in the profession as well as educational experiences through local, regional, and national conferences.

Think About It ———————————— *Journal Entry* **10.9**

Before you start to dig into this chapter, take a moment to answer the following questions:

1. Have you decided on a career, or are you leaning strongly toward one?

   Nope

2. If yes, why have you chosen this career? (Was your decision influenced by anybody or anything?)

   My Dad made m

3. If no, are there any careers you're considering as possibilities? What are they?

   In beauty

The Importance of Career Planning

College graduates in the 21st century are likely to continue working until age 75 (Herman, 2000). Once you enter the workforce full time, you'll spend most of the remaining waking hours of your life working. The only other single activity that you'll spend more time doing in your lifetime is sleeping. When you consider that such a sizable portion of your life is spent working and that your career can strongly influence your sense of personal identity and self-esteem, it becomes apparent that career choice is a critical process that should begin early in your college experience.

Remember

When you're doing career *planning, you're also doing* life *planning because you are planning how you will spend most of the waking hours of your future.*

Even if you've decided on a career that you were dreaming about since you were a preschooler, the process of career exploration and planning is not complete because you still need to decide on what specialization within that career you'll pursue. For example, if you're interested in pursuing a career in law, you'll need to eventually decide what branch of law you wish to practice (e.g., criminal law, corporate law, or family law). You'll also need to decide what employment sector or type of industry you would like to work in, such as nonprofit, for-profit, education, or government. Thus, no matter how certain or uncertain you are about your career path, you'll need to begin exploring career options and start taking your first steps toward formulating a career development plan.

Strategies for Career Exploration and Development

Reaching an effective decision about a career involves the same four steps you used in the goal-setting process (see Chapter 5):

1. **Awareness of yourself.** Your personal abilities, interests, needs, and values.

2. **Awareness of your options.** The variety of career fields available to you.

3. **Awareness of what best "fits" you.** The careers that best match your personal abilities, interests, needs, and values.

4. **Awareness of the process.** How to prepare for and gain entry into the career of your choice.

Step 1. Self-Awareness

The more you know about yourself, the better your choices and decisions will be. Self-awareness is a particularly important step to take when making career decisions because the career you choose says a lot about who you are and what you want from life. Your personal identity and life goals should not be based on or built around your career choice: it should be the other way around.

Remember

Your personal attributes and goals should be considered first because they provide the foundation on which you build your career choice and future life.

One way to gain greater self-awareness of your career interests is by taking psychological tests or assessments. These assessments allow you to see how your interests in certain career fields compare with those of other students and professionals who've experienced career satisfaction and success. These comparative perspectives can give you important reference points for assessing whether your level of interest in a career is high, average, or low relative to other students and working professionals. Your Career Development Center or Counseling Center is the place on campus where you can find these career-interest tests, as well as other instruments that allow you to assess your career-related abilities and values.

When making choices about a career, you may have to consider one other important aspect of yourself: your personal needs. A "need" may be described as something stronger than an interest. When you satisfy a personal need, you are doing something that makes your life more satisfying or fulfilling. Psychologists have identified several important human needs that vary in strength or intensity from person to person. Listed in Do It Now! 10.1 are personal needs that are especially important to consider when making a career choice.

10.1   DO IT **NOW!**

Personal Needs to Consider When Making Career Choices

As you read the needs listed here, make a note after each one indicating how strong the need is for you (high, moderate, or low).

1. **Autonomy.** The need to work independently without close supervision or control. Individuals high in this need may experience greater satisfaction working in careers that allow them to be their own bosses, make their own decisions, and control their own work schedules. Individuals low in this need may experience greater satisfaction working in careers that are more structured and involve working with a supervisor who provides direction, assistance, and frequent feedback.

2. **Affiliation.** The need for social interaction, a sense of belonging, and the opportunity to collaborate with others. Individuals high in this need may experience greater satisfaction working in careers that involve frequent interpersonal interaction and teamwork with colleagues or co-workers. Individuals low in this need may be more satisfied working alone or in competition with others.

Student *Perspective*

"To me, an important characteristic of a career is being able to meet new, smart, interesting people."

—First-year student

3. **Achievement.** The need to experience challenge and a sense of personal accomplishment. Individuals high in this need may be more satisfied working in careers that push them to solve problems, generate creative ideas, and continually learn new information or master new skills. Individuals low in this need may be more satisfied with careers that don't continually test their abilities and don't repeatedly challenge them to stretch their skills with new tasks and different responsibilities.

Student *Perspective*

"I want to be able to enjoy my job and be challenged by it at the same time. I hope that my job will not be monotonous and that I will have the opportunity to learn new things often."

—First-year student

4. **Recognition.** The need for high rank, status, and respect from others. Individuals high in this need may crave careers that are prestigious in the eyes of friends, family, or society. Individuals with a low need for recognition would feel comfortable working in a career that they find personally fulfilling, without being concerned about how impressive or enviable their career appears to others.

5. **Sensory stimulation.** The need to experience variety, change, and risk. Individuals high in this need may be more satisfied working in careers that involve frequent changes of pace and place (e.g., travel), unpredictable events (e.g., work tasks that vary considerably), and moderate stress (e.g., working under pressure of competition or deadlines). Individuals with a low need for sensory stimulation may feel more comfortable working in careers that involve regular routines, predictable situations, and minimal amounts of risk or stress.

Student *Perspective*

"For me, a good career is very unpredictable and interest-fulfilling. I would love to do something that allows me to be spontaneous."

—First-year student

"Don't expect a recluse to be motivated to sell, a creative thinker to be motivated to be a good proofreader day in and day out, or a sow's ear to be happy in the role of a silk purse."

—Pierce Howard, *The Owner's Manual for the Brain* (2000)

Think About It ———————————— Journal Entry 10.10

1. Which of the five needs in Do It Now! 10.1 did you indicate as being strong personal needs? Why?

   Autonomy, Affiliation,

2. What career or careers do you think would best match your strongest needs?

   Cosmotology

   teacher

Author's Experience

While enrolled in my third year of college with half of my degree completed, I had an eye-opening experience. I wish this experience had happened in my first year, but better late than never. Although I had chosen a career during my first year of college, my decision-making process was not systematic and didn't involve critical thinking. I chose a major based on what sounded prestigious and would pay me the most money. Although these are not necessarily bad factors, my failure to use a systematic and reflective process to evaluate these factors was bad. In my junior year of college I asked one of my professors why he decided to get his Ph.D. and become a professor. He simply answered, "I wanted autonomy." This was an epiphany for me. He explained that when he looked at his life he determined that he needed a career that offered independence, so he began looking at career options that would offer that. After that explanation, *autonomy* became my favorite word, and this story became a guiding force in my life. After going through a critical self-awareness process, I determined that autonomy was exactly what I desired and a professor is what I became.

Aaron Thompson

Student Perspective

"I think that a good career has to be meaningful for a person. It should be enjoyable for the most part [and] it has to give a person a sense of fulfillment."

—First-year student

Taken altogether, four aspects of yourself should be considered when exploring careers: your personal abilities, interests, values, and needs. As illustrated in Figure 10.3, these four pillars provide a solid foundation for effective career choices and decisions. You want to choose a career that you're good at, interested in, and passionate about and that fulfills your personal needs.

Lastly, since a career choice is a long-range decision that involves life beyond college, self-awareness should involve not only reflection on who you are now but also self-projection—reflecting on how you see yourself in the future. When you engage in the process of self-projection, you begin to see a connection between where you are now and where you want or hope to be.

FIGURE 10.3

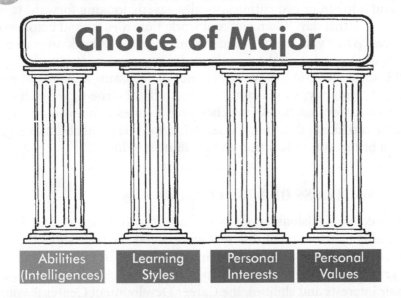

Abilities (Intelligences) | Learning Styles | Personal Interests | Personal Values

Personal Characteristics Providing the Foundation for Effective Career Choice

Think About It ——————— *Journal Entry* 10.11

Project yourself 10 years into the future and visualize your ideal career and life.

1. What are you spending most of your time doing during your typical workday?

    Homework, studying, relaxing

2. Where and with whom are you working?

    No where

3. How many hours are you working per week?

    30

4. Where are you living?

    With my parents

5. Are you married? Do you have children?

    No

6. How does your work influence your home life?

    If I dont go to school I get kicked out.

Ideally, your choice of a career should be one that leads to the best-case future scenario in which your typical day goes something like this: You wake up in the morning and hop out of bed enthusiastically, eagerly looking forward to what you'll be doing at work that day. When you're at work, time flies by, and before you know it, the day's over. When you return to bed that night and look back on your day, you feel good about what you did and how well you did it.

For this ideal scenario to have any chance of becoming a reality, or even coming close to reality, you have to select a career path that is true to yourself—a path that leads you to a career that closely matches your abilities (what you do well), your interests (what you like to do), your values (what you feel good about doing), and your needs (what brings you satisfaction and fulfillment in life).

Step 2. Awareness of Your Options

To make effective decisions about your career path, you need to have accurate knowledge about the nature of different careers and the realities of the work world. The Career Development Center is the first place to go for this information and help with career exploration and planning. In addition to helping you explore your personal career interests and abilities, the Career Development Center is your key campus resource for learning about the nature of different careers and for strategies on locating career-related work experiences.

If you were to ask people to name as many careers as they can, they wouldn't come close to naming the 900 career titles listed by the federal government in its Occupational Information Network. Many of these careers you may have never heard of, but some of them may represent good career options for you. You can learn about careers through nine major routes or avenues:

- Reading about them in books or online
- Becoming involved in cocurricular programs on campus related to career development
- Taking career development courses
- Interviewing people in different career fields
- Observing (shadowing) people at work in different careers
- Interning
- Participating in a co-op program
- Volunteering
- Working part-time

Author's Experience

When my sister was in the last year of her nursing degree, she decided she wanted to be a pediatric nurse and work at one of the top 10 pediatric hospitals in the country. At the time, I lived in a city with an excellent pediatric hospital. My sister decided to come visit me for an extended weekend and made appointments to shadow different units in that hospital on her visit. She fell in love with the place and decided she definitely wanted to work there! A few months later, when she was in her last semester of school, that hospital called her and asked if she wanted to come and interview for jobs on all four units. They'd been just as impressed with her when she shadowed as she was with them, and they made a note on her resume to call her when she was close to graduating. She interviewed and was offered all four jobs! It turned out her shadowing experience actually ended up being a "pre-interview," and she had a job before she even graduated!

— *Julie McLaughlin*

Resources on Careers

Your Career Development Center and your College Library are campus resources where you can find a wealth of reading material on careers, either in print or online. Listed here are some of the most useful sources of written information on careers:

- *Dictionary of Occupational Titles* (www.occupationalinfo.org). This is the largest printed resource on careers; it contains concise definitions of over 17,000 jobs. It also includes information on:
  - work tasks that people in the career typically perform regularly;
  - types of knowledge, skills, and abilities that are required for different careers;
  - interests, values, and needs of individuals who find working in particular careers to be personally rewarding; and
  - background experiences of people working in different careers that qualified them for their positions.

- *Occupational Outlook Handbook* (www.bls.gov/oco). This is one of the most widely available and used resources on careers. It contains descriptions of approximately 250 positions, including information on the nature of work, work conditions, places of employment, training or education required for career entry and advancement, salaries, careers in related fields, and additional sources of information about particular careers (e.g., professional organizations and governmental agencies). A distinctive feature of this resource is that it contains information about the future employment outlook for different careers.

- *Encyclopedia of Careers and Vocational Guidance* (Chicago: Ferguson Press). As the name suggests, this is an encyclopedia of information on qualifications, salaries, and advancement opportunities for various careers.

- Occupational Information Network (O*NET) Online (online.onetcenter.org). This is America's most comprehensive source of online information about careers. It contains an up-to-date set of descriptions for almost 1,000 careers, plus lots of other information similar to what you would find in the *Dictionary of Occupational Titles*.

In addition to these general sources of information, your Career Development Center and College Library should have books and other published materials related to specific careers or occupations (e.g., careers for English majors).

You can also learn a lot about careers by simply reading advertisements for position openings in your local newspaper or online, such as at www.careerbuilder.com and www.monstertrak.com. When reading position descriptions, make special note of the tasks, duties, or responsibilities they involve and ask yourself whether these positions are compatible with your personal profile of abilities, interests, needs, and values.

Career Planning and Development Programs

Periodically during the academic year, cocurricular programs devoted to career exploration and career preparation are likely to be offered on your campus. For example, the Career Development Center may sponsor career exploration or career planning workshops that you can attend for free. Also, the Career Development Center may organize a career fair on campus, at which professionals working in different career fields are given booths on campus where you can visit with them and ask questions about their careers. Research indicates that career development workshops offered on campus are effective in helping students plan for and decide on a career (Brown & Krane, 2000; Hildenbrand & Gore, 2005).

Career Development Courses

Many colleges offer career development courses for elective credit. These courses typically include self-assessment of your career interests, information about different careers, and strategies for career preparation. You should be doing career planning, so why not do it by taking a career development course that rewards you with college credit for doing it? Studies show that students who participate in career development courses experience significant benefits in terms of their career choice and career development (Pascarella & Terenzini, 2005).

Informational Interviews

One of the best and most overlooked ways to get accurate information about careers is to interview professionals who are working in career fields. Career development specialists refer to this strategy as informational interviewing. Don't assume that working professionals would not be interested in taking time out of their day to speak with a student. Most are willing to be interviewed about their careers; they often enjoy it (Crosby, 2002).

Informational interviews provide you inside information about what careers are like because you're getting that information directly from the horse's mouth. It also helps you gain experience and confidence in interview situations, which may help you prepare for future job interviews. Furthermore, if you make a good impression during informational interviews, the people you interview may suggest that you contact them again after graduation in case there are position openings. If there are openings, you might find yourself being the interviewee instead of the interviewer (and you might find yourself a job).

Because interviews are a valuable source of information about careers and provide possible contacts for future employment, we strongly recommend that you complete the information interview assignment included at the end of this chapter.

| Think About It — | *Journal Entry* **10.12** |

If you were to observe or interview a working professional in a career that interests you, what position would that person hold?

Makeup artist.

_____

_____

_____

_____

_____

_____

Career Observation (Shadowing)

In addition to learning about careers from reading and interviews, you can experience careers more directly by placing yourself in workplace situations or work environments that allow you to observe workers performing their daily duties. Two college-sponsored programs may be available on your campus that would allow you to observe working professionals:

- **Job Shadowing Programs.** These programs allow you to follow ("shadow") and observe a professional during a typical workday.
- **Career Development Center.** Learn about what job shadowing programs may be available on your college campus. If none are available in a career field that interests you, consider finding one on your own by using strategies similar to those we recommend for informational interviews at the end of this chapter. The only difference is that instead of asking the person for an interview, you'd be asking whether you could observe that person at work. The same person who gave you an informational interview might be willing to allow such observation. Keep in mind that one or two days of observation will give you some firsthand information about a career, but will not give you firsthand experience in that career.

Internships and Co-Ops

In contrast to job shadowing, where you observe someone at work, an internship program immerses you in the work itself and gives you the opportunity to perform career-related work duties. A distinguishing feature of internships is that you can receive academic credit and sometimes financial compensation for the work you do. An internship usually totals 120 to 150 work hours, which may be completed at the same time you're enrolled in a full schedule of classes or when you're not taking classes (e.g., during summer term).

An advantage of an internship is that it enables college students to avoid the classic catch-22 situation they often run into when interviewing for their first career positions after graduation. The interview scenario usually goes something like this: The potential employer asks the college graduate, "What work experience have you had in this field?" The recent graduate replies, "I haven't had any work experience because I've been a full-time college student." This scenario can be avoided if you complete an internship during your college experience, which allows you to say, "Yes, I do have work experience in this field." We encourage you to participate in an internship while in college because it will enable you to beat the "no experience" rap after graduation and distinguish yourself from many other college graduates. Research shows that students who have internships while in college are more likely to develop career-relevant work skills and find employment immediately after college graduation (Pascarella & Terenzini, 2005).

Internships are typically available to college students during their junior or senior year; however, there may be internships available to first- and second-year students on your campus. You can also pursue internships on your own. Published guides describe various career-related internships, along with information on how to apply for them (e.g., *Peterson's Internships* and the *Vault Guide to Top Internships*). You could also search for internships on the Web (e.g., www.internships.com and www.vaultreports.com). Another good resource for possible information on internships is the local chamber of commerce in the town or city where your college is located or in your hometown.

Another option for gaining firsthand work experience is enrolling in courses that allow you to engage in hands-on learning related to your career interest. For instance, if you're interested in working with children, courses in child psychology or early childhood education may offer experiential learning opportunities in a preschool or daycare center on campus.

A co-op is similar to an internship, but involves work experience that lasts longer than one academic term and often requires students to stop their coursework temporarily to participate in the program. However, some co-op programs allow you to continue to take classes while working part time at a co-op position; these are sometimes referred to as parallel co-ops. Students are paid for participating in co-op programs (Smith, 2005).

The value of co-ops and internships is strongly supported by research, which indicates that students who have these experiences during college:

- Are more likely to report that their college education was relevant to their career;
- Receive higher evaluations from employers who recruit them on campus;
- Have less difficulty finding initial positions after graduation;
- Are more satisfied with their first career positions after college;
- Obtain more prestigious positions after graduation; and
- Report greater job satisfaction (Gardner, 1991; Knouse, Tanner, & Harris, 1999; Pascarella & Terenzini, 1991, 2005).

In one statewide survey that asked employers to rank various factors they considered important when hiring new college graduates, internship or cooperative education programs received the highest ranking (Education Commission of the States, 1995). Furthermore, employers report that if full-time positions open up in their organization or company, they usually turn first to their own interns and co-op students (National Association of Colleges & Employers, 2003).

Volunteer Service

Engaging in volunteerism not only helps your community, but also helps you by giving you the opportunity to explore different work environments and gain work experience in career fields that relate to your area of service. For example, volunteer service to different age groups (e.g., children, adolescents, or the elderly) and service in different environments (e.g., hospital, school, or laboratory) can provide you with firsthand work experience and simultaneously give you a chance to test your interest in possibly pursuing future careers related to these different age groups and work environments. (To get a sense of the range of service opportunities that may be available to you, go to www.usa.service.org.)

Author's Experience

As an academic advisor, I was once working with two first-year students, Kim and Christopher. Kim was thinking about becoming a physical therapist, and Chris was thinking about becoming an elementary school teacher. I suggested to Kim that she visit the hospital near our college to see whether she could do volunteer work in the physical therapy unit. The hospital did need volunteers, so she volunteered in the physical therapy unit and loved it. That volunteer experience confirmed for her that physical therapy was what she should pursue as a career. She completed a degree in physical therapy and is now a professional physical therapist.

I suggested to Chris, the student who was thinking about becoming an elementary school teacher, that he visit some local schools to see whether they could use a volunteer teacher's aide. One of the schools did need his services, and Chris volunteered as a teacher's aide for about 10 weeks. At the halfway point during his volunteer experience, he came into my office to tell me that the kids were just about driving him crazy and that he no longer had any interest in becoming a teacher. He ended up majoring in communications.

Kim and Chris were the first two students I advised to get involved in volunteer work to test their career interests. Their volunteer experiences proved so valuable for helping both of them make a career decision that I now encourage all students I advise to get volunteer experience in the fields they're considering for future careers.

Joe Cuseo

Volunteer service also enables you to network with professionals outside of college who may serve as excellent references and resources for letters of recommendation for you. Furthermore, if these professionals are impressed with your volunteer work, they may become interested in hiring you part-time while you're still in college or full time when you graduate.

It may be possible to do volunteer work on campus by serving as an informal teaching assistant or research assistant to a faculty member. Such experiences are particularly valuable for students intending to go to graduate school. If you have a good relationship with any faculty members who are working in an academic field that interests you, consider asking them whether they would like some assistance (e.g., with their teaching or research responsibilities). Your volunteer work for a college professor could lead to making a presentation with your professor at a professional conference or even result in your name being included as a coauthor on an article published by the professor.

Think About It ———————————————— *Journal Entry* 10.13

Have you done volunteer work? If you have, did you learn anything from your volunteer experiences that might help you decide which types of work best match your interests or talents?

No.

_____

_____

_____

_____

_____

_____

Jobs that you hold during the academic year or during summer break should not be overlooked as potential sources of career information and as resume-building experience. Part-time work can provide opportunities to learn or develop skills that may be relevant to your future career, such as organizational skills, communication skills, and the ability to work effectively with co-workers from diverse backgrounds or cultures.

Also, work in a part-time position may eventually turn into a full-time career. The following personal story illustrates how this can happen.

It might also be possible for you to obtain part-time work experience on campus through your school's work-study program. A work-study job allows you to work at your college in various work settings, such as the Financial Aid Office, College Library, Public Relations Office, or Computer Services Center, and often allows you to build your employment schedule around your academic schedule. On-campus work can provide you with valuable career-exploration and resume-building experiences, and the professionals for whom you work can serve as excellent references for letters of recommendation to future employers. To see whether you are eligible for your school's work-study program, visit the Financial Aid Office on your campus.

Learning about careers through firsthand experience in actual work settings (e.g., shadowing, internships, volunteer services, and part-time work) is critical to successful career exploration and preparation. You can take a career-interest test, or you can test your career interest through actual work experiences. There is simply no substitute for direct, hands-on experience for gaining knowledge about careers. These firsthand experiences represent the ultimate career-reality test. They allow you direct access to information about what careers are really like, as opposed to how they are portrayed on TV or in the movies, which often paint an inaccurate or unrealistic picture of careers, making them appear more exciting or glamorous than they are.

In summary, firsthand experiences in actual work settings equip you with five powerful career advantages:

- Learn about what work is like in a particular field;
- Test your interest and skills for certain types of work;
- Strengthen your resume by adding experiential learning to academic (classroom) learning;
- Acquire contacts for letters of recommendation; and
- Network with employers who may refer or hire you for a position after graduation.

"Give me a history major who has done internships and a business major who hasn't, and I'll hire the history major every time."

—William Ardery, senior vice president, investor communications company (quoted in *The New York Times*)

Be sure to use your campus resources (e.g., the Career Development Center, Counseling Center, and Financial Aid Office), your local resources (e.g., chamber of commerce), and your personal contacts (family and friends) to locate and participate in work experiences that relate to your career interests. When you land an internship, work hard at it, learn as much as you can from it, and build relationships with as many people as possible at your internship site, because these are the people who can provide you with future contacts, references, and referrals.

Think About It ——————————— Journal Entry 10.14

1. Have you learned anything from your firsthand work experiences that may influence your future career plans?

   Nope

2. If you could get firsthand work experience in any career field right now, what career would it be? Why?

   Cosmotology Because you need to build up your clients.

Step 3. Awareness of What Best Fits You

When considering career options, don't buy into either of the following common myths about careers, which can lead students to poor career decisions.

Myth 1. Once you've decided on a career, you have decided on what you'll be doing for the rest of your life. This is simply and totally false. The term *career* derives from the same root word as *racecourse*. Like a racecourse, a career involves movement that typically takes different turns and twists, and as in any race, it's not how fast you start but how strong you finish that matters most. This ability to move and change direction is what distinguishes a professional career from a dead-end job. Americans average four careers in a lifetime; it's also estimated that today's college graduates will change jobs 12 to 15 times, which will span three to five career fields (U.S. Bureau of Labor Statistics, 2005). These statistics may be surprising because you're probably going to college with the idea that you're preparing for a particular career. However, these results become less surprising when you consider that the general education component of your college experience provides you with versatile, transferable skills that can qualify you for different positions in various career fields.

Myth 2. You need to pick a career that's in demand and that will get you a job with a good starting salary right after graduation. Looking only at careers that are "hot" now and have high starting salaries can distract you from looking at yourself and cause you to overlook a more important question: are these careers truly compatible with your personal abilities, interests, needs, and values? Starting salaries and available job openings are external factors that can be easily seen and counted; thus, they may get more attention and receive more weight in the decision-making process than qualities that are harder to see and put a number on, such as inner characteristics. In the case of career decision making, this can result in college students choosing careers based exclusively on external factors (salaries and openings) without giving equal (or any) attention to such internal factors as personal abilities, interests, and values. This can lead some college graduates to enter careers that eventually leave them bored, frustrated, or dissatisfied.

The number of job offers you receive immediately after graduation and the number of dollars you earn as a starting salary in your first position are short-term (and shortsighted) standards for judging whether you've made a good career choice. Remember that there's a critical difference between career *entry* and career *advancement*. Some college graduates may not bolt out of the starting gate and begin their career paths with well-paying first positions, but they will steadily work their way up the career ladder and be promoted to more advanced positions than graduates who start out with higher salaries.

Criteria (Standards) to Consider When Evaluating Career Options

Effective decision making requires you to identify all important factors that should be considered when evaluating your options and determine how much weight (influence) each of these factors should carry. As we emphasize throughout this chapter, the factor that should carry the greatest weight in career decision making is the match between your choice and your personal abilities, interests, needs, and values.

Suppose you discover more than one career option that's compatible with these four dimensions of yourself. What other aspects of a career should be considered to help you reach a decision and make a selection? Many people would probably say salary, but as the length of the following list suggests, other important aspects or characteristics of careers should be factored into your decision-making process.

- **Work conditions.** Work conditions include such considerations as:
  - the nature of the work environment (e.g., physical and social environment);
  - the geographical location of the work (e.g., urban, suburban, or rural);
  - the work schedule (e.g., number of hours per week and flexibility of hours); and
  - work-related travel (e.g., opportunities to travel, frequency of travel, and locations traveled to).
- **Career entry.** Can you enter into the career without much difficulty, or does the supply of people pursuing the career far exceed the demand (e.g., professional acting or athletes)? If a career is highly competitive and difficult to gain entry into, it doesn't mean you should automatically give up on it; however, it does mean you should have an alternative career to fall back on until you can (or in case you can't) catch a break that will allow you to break into your ideal career.
- **Career advancement (promotion).** An ideal first job educates and prepares you to advance to an even better one. Will the career you're considering provide you with opportunities for promotion to more advanced positions?
- **Career mobility.** Is it easy to move out of the career and into a different career path? This may be an important factor to consider because careers may rise or fall in demand; furthermore, your career interests or values may change as you gain more work and life experience.
- **Financial benefits.** Financial considerations include salary—both starting salary and expected salary increases with greater work experience or advancement to higher positions. However, they also include fringe benefits, such as health insurance, paid vacation time, paid sick-leave time, paid maternity- or paternity-leave time, paid tuition for seeking advanced education, and retirement benefits.

- **Impact of the career on your personal life.** How would the career affect your family life, your physical and mental health, and your self-concept or self-esteem? Remember that your life should not be built around your career: your career should be built around your life. Your means of making a living and other important aspects of yourself need to be considered simultaneously when making career choices, because the nature of your work will affect the nature (and quality) of your life.

"The French work to live, but the Swiss live to work."
—French proverb

> **Remember**
>
> *A good career decision should involve more than salary and should take into consideration how the career will affect all dimensions of your self (social, emotional, physical, etc.) throughout all stages of your adult life: young adulthood, middle age, and late adulthood. It's almost inevitable that your career will affect your identity, the type of person you become, how you will balance the demands of work and family, and how well you will serve others beyond yourself. An effective career decision-making process requires you to make tough and thoughtful decisions about what matters most to you.*

"Money is a good servant but a bad master."
—French proverb

Think About It ————————— Journal Entry 10.15

Answer the following questions about a career that you're considering or have chosen:

1. What is the career?

    Cosmotology

2. Why are you considering this career? (What led or caused you to become interested in it?)

    I love it.

3. Would you say that your interest in this career is motivated primarily by intrinsic factors—that is, factors "inside" of you, such as your personal abilities, interests, needs, and values? Or, would you say that your interest in the career is influenced more heavily by extrinsic factors—that is, factors "outside" of you, such as starting salary, pleasing parents, meeting family expectations, or meeting an expected role for your gender (male role or female role)? Why?

    I love making he and people look better

4. If money was not an issue and you could earn a comfortable living in any career, would you choose the same career? Why or why not? What career would you choose?

    Yes. I would do the same, Cosmotology.

Step 4. Awareness of the Process

Whether you're keeping your career options open or you've already decided on a particular career, you can start preparing for career success by using the following strategies.

Self-Monitoring: Watching and Tracking Your Personal Skills and Positive Qualities

Don't forget that *learning* skills are also *earning* skills. The skills you're acquiring in college may appear to be just *academic* skills, but they're also *career* skills. For instance, when you're in the process of completing academic tasks such as taking tests and writing papers, you're using various career-relevant skills (e.g., analyzing, organizing, communicating, and problem solving).

Many students think that a college diploma or certificate is an automatic passport to a good job and career success (Ellin, 1993; Sullivan, 1993). However, for most employers of college graduates, what matters most is not only the credential but also the skills and personal strengths an applicant brings to the position (Education Commission of the States, 1995). You can start building these skills and strengths by self-monitoring (i.e., watching yourself and keeping track of the skills you're using and developing during your college experience). Skills are mental habits, and like all other habits that are repeatedly practiced, their development can be so gradual that you may not even notice how much growth is taking place—perhaps somewhat like watching grass grow. Thus, career development specialists recommend that you consciously track your skills to remain aware of them and to put you in a position to "sell" them to potential employers (Lock, 2000).

One strategy you can use to track your developing skills is to keep a career-development journal in which you note academic tasks and assignments you've completed, along with the skills you used to complete them. Be sure to record skills in your journal that you've developed in nonacademic situations, such as those skills used while performing part-time jobs, personal hobbies, cocurricular activities, or volunteer services. Since skills are actions, it's best to record them as action verbs in your career-development journal.

The key to discovering career-relevant skills and qualities is to get in the habit of stepping back from your academic and out-of-class experiences to reflect on what skills and qualities these experiences entailed and then get them down in writing before they slip your mind. You're likely to find that many personal skills you develop in college will be the same ones that employers will seek in the workforce.

Author's Experience

After class one day, I had a conversation with a student (Max) about his personal interests. He said he was considering a career in the music industry and was now working part-time as a disc jockey at a nightclub. I asked him what it took to be a good disc jockey, and in less than five minutes of conversation, we discovered many more skills were involved in doing his job than either of us had realized. He was responsible for organizing three to four hours of music each night he worked; he had to read the reactions of his audience (customers) and adapt or adjust his selections to their musical tastes; he had to arrange his selections in a sequence that periodically varied the tempo (speed) of the music he played throughout the night; and he had to continually research and update his music collection to track the latest trends in hits and popular artists. Max also said that he had to overcome his fear of public speaking to deliver announcements that were a required part of his job.

Although we were just having a short, friendly conversation after class about his part-time job, Max wound up reflecting on and identifying multiple skills he was using on the job. We both agreed that it would be a good idea to get these skills down in writing so that he could use them as selling points for future jobs in the music industry or in any industry.

Joe Cuseo

10.2 DO IT NOW!

Personal Skills Relevant to Successful Career Performance

The following behaviors represent a sample of useful skills that are relevant to success in various careers (Bolles, 1998). As you read these skills, underline or highlight any of them that you have performed, either inside or outside of school.

advising	assembling	calculating	coaching	coordinating
creating	delegating	designing	evaluating	explaining
initiating	mediating	measuring	motivating	negotiating
operating	planning	producing	proving	researching
resolving	sorting	summarizing	supervising	synthesizing
translating				

In addition to tracking your developing skills, track your positive traits or personal qualities. While it's best to record your skills as action verbs because they represent actions that you can perform for anyone who hires you, it may be best to track your attributes as adjectives because they describe who you are and what personal qualities you can bring to the job. Do It Now! 10.3 gives a sample of personal traits and qualities that are relevant to success in multiple careers. As you read these traits, underline or highlight any of them that you feel you possess or will soon possess.

10.3 DO IT NOW!

Personal Traits and Qualities Relevant to Successful Career Performance

broad-minded	cheerful	congenial	conscientious	considerate
courteous	curious	dependable	determined	energetic
enthusiastic	ethical	flexible	imaginative	industrious
loyal	observant	open-minded	outgoing	patient
prepared	persistent	persuasive	positive	precise
productive	punctual	reasonable	reflective	sincere
tactful	thorough			

Remember

Keeping track of your developing skills and your positive qualities is as important to your successful entry into a future career as completing courses and compiling credits.

Self-Marketing: Packaging and Presenting Your Personal Strengths and Achievements

To convert your college experience into immediate employment, it might be useful to view yourself (a college graduate) as a product and employers as intentional customers who may be interested in making a purchase (of your skills and attributes). As a first-year student, it could be said that you're in the early stages of the product-development process. Now is the time to begin the process so that by the time you graduate, your finished product (you) will be one that employers notice and become interested in purchasing.

An effective self-marketing plan is one that gives employers a clear idea of what you can bring to the table and do for them. This should increase the number of job offers you receive and increase your chances of finding a position that best matches your interests, talents, and values.

You can effectively advertise or market your personal skills, qualities, and achievements to future employers through the following channels:

- College transcript
- Cocurricular experiences
- Personal portfolio
- Personal resume
- Letters of application (a.k.a. cover letters)
- Letters of recommendation (a.k.a. letters of reference)
- Networking
- Personal interview

These are the primary tools you will use to showcase yourself to employers and employers will use to evaluate you. Here's how you can strategically prepare for and sharpen these tools to maximize their effectiveness.

College Transcript

A college transcript is a listing of all courses you enrolled in and the grades you received in those courses. Two pieces of information included on your college transcript can influence employers' hiring decisions or admissions committee decisions about your acceptance to a four-year college, graduate, or professional school: (1) the grades you earned in your courses, and (2) the types of courses you completed.

Simply stated, the better your grades in college, the better your employment prospects after college. Research on college graduates indicates that the higher their grades, the higher:

- The prestige of their first job;
- Their total earnings; and
- Their job mobility.

This relationship between college grades and career success exists for students at all types of colleges and universities, regardless of the reputation or prestige of the institution they attend (Pascarella & Terenzini, 1991, 2005).

The particular types of courses listed on your college transcript can also influence employment and acceptance decisions. Listed here the types of courses that should strengthen your college transcript.

- **Honors courses.** If you achieve excellent grades during your first year, you may apply or be recommended for the honors program at your campus and take more academically challenging courses. If you qualify for the honors program, we recommend that you accept the challenge. Even though A grades may be more difficult to achieve in honors courses, the presence of these courses on your college transcript clearly shows that you were admitted to the honors program and were willing to accept this academic challenge.

- **Leadership courses.** Many employers hire college graduates with the hope or expectation that they will advance and eventually assume important leadership positions in the company or organization. Although a leadership course is not likely to be required for general education, or for your major, it is an elective course that will develop your leadership skills and the impressiveness of your college transcript.

- **International and cross-cultural courses.** Courses whose content crosses national and cultural boundaries are often referred to as international and cross-cultural courses. These courses are particularly pertinent to success in today's world, in which there is more international travel, more interaction among citizens from different countries, and more economic interdependence among nations than at any other time in world history (Office of Research, 1994). As a result of these developments, employers now place higher value on employees with international knowledge and foreign language skills (Fixman, 1990; Office of Research, 1994). Taking courses that have an international focus, or that focus on cross-cultural comparisons, helps you develop a global perspective that can improve the quality of your college degree and increase the attractiveness of your college transcript to potential employers.

- **Diversity (multicultural) courses.** America's workforce is more ethnically and racially diverse today than at any other time in the nation's history, and it will grow even more so in the years ahead (U.S. Bureau of Labor Statistics, 2005). Successful career performance in today's diverse workforce requires sensitivity to human differences and the ability to relate to people from different cultural backgrounds (National Association of Colleges & Employers, 2003; Smith, 1997). College courses relating to diversity awareness and appreciation, or courses emphasizing multicultural interaction and communication, can be valuable additions to your college transcript that should strengthen your career preparation, placement, and advancement.

Co-Curricular Experiences

Participation in student clubs, campus organizations, and other types of co-curricular activities can be a valuable source of experiential learning that can complement classroom-based learning and contribute to your career preparation and development. A sizable body of research supports the value of co-curricular experiences for career success (Astin, 1993; Kuh, 1993; Pascarella & Terenzini, 1991, 2005). Strongly consider getting involved in co-curricular life on your campus, especially involvement with co-curricular experiences that:

- Allow you to develop leadership and helping skills (e.g., leadership retreats, student government, college committees, peer counseling, or peer tutoring);
- Enable you to interact with others from diverse ethnic and racial groups (e.g., multicultural club or international club), and
- Provide you with out-of-class experiences related to your academic major or career interests (e.g., student clubs in your college major or intended career field).

Keep in mind that co-curricular experiences are also resume-building experiences that provide solid evidence of your commitment to the college community outside the classroom. Be sure to showcase these experiences to prospective employers.

Also, the campus professionals with whom you may interact while participating in co-curricular activities (e.g., the director of student activities or dean of students) can serve as valuable references for letters of recommendation to future employers or graduate and professional schools.

Personal Portfolio

You may have heard the word *portfolio* used to mean a collection of artwork that professional artists put together to showcase or advertise their artistic talents. However, a portfolio can be a collection of any materials or products that illustrates an individual's skills and talents or demonstrates an individual's educational and personal development. For example, a portfolio could include such items as:

- Outstanding papers, exam performances, research projects, or lab reports;
- Artwork, photos from study abroad, service learning, or internships experiences;
- Video footage of oral presentations or theatrical performances;
- CDs of musical performances;
- Assessments from employers or coaches; and
- Letters of recognition or commendation.

You can start the process of portfolio development right now by saving your best work and performances. Store them in a traditional portfolio folder, or save them on a computer disc to create an electronic portfolio. Another option would be to create a Web site and upload your materials there. Eventually, you should be able to build a well-stocked portfolio that documents your skills and demonstrates your development to future employers or future schools. You can start to develop an electronic portfolio now by completing the Creating an Electronic Portfolio exercise at the end of this chapter.

Letters of Application (a.k.a. Cover Letters)

You write a letter of application when applying for a position opening or for acceptance to a school. When writing these letters, be sure that you demonstrate awareness and knowledge of:

- Yourself (e.g., your personal interests, abilities, and values);
- The organization or institution to which you are applying (e.g., showing that you know something specific about its purpose, philosophy, programs, and the position you are applying for); and
- The match or fit between you and the organization (e.g., between the skills and qualities you possess and those that the position requires).

Focusing on these three major points should make your letter complete and will allow the letter to flow sequentially from a focus on *you*, to a focus on *them*, to a focus on the *relationship* between you and them. Here are some suggestions for developing each of these three points in your letter of application.

10.4   DO IT **NOW**

Constructing a Resume

Use this skeletal resume as an outline or template for beginning construction of your own resume and for setting your future goals. (If you have already developed a resume, use this template to identify and add categories that may be missing from your current one.)

Name (First, Middle, Last)

Current Addresses: Permanent Addresses:

Postal Address   Postal Address

E-mail address   E-mail address

Phone no.   Phone no.

EDUCATION: Name of College or University, City, State

Degree Name (e.g., Bachelor of Science)

College Major (e.g., Accounting)

Graduation Date, GPA

RELATED WORK   Position Title, City, State   Start and stop dates

EXPERIENCES: (Begin the list with the most recent
                             position dates held.)

(List skills used or developed.)

VOLUNTEER (COMMUNITY SERVICE)
EXPERIENCES:

(List skills used or developed.)

NOTABLE COURSEWORK:
(e.g., leadership, international, or interdisciplinary courses)

CO-CURRICULAR EXPERIENCES:
(e.g., student government or peer leadership)
(List skills used or developed.)

PERSONAL SKILLS AND POSITIVE QUALITIES:
(List as bullets. Be sure to include those that are especially relevant to the position for which you're applying.)

HONORS/AWARDS: (In addition to those received in college, you may include those received in high school.)

- **Organize information about yourself into a past-present-future sequence of personal development.** For instance, point out the following:
    - Where you have been—your past history or background experiences that qualify you to apply for the position (academic, co-curricular, and work experiences).
    - Where you are now—why you've decided to apply for the position today.
    - Where you intend to go—what you hope to do or accomplish for the employer once you get there.

Taking this past-present-future approach to organizing your letter should result in a smooth, well-sequenced flow of information about you and your development. Also, by focusing on where you've been and where you're going, you demonstrate your ability to reflect on the past and project to the future.

When describing yourself, try to identify specific examples or concrete illustrations of your positive qualities and areas in which you have grown or improved in recent years. While it is important to highlight all your major strengths, this doesn't necessarily mean you should ignore or cover up areas in which you feel you still need to improve or develop. No human is perfect; one indication of someone with a healthy self-concept is that person's ability to recognize and acknowledge both personal strengths and areas in which further improvement or development is needed. Including a touch of honest self-assessment in your letter of application demonstrates both sincerity and integrity. It should also reduce the risk that your letter will be perceived as a "snow job" that pours on mounds and pounds of self-flattery without an ounce of personal humility.

- **Do some advance research about the particular organization to which you're applying.** In your letter of application, mention some aspects or characteristics of the organization that you've learned about, such as one of its programs that impressed you or attracted your interest. This sends the message that you have taken the time and initiative to learn something about the organization, which says something positive about you.
- **Make it clear why you feel there is a good fit or match between you and the organization to which you've applied.** When applying for a position, your first objective is to focus on what you can do for the organization rather than what it can do for you or what's in it for you. Point out how your qualities, skills, interests, or values are in line with the organization's needs or goals. By doing some research on the particular institution or organization that you're applying to, and by including this information in your letter of application, you also distinguish your application from the swarms of standard "form letters" that companies receive from other applicants.

Letters of Recommendation (a.k.a. Letters of Reference)

Personal letters of recommendation can be a powerful way to document your strengths and selling points. To maximize the power of your personal recommendations, give careful thought to:

- Who should serve as your references;
- How to approach them; and
- What to provide them.

Strategies for improving the quality of your letters of recommendation are suggested in Do It Now! 10.5.

10.5

The Art and Science of Requesting Letters of Recommendation: Effective Strategies and Common Courtesies

1. **Select recommendations from people who know you well.** Think about individuals with whom you've had an ongoing relationship, who know your name, and who know your strengths: for example, an instructor who you've had for more than one class, an academic advisor whom you see often, or an employer whom you've worked for over an extended period.

2. **Seek a balanced blend of letters from people who have observed you perform in different settings or situations.** The following are settings in which you may have performed well and people who may have observed your performance in these settings:
   - The classroom—a professor who can speak to your academic performance.
   - On campus—a student life professional for a co-curricular reference who can comment on your contributions outside the classroom.
   - Off campus—a professional for whom you've performed volunteer service, part-time work, or an internship.

3. **Pick the right time and place to make your request.** Be sure to make your request well in advance of the letter's deadline date (e.g., at least two weeks). First ask whether the person is willing to write the letter, and then come back with forms and envelopes. Do not approach the person with these materials in hand, because this may send the message that you have assumed or presumed the person will automatically say "yes." (This is not the most socially sensitive message to send someone whom you're about to ask for a favor.) Lastly, pick a place where the person can give full attention to your request. For instance, make a personal visit to the person's office, rather than making the request in a busy hallway or in front of a classroom full of students.

4. **Waive your right to see the letter.** If the school or organization to which you're applying has a reference-letter form that asks whether or not you want to waive (give up) your right to see the letter, waive your right—as long as you feel reasonably certain that you will be receiving a good letter of recommendation. By waiving your right to see your letter of recommendation, you show confidence that the letter to be written about you will be positive, and you assure the person who reads the letter that you didn't inspect or screen it to make sure it was a good one before sending it.

5. **Provide your references with a fact sheet about yourself.** Include your experiences and achievements—both inside and outside the classroom. This will help make your references' job a little easier by providing points to focus on. More importantly, it will help you because your letter becomes more powerful when it contains concrete examples or illustrations of your positive qualities and accomplishments. On your fact sheet, be sure to include any exceptionally high grades you may have earned in certain courses, as well as volunteer services, leadership experiences, special awards or forms of recognition, and special interests or talents that relate to your academic major and career choice. Your fact sheet is the place and time for you to "toot your own horn," so don't be afraid of coming across as a braggart or egotist. You're not being conceited—you're just showcasing your strengths.

6. **Provide your references with a stamped, addressed envelope.** This is a simple courtesy that makes their job a little easier and demonstrates your social sensitivity.

7. **Follow up with a thank-you note.** Thank your references at about the time when your letter of recommendation should be sent.

   This is the right thing to do because it shows your appreciation; it's also the smart thing to do because if the letter hasn't been written yet, the thank-you note serves as a gentle reminder for your reference to write the letter.

8. **Let your references know the outcome of your application** (e.g., your admission to a school or acceptance of a job offer). This is the courteous thing to do, and your references are likely to remember your courtesy, which could strengthen the quality of any future letters they may write for you.

1. Have you met a faculty member or other professional on campus who knows you well enough to write a personal letter of recommendation for you?

    Maybe.

2. If yes, who is this person, and what position does he or she hold on campus?

    My old teacher. Had her for 3-4 yrs.

Networking

Would it surprise you to learn that 80 percent of jobs are never advertised? This means that the jobs you see listed in a classified section of the newspaper and posted in a Career Development Center or employment center represent only 20 percent of available openings at any given time. Almost one-half of all job hunters find employment through people they know or have met, such as friends, family members, and casual acquaintances. When it comes to locating positions, *whom* you know can be as important as *what* you know or how good your resume looks. Consequently, it's important to continually expand the circle of people who are aware of your career interests and abilities, because they can be a valuable source of information about employment opportunities.

Also, be sure to share copies of your resume with friends and family members, just in case they come in contact with employers who are looking for somebody with your career interests and qualifications.

Personal Interview

A personal interview is your opportunity to make a positive in-person impression. You can make a strong first impression during any interview by showing that you've done your homework and have come prepared. In particular, you should come to the interview with knowledge about yourself and your audience.

You can demonstrate knowledge about yourself by bringing a mental list of your strongest selling points to the interview and being ready to speak about them when the opportunity arises. You can demonstrate knowledge of your audience by doing some homework on the organization you are applying to, the people who are likely to be interviewing you, and the questions they are likely to ask you. Try to acquire as much information about the organization and its key employees as is available to you online and in print. When you know your audience (who your interviewers are likely to be and what they're likely to ask), and when you know yourself well (what about yourself you're going to say), you should then be ready to answer what probably is the most important interview question of all: "What can *you* do for *us?*"

To prepare for interviews, visit your Career Development Center and inquire about questions that are commonly asked during personal interviews. You might also try to speak with seniors who have interviewed with recruiters and ask them whether certain questions tended to be frequently asked. Once you begin to participate in actual interviews, make note of the questions you are asked. Although you may be able to anticipate some of the more general questions that are asked in almost any interview, there likely will be unique questions asked of you that relate specifically to your personal qualifications and experiences. If these questions are asked in one of your interviews, there's a good chance they'll be asked in a future interview. As soon as you complete an interview, mentally review it and attempt to recall the major questions you were asked before they slip your mind. Consider developing an index-card catalog of questions that you've been asked during interviews, with the question on one side and your prepared response on the reverse side. By being better prepared for personal interviews, you'll increase the quality of your answers and decrease your level of anxiety. You should also have a list of questions to ask at the interview. This shows that you are interested and did your homework. Finally, remember to dress appropriately for an interview. If you are unsure how to dress, consult a professional you trust on campus.

Lastly, remember to send a thank-you note to the person who interviewed you. This is not only the courteous thing to do, but also the smart thing to do because it demonstrates your interpersonal sensitivity and reinforces the person's memory of you.

Technology and Career Placement

Once you start looking for a job, internship, or co-op, it is very important to consider how you use technology:

1. **Your e-mail address.** Make sure it is professional and would not offend anyone.
2. **Your cell phone.** Consider your "ringback tone." If it is music that has offensive language, remove it. Also, make sure your voice mail message is short and professional. Time is precious and people don't want to listen to a two-minute voice mail message, no matter what it is about.
3. **Facebook, Twitter, etc.** Make sure anything you post would not turn off any potential employers. Even if your page is marked "private," employers are hiring people to get all the dirt on you!

It is important when you are looking for a job to put your best self out there; this includes your digital self.

Summary and Conclusion

Here is a snapshot of the points that were made in this chapter:

- Changing your educational goal is not necessarily a bad thing; it may represent your discovery of another field that's more interesting to you or that's more compatible with your personal interests and talents.
- Several myths exist about the relationship between college majors and careers that need to be dispelled:
  - **Myth 1.** When you choose your major, you're choosing your career.
  - **Myth 2.** After a bachelor's degree, any further education must be in the same field as your college major.
  - **Myth 3.** You should major in business because most college graduates work in business settings.

- - **Myth 4.** If you major in a liberal arts field, the only career available is teaching.
  - **Myth 5.** Specialized skills are more important for career success than general skills.
- You should be aware of two important elements when choosing your major: your form or forms of multiple intelligence (your mental strengths or talents) and your learning style (your preferred way of learning).
- Strategically select your courses in a way that contributes most to your educational, personal, and professional development. Choose your elective courses with one or more of the following purposes in mind:
  - Choose a major or confirm whether your first choice is a good one.
  - Acquire a minor or build a concentration that will complement your major.
  - Broaden your perspectives on the world around you.
  - Become a more balanced or complete person.
  - Handle the practical life tasks that face you now and in the future.
  - Strengthen your career development and employment prospects after graduation.

With higher education comes more freedom of choice and a greater opportunity to determine your own academic course of action. Employ it and enjoy it—use your freedom strategically to make the most of your college experience and college degree.

In national surveys, employers rank attitude of the job applicant as the number one factor in making hiring decisions; they rate is higher in importance than such factors as reputation of the applicant's school, previous work experience, and recommendations of former employers (Education Commission of the States, 1995; Institute for Research on Higher Education, 1995). Graduating from college with a diploma or certificate may make you a more competitive job candidate, but you still have to compete by documenting and selling your strengths and skills. Your diploma or certificate doesn't work like a merit badge or passport that you flash to gain automatic access to an ideal job. Your college experience will open career doors, but it's your attitude, initiative, and effort that will enable you to step through those doors and into a successful career.

Learning More through the World Wide Web

Internet-Based Resources for Further Information on Educational Planning and Decision Making

For additional information related to the ideas discussed in this chapter, we recommend the following Web sites:

www.mymajors.com

www.princetonreview.com/majors.aspx

www.eace.org/networks/liberalarts.html

www.internships.com

www.vaultreports.com

mappingyourfuture.org/PlanYourCareer/

www.monster.com

www.salary.com

10.1 Planning General Education

- Look at your college catalog. If you don't have a copy, you may be able to access it online or obtain a copy from your academic advisor or Registrar's Office. Use the index in the catalog to find the general education requirements at your college. You're likely to find that general education requirements are organized into academic divisions of knowledge that make up the college curriculum, such as humanities, fine arts, and natural sciences. Within each of these academic divisions, you'll see courses listed that fulfill the general education requirement for that particular division. In some cases, you'll have no choice about what courses you must take to fulfill the general education requirement, but in most cases, you'll have the freedom to choose from a group of courses. Read the course descriptions to get an idea about what each course covers, and choose those courses that are most relevant to your educational and career plans or to your interests in fields that you might consider choosing as a major.

- Record the courses you plan to take to fulfill your general education requirements on the following form. (Remember that courses you are taking this term may be fulfilling certain general education requirements, so be sure to include them on the form.)

General Education Planning Form

Academic Division: _Echs Boo_

General education courses you plan to take to fulfill requirements in this division:

(Record the course number and course title)

Academic Division: _English 1150_

General education courses you plan to take to fulfill requirements in this division:

Academic Division: _Psych 1010_

General education courses you plan to take to fulfill requirements in this division:

Academic Division: _echs 1000_

General education courses you plan to take to fulfill requirements in this division:

Academic Division: _____Math___115_

General education courses you plan to take to fulfill requirements in this division:

Academic Division: _____Englis___1000_

General education courses you plan to take to fulfill requirements in this division:

10.2 Planning for a College Major and Transfer to a Four-Year College

In the preceding exercise, you made a plan for the general education component of your college experience. Now consider developing a tentative plan for a college major or specialized field of study. Even if you don't think you're going to transfer to a four-year college and complete a bachelor's degree, it's still a good idea to complete this exercise because it'll give you an idea about what it would take to get such a degree. It's possible that when you see it all laid out in a plan, you might be motivated to pursue a bachelor's degree—if not right now, then perhaps at a later point in your life.

1. Go to your college catalog and use its index to locate pages containing information related to the major you have chosen or are considering. If you are undecided, select a field that you might consider as a possibility. To help you identify possible majors, you can use your catalog or go online and complete the short interview at the www.mymajors.com Web site.

    The point of this exercise is not to force you to commit to a major now, but to familiarize you with the process of developing a plan, thereby putting you in a position to apply this knowledge when you reach a final decision about the major you intend to pursue. Even if you don't yet know what your final destination may be with respect to a college major, creating this educational plan will keep you moving in the right direction.

2. Once you've selected a major for this assignment, look at the catalog of the four-year college to which you plan to transfer to identify the courses that are required for the major you have selected. Use the form that follows to list the number and title of each course required by the major.

    You'll find that you must take certain courses for the major; these are often called core requirements. For instance, at most colleges, all business majors must take microeconomics. You will likely discover that you can choose other required courses from a menu or list of options (e.g., "choose any three courses from the following list of six courses"). Such courses are often called restricted electives in the major. When you find restricted electives in the major you've selected, read the course descriptions and choose those courses from the list that appeal most to you. Simply list the numbers and titles of these courses on the planning form. (You don't need to write down all choices listed in the catalog.)

    College catalogs can sometimes be tricky to navigate or interpret, so if you run into any difficulty, don't panic. Seek help from an academic advisor. Your campus may also have a degree audit program available, which allows you to track major requirements electronically. If so, take advantage of it.

College Major Planning Form

Major Selected: __Cosmetology__

Core Requirements in the Major
(Courses in your major that you must take)

Course #	Course Title		Course #	Course Title
07	Hair			
09	Skin			
10	makup			
12	nails			

Restricted Electives in the Major
(Courses required for your major that you choose to take from a specified list)

Course #	Course Title		Course #	Course Title
01	Biology			

Self-Assessment Questions

1. Looking over the courses required for the major you've selected, would you still be interested in majoring in this field?

   Yes

2. Were there courses required by the major that you were surprised to see or that you did not expect would be required?

   No

3. Are there questions that you still have about this major?

   Nope!

10.3 Developing a Comprehensive Transfer and Graduation Plan

A comprehensive, long-range graduation plan includes all three types of courses you need to complete a college degree:

1. General education requirements

2. Major requirements

3. Free electives

In the preceding exercises, you planned for your required general education courses and required courses in your major. The third set of courses you'll take in college that count toward your degree consists of courses called free electives—courses that are not required for general education or your major but that you freely choose from any of the courses listed in your college catalog. By combining your general education courses, major courses, and free elective courses, you can create a comprehensive, long-term transfer and graduation plan.

Use the form on p. 333 to develop this complete educational plan. Use the slots to pencil in the general education courses you're planning to take to fulfill your general education requirements, your major requirements, and your free electives. Since this may be a tentative plan, it's probably best to use a pencil when completing it in case you need to make modifications to it.

Notes

1. If you have not decided on a major, a good strategy might be to concentrate on taking liberal arts courses to fulfill your general education requirements during your first year of college. This will open more slots in your course schedule during your sophomore year. By that time, you may have a better idea of what you want to major in, and you can fill these open slots with courses required by your major. This may be a particularly effective strategy if you choose to major in a field that has many lower-division (freshman and sophomore) requirements that have to be completed before you can be accepted as a transfer student in that major. (These lower-division requirements are often referred to as premajor requirements.)

2. Keep in mind that the course number indicates the year in the college experience that the course is usually taken. Courses numbered in the 100s (or below) are typically taken in the first year of college, 200-numbered courses in the sophomore year, 300-numbered courses in the junior year, and 400-numbered courses in the senior year. Also, be sure to check whether the course you're planning to take has any prerequisites—courses that need to be completed before you can enroll in the course you're planning to take. For example, if you are planning to take a course in literature, it is likely that you cannot enroll in it until you have completed at least one prerequisite course in writing or English composition.

3. To complete a college degree in four years, you should complete about 30 credits each academic year. Summer term is considered part of an academic year, and we encourage you to use that term to help keep you on a four-year timeline.

4. Check with an academic advisor to see whether your college and the four-year college to which you're planning to transfer have developed a projected plan of scheduled courses, which indicates the academic term when courses listed in the catalog are scheduled to be offered (e.g., fall, spring, or summer) for the next two to three years. If such a long-range plan of scheduled courses is available, take advantage of it because it will enable you to develop a personal educational plan that includes not only what courses you will take but also when you will take them. This can be an important advantage because some courses you may need for graduation will not be offered every term. We strongly encourage you to inquire about and acquire any long-range plan of scheduled courses that may be available and use it when developing your long-range graduation plan.

5. Don't forget to include out-of-class learning experiences as part of your educational plan, such as volunteer service, internships, and study abroad.

Your long-range graduation plan is not something set in stone that can never be modified. Like clay, its shape can be molded and changed into a different form as you gain more experience with the college curriculum. Nevertheless, your creation of this initial plan will be useful because it will provide you with a blueprint to work from. Once you have created slots specifically for your general education requirements, your major courses, and your electives, you have accounted for all the categories of courses you will need to complete to graduate. Thus, if changes need to be made to your plan, they can be easily accommodated by simply substituting different courses into the slots you've already created for these three categories.

Remember

The purpose of this long-range planning assignment is not to lock you into a rigid plan, but to give you a telescope for viewing your educational future and a map for reaching your educational goals.

Long-Range Transfer and Graduation Planning Form

STUDENT: Amanda Noble   ID NO.: 1128988

MAJOR: Cosmetology   MINOR: Child development

TERM: 1		TERM:		TERM:		TERM:	
Course	Units	Course	Units	Course	Units	Course	Units
Makeup	1						
Hair	2						
Skin	1						
Nails	1						
TOTAL		TOTAL		TOTAL		TOTAL	

TERM:		TERM:		TERM:		TERM:	
Course	Units	Course	Units	Course	Units	Course	Units
TOTAL		TOTAL		TOTAL		TOTAL	

TERM:		TERM:		TERM:		TERM:	
Course	Units	Course	Units	Course	Units	Course	Units
TOTAL		TOTAL		TOTAL		TOTAL	

TERM:		TERM:		TERM:		TERM:	
Course	Units	Course	Units	Course	Units	Course	Units
TOTAL		TOTAL		TOTAL		TOTAL	

		CO-CURRICULAR EXPERIENCES	SERVICE LEARNING AND INTERNSHIP EXPERIENCES
Advisor's Signature	Date:		
Student's Signature	Date:		
Notes:			

Self-Assessment Questions

1. Do you think this was a useful assignment? Why or why not? *No, didn't really help*

2. Do you see any way in which this assignment could be improved or strengthened? *No*

3. Did completing this long-range graduation plan influence your educational plans in any way? *Nope.*

10.4 Conducting an Informational Interview

To learn accurate information about a career that interests you, interview working professionals in that career—a career-exploration strategy known as informational interviewing. An informational interview enables you to:

- Learn what a career is really like;

- Network with professionals in the field; and

- Become confident in interview situations and prepare for later job interviews.

Self-Assessment Questions

1. Select a career that you may be interested in pursuing. Even if you are currently keeping your career options open, pick a career that might be a possibility. You can use the resources cited on p. 309 in this chapter to help you identify a career that may be most appealing to you.

2. Find someone who is working in the career you selected and set up an informational interview with that person. To help locate possible interview candidates, consider members of your family, friends of your family members, and family members of your friends. Any of these people may be working in the career you selected and may be good interview candidates, or they may know others who could be good candidates. The Career Development Center on your campus may also be able to provide you with graduates of your college or professionals working in the local community near your college who are willing to talk about their careers with students. Lastly, you might consider using the Yellow Pages or the Internet to find names and addresses of possible candidates. Send them a short letter or e-mail asking about the possibility of scheduling a short interview. Mention that you would be willing to conduct the interview in person or by phone, whichever would be more convenient for them. If you do not hear back within a reasonable period (e.g., within a couple of weeks), send a follow-up message; if you do not receive a response to the follow-up message, then consider contacting someone else.

3. Conduct an informational interview with the professional who has agreed to speak with you. Consider using the following suggested strategies.

10.5 Suggested Strategies for Conducting Informational Interviews

First, thank the person for taking the time to speak with you. This should be the first thing you do after meeting the person, before you officially begin the interview.

Prepare your interview questions in advance. Here are some questions that you might consider asking:

1. How did you decide on your career?

2. What qualifications or prior experiences did you have that enabled you to enter your career?

3. How does someone find out about openings in your field?

4. What steps did you take to find your current position?

5. What advice would you give to beginning college students about things they could start doing now to help them prepare to enter your career?

6. During a typical day's work, what do you spend most of your time doing?

7. What do you like most about your career?

8. What are the most difficult or frustrating aspects of your career?

9. What personal skills or qualities do you see as being critical for success in your career?

10. How does someone advance in your career?

11. Are there any moral issues or ethical challenges that tend to arise in your career?

12. Are members of diverse groups likely to be found in your career? (This is an especially important question to ask if you are a member of an ethnic, racial, or gender group that is underrepresented in the career field.)

13. What impact does your career have on your home life or personal life outside of work?

14. If you had to do it all over again, would you choose the same career?

15. Would you recommend that I speak with anyone else to obtain additional information or a different perspective on this career field? (If the answer is "yes," you may follow up by asking, "May I mention that you referred me?") This question is recommended because it's always a good idea to obtain more than one person's perspective before making an important choice or decision, especially one that can have a major influence on your life, such as your career choice.

Take notes during the interview. This not only benefits you by helping you remember what was said, but also sends a positive message to the person you're interviewing by showing that the person's ideas are important and worth writing down.

If the interview goes well, you could ask whether it might be possible to observe or shadow your interviewee during a day at work.

Self-Assessment Questions

After completing your interview, take a moment to reflect on it and answer the following questions:

1. What information did you receive that impressed you about this career?

2. What information did you receive that distressed (or depressed) you about this career?

3. What was the most useful thing you learned from conducting this interview?

4. Knowing what you know now, would you still be interested in pursuing this career? If yes, why? If no, why not?

Dazed and Confused: General Education versus Career Specialization

Joe Tech was looking forward to college because he thought he would have freedom to select the courses he wanted and the opportunity to get into the major of his choice (computer science). However, he is shocked and disappointed with his first-term schedule of classes because it consists mostly of required general education courses that do not seem to relate to his major, and some of these courses are about subjects that he already took in high school (English, history, and biology). He's beginning to think he would be better off moving off the transfer track and getting a technical degree so that he could finish sooner, get into the computer industry, and start earning money.

Discussion Questions

1. What do you see as the potential advantages and disadvantages of Joe pursuing a technical degree instead of a four-year college degree?

   He maybe not get a job or made limited.

2. Can you relate to Joe, or do you know of students who feel as he does?

   I can relate. You just have to wait a little longer.

3. Do you see any way Joe might strike a balance between pursuing his career interest and obtaining his college degree so that he can pursue both goals at the same time?

   Yes. Just wait and do as told.

Career Choice: Conflict and Confusion

Josh is a first-year student whose family has made a great financial sacrifice to send him to college. He deeply appreciates the tremendous commitment his family has made to his education and wants to pay them back as soon as possible. Consequently, he has been looking into careers that offer the highest starting salaries to college students immediately after graduation. Unfortunately, none of these careers seem to match Josh's natural abilities and personal interests, so he's conflicted, confused, and starting to get stressed out. He knows he'll have to make a decision soon because the careers with high starting salaries involve majors that have many course requirements, and if he expects to graduate in a reasonable period, he'll have to start taking some of these courses during his first year.

Discussion Questions

1. If you were Josh, what would you do?

   Do something he likes

2. Do you see any way that Josh might balance his desire to pay back his parents as soon as possible with his desire to pursue a career that's compatible with his interests and talents?

   Nope. Just wait.

3. What other questions or factors do you think Josh should consider before making his decision?

   Will he like his job still in twenty years.

Chapter 10 Reflection

What is your ideal career?

Cosmotologist

What would your work day be like?

Doing hair, makeup, nails, etc.

Make a **detailed** plan for how you can get to this career.

go to School

get a job

Make your own customers.

What are some things you can utilize from this chapter to make it happen?

Make your own dreams happen
and be realistic

Welcome to Macomb Community College!

My name is Linda Bajdo, and I am a psychology professor at Macomb Community College. I teach a variety of courses, including Introduction to Psychology, Psychological Statistics, Human Sexuality, Psychology of Gender, and Industrial and Organizational Psychology. I am naturally very curious, which is why I enjoy teaching so many different courses and getting to know all of my students each semester.

One of the things I really like about Macomb Community College is the diversity among our students. As people, our identities include factors such as race, ethnicity, social class, language, gender, sexual orientation, age, ability, and religion. Even though we may not realize it, these identities often serve as lenses through which we experience the world and other people.

I grew up in a suburb of Detroit that was not very diverse at all. Everyone pretty much looked like me, talked like me, and lived in homes that were similar to mine. My parents taught me that every person should be treated with dignity and respect and that prejudice and discrimination were wrong. Despite my limited experiences, I left for college confident that I was open minded about others and would not allow stereotypes to influence my feelings and behavior.

In one of my classes during my first year of college, I was assigned to work on a project about personal finance with a woman who had recently come to the United States from Uganda. I am embarrassed to admit that my heart sank. I was worried that we would have difficulty communicating because of the language barrier, or that because I was a "traditional student" and she was a few years older, we would not have anything in common and therefore would not have fun working together. Worst of all, I wondered whether she would have enough knowledge about the United States to contribute to a project about personal finance. So much for avoiding the use of stereotypes in my judgment! It turned out that I was so wrong about so many things. My partner knew a great deal more about managing finances than I did since she was married with a family and was accustomed to managing her own finances in multiple currencies. We did have some trouble communicating at first, but once we got used to each others' accents, we were able to understand each other well enough. Although we did not have much in common in terms of our life experiences, we did both want to succeed with our project. As I look back, I wonder whether her heart sank when she found out that she was assigned to work with someone so limited in her life experiences! If so, I am grateful that she treated me with such patience and kindness. During the course of our work together, I discovered that my partner was interesting, kind, funny, and smart. We did a great job on our project and both of us were proud of the result.

No lesson my parents could have taught me compared with my actual experience working with someone who was different from me. I learned something about myself that made me uncomfortable and that changed me. Since then, I am more aware of my own "lenses" and how they might influence my interpretations of events and other people. I make it a point to interact with people who are not "just like me," and

I try to avoid making snap judgments about them. At Macomb, you have the opportunity to do the same thing. Go out of your way to interact with people whose identities are different from yours. Be open minded enough to learn from each individual you encounter, and try to recognize how your "lenses" may actually cloud your point of view and limit your experiences. Obviously, I think that the knowledge you gain in your classes is important to your future success (I am a teacher, after all!). I also think that the things you learn when you step out of your comfort zone are just as important—and perhaps even more important—to your success as a person.

I am Linda Bajdo and I am Macomb.

Diversity and the Community College Experience

Appreciating the Value of Human Differences for Promoting Learning and Personal Development

THOUGHT STARTER | *Journal Entry* **11.1** | **LEARNING GOAL**

To appreciate the value of human differences and acquire skills for making the most of diversity in college and beyond.

Complete the following sentence:

When I hear the word *diversity*, the first thoughts that come to my mind are . . .

Different people and things

The Spectrum of Diversity

The word *diversity* derives from the Latin root *diversus*, meaning "various." Thus, human diversity refers to the variety of differences that exist among the people that comprise humanity (the human species). In this chapter, we use *diversity* to refer primarily to differences among the major groups of people who, collectively, comprise humankind or humanity. The relationship between diversity and humanity is represented visually in Figure 11.1.

The relationship between humanity and human diversity is similar to the relationship between sunlight and the spectrum of colors. Just as the sunlight passing through a prism is dispersed into all groups of colors that make up the visual spectrum, the human species that's spread across the planet is dispersed into all groups of people that make up the human spectrum (humanity).

As you can see in Figure 11.1, groups of people differ from one another in numerous ways, including physical features, religious beliefs, mental and physical abilities, national origins, social backgrounds, gender, sexual orientation, and other personal dimensions.

"We are all brothers and sisters. Each face in the rainbow of color that populates our world is precious and special. Each adds to the rich treasure of humanity."

—Morris Dees, civil rights leader and cofounder of the Southern Poverty Law Center

FIGURE 11.1

SPECTRUM
of
DIVERSITY

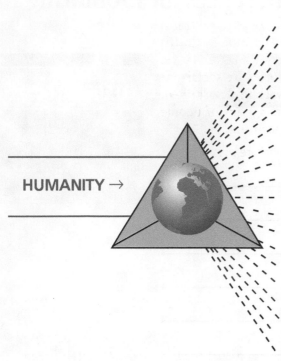

HUMANITY →

Gender (male-female)
Age (stage of life)
Race (e.g., White, Black, Asian)
Ethnicity (e.g., Native American, Hispanic, Irish, German)
Socioeconomic status (job status/income)
National citizenship (citizen of U.S. or another country)
Native (first-learned) language
National origin (nation of birth)
National region (e.g., raised in north/south)
Generation (historical period when people are born and live)
Political ideology (e.g., liberal/conservative)
Religious/spiritual beliefs (e.g., Christian/Buddhist/Muslim)
Family status (e.g., single-parent/two-parent family)
Marital status (single/married)
Parental status (with/without children)
Sexual orientation (heterosexual/homosexual/bisexual)
Physical ability/disability (e.g., able to hear/hearing impaired)
Mental ability/disability (e.g., mentally able/challenged)
Learning ability/disability (e.g., absence/presence of dyslexia)
Mental health/illness (e.g., absence/presence of depression)

_ _ _ _ _ _ = dimension of diversity

*This list represents some of the major dimensions of human diversity; it does not represent a complete list of all possible forms of human diversity. Also, disagreement exists about certain dimensions of diversity (e.g., whether certain groups should be considered races or ethnic groups).

© Kendall Hunt

Humanity and Diversity

Think About It ———————————— Journal Entry 11.2

Look at the diversity spectrum in Figure 11.1 and look over the list of groups that make up the spectrum. Do you notice any groups that are missing from the list that should be added, either because they have distinctive backgrounds or because they have been targets of prejudice and discrimination?

Nope

Since diversity has been interpreted (and misinterpreted) in different ways by different people, we begin by defining some key terms related to diversity that should lead to a clearer understanding of its true meaning and value.

What Is Race?

A racial group (race) is a group of people who share some distinctive physical traits, such as skin color or other facial characteristics. The U.S. Census Bureau (2010) identifies four races: White, Black, Asian, and American Indian or Alaska Native. However, as Anderson and Fienberg (2000) caution, racial categories are social-political constructs (concepts) that are not scientifically based but socially determined. There continues to be disagreement among scholars about what groups of people constitute a human "race" or whether distinctive races exist (Wheelright, 2005). No specific genes differentiate one race from another. In other words, you couldn't do a blood test or any type of internal genetic test to determine a person's race. Humans have simply decided to categorize people into races on the basis of certain external differences in physical appearance, particularly the color of their outer layer of skin. The U.S. Census Bureau could just as easily have divided people into categories based on such physical characteristics as eye color (blue, brown, and green) or hair texture (straight, wavy, curly, and frizzy).

Author's Experience My mother was from Alabama and was dark in skin color, with high cheekbones and long curly black hair. My father stood approximately six feet tall and had light brown straight hair. His skin color was that of a Western European with a slight suntan. If you did not know that my father was of African American descent, you would not have thought of him as Black. All of my life I have thought of myself as African American, and all of the people who are familiar with me thought of me as African American. I have lived half of a century with that as my racial description. Several years ago, after carefully looking through records available on births and deaths in my family history, I discovered that fewer than 50 percent of my ancestors were of African lineage. Biologically, I am no longer Black. Socially and emotionally, I still am. Clearly, race is more of a social concept than a biological fact.

Aaron Thompson

The differences in skin color that now occur among humans are likely due to biological adaptations that evolved over long periods among groups of humans who lived in regions of the world with different climatic conditions. For instance, darker skin tones developed among humans who inhabited and reproduced in hotter regions nearer the equator (e.g., Africa), where darker skin enabled them to adapt and survive by providing their bodies with better protection from the potentially damaging effects of the sun (Bridgeman, 2003) and allowing their bodies to better use the vitamin D supplied by sunlight (Jablonski & Chaplin, 2002). In contrast, lighter skin tones developed over time among humans inhabiting colder climates that were farther from the equator (e.g., Scandinavia) to enable their bodies to absorb greater amounts of sunlight, which was in shorter supply in their region of the world.

While humans may display diversity in skin color or tone, the biological reality is that all members of the human species are remarkably similar. More than 98 percent of the genes that make up humans from different racial groups are the same (Bridgeman, 2003; Molnar, 1991). This large amount of genetic overlap among humans accounts for the many similarities that exist, regardless of what differences in color appear at the surface of skin. For example, all humans have similar external features that give them a "human" appearance and clearly distinguish people from other animal species, all humans have internal organs that are similar in structure and function, and no matter what the color of the outer layer of skin, when it's cut, all humans bleed in the same color.

Author's Experience   I was proofreading this chapter while sitting in a coffee shop in the Chicago O'Hare airport. I looked up from my work for a second and saw what appeared to be a White girl about 18 years old. As I lowered my head to return to my work, I did a double-take to look at her again because something about her seemed different or unusual. When I looked at her more closely the second time, I noticed that although she had light skin, the features of her face and hair appeared to be those of an African American. After a couple of seconds of puzzlement, I figured it out: she was an *albino* African American. That satisfied me for the moment, but then I began to wonder: Would it still be accurate to say that she was "Black" even though her skin was light? Would her hair and facial features be sufficient for her to be considered or classified as Black? If yes, then what about someone who had a dark skin tone but did not have the typical hair and facial features characteristic of Black people? Is skin color the defining feature of being African American, or are other features equally important? I was unable to answer these questions, but I found it amusing that these thoughts were taking place while I was working on a book dealing with diversity. Later, on the plane ride home, I thought again about that albino African American girl and realized that she was a perfect example of how classifying people into races is based not on objective, scientifically determined evidence but on subjective, socially constructed categories.

— *Joe Cuseo*

Think About It ——————————— *Journal Entry* 11.3

What race do you consider yourself to be? Would you say you identify strongly with your race, or are you rarely conscious of it? Explain.

White. Yes I do identify.

What Is Culture?

Culture may be defined as a distinctive pattern of beliefs and values learned by a group of people who share the same social heritage and traditions. In short, culture is the whole way in which a group of people has learned to live (Peoples & Bailey, 1998); it includes style of speaking (language), fashion, food, art, music, values, and beliefs.

A major advantage of culture is that it helps bind its members together into a supportive, tight-knit community; however, it can also blind them to other cultural perspectives. Since culture shapes the way people think, it can cause groups of people to view the world solely through their own cultural lens or frame of reference

Cultural differences can exist within the same society (multicultural society), within a single nation (domestic diversity), or across different nations (international diversity).

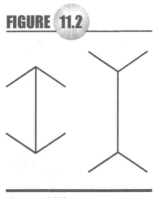

FIGURE 11.2

Optical Illusion

(Colombo, Cullen, & Lisle, 1995). Optical illusions are a good illustration of how cultural perspectives can blind people or lead them to inaccurate perceptions. For instance, compare the lengths of the two lines in Figure 11.2.

If you perceive the line on the right to be longer than the line on the left, welcome to the club. Virtually all Americans and people from Western cultures perceive the line on the right to be longer. Actually, both lines are equal in length. (If you don't believe it, take out a ruler and check it out.) Interestingly, this perceptual error is not made by people from non-Western cultures that live in environments populated with circular structures rather than structures with linear patterns and angled corners, like Westerners use (Segall, Campbell, & Herskovits, 1966).

The key point underlying this optical illusion is that cultural experiences shape and sometimes distort perceptions of reality. We think we are seeing things objectively or "as they really are," but we are often seeing things subjectively from our limited cultural vantage point. Being open to the viewpoints of diverse people who perceive the world from different cultural vantage points widens our range of perception and helps us overcome our "cultural blind spots." As a result, we tend to perceive the world around us with greater clarity and accuracy.

Remember

The reality of our own culture is not the reality of other cultures. Our perceptions of the outside world are shaped (and sometimes distorted) by our prior cultural experiences.

What Is an Ethnic Group?

An ethnic group (ethnicity) is a group of people who share the same culture. Thus, *culture* refers to *what* an ethnic group has in common and *ethnic group* refers to a group of people *who* share the same culture. Unlike a racial group, whose members share physical characteristics that they are born with and that have been passed on biologically, an ethnic group's shared characteristics have been passed on through socialization—that is, their common characteristics have been *learned* or acquired through shared social experiences.

Currently, European Americans are the majority ethnic group in the United States because they account for more than 50 percent of the American population. Native Americans, African Americans, Hispanic Americans, and Asian Americans are considered to be ethnic minority groups because each of these groups represents less than 50 percent of the American population.

| Think About It | *Journal Entry* **11.4** |

Which ethnic group or groups do you belong to or identify with? What are the most common cultural values shared by your ethnic group or groups?

White, Polish art italian

As with the concept of race, whether a particular group of people is defined as an ethnic group can be arbitrary, subjective, and interpreted differently by different groups of people. Currently, the only races recognized by the U.S. Census Bureau are White, Black, and Asian; Hispanic is not defined as a race but is classified as an ethnic group. However, among those who checked "some other race" in the 2000 census, 97 percent were Hispanic. This fact has been viewed by Hispanic advocates as a desire for their "ethnic" group to be reclassified as a racial group (Cianciotto, 2005).

This disagreement illustrates how difficult it is to conveniently categorize groups of people into particular racial or ethnic groups. The United States will continue to struggle with this issue because the ethnic and racial diversity of its population is growing and members of different ethnic and racial groups are forming cross-ethnic and interracial families. Thus, it is becoming progressively more difficult to place people into distinct categories based on their race or ethnicity. For example, by 2050, the number of people who will identify themselves as being of two or more races is projected to more than triple, growing from 5.2 million to 16.2 million (U.S. Census Bureau, 2008).

What Is Humanity?

It is important to realize that human *variety* and human *similarity* exist side by side and complement each other. Diversity is a "value that is shown in mutual respect and appreciation of similarities and differences" (Public Service Enterprise Group, 2009.) Experiencing diversity not only enhances our appreciation of the unique features of different cultures, but also provides us with a larger perspective on the universal aspects of the human experience that are common to all humans, no matter what their particular cultural background may be. For example, despite our racial and cultural differences, all people express the same emotions with the same facial expressions (see Figure 11.3).

FIGURE 11.3

Humans all over the world display the same facial expressions when experiencing certain emotions. See if you can detect the emotions being expressed in the following faces. (To find the answers, turn your book upside down.)

All images © JupiterImages Corporation.

Answers: The emotions shown. Top, left to right: anger, fear, and sadness. Bottom, left to right: disgust, happiness, and surprise.

Think About It — Journal Entry 11.5

List three human experiences that you think are universal—that is, they are experienced by all humans in all cultures:

1. _spending time with family_
2. _Bullying_
3. _being made fun of_

Other human characteristics that anthropologists have found to be shared across all groups of people in every corner of the world include storytelling, poetry, adornment of the body, dance, music, decoration of artifacts, families, socialization of children by elders, a sense of right and wrong, supernatural beliefs, explanations of diseases and death, and mourning of the dead (Pinker, 1994). Although different ethnic groups may express these shared experiences in different ways, these universal experiences are common to all humans.

Remember

Diversity represents variations on the common theme of humanity. Although people have different cultural backgrounds, they are still cultivated from the same soil—they are all grounded in the common experience of being human.

"We are all the same, and we are all unique."

—Georgia Dunston, African American biologist and research specialist in human genetics

Thus, different cultures associated with different ethnic groups may be viewed simply as variations on the same theme: being human. You may have heard the question "We're all human, aren't we?" The answer to this important question is "yes and no." Yes, we are all the same, but not in the same way.

A good metaphor for understanding this apparent contradiction is to visualize humanity as a quilt in which we are all joined together by the common thread of humanity—by the common bond of being human. Yet the different patches that make up the quilt represent diversity—the distinctive or unique cultures that comprise our common humanity. The quilt metaphor acknowledges the identity and beauty of all cultures. It differs from the old American melting pot metaphor, which viewed differences as something that should be melted down or eliminated, or the salad bowl metaphor, which suggested that America is a hodgepodge or mishmash of different cultures thrown together without any common connection. In contrast, the quilt metaphor suggests that the cultures of different ethnic groups should be recognized and celebrated. Nevertheless, our differences can be woven together to create a unified whole—as in the Latin expression *E pluribus unum* ("Out of many, one"), the motto of the United States, which you will find printed on all U.S. coins.

"We have become not a melting pot but a beautiful mosaic."

—Jimmy Carter, 39th president of the United States and winner of the Nobel Peace Prize

To appreciate diversity and its relationship to humanity is to capitalize on the power of our differences (diversity) while still preserving our collective strength through unity (humanity).

Remember

By learning about diversity (our differences), we simultaneously learn about our commonality (our shared humanity).

Author's Experience   When I was 12 years old and living in New York City, I returned from school one Friday afternoon and my mother asked me if anything interesting happened at school that day. I mentioned to her that the teacher went around the room, asking students what we had eaten for dinner the night before. At that moment, my mother began to become a bit agitated and nervously asked me, "What did you tell the teacher?" I said, "I told her and the rest of the class that I had pasta last night because my family always eats pasta on Thursdays and Sundays." My mother exploded and fired back at me, "Why couldn't you tell her that we had steak or roast beef?" For a moment, I was stunned and couldn't figure out what I had done wrong or why I should have lied about eating pasta. Then it suddenly dawned on me: My mother was embarrassed about being an Italian American. She wanted me to hide our family's ethnic background and make it sound like we were very "American." After this became clear to me, a few moments later, it also became clear to me why her maiden name was changed from the Italian-sounding DeVigilio to the more American-sounding Vigilis and why her first name was changed from Carmella to Mildred. Her family wanted to minimize discrimination and maximize their acculturation (absorption) into American culture.

I never forgot this incident because it was such an emotionally intense experience. For the first time in my life, I became aware that my mother was ashamed of being a member of the same group to which every other member of my family belonged, including me. After her outburst, I felt a combined rush of astonishment and embarrassment. However, these feelings eventually faded and my mother's reaction ended up having the opposite effect on me. Instead of making me feel inferior or ashamed about being Italian American, her reaction that day caused me to become more aware of, and take more pride in, my Italian heritage.

As I grew older, I also grew to understand why my mother felt the way she did. She grew up in America's "melting pot" era—a time when different American ethnic groups were expected to melt down and melt away their ethnicity. They were not to celebrate diversity: they were to eliminate it.

— *Joe Cuseo*

What Is Individuality?

It's important to keep in mind that *individual* differences within the same racial or ethnic group are greater than the *average* differences between two different groups. For example, although you live in a world that is conscious of differences among races, differences in physical attributes (e.g., height and weight) and behavior patterns (e.g., personality characteristics) among individuals within the same racial group are greater than the average differences among various racial groups (Caplan & Caplan, 1994).

As you proceed through this book, keep in mind the following distinctions among humanity, diversity, and individuality:

- **Diversity.** We are all members of *different groups* (e.g., different gender and ethnic groups).
- **Humanity.** We are all members of the *same group* (the human species).
- **Cultural competence.** The ability to *appreciate and capitalize* on human differences by interacting effectively with people from diverse cultural backgrounds.
- **Individuality.** We are all *unique individuals* who differ from other members of any group to which we may belong.

"Every human is, at the same time, like all other humans, like some humans, and like no other human."

—Clyde Kluckhohn, American anthropologist

Major Forms or Types of Diversity

International Diversity

Moving beyond our particular countries of citizenship, we are also members of an international world that includes multiple nations. Global interdependence and international collaboration are needed to solve current international problems, such as global warming and terrorism. Communication and interaction across nations are now greater than at any other time in world history, largely because of rapid advances in electronic technology (Dryden & Vos, 1999; Smith, 1994). Economic boundaries between nations are also breaking down due to increasing international travel, international trading, and development of multinational corporations. Today's world really is a "small world after all," and success in it requires an international perspective. By learning from and about different nations, you become more than a citizen of your own country; you become cosmopolitan—a citizen of the world.

Taking an international perspective allows you to appreciate the diversity of humankind. If it were possible to reduce the world's population to a village of precisely 100 people, with all existing human ratios remaining the same, the demographics of this "world village" would look something like this:

61 would be Asians, 13 Africans, 12 Europeans, 9 Latin Americans, and 5 from the USA and Canada
50 would be male, 50 would be female
75 would be non-white; 25 white
67 would be non-Christian; 33 would be Christian
80 would live in substandard housing
16 would be unable to read or write
50 would be malnourished and 1 dying of starvation
33 would be without access to a safe water supply
39 would lack access to improved sanitation
24 would not have any electricity (and of the 76 that did have electricity, most would only use it for light at night)
 8 people would have access to the Internet
 1 would have a college education
 1 would have HIV
 2 would be near birth; 1 near death
 5 would control 32 percent of the entire world's wealth; all 5 would be U.S. citizens
48 would live on less than US$ 2 a day
20 would live on less than US$ 1 a day

Source: Family Care Foundation (2005).

Ethnic and Racial Diversity

America is rapidly becoming a more racially and ethnically diverse nation. In 2008, the minority population in the United States reached an all-time high of 34 percent of the total population. The population of ethnic minorities is now growing at a much faster rate than the White majority. This trend is expected to continue, and by the middle of the 21st century, the minority population will have grown from one-third of the U.S. population to more than one-half (54 percent), with more than 60 percent of the nation's children expected to be members of minority groups (U.S. Census Bureau, 2008).

By 2050, the U.S. population is projected to be more than 30 percent Hispanic (up from 15 percent in 2008), 15 percent Black (up from 13 percent), 9.6 percent Asian (up from 5.3 percent), and 2 percent Native American (up from 1.6 percent). The native Hawaiian and Pacific Islander population is expected to more than double between 2008 and 2050. In the same time frame, the percentage of Americans who are White will drop from 66 percent (2008) to 46 percent (2050). As a result of these population trends, ethnic and racial minorities will become the "new majority" because they will constitute the majority of Americans by the middle of the 21st century. (See Figure 11.4.)

Socioeconomic Diversity

Diversity also appears in the form of socioeconomic status or social class, which is typically stratified (divided) into lower, middle, and upper classes, depending on

FIGURE 11.4

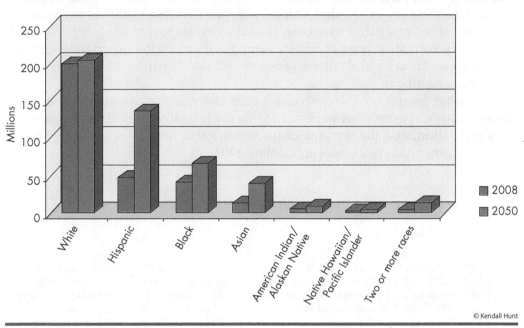

© Kendall Hunt

The "New Majority"

level of education and income. Groups occupying lower social strata have significantly fewer social and economic opportunities or privileges (Feagin & Feagin, 2007).

According to U.S. Census figures, the wealthiest 20 percent of the American population controls approximately 50 percent of the country's total income, and the 20 percent of Americans with the lowest income controls only 4 percent of the nation's income. Sharp discrepancies also exist in income level among different racial, ethnic, and gender groups. In 2007, Black households had the lowest median income ($33,916), compared to a median income of $54,920 for non-Hispanic White households (Annual Social and Economic Supplement, 2008).

Poverty continues to be a problem in America. In 2007, 12.5 percent of Americans (37.3 million people) lived below the poverty line, making the United States one of the most impoverished of all developed countries in the world (Shah, 2008). Although all ethnic and racial groups experience poverty, minority groups experience poverty at significantly higher rates than the White majority. In 2007, poverty rates for different ethnic and racial groups were as follows:

- Whites: 8.2 percent
- Asians: 10.2 percent
- Hispanics: 21.5 percent
- Blacks: 24.5 percent

Source: U.S. Census Bureau (2008).

It's estimated that 600,000 families and 1.25 million children are now homeless, accounting for roughly 50 percent of the homeless population. Typically, these families comprise a mother and two children under the age of five (National Alliance to End Homelessness, 2007).

Generational Diversity

Humans are also diverse with respect to the generation in which they grew up. *Generation* refers to a group of individuals born during the same historical period whose attitudes, values, and habits have been shaped by events that took place in the world during their formative years of development. Each generation experiences different historical events, so it's likely that generations will develop different attitudes and behaviors as a result.

Snapshot Summary 11.1 provides a brief summary of the major generations, the key historical events that occurred during the formative periods of the people in each generation, and the personal characteristics that have been associated with a particular generation (Lancaster & Stillman, 2002).

Snapshot Summary

11.1 Generational Diversity

- **The Traditional Generation, a.k.a. the Silent Generation** (born 1922–1945). This generation was influenced by events such as the Great Depression and World Wars I and II. Characteristics associated with this generation include loyalty, patriotism, respect for authority, and conservatism.

- **The Baby Boomer Generation** (born 1946–1964). This generation was influenced by events such as the Vietnam War, Watergate, and the human rights movement. Characteristics associated with this generation include idealism, importance of self-fulfillment, and concern for equal rights.

- **Generation X** (born 1965–1980). This generation was influenced by Sesame Street, the creation of MTV, AIDS, and soaring divorce rates that produced the first "latchkey children"—youngsters who let themselves into their homes after school with their own keys because their mothers were working outside the home. Characteristics associated with this generation include self-reliance, resourcefulness, and being comfortable with change.

- **Generation Y, a.k.a. Millennials** (born 1981–2002). This generation was influenced by the September 11, 2001, terrorist attack on the United States, the shooting of students at Columbine High School, and the collapse of the Enron Corporation. Characteristics associated with this generation include a preference for working and playing in groups, being technologically savvy, and a willingness to provide volunteer service in their community (the civic generation). They are also the most ethnically diverse generation, which may explain why they are more open to diversity and see it as a positive experience.

Diversity and the College Experience

There are more than 3,000 public and private colleges in the United States. They vary in size (small to large) and location (urban, suburban, and rural), as well as in their purpose or mission (research universities, comprehensive state universities, liberal arts colleges, and community colleges). This variety makes the American higher education system the most diverse and accessible in the world. The diversity of educational opportunities in American colleges and universities reflects the freedom of opportunity in the United States as a democratic nation (American Council on Education, 2008).

The U.S. system of higher education is also becoming more diverse with respect to the people enrolled in the system. (See Snapshot Summary 11.2 for recent statistics related to diversity in U.S. community colleges.) The ethnic and racial diversity of students in American colleges and universities is rapidly rising. In 1960, Whites made up almost 95 percent of the total college population; in 2005, that percentage

Snapshot Summary

11.2 Diversity in America's Community Colleges

58% of community college students are women

53% are 22 years of age or older

Among full-time students, 50% are employed part-time and 27% are employed full-time

Among part-time students, 50% are employed full-time and 33% are employed part-time

39% are the first in their family to attend college

36% are members of a minority ethnic or racial group

17% are single parents

Source: American Association of Community Colleges (2009).

had decreased to 69 percent. At the same time, there was an increase in the percentage of Asian, Hispanic, Black, and Native American students attending college (Chronicle of Higher Education, 2003).

The rise in ethnic and racial diversity on American campuses is particularly noteworthy when viewed in light of the historical treatment of minority groups in the United States. In the early 19th century, education was not a right but a privilege available only to those who could afford to attend private schools. Members of certain minority groups were left out of the educational process altogether or were forced to be educated in racially segregated settings. For example, Americans of color were once taught in separate, segregated schools that were typically inferior in terms of educational facilities. This continued until the groundbreaking U.S. Supreme Court ruling in *Brown v. Board of Education* in 1954, which changed the face of education for people of color by ruling that "separate educational facilities are inherently unequal." The decision made it illegal for Kansas and 20 other states to deliver education in segregated classrooms.

"Of all the civil rights for which the world has struggled and fought for 5,000 years, the right to learn is undoubtedly the most fundamental."

—W. E. B. DuBois, African American sociologist, historian, and civil rights activist

Think About It ——————————— Journal Entry 11.6

1. Are you the first in your family to attend college?

No

2. Whether yes or no, how does that make you feel?

I dont mind

Author's Experience My mother was a direct descendent of slaves and moved with her parents from the Deep South at the age of 17. My father lived in an all-Black coal mining camp, into which my mother and her family moved in 1938. My father remained illiterate because he was not allowed to attend public schools in eastern Kentucky.

In the early 1960s my brother, my sister, and I were integrated into the White public schools. Physical violence and constant verbal harassment caused many other Blacks to forgo their education and opt for jobs in the coal mines at an early age. But my father remained constant in his advice to me: "It doesn't matter if they call you n____; but don't you ever let them beat you by walking out on your education." He would say to me, "Son, you will have opportunities that I never had. Just remember, when you do get that education, you'll never have to go in those coal mines and have them break your back. You can choose what you want to do, and then you can be a free man."

My parents, who could never provide me with monetary wealth, truly made me proud of them by giving me the gift of insight and an aspiration for achievement.

— *Aaron Thompson*

Think About It ———————————— *Journal Entry* **11.7**

1. What diverse groups do you see represented on your campus?

   Different ages and ethnicity

   _____

   _____

2. Are there groups on your campus that you did not expect to see or to see in such large numbers?

   No.

   _____

   _____

3. Are there groups on your campus that you expected to see but do not see or see in smaller numbers than you expected?

   yes. More older people

   _____

   _____

The Benefits of Experiencing Diversity

Diversity Promotes Self-Awareness

Learning from people with diverse backgrounds and experiences sharpens your self-knowledge and self-insight by allowing you to compare and contrast your life experiences with others whose life experiences differ sharply from your own. This comparative perspective gives you a reference point for viewing your own life, which places you in a better position to see more clearly how your unique cultural background has influenced the development of your personal beliefs, values, and lifestyle. By viewing your life in relation to the lives of others, you see more clearly what is distinctive about yourself and how you may be uniquely advantaged or disadvantaged.

When students around the country were interviewed about their diversity experiences in college, they reported that these experiences often helped them learn more about themselves and that their interactions with students from different races and ethnic groups produced "unexpected" or "jarring" self-insights (Light, 2001).

Remember

The more opportunities you create to learn from others who are different from yourself, the more opportunities you create to learn about yourself.

Diversity Stimulates Social Development

Interacting with people from various groups widens your social circle. By widening the pool of people with whom you have contact, you increase your capability and confidence in relating to people with varied life experiences, as well as your ability to converse with people on a wider range of topics. Just as seeking variety in what you eat provides greater stimulation to your taste buds, seeking variety in the people with whom you interact stimulates your social life and social skills. Research indicates that students who have more diversity experiences in college report higher levels of satisfaction with their college experience (Astin, 1993).

Diversity Enriches a College Education

Diversity magnifies the power of a college education because it helps liberate you from the tunnel vision of ethnocentric (culture-centered) and egocentric (self-centered) thinking, enabling you to get beyond yourself and your own culture to see yourself in relation to the world around you. Just as the various subjects you take in the college curriculum open your mind to multiple perspectives, so does your experience with people from varied backgrounds; it equips you with a wide-focus lens that allows you to take a multicultural perspective. A multicultural perspective helps you become aware of cultural "blind spots" and avoid the dangers of groupthink—the tendency for tight, like-minded groups of people to think so much alike that they overlook flaws in their own thinking that can lead to poor choices and faulty decisions (Janis, 1982).

Diversity Strengthens Learning and Critical Thinking

Research consistently shows that we learn more from people who are different from us than we do from people who are similar to us (Pascarella, 2001; Pascarella & Terenzini, 2005). When your brain encounters something that is unfamiliar or different than you're accustomed to, you must stretch beyond your mental comfort zone and work harder to understand it because doing so forces you to compare and contrast it to what you already know (Acredolo & O'Connor, 1991; Nagda, Gurin, & Johnson, 2005). This mental "stretch" requires the use of extra psychological effort and energy, which strengthens and deepens learning.

Student *Perspective*

"I remember that my self-image was being influenced by the media. I got the impression that women had to look a certain way. I dyed my hair, wore different clothes, more makeup . . . all because magazines, TV, [and] music videos 'said' that was beautiful. Luckily, when I was 15, I went to Brazil and saw a different, more natural beauty and came back to America more as myself. I let go of the hold the media image had on me."

—First-year college student

"Variety is the spice of life."
—American proverb

Vive la différence! ("Long live difference!")
—French saying

"Without exception, the observed changes [during college] involve greater breadth, expansion, and appreciation for the new and different."
—Ernest Pascarella and Pat Terenzini, *How College Affects Students* (2005)

"When all men think alike, no one thinks very much."
—Walter Lippmann, distinguished journalist and originator of the term *stereotype*

Diversity Promotes Creative Thinking

Experiences with diversity supply you with a broader base of knowledge and wider range of thinking styles that better enable you to think outside your own cultural box or boundaries. In contrast, limiting your number of cultural vantage points is akin to limiting the variety of mental tools you can use to solve new problems, thereby limiting your creativity.

Drawing on different ideas from people with diverse backgrounds and bouncing your ideas off them is a great way to generate energy, synergy, and serendipity—unanticipated discoveries and creative solutions. People who approach problems from diverse perspectives are more likely to look for and discover "multiple partial solutions" (Kelly, 1994). Diversity expands students' capacity for viewing issues or problems from multiple vantage points, equipping them with a wider variety of approaches to solving unfamiliar problems they may encounter in different contexts and situations.

Diversity Enhances Career Preparation and Success

Learning about and from diversity has a practical benefit: it better prepares you for the world of work. Whatever career you may choose to pursue, you are likely to find yourself working with employers, employees, co-workers, customers, and clients from diverse cultural backgrounds. America's workforce is now more diverse than at any other time in the nation's history, and it will grow ever more diverse. For example, the percentage of America's working-age population that represents members of minority groups is expected to grow from 34 percent in 2008 to 55 percent in 2050 (U.S. Bureau of Labor Statistics, 2008).

In addition to increasing diversity in America, today's work world is characterized by a global economy. Greater economic interdependence among nations, more international trading (imports and exports), more multinational corporations, and almost-instantaneous worldwide communication increasingly occur—thanks to advances in the World Wide Web (Dryden & Vos, 1999; Smith, 1994). Because of these trends, employers of college graduates now seek job candidates with the following skills and attributes: sensitivity to human differences, the ability to understand and relate to people from different cultural backgrounds, international knowledge, and foreign language skills (Fixman, 1990; National Association of Colleges & Employers, 2003; Office of Research, 1994; Smith, 1997). In one national survey, policymakers, business leaders, and employers all agreed that college graduates should be more than just "aware" or "tolerant" of diversity: they should have *experience* with diversity (Education Commission of the States, 1995).

The wealth of diversity on college campuses today represents an unprecedented educational opportunity. You may never again be a member of a community that includes so many people from such a rich variety of backgrounds. Seize this opportunity! You're now in the right place at the right time to experience the people and programs that can infuse and enrich the quality of your college education with diversity.

Stumbling Blocks and Barriers to Experiencing Diversity

Stereotypes

The word *stereotype* derives from a combination of two roots: *stereo* (to look at in a fixed way) and *type* (to categorize or group together, as in the word *typical*). Thus, stereotyping is viewing individuals of the same type (group) in the same (fixed) way.

In effect, stereotyping ignores or disregards a person's individuality; all people who share a similar group characteristic (e.g., race or gender) are viewed as having the same personal characteristics, as in the expression, "You know what they are like; they're all the same." Stereotypes involve bias, which literally means "slant." A bias can be either positive or negative. Positive bias results in a favorable stereotype (e.g., "Italians are great lovers"); negative bias produces an unfavorable stereotype (e.g., "Italians are in the Mafia"). Snapshot Summary 11.3 lists some common stereotypes.

Snapshot Summary

11.3 Examples of Common Stereotypes

Muslims are terrorists.

Whites can't jump (or dance).

Blacks are lazy.

Asians are brilliant in math.

Irish are alcoholics.

Gay men are feminine; lesbian women are masculine.

Jews are cheap.

Hispanic men are abusive to women.

Men are strong.

Women are weak.

Think About It ——————— Journal Entry 11.8

1. Have you ever been stereotyped, such as based on your appearance or group membership? If so, how did it make you feel and how did you react?

   Yes, white girl. Annoyed

2. Have you ever unintentionally perceived or treated someone in terms of a group stereotype rather than as an individual? What assumptions did you make about that person? Was that person aware of, or affected by, your stereotyping?

   Yes. That was actually millavit.

Whether you are male or female, don't let gender stereotypes limit your career options.

Author's Experience

When I was six years old, I was told by another six-year-old from a different racial group that all people of my race could not swim. That six-year-old happened to be of a different racial group. Since I could not swim at that time and she could, I assumed she was correct. I asked a boy, who happened to be of the same racial group as that little girl, if that statement were true; he responded: "Yes, it is true." Since I was from an area where few other African Americans were around to counteract this belief about Blacks, I bought into this stereotype for a long time until I finally took swimming lessons as an adult. I am now a lousy swimmer after many lessons because I did not even attempt to swim until I was an adult. The moral of this story is that group stereotypes can limit the confidence and potential of individuals who are members of the stereotyped group.

— Aaron Thompson

"Let us all hope that the dark clouds of racial prejudice will soon pass away and the deep fog of misunderstanding will be lifted from our fear-drenched communities, and in some not too distant tomorrow the radiant stars of love and brotherhood will shine over our great nation."

—Martin Luther King, Jr., civil rights activist and clergyman

Prejudice

If virtually all members of a stereotyped group are judged or evaluated in a negative way, the result is prejudice. (The word *prejudice* literally means to "pre-judge.") Technically, prejudice may be either positive or negative; however, the term is most often associated with a negative prejudgment or stigmatizing—associating inferior or unfavorable traits with people who belong to the same group. Thus, prejudice may be defined as a negative judgment, attitude, or belief about another person or group of people, which is formed before the facts are known. Stereotyping and prejudice often go hand in hand because individuals who are placed in a negatively stereotyped group are commonly prejudged in a negative way.

Someone with a prejudice toward a group typically avoids contact with individuals from that group. This enables the prejudice to continue unchallenged because there is little or no chance for the prejudiced person to have positive experiences with a member of the stigmatized group that could contradict or disprove the prejudice. Thus, a vicious cycle is established in which the prejudiced person continues to avoid contact with individuals from the stigmatized group, which, in turn, continues to maintain and reinforce the prejudice.

> "'See that man over there?'
> 'Yes.'
> 'Well, I hate him.'
> 'But you don't know him.'
> 'That's why I hate him.'"
>
> —Gordon Allport, *The Nature of Prejudice* (1954)

Discrimination

Literally translated, the term *discrimination* means "division" or "separation." Whereas prejudice involves a belief or opinion, discrimination involves an *action* taken toward others. Technically, discrimination can be either negative or positive—for example, a discriminating eater may be careful about eating only healthy foods. However, the term is most often associated with a negative action that results in a prejudiced person treating another person, or group of people, in an unfair way. Thus, it could be said that discrimination is prejudice put into action. Hate crimes are examples of extreme discrimination because they are acts motivated solely by prejudice against members of a stigmatized group. Victims of hate crimes may have their personal property damaged or they may be physically assaulted, sometimes referred to as "gay bashing" if the victim is a homosexual. Other forms of discrimination are more subtle and may take place without people being fully aware that they are discriminating. For example, evidence shows that some White, male college professors tend to treat female students and students from ethnic or racial minority groups differently than they do males and nonminority students. In particular, females and minority students in classes taught by White, male instructors tend to:

> "A lot of us never asked questions in class before—it just wasn't done, especially by a woman or a girl, so we need to realize that and get into the habit of asking questions and challenging if we want to—regardless of the reactions of the profs and other students."
>
> —Adult female college student (Wilkie & Thompson, 1993)

- Receive less eye contact from the instructor;
- Be called on less frequently in class;
- Be given less time to respond to questions asked by the instructor in class; and
- Have less contact with the instructor outside of class (Hall & Sandler, 1982, 1984; Sedlacek, 1987; Wright, 1987).

In most of these cases, the discriminatory treatment received by these female and minority students was subtle and not done consciously or deliberately by the instructors (Green, 1989). Nevertheless, these unintended actions are still discriminatory, and they may send a message to minority and female students that their ideas are not worth hearing or that they are not as capable as other students (Sadker & Sadker, 1994).

> "The best way to beat prejudice is to show them. On a midterm, I got 40 points above the average. They all looked at me differently after that."
>
> —Mexican American student (Nemko, 1988)

Think About It ——————— *Journal Entry* 11.9

Prejudice and discrimination can be subtle and only begin to surface when the social or emotional distance among members of different groups grows closer. Rate your level of comfort (high, moderate, or low) with the following situations.

Someone from another racial group:

1. Going to your school	high moderate low
2. Working in your place of employment	high moderate low
3. Living on your street as a neighbor	high moderate low

4. Living with you as a roommate   high   moderate   (low)
5. Socializing with you as a personal friend   (high)   moderate   low
6. Being your most intimate friend or romantic
   partner or   high   moderate   (low)
7. Being your partner in marriage   high   moderate   low

For any item you rated "low," what do you think was responsible for the low rating?

I dont know

Snapshot Summary

11.4 Stereotypes and Prejudiced Belief Systems about Group Inferiority

- **Ableism.** Prejudice or discrimination toward people who are disabled or handicapped—physically, mentally, or emotionally. For example, someone shows ableism by avoiding interaction with handicapped people because of anxiety about not knowing what to say or how to act around them.

- **Ageism.** Prejudice or discrimination based on age, particularly toward the elderly. For example, an ageist might believe that all "old" people are bad drivers with bad memories.

"The Constitution of the United States knows no distinction between citizens on account of color."

—Frederick Douglass, abolitionist, author, advocate for equal rights for all people, and former slave

- **Anti-Semitism.** Prejudice or discrimination toward Jews or people who practice the religion of Judaism. For example, someone could claim to hate Jews because they're the ones who "killed Christ."

- **Classism.** Prejudice or discrimination based on social class, particularly toward people of low socio-economic status. For example, a classist might focus only on the contributions made by politicians and wealthy industrialists to America, ignoring the contributions of poor immigrants, farmers, slaves, and pioneer women.

- **Ethnocentrism.** Considering one's own culture or ethnic group to be "central" or "normal," and viewing different cultures as "deficient" or "inferior." For example, people who are ethnocentric might claim that another culture is "weird" or "abnormal" for eating certain animals that they consider unethical to eat, even though they eat certain animals that the other culture would consider unethical to eat.

Student *Perspective*

"I would like to change the entire world, so that we wouldn't be segregated by continents and territories."

—College sophomore

- **Genocide.** Mass murdering of one group by another group. An example is the Holocaust during World War II, in which millions of Jews were murdered. Other examples include the murdering of Cambodians under the Khmer Rouge, the murdering of Bosnian Muslims in the former country of Yugoslavia, and the slaughter of the Tutsi minority by the Hutu majority in Rwanda.

Student
Perspective

"Most religions dictate that theirs is the only way, and without believing in it, you cannot enter the mighty Kingdom of Heaven. Who are we to judge? It makes more sense for God to be the only one mighty enough to make that decision. If other people could understand and see from this perspective, then many religious arguments could be avoided."

—First-year student

- **Heterosexism.** Belief that heterosexuality is the only acceptable sexual orientation. For example, using the slang "fag" or "queer" as an insult or put-down or believing that gays should not have the same legal rights and opportunities as heterosexuals shows heterosexism.
- **Homophobia.** Extreme fear or hatred of homosexuals. For example, people who engage in gay bashing (acts of violence toward gays) or who create and contribute to antigay Web sites show homophobia.
- **Nationalism.** Excessive interest and belief in the strengths of one's own nation without acknowledging its mistakes or weaknesses, the needs of other nations, or the common interests of all nations. For example, "blind patriotism" blinds people to the shortcomings of their own nation, causing patriots to view any questioning or criticism of their nation as disloyalty or "unpatriotic" (as in the slogans "America: right or wrong" and "America: love it or leave it!").

- **Racism.** Prejudice or discrimination based on skin color. For example, Cecil Rhodes (Englishman and empire builder of British South Africa), once claimed, "We [the British] are the finest race in the world and the more of the world we inhabit the better it is for the human race." Currently, racism is exemplified by the Ku Klux Klan, a domestic terrorist group that believes in the supremacy of the White race and considers all other races to be inferior.
- **Regionalism.** Prejudice or discrimination based on the geographical region of a nation in which an individual has been born and raised. For example, a Northerner might think that all Southerners are racists.
- **Religious bigotry.** Denying the fundamental human right of other people to hold religious beliefs or to hold religious beliefs that differ from one's own. For example, an atheist might force nonreligious (secular) beliefs on others, or a member of a religious group may believe that people who hold different religious beliefs are immoral or sinners.
- **Sexism.** Prejudice or discrimination based on sex or gender. For example, a sexist might believe that no one should vote for a female president because she would be too "emotional."
- **Terrorism.** Intentional acts of violence against civilians that are motivated by political or religious prejudice. An example would be the September 11, 2001, attacks on the United States.
- **Xenophobia.** Extreme fear or hatred of foreigners, outsiders, or strangers. For example, someone might believe that all immigrants should be kept out of the country because they will increase the crime rate.

Think About It — *Journal Entry* **11.10**

1. Have you ever held a prejudice against a particular group of people?

   _____ Yes _____

2. If you have, what was the group, and how do you think your prejudice developed?

   _____ Any _____

   _____

   _____

   _____

   _____

   _____

Student
Perspective

"I grew up in a very racist family. Even just a year ago, I could honestly say 'I hate Asians' with a straight face and mean it. My senior AP language teacher tried hard to teach me not to be judgmental. He got me to be open to others, so much so that my current boyfriend is half Chinese!"

—First-year college student

The following practices and strategies may be used to accept and appreciate individuals from other groups toward whom you may hold prejudices, stereotypes, or subtle biases that bubble beneath the surface of your conscious awareness:

1. **Consciously avoid preoccupation with physical appearances.** Go deeper and get beneath the superficial surface of appearances to judge people not in terms of how they look, but in terms of who they are and how they act. Remember the old proverb "It's what's inside that counts." Judge others by the quality of their personal character, not by the familiarity of their physical characteristics.

2. **Perceive each person with whom you interact as a unique human being.** Make a conscious effort to see each person with whom you interact not merely as a member of a group, but as a unique individual. Form your impressions of each person case by case rather than by using some rule of thumb.

This may seem like an obvious and easy thing to do, but research shows that humans have a natural tendency to perceive and conceive of individuals who are members of unfamiliar groups as being more alike (or all alike) than members of their own group (Taylor, Peplau, & Sears, 2006). Thus, you may have to consciously resist this tendency to overgeneralize and "lump together" individuals into homogeneous groups and make an intentional attempt to focus on treating each person you interact with as a unique human.

> **Remember**
>
> *While it is valuable to learn about different cultures and the common characteristics shared by members of the same culture, differences exist among individuals who share the same culture. Don't assume that all individuals from the same cultural background share the same personal characteristics.*

Interacting and Collaborating with Members of Diverse Groups

Once you overcome your biases and begin to perceive members of diverse groups as unique individuals, you are positioned to take the next step of interacting, collaborating, and forming friendships with them. Interpersonal contact between diverse people takes you beyond multicultural awareness and moves you up to a higher level of diversity appreciation that involves intercultural interaction. When you take this step to cross cultural boundaries, you transform diversity appreciation from a value or belief system into an observable action and way of living.

Your initial comfort level with interacting with people from diverse groups is likely to depend on how much experience you have had with diversity before college. If you have had little or no prior experience interacting with members of diverse groups, it may be more challenging for you to initiate interactions with diverse students on campus.

However, if you have had little or no previous experience with diversity, the good news is that you have the most to gain from experiencing diversity. Research consistently shows that when humans experience social interaction that differs radically from their prior experiences, they gain the most in terms of learning and cognitive development (Piaget, 1985; Acredolo & O'Connor, 1991).

Think About It ———————— Journal Entry 11.11

Rate the amount or variety of diversity you have experienced in the following settings:

1. The high school you attended   high   moderate   low
2. The college or university you now attend   high   moderate   low
3. The neighborhood in which you grew up   high   moderate   low
4. Places where you have worked or been employed   high   moderate   low

Which setting had the most and which had the least diversity?

work   _hometown_

_____

_____

What do you think accounts for this difference?

Nothing

_____

_____

_____

_____

_____

_____

What follows is a series of strategies for meeting and interacting with people from diverse backgrounds:

1. **Intentionally create opportunities for interaction and conversation with individuals from diverse groups.** Consciously resist the natural tendency to associate only with people who are similar to you. One way to do this is by intentionally placing yourself in situations where individuals from diverse groups are nearby and potential interaction can take place. Research indicates that meaningful interactions and friendships are more likely to form among people who are in physical proximity to one another (Latané, Liu, Nowak, Bonevento, & Zheng, 1993). Studies show that stereotyping and prejudice can be sharply reduced if contact between members of different racial or ethnic groups is frequent enough to allow time for the development of friendships (Pettigrew, 1998). You can create this condition in the college classroom by sitting near students from different ethnic or racial groups or by joining them if you are given the choice to select whom you will work with in class discussion groups and group projects.

2. **Take advantage of the Internet to "chat" with students from diverse groups on your campus or with students in different countries.** Electronic communication can be a more convenient and more comfortable way to initially interact with members of diverse groups with whom you have had little prior experience.

After you've communicated successfully *online,* you may then feel more comfortable about interacting with them *in person.* Online and in-person interaction with students from other cultures and nations can give you a better understanding of your own culture and country, as well as increase awareness of its customs and values that you may have taken for granted (Bok, 2006).

3. **Seek out the views and opinions of classmates from diverse backgrounds.** For example, during or after class discussions, ask students from different backgrounds if there was any point made or position taken in class that they would strongly question or challenge. Seeking out divergent (diverse) viewpoints has been found to be one of the best ways to develop critical thinking skills (Kurfiss, 1988).

4. **Join or form discussion groups with students from diverse backgrounds.** You can gain exposure to diverse perspectives by joining or forming groups of students who differ from you in terms of such characteristics as gender, age, race, or ethnicity. You might begin by forming discussion groups composed of students who differ in one way but are similar in another way. For instance, form a learning group of students who have the same major as you do but who differ with respect to race, ethnicity, or age. This strategy gives the diverse members of your group some common ground for discussion (your major) and can raise your group's awareness that although you may be members of different groups, you can, at the same time, be similar with respect to your educational goals and life plans.

Remember

Including diversity in your discussion groups not only provides social variety, but also promotes the quality of the group's thinking by allowing its members to gain access to the diverse perspectives and life experiences of people from different backgrounds.

5. **Form collaborative learning teams.** A learning team is more than a discussion group or a study group. It moves beyond discussion to collaborative learning—in other words, members of a learning team "colabor" (work together) as part of a joint and mutually supportive effort to reach the same goal. Studies show that when individuals from different ethnic and racial groups work collaboratively toward the attainment of a common goal, it reduces racial prejudice and promotes interracial friendships (Allport, 1954; Amir, 1976). These positive findings may be explained as follows: if individuals from diverse groups work together on the same team, no one is a member of an "out" group: instead, all are members of the same "in" group (Pratto et al., 2000; Sidanius et al., 2000).

Summary and Conclusion

Diversity refers to differences among groups of people who, together, comprise humanity. Experiencing diversity enhances our appreciation of the unique features of different cultures, and it provides us with a larger perspective on those aspects of the human experience that are common to all people, no matter what their particular cultural background happens to be.

Culture is a distinctive pattern of beliefs and values learned by a group of people who share the same social heritage and traditions. A major advantage of culture is that it helps bind groups of people into supportive, tight-knit communities. However, it can also lead its members to view the world solely through their own cultural lens, known as ethnocentrism, which can blind them from seeing the world and from taking on other cultural perspectives. Ethnocentrism can contribute to stereo-typing—viewing individual members of the same group in the same way and think-ing they all have similar personal characteristics.

If members of a stereotyped group are judged or evaluated in a negative way, the result is prejudice—a negative prejudgment about another person or group of peo-ple, which is formed before the facts are known. Stereotyping and prejudice often go hand in hand because if the stereotype is negative, individual members of the stereo-typed group are then prejudged in a negative way. Discrimination takes prejudice one step further by converting the negative prejudgment into action that results in unfair treatment of others. Thus, discrimination is prejudice put into action.

If stereotyping and prejudice are overcome, you are then positioned to experi-ence diversity and reap its multiple benefits, which include sharpened self-aware-ness, social stimulation, broadened personal perspectives, deeper learning and higher-level thinking, and career success.

College campuses today have such diversity that the educational opportunities available are unprecedented. This may be the only time in your life when you are part of an organization or community that includes so many diverse members. Seize this unique opportunity to experience the diversity of people and programs available to you and profit from the power of diversity.

Learning More through the World Wide Web

Internet-Based Resources for Further Information on Diversity

For additional information related to the ideas discussed in this chapter, we recom-mend the following Web sites:

www.tolerance.org

www.amnesty.org

www.amnesty.org/en/universal-declaration-human-rights-anniversary/declaration-text

11.1 Multigroup Self-Awareness

You can be members of multiple groups at the same time, and your membership in these groups can influence your personal development and self-identity. In the figure that follows, consider the shaded center circle to be yourself and the six nonshaded circles to be six groups you belong to that you think have influenced your personal development or personal identity.

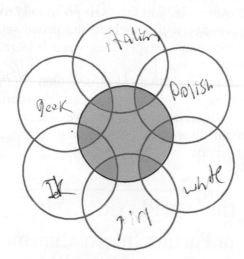

© Kendall Hunt

Fill in the nonshaded circles with the names of groups to which you belong that have had the most influence on your personal development. You can use the diversity spectrum that appears on the first page of this chapter to help you identify different groups. Do not feel you have to come up with six groups and fill all six circles. What is more important is to identify those groups that have had a significant influence on your personal development or identity.

Self-Assessment Questions

1. Which one of your groups has had the greatest influence on your personal identity, and why?
   girl, I like being it.

2. Have you ever felt limited or disadvantaged by being a member of any group or groups?
   No

3. Have you ever felt that you experienced advantages or privileges because of your membership in any group or groups? *No*

11.2 Switching Group Identity

Imagine you were to be born again as a member of a different racial or ethnic group.

1. What group would you want it to be? Why? *British, its cool.*

2. With your new group identity, what things would change in your personal life?
   Be more outgoing

3. What things would remain the same in your life even though your group identity has changed?
   Everything

Source: Adapted from University of New Hampshire Office of Residential Life (2001).

11.3 Intercultural Interview

Find a student, faculty member, or administrator on campus whose cultural background is different from yours, and ask if you can interview that person about his or her culture. Use the following questions in your interview:

1. How is "family" defined in your culture, and what are the traditional roles and responsibilities of different family members? *Immediate family*

2. What are the traditional gender (male vs. female) roles associated with your culture? Are they changing? *Man + women yes*

3. What is your culture's approach to time? (Is there an emphasis on punctuality? Is doing things fast valued or frowned upon?) *yes*

4. What are your culture's staple foods or favorite foods? *Chicken, meat, stuff like that*

5. What cultural traditions or rituals are highly valued and commonly practiced? *christianity*

6. What special holidays are celebrated? *Christmas, thanksgiving, easter*

11.4 Hidden Bias Test

Go to www.tolerance.org/activity/test-yourself-hidden-bias and take one or more of the hidden bias tests on the Web site. These tests assess subtle bias with respect to gender, age, Native Americans, African Americans, Asian Americans, religious denominations, sexual orientations, disabilities, and body weight. You can assess whether you have a bias toward any of these groups.

Self-Assessment Questions

1. Did the results reveal any bias that you were unaware of? *yes*

2. Did you think the assessment results were accurate or valid? *yes*

3. What do you think best accounts for or explains your results? *Im me*

4. If your parents and best friends took the test, how do you think their results would compare with yours? *Parents would be racist Friend same as me*

Hate Crime: A Racially Motivated Murder

Jasper County, Texas, has a population of approximately 31,000 people. In this county, 80 percent of the people are White, 18 percent are Black, and 2 percent are of other races. The county's poverty rate is considerably higher than the national average, and its average household income is significantly lower. In 1998, the mayor, president of the Chamber of Commerce, and two councilmen were Black. From the outside, Jasper appeared to be a town with racial harmony, and its Black and White leaders were quick to state there was racial harmony in Jasper.

However, on June 7, 1998, James Byrd Jr., a 49-year-old African American male, was walking home along a road one evening and was offered a ride by three White males. Rather than taking Byrd home, Lawrence Brewer (31), John King (23), and Shawn Berry (23), three individuals linked to White supremacist groups, took Byrd to an isolated area and began beating him. They then dropped his pants to his ankles, painted his face black, chained Byrd to their truck, and dragged him for approximately three miles. The truck was driven in a zigzag fashion to inflict maximum pain on the victim. Byrd was decapitated after his body collided with a culvert in a ditch alongside the road. His skin, arms, genitalia, and other body parts were strewn along the road, while his torso was found dumped in front of a Black cemetery. Medical examiners testified that Byrd was alive for much of the dragging incident.

While in prison awaiting trial, Brewer wrote letters to King and other inmates. In one letter, Brewer wrote: "Well, I did it and am no longer a virgin. It was a rush and I'm still licking my lips for more." Once the trials were completed, Brewer and King were sentenced to death. Both Brewer and King, whose bodies were covered with racist tattoos, had been on parole before the incident, and they had previously been cellmates. King had spent an extensive amount of time in prison, where he began to associate with White males in an environment in which each race was pitted against the other.

As a result of the murder, Byrd's family created the James Byrd Foundation for Racial Healing in 1998. On January 20, 1999, a wrought iron fence that separated Black and White graves for more than 150 years in Jasper Cemetery was removed in a special unity service. Members of the racist Ku Klux Klan have since visited the gravesite of Byrd several times, leaving racist stickers and other marks that have angered the Jasper community and Byrd's family.

Sources: *San Antonio Express News* (September 17, 1999), *Louisiana Weekly* (February 3, 2003), *Houston Chronicle* (June 14, 1998).

Discussion Questions

1. What factors do you think were responsible for causing this incident to take place?

2. Could this incident have been prevented? If yes, how? If no, why not?

3. What do you think will be the long-term effects of this incident on the town?

4. How likely do you think it is that an incident like this could take place in your hometown or near your college campus?

5. If this event took place in your hometown, how would you and members of your family and community react?

Chapter 11 Reflection

After reading this chapter, has your definition of *diversity* changed? Explain.

List and describe five ways appreciating diversity will assist you in being successful in college and/or in life.

1.

2.

3.

4.

5.

Are there any areas of diversity you feel you need to be more comfortable with? What are the areas and HOW will you become more comfortable with them?

Welcome to Macomb Community College!

My name is Pat Lathers, and I am part-time faculty, teaching English as a Second Language (ESL) with the Workforce & Continuing Education (WCE) program at Macomb Community College. English as a Second Language includes grammar, reading, writing, and conversation. My students come from various backgrounds and nationalities (different countries). I have found from my experience that you can be successful in your studies if you work hard, study, and become aware of the resources available to help.

There are some things in life that you can control; and some things that you can't. You can't control whether or not you are the smartest person in your class. What you can control is how hard you work. Because I had a reputation as a hard worker in everything I did, I was given a scholarship to study in the U.S. at Northwest University near Seattle, Washington. To pay for room and board, I worked in the administration offices. I apply the same attitude whether I am a student or a teacher and encourage my students to do the same.

Because of my busy schedule, I soon found that simply studying and working hard wasn't going to be enough. I needed to learn strategies to study smart and be more efficient with my time. That is where Professor K. came in. He taught me to scan and skim reading assignments. Even I don't have a photographic memory like he does—he can read a 400-page novel in about 45 minutes! His strategies helped me improve my reading and reduce my study time. He also shared how to look up background information on topics to enhance understanding while I read. In addition, I learned that I am more of a visual learner, so I learned some ideas for taking study material and making it more visually appealing and easier to remember.

I also found that it is important to be aware of the resources around you. For instance, the library at the small college I attended was good, but not great. Therefore, I learned that I could take a bus for $1 on Saturdays from our campus to the world-class library at the University of Washington. In my classes here at Macomb, I am constantly helping students make appointments with counselors, get a library card, interact with other students, and learn the registration process. There are many resources Macomb makes available to help students be successful. Learning about those resources early helps a student make them a part of their overall strategy.

I was able to finish my four years of college in three years while taking a full-time load and working a job, because I stayed organized and followed the above strategies. In my graduate studies in Reading, I learned many other techniques that I pass on to my students. I hope that I can pass on my love of reading and studying by setting an example of hard work, smart study strategies, and helping others find and use resources that are available to them.

I am Pat Lathers and I am Macomb.

Social and Emotional Intelligence

Relating to Others and Regulating Emotions

THOUGHT STARTER | *Journal Entry* **12.1** | **LEARNING GOAL**

When you think about someone who's "intelligent," what personal characteristics come to mind? Why?

Smart, knowledgeable etc. because thats what it means.

The Importance of Interpersonal Relationships for Success, Health, and Happiness

Interpersonal relationships can be a source of social support that promotes success, or a source of social conflict that distracts you from focusing on and achieving your personal goals. As a new college student, you may find yourself surrounded by multiple social opportunities. One of the adjustments you'll need to make is finding a healthy middle ground between too much and too little socializing, as well as forming solid interpersonal relationships that support rather than sabotage your educational success.

Social intelligence, a.k.a. interpersonal intelligence, is the ability to relate effectively to others and is considered to be a major form of human intelligence (Gardner, 1993; Goleman, 2006). Emotional intelligence is emotional self-awareness or empathy (sensitivity to the emotions of others). Both social and emotional intelligence are better predictors of personal and professional success than is intellectual ability (Goleman, 1995, 2006).

Social Intelligence

Studies show that people who have stronger social support networks have a longer life expectancy (Giles, Glonek, Luszcz, & Andrews, 2005) and are more likely to re-

Student
Perspective

"I have often found conflict in living a balanced academic and social life. I feel that when I am enjoying and succeeding in one spectrum, I am lagging in the other."

—First-year student

"I will pay more for the ability to deal with people than any other ability under the sun."

—John D. Rockefeller, American industrialist and philanthropist and once the richest man in the world

port being happy (Myers, 1993). The development of a strong social support system is particularly important in today's high-tech world of virtual reality and online (vs. in-person) communication, both of which make it easier to avoid direct contact, not form human connections with others, and increase the risk of isolation, loneliness, and social avoidance (Putman, 2000).

Think About It ——————————— *Journal Entry* 12.2

Who are the people in your life that you tend to turn to for social support when you are experiencing stress or need personal encouragement? Why?

My mom or my friends

Improving the Quality of Interpersonal Relationships

The quality of your interpersonal relationships rests on two skills: (1) communica-tion skills, or how well you send and receive information when interacting with oth-ers (verbally and nonverbally), and (2) human relations skills, or how well you relate to and treat people, i.e., "people skills."

Listed here are our top recommendations for strengthening your interpersonal communication skills. Some strategies may appear to be basic and obvious, but they're also powerful. It may be that because they are so basic, people overlook them and forget to use them consistently. Don't be fooled by the seeming simplicity of the following suggestions, and don't underestimate their social impact.

Strategies for Improving the Quality of Interpersonal Communication

1. **Work hard at being a good listener.** Studies show that listening is the most fre-quent human communication activity, followed, in order, by reading, speaking, and writing (Newton, 1990; Purdy & Borisoff, 1996). One study found that col-lege students spend an average of 52.5 percent of each day listening (Barker & Watson, 2000). Being a good listener is one of the top characteristics mentioned by people when they cite the positive features of their best friends (Berndt, 1992). Listening is also one of the top skills employers look for when hiring and pro-moting employees (Maes, Weldy, & Icenogle, 1997; Winsor, Curtis, & Stephens, 1997).

Human relations experts often recommend that people talk less, listen more, and listen more effectively (Nichols, 1995; Nichols & Stevens, 1957). Being a good listener is easier said than done because the ability to listen closely and sensitively is a challenging mental task. Studies show that listening comprehension for spoken messages is less than 50 percent (Nichols & Stevens, 1957; Wolvin & Coakley, 1993), which is not surprising considering that listeners have only one chance to understand words spoken to them. People cannot replay a message delivered in person like they can reread words in print. Studies also show that a person can understand spoken language at a rate almost four times faster than the average person speaks (Adler & Towne, 2001), which leaves our minds plenty of spare time to drift off to something else (e.g., think about what to say next). Since you're not actively doing something while listening, you can easily fall prey to passive listening, whereby you can give others the impression that you're focused on their words but your mind is partially somewhere else. When listening, you need to remain aware of this tendency to drift off and to actively fight it by devoting your full attention to others when they're speaking. Two key strategies for doing so are: (1) focus your attention on what the speaker is saying rather than on what you're going to say next, and (2) actively engage with the speaker's message by occasionally asking questions or seeking clarification about what is being said.

Remember

When you listen closely to those who speak to you, you send them the message that you respect their ideas and that they're worthy of your undivided attention.

2. **Be conscious of the nonverbal messages you send while listening.** Whether or not you're truly listening is often communicated silently through nonverbal body language. It's estimated that 90 percent of communication is nonverbal, because human body language often communicates stronger and truer messages than spoken language (Mehrabian, 1972). Researchers who study lying have identified one of the best ways to detect whether people are telling the truth: see whether their body language matches their spoken language. For example, if people say they're excited or enthusiastic about an idea you're communicating to them but their nonverbal communication indicates otherwise (e.g., their eyebrows don't rise and they sit motionless), you have good reason to doubt their sincerity (Eckman & Friesen, 1969).

"The most important thing in communication is to hear what isn't being said."
—Peter F. Drucker, Austrian author and founder of the study of management

When it comes to listening, body language may be the best way to communicate interest in the speaker's words, as well as interest in the person who's doing the speaking. Similarly, if you are speaking, awareness of your listeners' body language can provide important clues about whether you're holding or losing their interest.

A good mnemonic device (memory-improvement method) for remembering the nonverbal signals you should send others while listening is the acronym SOFTEN, in which each letter stands for an effective nonverbal message:

S = **Smile.** Smiling suggests interest and acceptance, but do it periodically, not continually. (A permanent smile can come across as an artificial pose.)
Sit still. Fidgeting and squirming send the message that the speaker is making you feel anxious or bored.

O = **Open posture.** Avoid closed-posture positions, such as crossing your arms or folding your hands; they can send a message that you're not open to what the speaker is saying or passing judgment on what's being said.

F = **Forward lean.** Leaning back can send a signal that you're not "into" what the person is saying or evaluating (psychoanalyzing) the person saying it. **Face the speaker directly.** Line up both shoulders with the speaker rather than turning one shoulder away, as if to give the speaker the cold shoulder.

T = **Touch.** A light touch on the arm or hand can be a good way to communicate warmth, but no rubbing, stroking, or touching in ways that could be interpreted as inappropriate intimacy (or sexual harassment).

E = **Eye contact.** Lack of eye contact sends the message that you're looking around for something more interesting or stimulating than the speaker. However, don't make continual or relentless eye contact because that borders on staring or glaring. Instead, strike a happy medium by making *periodic* eye contact.

N = **Nod your head.** Slowly and periodically, not rapidly and repeatedly—this sends the message that you want the speaker to hurry up and finish up so you can start talking.

Sending positive nonverbal signals when listening encourages others to become more self-confident and enthusiastic speakers, which not only benefits them but also benefits the listener. Listening to speakers who are more self-confident and animated makes listening less challenging and more stimulating.

3. **Be open to different topics of conversation.** Don't be a closed-minded or selective listener who listens to people like you're listening to the radio—selecting or tuning into only those conversational topics that reflect your favorite interests or personal points of view but tuning out everything else.

> **Remember**
> _____
> *People learn most from others whose interests and viewpoints don't necessarily match their own. Ignoring or blocking out information and ideas about topics that don't immediately interest you or support your particular perspective is not only a poor social skill but also a poor learning strategy.*

If people express viewpoints that you don't agree with, you don't have to nod in agreement; however, you still owe them the courtesy of listening to what they have to say (rather than shaking your head, frowning, or interrupting them). This isn't just a matter of social etiquette: it's a matter of social ethics. After others finish expressing their point of view, you should then feel free to express your own. Your informed opinions are worth expressing, as long as you don't express them in an opinionated way—that is, stating them so strongly that it sounds like your viewpoints are the only rational or acceptable ones while all others are inferior or insane (Gibb, 1961). Opinionated expression is likely to immediately end a potentially useful discussion or a possible future relationship.

Think About It ——————————— Journal Entry 12.3

On what topics do you hold strong opinions? Why?

equality, Anything thats changing and people dont agree on

When you express these opinions, how do others usually react to you?

They get mad that im not like them.

Human Relations Skills (a.k.a. People Skills)

In addition to communicating and conversing well with others, one element of managing interpersonal relationships involves how well you relate to and treat people. You can use several strategies to improve this broader set of human relations or people skills.

1. **Remember the names of people you meet.** Remembering people's names communicates to others that you know them as individuals. It makes each person you meet feel less like an anonymous face in a crowd and more like a special and unique individual with a distinctive identity.

   Although people commonly claim they don't have a good memory for names, no evidence shows that the ability to remember names is an inherited trait that people are born with and have no control over; instead, it's a skill that can be developed through personal effort and employment of effective learning and memory strategies.

   You can use the following strategies for remembering names:

   - Consciously pay attention to the name of each person you meet. Make a conscious effort to listen for the person's name rather than focus on the impression you're making on that person, the impression the individual is making on you, or what you're going to say next.

"We should be aware of the magic contained in a name. The name sets that individual apart; it makes him or her unique among all others. Remember that a person's name is to that person the sweetest and most important sound in any language."

—Dale Carnegie, author of the bestselling book *How to Win Friends and Influence People* (1936) and founder of the Dale Carnegie Course, a worldwide program for business based on his teachings

- Reinforce your memory for a new name by saying it or rehearsing it within a minute or two after you first hear it. For instance, if your friend Gertrude has just introduced you to Geraldine, you might say: "Geraldine, how long have you known Gertrude?" By using a person's name soon after you've heard it, you intercept memory loss when forgetting is most likely to occur—immediately after you acquire new information (Underwood, 1983).
- Strengthen your memory of an individual's name by associating it with other information learned about the person. For instance, you can associate the person's name with: (1) your first impression of the individual's personality, (2) a physical characteristic of the person, (3) your topic of conversation, (4) the place where you met, or (5) a familiar word that rhymes with the person's name. By making a mental connection between the person's name and some other piece of information, you help your brain form a physical connection, which is the biological foundation of human memory.

Remember

Developing the habit of remembering names is not only a social skill that can improve your interpersonal interactions and bring you friends, but also a powerful professional tool that can promote your career success in whatever field you may pursue.

In business, remembering people's names can help recruit and retain customers; in politics, it can win votes; and in education, it can promote the teacher's connection and rapport with students.

2. **Refer to people by name when you greet and interact with them.** When you greet a person, be sure to use the person's name in your greeting. Saying, "Hi, Waldo," will mean a lot more to Waldo than simply saying "Hi" or, worse yet, "Hi, there"—which sounds like you're just acknowledging something "out there" that could be either a human or an inanimate object. By continuing to use people's names after you've learned them, you continue to send them the message that you haven't forgotten their unique identities and you continue to strengthen your memory of their names.

3. **Show interest in others by remembering information about them.** Ask people questions about their personal interests, plans, and experiences. Listen closely to their answers, especially to what seems most important to them, what they care about, or what intrigues them, and introduce these topics when you have conversations with them. For one person that topic may be politics, for another it may be sports, and for another it may be relationships. When you see people again, ask them about something they brought up in your last conversation. Try to get beyond the standard, generic questions that people routinely ask after they say "Hello" (e.g., "What's going on?"). Instead, ask about something specific you discussed with them last time you spoke (e.g., "How did that math test go that you were worried about last week?"). This sends a clear message to others that you remember them and care about them. Your memory often reflects your priorities—you're most likely to remember what's most important to you. When you remember people's names and something about them, it lets them know that they're a high priority to you. Furthermore, you're likely to find that others start showing more interest in you after you show interest in them. Another surprising thing may happen when you ask questions that show interest in others: people are likely to say you're a great conversationalist and a good friend.

Author's Experience One of my most successful teaching strategies is something I do on the first day of class. I ask my students to complete a student information sheet that includes their name and some information relating to their past experiences, future plans, and personal interests. I answer the same questions I ask my students, writing my information on the board while they write theirs on a sheet of paper. (This allows them to get to know me while I get to know them.) After I've collected all their information sheets, I call out the names of individual students, asking each student to raise a hand when his or her name is called so that I can associate the name and the student's face. To help me remember the names, as I call each name I rapidly jot down a quick word or abbreviated phrase next to the student's name for later review (e.g., a distinctive physical feature or where the student's seated).

I save the student information sheets and refer back to them throughout the term. For example, I record the student's name and strongest interest on a sticky note and attach the note to my class notes near topics I'll be covering during the term that relate to the student's interest. When I get to that topic in class (which could be months later), I immediately see the student's name posted by it. When I begin to discuss the topic, I mention the name of the student who had expressed interest in it on the first day of class (e.g., "Gina, we're about to study your favorite topic"). Students often perk up when I mention their names in association with their preferred topics; plus, they're often amazed by my apparent ability to remember so much later in the term the personal interests that they shared on the first day of class. Students never ask how I remember their personal interests, so they're not aware of my sticky note strategy. Instead, they just think I have an extraordinary social memory and social sensitivity (which is just fine with me).

— *Joe Cuseo*

Strategies for Meeting People and Forming Friendships

An important aspect of the college experience is meeting new people, learning from them, and forming lifelong friendships. Here are some practical strategies for increasing the quantity and variety of the people you meet and the quality of friendships you form.

1. **Place yourself in situations and locations where you will come in regular contact with others.** Social psychologists have found that the origin of friendships is physical proximity—people are more likely to become friends if they continually find themselves in the same place at the same time (Latané et al., 1995). You can apply this principle by spending as much time on campus as possible and spending time in places where others are likely to be present (e.g., by eating your meals in the student cafeteria and studying in the college library). If you are a commuter student, try to make your college experience as similar as possible to that of a residential student: for example, try to spend study time and social time on campus (e.g., attending campus social or cultural events).

2. **Put yourself in social situations where you're likely to meet people who have similar interests, goals, and values.** Research supports the proverb, "Birds of a feather flock together." People tend to form friendships with others who share similar interests, values, or goals (AhYun, 2002). When two people have something in common, they're more likely to become friends because they're more likely to enjoy spending time together doing things that relate to their common interests. They're also more likely to get along with each other because they reinforce or validate each other's personal interests and values (Festinger, 1954; Suls, Martin, & Wheeler, 2002).

© pixinity, 2013. Under license from Shutterstock, Inc.

An important aspect of the college experience is meeting new people and forming lasting friendships.

One straightforward way to find others with whom you have something in common is by participating in clubs and organizations on campus that reflect your interests and values. If you cannot find one, start one of your own. Also, regularly check your college newspaper, posted flyers on campus, and the Student Information Desk in your Student Activities Center to keep track of social events that are more likely to attract others who share your interests, values, or goals.

3. **Meeting others through a social Web site.** Facebook and other social Web sites represent another type of venue through which you can network with other college students. You can use this electronic medium to meet new people, join groups on campus, and check for announcements of parties or other social events. However, be careful about the people you respond to, and be careful about what you post on your page or "wall." Reports indicate that both schools and employers are checking students' Facebook entries and using that information to help them decide whether to accept or reject applicants (Palank, 2006).

Romantic Relationships

Romantic relationships begin through the process of dating. Research shows that college students take different approaches to dating, ranging from not dating at all to dating with the intent of exploring or cementing long-term relationships. Following is a summary of the major forms or purposes of college dating.

The different approaches to dating described in Snapshot Summary 12.1 don't always occur separately or independently: they may be blended or combined. Romantic relationships may also evolve or grow into different stages with the passage of time. Described are the characteristics of two major stages that often take place in the evolution or maturation of romantic love.

Snapshot Summary

12.1 Approaches to Dating

Postpone dating. Students who adopt this approach feel that the demands of college work and college life are too time-consuming to take on the additional social and emotional burden of dating while in college.

Student
Perspectives

"Relationships take time and patience, and in college, both of these can be very limited."

—College student quoted in Kucewicz (2001)

"It's hard enough to have fun here with all the work you have to do. There's no reason to have the extra drama [of dating] in your life."

—College sophomore quoted in Sax (2003)

Hooking up. Students who prefer this approach believe that formal dating is unnecessary; they feel that their social and sexual needs are better met more casually by associating with friends and acquaintances. Instead of going out on a one-on-one date, they prefer to first meet and connect with romantic partners in larger group settings, such as college parties.

Casual dating. Students taking this approach go out on dates primarily for the purpose

"Now all a guy has to do to hookup on a Saturday night is to sit on the couch long enough at a party. Eventually a girl will plop herself down beside him . . . he'll make a joke, she'll laugh, their eyes will meet, sparks will fly, and the mission is accomplished. And you want me to tell this guy to call a girl, spend $100 on dinner and hope for a goodnight kiss."

—College student quoted in Beckett (2003)

of enjoying themselves, but not getting "tied down" to any particular person. These "casual daters" prefer to go out on a series of successive dates with different partners, and they may date different individuals at the same time. Their primary goal is to meet new people and discover what characteristics they find attractive in others.

Exclusive dating. Students adopting this approach prefer to date only one person for an extended period of time. Although marriage is not the goal, exclusive dating takes casual dating one step further. This form of dating may help the partners develop a clearer idea of what characteristics they may seek in an ideal spouse or long-term mate.

Courtship. This form of dating is intended to continue the relationship until it culminates in marriage or a formal, long-term commitment.

Source: Adapted from research reviewed by Seirup (2004).

Think About It — *Journal Entry* 12.4

How would you define love?

Somebody caring about you and not themselves.

Would you say that love is a feeling, an action, or both? Explain.

Both. Love makes you do stupid things.

(continued)

What do you think are the best signs that two people are in love?

That they are comfortable with eachother

What would you say is the most common reason people fall out of love?

They dont it just happens

Research reveals that romantic love involves two stages: infatuation and mature love.

Stage 1. Passionate Love (Infatuation)

This stage of romantic love is often characterized by the following features:

- **Impulsive.** Partners quickly or suddenly fall into love or are swept off their feet (e.g., "love at first sight").
- **Obsessive.** Partners can't stop thinking about each other.
- **Physical.** Heavy emphasis is placed on physical elements of the relationship. For example, lots of attention is focused on the partner's physical appearance or attractiveness, and the partners experience a high level of physical arousal and passion (i.e., erotic love in which lust and love are closely connected).
- **Emotional.** Intense emotion is characterized by a "rush" of chemical changes in the body (similar to a drug-induced state), including:
  a. Release of the hormone adrenaline that triggers faster rates of heartbeat and breathing; and
  b. Increased production of brain chemicals (e.g., dopamine) that trigger feelings of excitement, euphoria, joy, and general well-being (Bartels & Zeki, 2000).

The intensity of this emotional and chemical experience decreases with time, typically leveling off within a year after the couple has been together. The decrease in emotional intensity experienced by romantic partners after their relationship continues for an extended period is similar to the buildup of tolerance to a drug after continued use (Peele & Brodsky, 1991).

- **Idealistic.** The partner and the relationship are perceived as perfect. For example, the partners may say things like "We're perfect for each other," "Nobody else has a relationship like ours," and "We'll be together forever." This is the stage where love can be "blind"—the partner's most obvious flaws and weaknesses aren't acknowledged or even seen. As in the psychological defense mechanism of denial, the lover pushes out of conscious any awareness of the partner's personal shortcomings or any problems that may threaten the security of the relationship.

- **Attached and dependent.** The lovers feel insecure and cannot bear being separated (e.g., "I can't live without him"). This type of attachment and dependence follows the principle "I love you because I am loved" and "I love you because I need you." Thus, it may be difficult to determine whether the person is in love with the partner or is in love with the feeling of being in love or being loved (Fromm, 1970).

- **Possessive and jealous.** The lover expects exclusive rights to the partner and may become suspicious of the partner or those who interact with the partner in a friendly or affectionate manner. This suspiciousness can sometimes border on illogical or irrational; for example, "insane jealousy" may be experienced, where the lover suspects infidelity in the partner when none exists.

- **Despairing.** "Love sickness" is often experienced if the relationship breaks up. For example, an intense depression or "love withdrawal" may follow the breakup that is similar to withdrawal from a pleasure-producing drug. Studies show that the most common cause of despair or depression among college students is a romantic breakup (Foreman, 2009).

- **Lust.** There is amazing physical chemistry and it is often the only thing the lovers can think about. These people often "can't keep their hands off each other." However, lust usually runs out and there is not much "love" lost in the relationship. Young people often confuse lust with love.

When partners are caught up in this intense stage of a romantic relationship, the quality of thinking can become seriously impaired, as reflected in expressions such as:

- "madly in love"—losing ability to think rationally;
- "love is blind"—failing to see obvious flaws in the partner; and
- "insanely jealous"—having irrational thoughts about the partner "cheating" (Bassham, Irwin, Nardone, & Wallace, 2005; Ruggiero, 2004; Wade & Tavris, 1990).

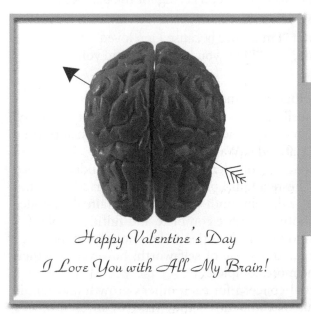

Happy Valentine's Day
I Love You with All My Brain!

Despite expressions like "I love you with all my heart," romantic love takes place in the human brain and is accompanied by major changes in the production of brain chemicals.

Stage 2. Mature Love

At the more advanced stage of a relationship, the partners gradually fall out of first-stage (puppy) love and gradually grow into a more mature stage of love that has the following characteristics:

- **Intimate.** Physical passion decreases. The "flames of the flesh" don't burn as intensely as in first-stage love, but a romantic afterglow continues. This afterglow is characterized by more emotional intimacy or closeness between the partners and greater self-disclosure, mutual trust, and honesty, which often enhance both the physical and the psychological qualities of the relationship (Viorst, 1998).

- **Balanced.** Less of an emotional high is experienced at this stage than during early stages of the relationship. For example, the mad rush of hormones and mass production of euphoria-producing brain chemicals is replaced by feelings of emotional serenity (mellowness) and emotional evenness (instead of emotional ups and downs). The love "rush" is replaced by a less intense but more consistently pleasant emotional state characterized by slightly elevated levels of different brain chemicals (endorphins rather than dopamine). Unlike infatuation or early-stage love, this pleasant emotional state doesn't decline with time; it may even grow stronger as the partners' relationship continues and matures (Bartels & Zeki, 2000).

- **Realistic.** At this more advanced stage of love, interest is focused broadly on the partner as a whole person rather than narrowly on the partner's physical qualities. Partners genuinely like one another as people and consider each other to be their "best" or "closest" friend. Partners have a realistic rather than an idealistic view of each other. Their respective strengths and weaknesses are recognized and accepted.

- **Altruistic.** The partners become less selfish and self-centered (egocentric) and become more selfless and other-centered (altruistic). Love moves beyond being just a noun—an emotion or feeling within the person (e.g., "I am in love"). It becomes an action verb—a way in which the partners act toward each other (e.g., "we love each other"). More emphasis is placed on caring for the partner than on being cared for. Mature love follows two principles:

  1. "I am loved because I love," not "I'm in love because I am loved"; and
  2. "I need you because I love you," not "I love you because I need you."

  (Fromme, 1980).

- **Trusting.** The partners have mutual trust and confidence in each other's commitment and aren't plagued by feelings of suspicion, distrust, or petty jealousy. Each partner may have interests and close friends outside the relationship without the other becoming jealous (Hatfield & Walster, 1985).

- **Independent and interdependent.** A complementary blend of independence and interdependence builds in the relationship—sometimes referred to as the paradox (contradiction) of love—whereby both partners maintain their independence and individuality yet both feel more complete and fulfilled when together. Both partners have their individual identities and do not expect the other to give them a personal identity and a sense of self-worth; however, together, their respective identities become more complete.

- **Caring.** The partners have mutual concern for each other's growth and fulfillment. Rather than being envious or competitive, they take joy in each other's personal success and accomplishments.

Think About It ——————————— *Journal Entry* **12.5**

Rate your degree of agreement or disagreement with the following statements:

"All you need is love."

strongly agree   agree   not sure   (disagree)   strongly disagree

Reason for rating:

You dont ned love

"Love is just a four-letter word."

strongly agree   (agree)   not sure   disagree   strongly disagree

Reason for rating:

It is

"Love stinks."

strongly agree   agree   not sure   (disagree)   strongly disagree

Reason for rating:

At some points it does but not always.

Unhealthy Relationships

When a relationship becomes unhealthy, there are often clear warning signs telling you it's time to end things for your own well-being. If you are feeling disrespected or controlled, or you are concerned for your safety, it's essential that you acknowledge and act upon these signals. Relationship violence—whether emotional, psychological, physical, or sexual—is *never* appropriate or acceptable. Neither is it an effective means for dealing with a dating conflict. If you are in such a situation, or you have a friend who is, addressing the violence immediately is of primary importance. (See Snapshot Summary 12.2 on page 387 for a summary of the major types of sexual abuse and violence.)

Sometimes victims and perpetrators don't recognize that they are in fact in a violent relationship because they don't identify the behaviors as abusive. Behaviors that characterize relationship violence include, but are not limited to, degrading language, dominating or dictating a partner's actions, and physical and/or sexual assault. Without such recognition, victims and perpetrators are likely to remain in their current relationship or have other such relationships that are more violent in the future.

Unfortunately, this type of violence is highly common among college-aged women and men. In fact, recent studies have reported that 13 to 42 percent of college students have experienced and/or perpetrated physical relationship violence. In another study, 88 percent of females and 81 percent of males reported being victims and/or perpetrators of psychological and/or emotional relationship violence. Also important to note is that relationship violence occurs among all segments of the college-aged population. When looking at the demographics of victims and perpetrators, studies show comparable rates among men and women and among members of all races, ethnicities, and socioeconomic groups. Comparable levels of occurrence have also been found among victims and perpetrators who are gay, bisexual, and straight. Taken together, these data highlight the unfortunate fact that relationship violence is all too common. Furthermore, they emphasize the need for such cases to be stopped before they escalate to even more dangerous levels.

Since victims of relationship violence often experience distress, and perhaps even trauma, it is critical that they seek help. Victims tend to be reluctant to do so, however, out of fear of embarrassment or retribution. If you find yourself in a violent relationship, it is important that you tell someone what is going on and get support. Don't let fear immobilize you. Talking to a trusted friend who has your health and safety in mind is a good place to start. Also, connecting with your college's Counseling Center is especially helpful so that you can get the trained assistance you might need. Counseling Centers are often staffed with professionals who have experience working with victims—and perpetrators—of relationship violence and will explain to you your rights as a victim. If the Center on your campus is not staffed with such experienced professionals, they are likely to help connect you to a center in your community that is.

Abusive Relationships

An abusive relationship may be defined as one in which one partner abuses the other physically, verbally, or emotionally. Abusive individuals often are dependent on their partners for their sense of self-worth. They commonly have low self-esteem and fear their partners will abandon them, so they attempt to prevent this abandonment by controlling their partners. Frequently, abusers feel powerless or weak in other areas of their lives and overcompensate by attempting to exert power and personal strength over their partners.

Potential signs of abuse:

- The abuser tries to dominate or control all aspects of the partner's life,
- The abuser frequently yells, shouts, intimidates, or makes physical threats,
- The abuser constantly puts down the partner and damages the partner's self-esteem,
- The abuser displays intense and irrational jealousy,
- The abuser demands affection or sex when the partner is not interested,
- The abuser isolates the partner so there is little or no support system,
- The abuser constantly questions the partner's whereabouts,
- The abused partner behaves differently and is more inhibited when the abuser is around, or
- The abused partner fears the abuser.

Strategies for Avoiding or Escaping Abusive Relationships

- Avoid relationship isolation by continuing to maintain social ties with friends outside of the relationship.
- Don't make excuses for or rationalize the abuser's behavior (e.g., he was under stress or he was drinking).

- Get an objective third-party perspective by asking close friends for their views on your relationship. (Love can be "blind," so it's possible to be in denial about an abusive relationship and not "see" what's really going on.)
- Speak with a professional counselor on campus to help you see your relationships more objectively and help you cope or escape from any relationship that you sense is becoming abusive.

References: ETR Associates (2000). *Acquaintance rape.* Santa Cruz, CA. ETR Associates (2001). *Sexual harassment.* Santa Cruz, CA. http://sexualviolence.uchicago.edu/daterape.shtml

---

Snapshot Summary

12.2 Sexual Harassment

This list explains various forms of abuse and violence experienced by both men and women. Note that these examples are not just physical or sexual in nature—emotional and psychological violence can be just as harmful to victims.

Sexual Harassment

Sexual harassment may be defined as unwelcome sexual advances or requests for sexual favors in exchange for a grade, job, or promotion. Harassment can take the following forms:

1. **Verbal** (e.g., sexual comments about your body or clothes; sexual jokes or teasing)
2. **Nonverbal** (e.g., staring or glaring at your body or obscene gestures)
3. **Physical** (e.g., contact by touching, pinching, or rubbing up against your body)

Recommendations for Dealing with Sexual Harassment

- Make your objections clear and firm. Tell the harasser directly that you are offended by the unwanted behavior and that you consider it sexual harassment.
- Keep a written record of any harassment. Record the date, place, and specific details about the harassing behavior.
- Become aware of the sexual harassment policy at your college, which is likely to be found in the Student Handbook or may be available from the Office of Human Resources on your campus.
- If you're unsure about whether you are experiencing sexual harassment or what to do, seek help from the Counseling Center or Human Resources.

Interpersonal Conflict

Disagreement and conflict among people are inevitable aspects of social life. Research shows that even the most happily married couples don't experience continual marital bliss, but have occasional disagreements and conflicts (Gottman, 1994). Thus, conflict is something you cannot expect to escape or eliminate; you can only hope to contain it, defuse it, and prevent it from reaching unmanageable levels. The effective interpersonal communication and human relations skills discussed in this chapter can help minimize conflicts. In addition to these general skills, the following set of strategies may be used to handle interpersonal conflict constructively and humanely.

Minimizing and Resolving Interpersonal Conflicts

1. **Pick the right place and time to resolve conflicts.** Don't discuss sensitive issues when you're fatigued, in a fit of anger, or in a hurry (Daniels & Horowitz, 1997), and don't discuss them in a public arena; deal with them only with the person involved. As the expression goes, "Don't air your dirty laundry in public." Addressing a conflict in public is akin to a public stoning; it's likely to embarrass or hu-

miliate the person with whom you are in conflict and cause him/her to resist or resent you.

2. **Decompress yourself before you express yourself.** When you have a conflict with someone, your ultimate objective should be to solve the problem, not to unload your anger and have an emotionally cathartic experience. Impulsively "dumping" on the other person may give you an immediate sense of relief, but it's not likely to produce permanent improvement in the other person's attitude or behavior toward you. Instead of unloading, take the load off—cool down and give yourself a little down time to reflect rationally before you react emotionally. For example, count to 10 and give your emotions time to settle down before you begin to say anything. Pausing for reflection also communicates to the other person that you're giving careful thought and attention to the matter rather than lashing out randomly.

   If the conflict is so intense that you're feeling incensed or enraged, it may be a good idea to slow things down by writing out your thoughts ahead of time. This strategy will give you time to organize and clarify your ideas by first talking silently to yourself (on paper) before talking out loud to the other person (in person).

3. **Give the person a chance to respond.** Just because you're angry doesn't mean that the person you're angry with must forfeit the right to free speech and self-defense. Giving the other person a chance to speak and be heard will increase the likelihood that you'll receive a cooperative response to your request. It will also prevent you from storming in, jumping the gun, and "pulling the trigger" too quickly before being sure you've got all the facts straight.

   After listening to the other person's response, check your understanding by summarizing it in your own words (e.g., "What I hear you saying is . . ."). This is an important first step in the conflict-resolution process because conflicts often revolve around a simple misunderstanding, failure to communicate, or communication breakdown. Sometimes just taking the time to hear where the other person is coming from before launching into a full-scale complaint or criticism can reduce or resolve the conflict.

4. **Acknowledge the person's perspectives and feelings.** After listening to the person's response, if you disagree with it, don't dismiss or discount the person's feelings. For instance, don't say, "That's ridiculous," or "You're not making any sense." Instead, say, "I see how you might feel that way, but . . ." or "I feel bad that you are under pressure, but . . .".

5. **If things begin to get nasty, call for a time-out or cease-fire, and postpone the discussion to allow both of you time to cool off.** When emotion and adrenaline run high, logic and reason often run low. This can result in someone saying something during a fit of anger that, in turn, stimulates an angry response from the other person; then the anger of both combatants continues to escalate and turns into an intense volley of verbal punches and counterpunches. For example, the conversation may end up something like this:

   Person A: "You're out of control."
   Person B: "No, I'm not out of control, you're just overreacting."
   Person A: "*I'm* overreacting, you're the one who's yelling!"
   Person B: "I'm not yelling, *you're* the one who's raising your voice!"

   Blow-by-blow exchanges such as these are likely to turn up the emotional heat so high that resolving the conflict is out of the question until both fighters back off, retreat to their respective corners, cool down, and try again later when neither one of them is ready to throw a knockout punch.

"Seek first to understand, then to be understood."

—Stephen Covey, international bestselling author of *The Seven Habits of Highly Effective People* (1990)

6. **Make your point assertively (not passively, aggressively, or passive-aggressively).** When you're passive, you don't stand up for your personal rights: you allow others to take advantage of you and push you around. You say nothing when you should say something. You say "yes" when you want to say "no." When you handle conflict passively, you become angry, anxious, or resentful about doing nothing and keeping it all inside. People refer to others who are passive as being a "doormat" or letting others walk all over them.

   When you're aggressive, you stand up for your rights but you also violate the rights of the other person by threatening, dominating, humiliating, or bullying that person. You use intense, emotionally loaded words to attack the person (e.g., "You spoiled brat" or "You're a sociopath"). You manage to get what you want but at the other person's expense. Later, you tend to feel guilty about overreacting or coming on too strong (e.g., "I knew I shouldn't have said that").

How Do I Make My Point?

If you tend to be passive, then you will make your point tentatively and nervously while being uncertain and apologetic about that point. You will be intimidated by others in the group and may not make your point at all.

If you tend to be aggressive, you will use a loud, intimidating voice. You will not take people disagreeing with your point lightly. You will use your body language to intimidate people into agreeing with your point and may lose your temper easily if they don't.

If you tend to be passive-aggressive, you will be upset or angry but will not let others see it. Instead, you will try to destroy the person or point that makes you angry behind the scenes. You will say openly that you agree with a point while looking for secret ways to be hostile toward that point.

If you tend to be assertive, you will listen to other points being made. You will be sure of the validity of your point and argue it reasonably and with respect. You will have a strong and sure voice and your tone will not be intimidating. You will not let others in the group be bullied because of their points of view. You will not lose control or lose your temper if people disagree.

Remember

Your goal is reconciliation, not retaliation.

When you're passive-aggressive, you get back or get even with the other person in an indirect and ineffective way by withholding or taking away something (e.g., not speaking to the other person or withdrawing all attention or affection).

In contrast, when you're assertive, you strike the middle ground between aggression and passivity. You handle conflict in a way that protects or restores your rights without taking away or stepping on the rights of the other person. You approach conflict in an even-tempered way rather than in an angry or agitated manner; you speak in a normal volume rather than yelling or screaming; and you communicate at a normal distance rather than getting up close and "into the face" of the other person involved in the conflict. You can resolve conflicts assertively by using the following four strategies:

1. **Focus on the specific behavior causing the conflict, not the person's general character.** Avoid labeling the person as "selfish," "mean," "inconsiderate," and so on. For instance, if you're upset because your roommate doesn't share in clean-

ing, stay away from aggressive labels such as "You slacker" or "You lazy bum." Attacking others with negative labels such as these does to the other person just what it sounds like: It gives the feeling of being attacked or verbally assaulted. This is likely to put the other person on the defensive and provoke a counterattack on one of your personal characteristics. Before you know it, you're likely to find yourself in a full-out war of words and mutual character assassinations that has escalated well beyond a small-scale skirmish about the specific behavior of one individual.

Rather than focusing on the person's general character, focus on the behaviors that are causing the problem (e.g., failing to do the dishes or leaving dirty laundry around the room). This will enable the other person to know exactly what actions need to be taken to take care of the problem. Furthermore, it's easier for others to change a specific behavior than it is to change their entire character, which would require a radical change in personality (or a frontal lobotomy).

2. **Use "I" messages to focus on how the other person's behavior or action affects you.** By using "I" messages, which focus on your perceptions and feelings, you send a message that's less accusatory and threatening (Narciso & Burkett, 1975). In contrast, "you" messages are more likely to make the other person defensive and put them on the offensive—ready to retaliate rather than cooperate (Gibb, 1991).

For instance, suppose you've received a course grade that's lower than what you think you earned or deserved and you decide to question your instructor about it. You should not begin by saying to the instructor, "*You* gave me the wrong grade," or "*You* made a mistake." These messages are likely to make your professor immediately ready to defend the grade you received. Your professor will be less threatened and more likely to listen to and consider your complaint if you initiate the conversation with an "I" statement, such as "I don't believe I received the correct grade" or "I think an error may have been made in my final grade."

"I" messages are less aggressive because you're targeting an issue, not a person (Jakubowski & Lange, 1978). By saying, "I feel angry when . . ." rather than "You make me angry when . . ." you send the message that you're taking responsibility for the way you feel rather than guilt-tripping the individual for making you feel that way (perhaps without the person even being aware of how you feel).

Lastly, when using "I" messages, try to describe what you're feeling as precisely as possible. "I feel neglected when you don't write or call" identifies what you're feeling more precisely than "I wish you'd be more considerate." Describing what you feel in specific terms increases the persuasive power of your message and reduces the risk that the other person will misunderstand or discount it.

Think About It ———————————————————————— *Journal Entry* **12.6**

Your classmates aren't carrying their weight on a group project that you're all supposed to be working on as a team; you're getting frustrated and angry because you're doing most of the work. What might be an "I" message that you could use to communicate your concern in a nonthreatening way that's likely to resolve this conflict successfully?

Saying I'm done so they can do the rest.

3. **Don't make absolute judgments or blanket statements.** Compare the following three pairs of statements:

   - "You're no help at all" versus "You don't help me enough."
   - "You never try to understand how I feel" versus "You don't try hard enough to understand how I feel."
   - "I always have to clean up" versus "I'm doing more than my fair share of the cleaning."

   The first statement in each of the preceding pairs is an absolute statement that covers all times, situations, and circumstances, without any room for possible exceptions. Such extreme, blanket criticisms are likely to put the criticized person on the defensive because they state that the person is lacking or deficient with respect to the behavior in question. The second statement in each pair states the criticism in terms of degree or amount, which is less likely to threaten the person's self-esteem (and is probably closer to the truth).

4. **Focus on solving the problem, not winning the argument.** Try not to approach conflict with the attitude that you're going to "get even" or "prove that you're right." Winning the argument but not persuading the person to change the behavior that's causing the conflict is like winning a battle but losing the war. Instead, approach the conflict with the attitude that it's a problem to be solved and that both parties can win—that is, both of you can end up with a better relationship in the long run if the issue is resolved.

   > "Don't find fault. Find a remedy."
   >
   > —Henry Ford, founder of Ford Motor Co. and one of the richest people of his generation

5. **Conclude your discussion of the conflict on a warm, constructive note.** By ending on a positive note, you assure that the other person knows there are no hard feelings and that you're optimistic the conflict can be resolved and your relationship can be improved.

6. **If the conflict is resolved because of some change made by the other person, express your appreciation for the individual's effort.** Even if your complaint was legitimate and your request was justified, the person's effort to accommodate your request shouldn't be taken for granted. At the least, you shouldn't react to a positive change in behavior by rubbing it in with comments such as "That's more like it" or "It's about time!"

   > "To keep your marriage brimming with love . . . when you're wrong, admit it; when you're right, shut up."
   >
   > —Ogden Nash, American poet

   Expressing appreciation to the other person for making a change in response to your request is not only a socially sensitive thing to do, but also a self-serving thing to do. By recognizing or reinforcing the other person's changed behavior, you increase the likelihood that the positive change in behavior will continue.

The Importance of Emotional Intelligence for Educational and Personal Success

The term *intrapersonal intelligence* refers to the ability to be aware of your feelings or emotions (Gardner, 1983). More recently, the term *emotional intelligence* has been coined to describe the ability to identify and monitor your emotions and to be aware of how your emotions are influencing your thoughts and actions (Goleman, 1995; Salovey & Mayer, 1990). Emotional intelligence has been found to be a better predictor of personal and occupational success than is performance on intellectual intelligence tests (Goleman, 1995). Research on college students indicates that those with higher emotional intelligence, such as the ability to identify their emotions and moods, are: (1) less likely to experience boredom (Harris, 2006), and (2) more able to focus their attention and get absorbed (in the zone) when completing challenging tasks (Wiederman, 2007). The connection between emotional intelligence and successful personal performance is further supported by research indicating that people who are able to control their emotions and use them to their advantage are more likely to persist longer at challenging tasks (Simunek, Schutte, Hollander, & McKenley, 2000) and to experience professional success (Goleman, 1995; Saarni, 1999). Success in college is a challenging task that will test your emotional strength and your ability to persist to task completion (graduation).

Research also indicates that experiencing positive emotions, such as optimism and excitement, promotes learning by increasing the brain's ability to take in, store, and retrieve information (Rosenfield, 1988). In one study involving nearly 4,000 first-year college students, it was found that students' level of optimism or hope for success during their first term on campus was a more accurate predictor of their first-year grades than was their SAT score or high school grade point average (Snyder et al., 1991). In contrast, negative emotions such as anxiety and fear can interfere with the brain's ability to store memories (Jacobs & Nadel, 1985), retrieve stored memories (O'Keefe & Nadel, 1985), and engage in higher-level thinking (Caine & Caine, 1991).

College students who score higher on tests of emotional intelligence and emotional management have been found to achieve higher GPAs at the end of their first year (Schutte et al., 1998). Additional research shows that new college students who take seminars or college success courses that include information on emotional control and emotional skill development are more likely to be successful during their first year of college (Schutte & Malouff, 2002).

Stress and Anxiety

"Future shock [is] the shattering stress and disorientation that we induce in individuals by subjecting them to too much change in too short a time."

—Alvin Toffler, American science-fiction author

© Kendall Hunt

Among the most common emotions that humans have to monitor, manage, and regulate are stress and anxiety. College students report higher levels of stress while in college than they did before college (Bartlett, 2002; Sax, 2003), and students entering college in recent years report higher levels of stress (Astin, Parrot, Korn, & Sax, 1997; Sax, Astin, Korn, & Mahoney, 1999) and lower levels of mental health (Kadison & DiGeronimo, 2004) than they have in years past. This increased level of stress may reflect that you're living in a world experiencing an unprecedented rate of technological change and information overload. Terms such as *Internet addiction* and *information fatigue syndrome* are now being used by psychologists to diagnose disorders involving, respectively, psychological dependency on the Internet and excess stress relating to information overload (Waddington, 1996; Young, 1996).

What exactly is stress? The biology of stress originates from the fight-or-flight reaction that's been wired into your body for survival purposes. This automatic reaction prepares you to handle danger or threat by flooding your body with chemicals (e.g., adrenaline) in the same way that ancient humans had to handle threats by engaging in fight or flight (escape) when confronted by life-threatening predators.

The word *stress* derives from a Latin root that means "to draw tight." Thus, stress isn't necessarily bad. For example, a tightened guitar string provides better sound than a string that's too lax or loose, a tightened bow delivers a more powerful arrow shot, and a tightened muscle provides more strength or speed. Such productive stress is sometimes referred to as *eustress*—deriving from the root *eu*, meaning "good" (as in the words *euphoria*, meaning "good mood," and *eulogy*, meaning "good words").

COUNSELING OFFICE
Hours: 24–7

Anxiety Disorders
Drug Addiction
Internet Addiction
Information Fatigue
Syndrome

Today's technological revolution and information explosion may be making life particularly stressful.

The "fight-or-flight" reaction occurs when we're under stress because it's a throwback to the time when ancient humans needed to fight with or flee from potential predators. Unlike that of other animals, our hair doesn't rise up and appear more intimidating to foes (but we still get "goose-bumps" when we're nervous, and we still refer to scary events as "hair-raising" experiences).

© Kendall Hunt

If you keep college stress at a moderate level, it can be a productive emotion that promotes your learning and personal development. Stress in moderate amounts can benefit your:

1. Physical performance (e.g., strength and speed);
2. Mental performance (e.g., attention and memory); and
3. Mood (e.g., hope and optimism).

Think About It ——————————— *Journal Entry* 12.7

Can you think of a situation in which you performed at a higher level because you were somewhat nervous or experienced a moderate amount of stress? Describe the situation.

Talking infront of others

However, if stress is extreme and continues for a prolonged period, it moves from being a productive to a destructive feeling. Using the guitar string as an analogy, if a guitar is strung too tight, the string is likely to snap or break—which isn't productive. Unproductive stress is often referred to as *distress*—from the root *dis* meaning "bad" (as in the words *discomfort* and *disease*). Extreme stress can create feelings of intense anxiety or anxiety disorders (e.g., panic attacks), and if a high level of stress persists for a prolonged period, it can trigger psychosomatic illness—tension-induced bodily disorders (from *psyche,* meaning "mind," and *soma,* meaning "body"). For instance, prolonged distress can trigger indigestion by increasing secretion of stomach acids or contribute to high blood pressure, a.k.a. hypertension. Prolonged stress can also suppress the immune system, leaving you more vulnerable to flu, colds, and other infectious diseases. Studies show that the immune systems of college students are suppressed (produce fewer antibodies) at stressful times during the academic term, such as midterms and finals (Jemott & Magloire, 1985; Kielcolt-Glaser & Glaser, 1986).

Research indicates that college students' stress levels tend to rise when they are experiencing a wave of exams, such as finals.

Excess stress can interfere with mental performance because the feelings and thoughts that accompany anxiety begin to preoccupy your mind and take up space in your working memory, leaving it with less capacity to process information you're trying to learn and retain. Studies also show that students experiencing higher levels of academic stress or performance anxiety are more likely to use ineffective surface approaches to learning that rely merely on memorization (Ramsden & Entwistle, 1981) rather than effective deep-learning strategies that involve seeking meaning and understanding. Furthermore, high levels of test anxiety are more likely to result in careless concentration errors on exams (e.g., overlooking key words in test questions) and can interfere with memory for information that's been studied (Jacobs & Nadel, 1985; O'Keefe & Nadel, 1985; Tobias, 1985).

Although considerable research points to the negative effects of excess stress, you still need to keep in mind that stress can work either for or against you: you can be either energized or sabotaged by stress depending on its level of intensity and the length of time it continues. You can't expect to stop or eliminate stress, nor should you want to; you can only hope to contain it and maintain it at a level where it's more productive than destructive. Many years of research indicate that personal performance is best when it takes place under conditions of moderate stress because this creates a sense of challenge. On the other hand, too much stress creates performance anxiety, and too little stress results in loss of intensity or indifference (Sapolsky, 2004; Yerkes & Dodson, 1908). (See Figure 12.1.)

FIGURE 12.1

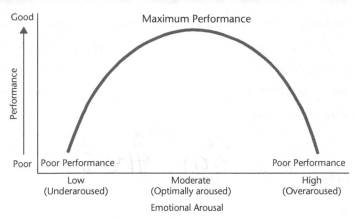

Moderate challenge that produces moderate stress often results in maximum (peak) performance.

Source: Williams, Landers, and Boutcher (1993).

Relationship between Arousal and Performance

Snapshot Summary 12.3 provides a short summary of the signs or symptoms of extreme stress, which indicate that stress has climbed to a level where it's creating distress or anxiety. If these are experienced, particularly for an extended period during which symptoms continue to occur for 2 or more weeks, action should be taken to reduce them.

Snapshot Summary

12.3 High Anxiety: Recognizing the Symptoms (Signs) of Distress

- **Jitteriness or shaking**, especially the hands
- **Accelerated heart rate or heart palpitations:** irregular heartbeat
- **Muscle tension:** tightness in the chest or upper shoulders or a tight feeling (lump) in the throat (the expressions "uptight" and "choking" stem from these symptoms of upper-body tension)
- **Body aches:** heightened muscle tension leading to tension headaches, backaches, or chest pain (in extreme cases, it can feel as if a heart attack is taking place)
- **Sweating**, especially sweaty (clammy) palms
- **Cold, pale hands or feet**, symptoms that have led to the expressions "white knuckles" and "cold feet" to describe someone who is very anxious
- **Dry mouth:** decreased production of less saliva (leading to the expression "cotton mouth" and the need for very nervous speakers to have water nearby)

- **Stomach discomfort or indigestion** due to increased secretion of stomach acid (the expression "feeling butterflies in my stomach" relates to this symptom)
- **Gastrointestinal discomfort**, e.g., stomach cramps, constipation, or diarrhea
- **Feeling faint or dizzy** due to constriction of blood vessels that decreases oxygen flow to the brain
- **Weakness and fatigue:** a sustained (chronic) state of arousal and prolonged muscle tension that becomes tiring
- **Menstrual changes:** missing or irregular menstrual periods
- **Difficulty sleeping:** insomnia or interrupted (fitful) sleep
- **Increased susceptibility to colds, flu, and other infections** due to suppression of the body's immune system that leads to more infections

Think About It ——————— *Journal Entry* 12.8

How would you rate your level of anxiety in the following situations?

1. Taking tests or exams   high   (moderate)   low
2. Interacting in social situations   high   moderate   (low)
3. Making decisions about the future   (high)   moderate   low

Why did you rate them this way?

Because some things are more important then others.

Snapshot Summary

12.4   Posttraumatic Stress Disorder: A Distinctive Form of Stress and Anxiety

Posttraumatic stress disorder (PTSD) is an anxiety disorder that arises after someone experiences a traumatic (dangerous or life-threatening) event, such as combat or sexual assault. It's natural to experience feelings of anxiety after such events, and the symptoms may last for weeks. However, if these feelings of anxiety do not gradually decline but remain or intensify over time and continue to interfere with the person's ability to carry out daily tasks, the person may be experiencing PTSD.

Symptoms of PTSD include the following:

- Constantly feeling tense or "on edge"
- Finding it difficult to concentrate
- Being easily startled
- Having difficulty sleeping
- Experiencing emotional numbness
- Having sudden outbursts of anger

- Blocking memories of the traumatic experience and events around the time of the experience
- Having flashbacks—reliving the trauma repeatedly and experiencing frightening thoughts and physical symptoms (e.g., a racing heart or sweating) that may occur spontaneously or be triggered by sights, sounds, or dreams that serve as reminders of the original traumatic experience
- Avoiding places, events, or objects that are reminders of the traumatic experience

If the preceding symptoms are occurring three or more months after a traumatic event, professional help should be sought. A good place to start would be the Counseling Center on campus or the PTSD Information Line at (802) 296-6300 (e-mail: ncptsd@va.gov).

Source: National Institute of Mental Health (2009).

Stress

You have not done well on your first few assignments and tests in college, and it's really starting to get to you. You feel as though there is no hope—you have no future—and soon you stop eating and sleeping. Your life seems to be spinning out of control. You continue to tell yourself that you will amount to nothing and it doesn't matter what you do, the situation is not going to change—you just can't do this school thing! You are ready to give up! Are you in control of this situation, or is someone else? What could you have done to stop yourself from getting to the point where you want to give up? What are some resources you could use to help yourself through this situation?

Research-Based Techniques for Stress Management

If you perceive your level of stress to be reaching a point where it's beginning to interfere with the quality of your performance or life, you need to take steps to reduce it. Listed here are three stress-management methods whose positive effects have been well documented by research in psychology and biology (Benson & Klipper, 1990; Everly, 1989; Lehrer & Woolfolk, 1993).

Deep (Diaphragmatic) Breathing

The type of breathing associated with excessive stress is hyperventilation—fast, shallow, and irregular breathing through the mouth rather than the chest. Breathing associated with relaxation is just the opposite—slow, deep, and regular breathing that originates from the stomach.

Breathing is something you usually do automatically or involuntarily; however, with some concentration and effort, you can control your breathing by controlling your diaphragm—the body's muscle that enables you to expand and contract your lungs. By voluntarily controlling your diaphragm muscle, you can slow your breathing rate, which, in turn, can bring down your stress level.

Your breathing rate is the pacesetter for the rate at which all other bodily systems operate. For example, when your breathing slows, your heart rate slows, your blood pressure goes down, and your muscle tension is reduced. Thus, if you slow your breathing, you produce a relaxation "wave" or "ripple effect" throughout your body. Deep breathing's ability to trigger relaxation across all systems of the body makes it one of the most powerful stress-management techniques available to you.

You can practice diaphragmatic breathing by inhaling and exhaling with your mouth closed (but without pressing your lips tightly together), keeping your chest still, and allowing your stomach to rise and fall at a slow, steady pace. To help you breathe this way, imagine a candle in front of you that you're blowing on and trying to make flicker without blowing it out. To be sure you're breathing through your stomach deeply and consistently, put one hand on your chest and make sure your chest remains still while you breathe; place your other hand on your stomach and make sure that it rises and falls as you breathe in and out, respectively.

If you practice diaphragmatic breathing consistently, it will soon become natural to you, and you'll be able to quickly shift into deep breathing any time you feel yourself becoming anxious or tense (e.g., before a big exam or speech).

Progressive Muscle Relaxation

This stress-management method is similar to stretching exercises used to relax and loosen muscles before and after physical exercise. To achieve total-body (head-to-

toe) muscle relaxation, progressively tense and release the five sets of muscles listed here. Hold the tension in each muscle area for about five seconds, and then release it slowly.

1. Wrinkle your forehead muscles, and then release them.
2. Shrug your shoulders up as if to touch your ears, and then drop them.
3. Make a fist with each hand, and then open both.
4. Tighten your stomach muscles, and then release them.
5. Tighten your toes by curling them under your feet, and then raise them as high as you can.

To help tense your muscles, imagine you're using them to push or lift a heavy object. When relaxing your muscles, take a deep breath and think or say, "Relax." By breathing deeply and thinking or hearing "Relax" each time you release your muscles, you associate the word with your muscles becoming relaxed. Then, if you find yourself in a stressful situation, you can take a deep breath, think or say, "Relax," and immediately release tension because that's what your muscles have been trained or conditioned to do.

Mental Imagery

You can use your visual imagination to create sensory experiences that promote relaxation. You can create your own relaxing "mental movie" or "imaginary DVD" by visually placing yourself in a calm, comfortable, and soothing setting. You can visualize ocean waves, floating clouds, floating in a warm sauna, or any sensory experience that tends to relax you. The more senses you use, the more real the scene will seem and the more powerful its relaxing effects will be. Try to use all of your senses—try to see it, hear it, smell it, and feel it. You can also use musical imagination to create calming background music that accompanies your visual image.

Lastly, when using your visual imagination, close your eyes and move your eyeballs upward as if you're looking at the sky or ceiling. Research indicates that this upward eye movement tends to trigger alpha waves—brain waves associated with a relaxed yet alert mental state (Liebertz, 2005a).

Author's Experience   My wife, Mary, is a kindergarten teacher. Whenever her young students start misbehaving and the situation becomes stressful (e.g., during lunchtime when the kids are running wildly, arguing vociferously, and screaming at maximum volume), Mary "plays" relaxing songs in her head. She reports that her musical imagination always works to soothe her nerves, enabling her to remain calm and even-tempered when she must confront children who need to be scolded or disciplined.

Joe Cuseo

Think About It ———————————— *Journal Entry* 12.9

What are the most common sources of stress for you?

everything

Would you say that you deal with stress well? Why or why not?

Nope. I freak out.

_____

_____

What strategies do you use to cope with stress?

Sleep

_____

_____

Stress-Reduction Strategies and Practices

In addition to formal stress management techniques, such as diaphragmatic breathing, progressive muscle relaxation, and mental imagery, you can use other habits and simple strategies to reduce stress.

1. **Exercise.** Exercise reduces stress by increasing the release of serotonin, a mellowing brain chemical that reduces feelings of tension (anxiety) and depression. Studies also show that people who exercise regularly tend to report feeling happier (Myers, 1993). Exercise also elevates mood by improving people's sense of self-esteem because it gives them a sense of accomplishment by improving their physical self-image. It is for these reasons that counselors and psychotherapists recommend exercise for patients experiencing milder forms of anxiety or depression (Johnsgard, 2004).

2. **Keep a journal of feelings and emotions.** Writing about our feelings in a personal journal can serve as an effective way to identify our emotions (one form of emotional intelligence) and provide a safe outlet for releasing steam and coping with stress. Writing about our emotions also enables us to become more aware of them, reducing the risk that we'll deny them and push them out of consciousness.

3. **Take time for humor and laughter.** Research on the power of humor for reducing tension is clear and convincing. In one study, college students were suddenly told they had to deliver an impromptu (off the top of their head) speech. This unexpected assignment caused students' heart rates to elevate to an average of 110 beats per minute during delivery of the speech. However, students who watched humorous episodes of sitcoms before delivering their impromptu speeches had an average heart rate during the speech that was significantly lower (80–85 beats per minute), suggesting that humor reduces anxiety (O'Brien, as cited in Howard, 2000). Research also shows that if the immune system is suppressed or weakened by stress, humor strengthens it by blocking the body's production of the stress hormone cortisol—a biochemical responsible for suppressing the immune system when we're stressed (Berk, as cited in Liebertz, 2005b).

"There are thousands of causes for stress, and one antidote to stress is self-expression. That's what happens to me every day. My thoughts get off my chest, down my sleeves, and onto my pad."

—Garson Kanin, American writer, actor, and film director

Depression

Along with anxiety, depression is the other emotional problem that most commonly afflicts humans and must be managed. Excess stress can turn into anxiety (a heightened state of tension, arousal, and nervous energy), or it can lead to depression (an emotional state characterized by a loss of optimism, hope, and energy). As its name implies, when people are depressed, their mood is "lowered" or "pushed down" (like depressing the accelerator in a car). In contrast to anxiety, which typically involves worrying about something that's currently happening or is about to happen (e.g., experiencing test anxiety before an upcoming exam), depression more often relates to something that's already happened. In particular, depression is often related to a loss, such as a lost relationship (e.g., departed friend, broken romance, or death of a family member) or a lost opportunity (e.g., losing a job, failing a course, or failing to be accepted into a major; Bowlby, 1980; Price, Choi, & Vinokur, 2002). It's natural and normal to feel dejected after losses such as these. However, if your dejection reaches a point where you can't concentrate and complete your day-to-day tasks, and if this continues for an extended period, you may be experiencing what psychologists call clinical depression (i.e., depression so serious that it requires professional help).

Snapshot Summary 12.5 provides a summary of symptoms or signs that may indicate the presence of depression. If these symptoms continue to occur for two or more weeks, action should be taken to relieve them.

Snapshot Summary

12.5 Recognizing the Symptoms (Signs) of Depression

- Feeling low, down, dejected, sad, or blue
- Pessimistic feelings about the future (e.g., expecting failure or feeling helpless or hopeless)
- Decreased sense of humor
- Difficulty finding pleasure, joy, or fun in anything
- Lack of concentration
- Loss of motivation or interest in things previously found to be exciting or stimulating
- Stooped posture (e.g., hung head or drawn face)
- Slower and softer speech rate
- Decreased animation and slower bodily movements

- Loss of energy
- Changes in sleeping patterns (e.g., sleeping more or less than usual)
- Changes in eating patterns (e.g., eating more or less than usual)
- Social withdrawal
- Neglect of physical appearance
- Consistently low self-esteem (e.g., thinking "I'm a loser")
- Strong feelings of worthlessness or guilt (e.g., thinking "I'm a failure")
- Suicidal thoughts (e.g., thoughts such as "I can't take it anymore," "People would be better off without me," or "I don't deserve to live")

Remember

There is a difference between feeling despondent or "down" and being depressed. When psychologists use the word depression, they're usually referring to clinical depression—a mood state so low that it's interfering with a person's ability to cope with day-to-day life tasks, such as getting to school or going to work.

Think About It ——————————— *Journal Entry* 12.10

Have you, or a member of your family, ever experienced clinical depression?

Maybe

What do you think was the primary cause or factor that triggered it?

Life sucks.

Strategies for Coping with Depression

Depression can vary widely in intensity. Moderate and severe forms of depression often require professional counseling or psychotherapy, and their cause often lies in genetic factors that involve inherited imbalances in brain chemistry.

The following strategies are offered primarily for milder cases of depression that are more amenable to self-help and self-control. These strategies may also be used with professional help or psychiatric medication to reduce the intensity and frequency of depression.

1. **Focus on the present and the future, not the past.** Consciously fight the tendency to dwell on past losses or failures, because you can no longer change or control them. Instead, focus on things you can still control, which are occurring now and will occur in the future.

2. **Deliberately make an effort to engage in positive or emotionally uplifting behavior when you're feeling down.** If your behavior is upbeat, your mind (mood) often follows suit. "Put on a happy face" may be an effective depression-reduction strategy because smiling produces certain changes in your facial muscles, which, in turn, trigger changes in brain chemistry that improve your mood (Liebertz, 2005b). In contrast, frowning activates a different set of facial muscles that reduces production of mood-elevating brain chemicals (Myers, 1993).

3. **Continue to engage in activities that are fun and enjoyable for you.** For example, continue to socialize with friends and engage in your usual recreational activities. Falling into the downward spiral of withdrawing from doing the things that bring you joy because you're too down to do them will bring you down even further by taking away the very things that bring you up. Interestingly, the root of the word *recreation* means "to re-create" or "create again," which suggests that recreation can revive, restore, and renew you—physically and emotionally.

4. **Try to continue accomplishing things.** By staying busy and getting things done when you feel down, you help boost your mood by experiencing a sense of accomplishment and boosting your self-esteem. Doing something nice for someone less fortunate than yourself can be a particularly effective way to elevate your mood, because it helps you realize that your issues are often far less serious and more manageable than the problems faced by others.

> "Yesterday is gone. Tomorrow has not yet come. We have only today. Let us begin."
>
> —Mother Teresa of Calcutta, Albanian Catholic nun and winner of the Nobel Peace Prize

> "The best way to cheer yourself up is to try to cheer somebody else up."
>
> —Samuel Clemens, a.k.a. Mark Twain, writer, lecturer, and humorist

"If you can laugh at it, you can survive it."

—Bill Cosby, American comedian, actor, and activist

One strategy for coping with depression is to write down the positive events in your life in a journal.

5. **Intentionally seek out humor and laughter. In addition to reducing anxiety, laughter can lighten and brighten a dark mood.** Furthermore, humor improves memory (Nielson, as cited in Liebertz, 2005a), which is an important advantage for people experiencing depression, because depression interferes with concentration and memory. Research supporting the benefits of humor for the body and mind is so well established that humor has become a legitimate academic field of study known as gelontology—the study of laughter (from the Greek *gelos* for "laughter" and *ology*, meaning "study of").

6. **Make a conscious effort to focus on your personal strengths and accomplishments.** Another way to drive away the blues is by keeping track of the good developments in your life. You can do this by keeping a positive events journal in which you note the good experiences in your life, including things you're grateful for, as well as your accomplishments and achievements. Positive journal entries will leave you with a visible, uplifting record that you can review anytime you're feeling down. Furthermore, a positive events journal can provide you with a starting point for developing a formal resume, portfolio, and personal strengths sheet, which you can provide to those who serve as your personal references and who write your letters of recommendation.

7. **If you're unable to overcome depression on your own, seek help from others.** College students are more likely than ever to seek professional help if they're feeling depressed (Kadison & DiGeronimo, 2004). This is good news because it suggests that seeking help is no longer viewed as a source of embarrassment or a sign of personal weakness; instead, today's college students are willing to share their feelings with others and improve the quality of their emotional life.

In some cases, you may be able to help yourself overcome emotional problems through personal effort and effective coping strategies. This is particularly true if you experience depression or anxiety in milder forms and for limited periods. However, overcoming more serious and long-lasting episodes of clinical depression or anxiety isn't as simple as people make it out to be when they glibly say, "Just deal with it," "Get over it," or "Snap out of it."

In mild cases of anxiety and depression, it's true that a person may be able to deal with or get over it, but in more serious cases, depression and anxiety may be strongly related to genetic factors that are beyond the person's control. The genes that trigger emotional problems often have a delayed effect; their influence doesn't kick in until the late teens and early 20s. Thus, individuals who may have experienced no emotional problems during childhood may begin to experience them for the first time while they're in college. These cases of depression and anxiety often cannot be solved by willpower alone because they're often related to underlying imbalances in brain chemicals caused by the individual's genetic makeup.

Certainly, you wouldn't tell a diabetic, "Come on; snap out of it. Get your insulin up." This sounds ridiculous because you know that this illness is caused by a chemical imbalance (shortage of insulin) in the body. Similarly, emotional disorders can be caused by a chemical imbalance (e.g., shortage of serotonin) in the brain. You wouldn't expect people suffering from diabetes to be able to exert self-control over a problem caused by their blood chemistry; similarly, you shouldn't expect people suffering from serious cases of emotional illness to be able to exert self-control over a problem caused by their brain chemistry.

When professional assistance is needed for depression, anxiety, or any other emotional problem, an effective (and convenient) place to start is the Counseling

Center on campus. Psychologists (who usually have earned their doctoral degrees in psychology, philosophy, or education) in this center are licensed to provide professional counseling, and they can make referrals to psychiatrists (who hold a doctorate in medicine) in case medication is needed.

Medications for emotional disorders are designed to compensate or correct chemical imbalances in the brain. Thus, taking medication for emotional disorders may be viewed as a way of helping the brain to produce chemicals that it should be producing on its own but isn't producing because of its genetic makeup. When humans experience intense physical pain, we understand and accept their need to take painkilling drugs (e.g., over-the-counter or prescription painkillers) to provide relief for their symptoms. Similarly, we should understand that humans experiencing intense emotional pain (e.g., depression or anxiety) may need to take psychiatric medication to provide relief for their symptoms.

Think About It — Journal Entry 12.11

If you thought you were experiencing a serious episode of anxiety or depression, would you feel comfortable seeking help from a professional?

yes.

If yes, why? If no, why not?

Not going to sink into a sad level

Summary and Conclusion

The quality of our interpersonal relationships is strengthened by our communication skills (verbal and nonverbal) and human relations (people) skills. We can improve our interactions and relationships by working hard at remembering the names and interests of people we meet, being good listeners, and being open to different topics of conversation. Romantic relationships are no exception. These begin through the process of dating. Research shows that college students take different approaches to dating, ranging from not dating at all to dating with the intent of exploring or cementing long-term relationships.

Interpersonal conflict is an inevitable aspect of social life; we can't completely eliminate it, but we can minimize and manage it with effective strategies that enable us to resolve conflicts assertively rather than aggressively, passively, or passive-aggressively.

Today's college students report higher levels of stress than students in years past. Strategies for reducing excess stress include formal stress-management techniques (e.g., diaphragmatic breathing and progressive muscle relaxation), good physical habits (e.g., exercising and reducing intake of caffeine or other stimulants), and positive ways of thinking (e.g., focusing on the present and the future, rather than the past, and making a conscious effort to focus on our personal strengths and accomplishments).

Intellectual ability is only one form of human intelligence. Social and emotional intelligence are at least as important for being successful, healthy, and happy. The strategies discussed in this chapter are not merely "soft skills": they're actually "hardcore" skills essential for success in college and beyond.

Interpersonal relationships are strengthened by communication skills (verbal and nonverbal) and human relations or people skills. You can improve the quality of your interpersonal communication and social relationships by:

- Being a good listener;
- Recognizing nonverbal messages you send while listening;
- Opening your mind to different topics of conversation;
- Recalling people's names;
- Greeting people by name when you interact with them; and
- Remembering information about others, thereby expressing interest in them.

Interpersonal conflict occurs throughout social life. However, you can minimize and manage such conflict by:

- Choosing the best place and time to resolve conflicts;
- Cooling off emotionally before expressing your thoughts verbally;
- Letting the person respond;
- Actively listening to the person's response;
- Making your point assertively rather than aggressively, passively, or both;
- Focusing on solving the problem rather than winning the argument;
- Ending the conversation on a warm, constructive note; and
- Expressing your appreciation for the person's effort to change in response to your request.

Today's college students report higher levels of stress than students in years past. Strategies that have been found effective for reducing excessive stress or anxiety include:

- Deep (diaphragmatic) breathing;
- Progressive muscle relaxation;
- Mental imagery;
- Journaling; and
- Humor and laughter.

Depression is another common emotional problem that people must manage. Self-help strategies for coping with depression include:

- Focusing on the present and the future rather than the past;
- Intentionally improving your mood by engaging in enjoyable or emotionally uplifting activities;
- Continuing to accomplish things, especially those that benefit others who are less fortunate;
- Seeking out humor and experiencing laughter;

- Consciously focusing on personal strengths and accomplishments; and
- Seeking help from others, including professional help if your depression reaches a debilitating level.

Communicating and relating effectively with others are important life skills and forms of human intelligence. Similarly, emotional intelligence—the ability to identify and manage emotions when dealing with others and remain aware of how emotions influence thoughts and actions—has been found to be an important life skill that influences academic, personal, and professional success. The research and strategies discussed in this chapter point strongly to the conclusion that the quality of relationships and emotional life plays a pivotal role in promoting success, health, and happiness.

Learning More through the World Wide Web

Internet-Based Resources for Further Information on Social and Emotional Intelligence

For additional information related to the ideas discussed in this chapter, we recommend the following Web sites:

Social Intelligence and Interpersonal Relationships:

humanresources.about.com/od/interpersonalcommunication1/

www.articles911.com/Communication/Interpersonal_Communication/

hodu.com/ECS-Menu1.shtml

Emotional Intelligence and Mental Health:

eqi.org/eitoc.htm

www.nimh.nih.gov/health/publications/index.shtml

12.1 Identifying Ways of Handling Interpersonal Conflict

Think of the social situation or relationship that is currently causing you the most conflict in your life. Describe how this conflict might be approached in each of the following ways:

1. Passively:

   talking to my dad

2. Aggressively:

   my dad yelling at me

3. Passive-aggressively:

   me talking to him

4. Assertively:

   Mother talking

(See pp. 387–391 for descriptions of each of these four approaches.)

Consider practicing the assertive approach by role-playing it with a friend or classmate and then applying it to the actual situation or relationship in your life in which you're experiencing conflict.

My boyfriend

Caught between a Rock and a Hard Place: Romantic versus Academic Commitments

Lauren has been dating her new boyfriend (Nick) for about two months. She's convinced this is the "real thing" and that she's definitely "in love." Lately, Nick has been asking her to skip class to spend more time with him. He tells Lauren, "If you really love me, you would do it for our relationship." Lauren feels that Nick truly loves her and wouldn't do anything to hurt her or interfere with her goals. So she figures that skipping a few classes to spend time with her boyfriend is the right choice. However, Lauren's grades soon start to slip; at the same time, Nick starts to demand that she spend even more time with him.

Discussion Questions

1. What concerns you most about Lauren's behavior? What concerns you most about Nick's behavior?

   she is focusing on a guy and not her life.

2. Would you agree with Lauren's decision to start skipping classes?

   Nope. Stupid

3. What might Lauren do to keep her grades up and still keep her relationship with Nick strong?

   Tell him he needs to wait.

4. If you were Lauren's friend, what advice would you give her?

   Tell him no or dump him.

5. If you were Nick's friend, what advice would you give him?

   Calm down you dont own her.

415

12.2 College Stress: Identifying Potential Sources and Possible Solutions

Read through the following 29 college stressors and rate them in terms of how stressful each one is for you on a scale from 1 to 5 (1 = lowest, 5 = highest):

Potential Stressors		Stress Rating			
Tests and exams	1	2	③	4	5
Assignments	1	②	3	4	5
Class workload	①	2	3	4	5
Pace of courses	1	2	③	4	5
Performing up to expectations	1	2	3	④	5
Handling personal freedom	①	2	3	4	5
Time pressure (e.g., not enough time)	1	2	3	4	⑤
Organizational pressure (e.g., losing things)	1	②	3	4	5
Living independently	①	2	3	4	5
The future	1	2	3	4	⑤
Decisions about a major or career	1	②	3	4	5
Moral and ethical decisions	1	②	3	4	5
Finding meaning in life	1	2	3	4	⑤
Emotional issues	①	2	3	4	5
Physical health	1	2	3	4	⑤
Social life	1	②	3	4	5
Intimate relationships	1	2	3	4	⑤
Sexuality	①	2	3	4	5
Family responsibilities	1	2	③	4	5
Family conflicts	1	2	3	4	⑤
Family pressure	1	2	3	4	⑤
Peer pressure	①	2	3	4	5
Loneliness or isolation	①	2	3	4	5
Roommate conflicts	①	2	3	4	5
Conflict with professors	①	2	3	4	5
Campus policies or procedures	①	2	3	4	5
Transportation	①	2	3	4	⑤
Technology	①	2	3	4	5
Safety	1	2	③	4	5

Review your ratings and write down three of your top (highest-rated) stressors. Identify: (1) a coping strategy you may use on your own to deal with that source of stress and (2) a campus resource you could use to obtain help with that source of stress.

Stressor: _____The Future_____

Personal coping strategy:

Talk it out, deal with it.

Campus resource:

counselr

Stressor: ____Emotional issues_____

Personal coping strategy:

Find a middle

Campus resource:

Counseler

Stressor: _____Living independently_____

Personal coping strategy:

Talk to family

Campus resource:

Counseler

Mental Wellness

Leo was really looking forward to college, but he was not prepared to handle the stress and anxiety that came along with it. In high school, his teachers always reminded him when things were due and he hardly had any homework. Now his instructors expect him to read that silly syllabus and he has so much homework he does not know where to start! He is starting to fall behind and gets anxious and nervous any time he goes to class. His heart starts to race and his palms get really sweaty. The further he falls behind, the worse his stress and anxiety get. Soon he stops going to class altogether because he gets so worked up he literally makes himself sick.

Discussion Questions

1. How realistic do you think this case is? Why?

Not realistic, you find time to do it.

2. What could Leo have done to calm himself down so that he was able to go to his classes and be successful?

Breathe, sleep, and do his homework.

3. What do you think is going to happen to Leo?

Drop all.

Chapter 12 Reflection

What is one healthy relationship you currently have that could positively affect your success in college? Explain.

your family

What is one unhealthy relationship that could negatively affect your success in college? Explain. How can you make this relationship healthy, or what are other options you might have?

your BF/GF —

Dump them

Think of a situation that is currently causing you stress. What is it? What are some ways you can address the situation so it will not cause you so much stress?

My Dad.

Don't talk to him.

End of the Course Reflection

Now that your First Year Experience course is coming to an end, take some time to reflect on and answer the following questions.

1. Look back at the three things you wanted to learn or accomplish through completing this course on page 25 of the Introduction. What were they? Have you learned or accomplished them? Explain.

2. Think back to the first day of this course. What type of person and student were you? How have you changed over the semester?

3. Has your approach to college changed as a result of this course? Explain.

4. Identify and describe four steps you will take to ensure your academic success in college.

5. If you had a chance to do this semester over again, what would you do differently?

6. What is the most important thing you have learned in this course? Why is it the most important?

7. What one piece of advice would you give to freshmen who will be taking this course next semester?

8. Write a paragraph on how this course has affected you as a college student.

Glossary

Ability (Aptitude): the capacity to do something well or to have the potential to do it well.

Academic Advisor: a professional who advises college students on course selection, helps students understand college procedures, and helps guide their academic progress toward completion of a college degree.

Academic Dismissal: denying a student continued college enrollment because of a cumulative GPA that remains below a minimum level (e.g., below 2.0).

Academic Probation: a period (usually one term) during which students with a GPA that is too low (e.g., less than 2.0) are given a chance to improve their grades; if a student's GPA does not meet or exceed the college's minimum requirement after this probationary period, that student may be academically dismissed from the college.

Academic Support Center: the place on campus where students can obtain individual assistance from professionals and trained peers to support and strengthen their academic performance.

Active Involvement: the amount of personal time devoted to learning in college and the degree of personal effort or energy (mental and physical) put into the learning process.

Administrator: someone whose primary responsibility is the governance of the college or a unit within the college, such as an academic department or student support service.

Career: the sum total of vocational experiences throughout an individual's work life.

Career Advancement: working up the career ladder to higher levels of decision-making responsibility and socioeconomic status.

Career Development Center: a key campus resource for learning about the nature of different careers and strategies on how to locate career-related work experiences.

Career Development Course: a college course that typically includes self-assessment of career interests, information about different careers, and strategies for career preparation.

Career Entry: gaining entry into a career and beginning a career path.

Citation: an acknowledgment of the source of any piece of information included in a written paper or oral report that doesn't represent original work or thoughts.

Co-Curricular Experience: the learning and development that occur outside the classroom.

Collaboration: the process of two or more people working interdependently toward a common goal that involves true teamwork, whereby teammates support one another's success and take equal responsibility for helping the team move toward its shared goal.

Communication Skills: skills necessary for accurate comprehension and articulate expression of ideas, which include reading, writing, speaking, listening, and multimedia skills.

Commuter Student: a college student who does not live on campus.

Concentration: a cluster of approximately three courses in the same subject area.

Concept: a larger system or network of related ideas.

Concept (Idea) Map: a visual diagram that represents or maps out main categories of ideas and their relationships in a visual-spatial format.

Cooperative Education (Co-op) Program: a program in which students gain work experience relating to their college major, either by stopping their coursework temporarily to work full-time at the co-op position or by continuing to take classes while working part-time at the co-op position.

Core Course: a course required of all students, regardless of their particular major.

Counseling Services: the personal counseling provided by professionals on campus that is designed to promote self-awareness and self-development in emotional and social aspects of life.

Cover (Application) Letter: a letter written by an applicant who is applying for an employment position or admission to a school.

Cramming: packing study time into one study session immediately before an exam.

Creative Thinking: a form of higher-level thinking that involves producing a new and different idea, method, strategy, or work product.

Critical Thinking: a form of higher-level thinking that involves making well-informed evaluations or judgments.

Culture: a distinctive pattern of beliefs and values learned by a group of people who share the same social heritage and traditions.

Cum Laude: graduating with honors (e.g., achieving a cumulative GPA of at least 3.3).

Cumulative Grade Point Average: a student's GPA for all academic terms combined.

Curriculum: the total set of courses offered by a college or university.

Dean's List: achieving an outstanding GPA for a particular term (e.g., 3.5 or higher).

Diversity: interacting with and learning from peers of varied backgrounds and lifestyles.

Diversity Appreciation: valuing the experiences of different groups of people and interest in learning more about them.

Diversity (Multicultural) Course: a course designed to promote diversity awareness and appreciation of multiple cultures.

Documentation: information sources that serve as references to support or reinforce conclusions in a written paper or oral presentation.

Elective: a course that students are not required to take but that they elect or choose to take.

Ethnic Group (Ethnicity): a group of people who share the same culture.

Experiential Learning: out-of-class experiences that promote learning and development.

Faculty: the collection of instructors on campus whose primary role is to teach courses that comprise the college curriculum.

Free Elective: a course that students may elect to enroll in, which counts toward a college degree but is not required for either general education or academic major.

Freshman 15: a phrase commonly used to describe the 15-pound weight gain that some students experience during their first year of college.

Full-Time Student: a student who typically enrolls in and completes at least 24 units per academic year.

Grade Points: the amount of points earned for a course, which is calculated by multiplying the course grade by the number of credits carried by the course.

Grade Point Average (GPA): the translation of students' letter grades into a numerical system, whereby the total number of grade points earned in all courses is divided by total number of course units.

Graduate School: a university-related education pursued after completing a bachelor's degree.

Grant: money received that does not have to be repaid.

Higher-Level Thinking: thinking at a higher or more complex level than merely acquiring factual knowledge or memorizing information.

Holistic (or Whole-Person) Development: the development of the total self, which includes intellectual, social, emotional, physical, spiritual, ethical, vocational, and personal development.

Human Diversity: the variety of differences that exist among people who comprise humanity (the human species).

Humanity: the common elements of the human experience shared by all humans.

Illustrate: to provide concrete examples or specific instances.

Informational Interview: an interview with a professional working in a career to obtain inside information on what the career is like.

Information Literacy: the ability to find, evaluate, and use information.

Intellectual (Cognitive) Development: acquiring knowledge and learning how to learn and how to think deeply.

Interest: something someone likes or enjoys doing.

International Student: a student attending college in one nation who is a citizen of another nation.

International Study (Study Abroad) Program: doing coursework at a college or university in another country.

Internship: a work experience related to a college major for which students receive academic credit and, in some cases, financial compensation.

Interpret: to draw a conclusion about something and support that conclusion with evidence.

Introspection: turning inward to gain deeper self-awareness of what has been done, what is being done, or what will be done.

Job Shadowing: a program that allows a student to follow (shadow) and observe a professional during a typical workday.

Justify: to back up arguments and viewpoints with evidence.

Leadership: the ability to influence people in a positive way (e.g., motivating peers to do their best) or the ability to produce positive change in an organization or institution (e.g., improving the quality of a school, business, or political organization).

Leadership Course: a course in which students learn how to advance and eventually assume important leadership positions in a company or organization.

Learning Community: a program in which the same group of students takes the same block of courses together during the same academic term.

Learning Habit: the usual approach, method, or technique a student uses while attempting to learn.

Learning Style: the way in which individuals prefer to perceive information (receive or take it in) and process information (deal with it once it has been taken in).

Liberal Arts: the component of a college education that provides the essential foundation or backbone for the college curriculum and is designed to equip students with a versatile set of skills to promote their success in any academic major or career.

Lifelong Learning Skills: skills that include learning how to learn and how to continue learning that can be used throughout the remainder of personal and professional life.

Magna Cum Laude: graduating with high honors (e.g., achieving a cumulative GPA of at least 3.5).

Major: the academic field students choose to specialize in while in college.

Mentor: someone who serves as a role model and personal guide to help students reach their educational or occupational goals.

Merit-Based Scholarship: money awarded on the basis of performance or achievement that does not have to be repaid.

Metacognition: thinking about the process of thinking.

Midterm: the midpoint of an academic term.

Minor: a second field of study that is designed to complement and strengthen a major, which usually consists of about half the number of courses required for a college major (e.g., six to seven courses are usually needed for a minor).

Mnemonic Device (Mnemonics): a specific memory-improvement method designed to prevent forgetting, which often involves such memory-improvement principles as meaning, organization, visualization, or rhythm and rhyme.

Multicultural Center: a place on campus designed to provide space for interaction among members of diverse cultural groups.

Multicultural Competence: the ability to understand cultural differences and to interact effectively with people from multiple cultural backgrounds.

Multidimensional Thinking: a form of higher-level thinking that involves taking multiple perspectives and considering multiple theories.

Multiple Intelligences: the notion that humans display intelligence or mental skills in many other forms besides their ability to perform on intellectual tests such as IQ and SAT tests.

Need: a key element of life planning that represents something stronger than an interest and makes a person's life more satisfying or fulfilling.

Need-Based Scholarship: money awarded to students on the basis of financial need that does not have to be repaid.

Netiquette: applying the principles of social etiquette and interpersonal sensitivity when communicating online.

Non-Traditional-Age (Reentry) Student: a student entering college who is not directly out of high school.

Online Resource: a resource that can be used to search for and locate information, including online card catalogs, Internet search engines, and electronic databases.

Oral Communication Skills: the ability to speak in a concise, confident, and eloquent fashion.

Oversubscribed (Impacted) Major: a major that has more students interested in it than there are openings for students to be accepted.

Paraphrase: restating or rephrasing information in original words.

Part-to-Whole Method: a study strategy that involves dividing study time into smaller parts or units and then learning these parts in several short, separate study sessions in advance of exams.

Part-Time Student: a student who typically enrolls in and completes less than 24 units per academic year.

Personal Reflection: the process deliberately and thoughtfully reviewing what has been learned and connecting it to what is already known.

Plagiarism: the deliberate or unintentional use of someone else's work without acknowledging it, giving the impression that it is original work.

Portfolio: a collection of work materials or products that illustrates an individual's skills and talents or demonstrates that individual's educational and personal development.

Prejudice: to prejudge members of the same group in the same way.

Primary Source: a firsthand source or original document.

Process-of-Elimination Method: a multiple-choice test-taking strategy that involves weeding out or eliminating choices that are clearly wrong and continuing to do so until the choices are narrowed down to one answer that seems to be the best choice available.

Procrastination: the tendency to postpone making a decision or taking action until the last moment.

Professional School: a formal education pursued after a bachelor's degree in school that prepares students for an "applied" profession (e.g., pharmacy, medicine, or law).

Prerequisite Course: a course that must be completed before students can enroll in a more advanced course.

Proofreading: a final microscopic form of editing that focuses on detecting mechanical errors relating to such things as referencing, grammar, punctuation, and spelling.

Race (Racial Group): a group of people who share some distinctive physical traits, such as skin color or other facial characteristics.

Recall Test Question: a type of test question that requires students to generate or produce the correct answer on their own, such as a short-answer question or an essay question.

Recitation (Reciting): a study strategy that involves verbally stating information to be remembered without looking at it.

Recognition Test Question: a type of test question that requires students to select or choose a correct answer from answers that are provided to them (e.g., multiple-choice, true-false, and matching questions).

Reconstruction: a process of rebuilding a memory part by part or piece by piece.

Reentry Student: a student who matriculated as a traditional (just out of high school) student but who left college to meet other job or family demands and has returned to complete a degree or obtain job training.

Reference (Referral) Letter: a letter of reference typically written by a faculty member, advisor, or employer for students who are applying for entry into positions or schools after college or for students during the college experience when they apply for special academic programs, student leadership positions on campus, or part-time employment.

Reflection: a thoughtful, personal review of what a person has already done, is in the process of doing, or is planning to do.

Research Skills: the ability to locate, access, retrieve, organize, and evaluate information from various sources, including library- and technology-based (computer) systems.

Restricted Elective: a course that falls into an area of study students must complete but can be chosen from a restricted set or list of possible courses that have been specified by the college.

Resume: a written summary or outline that effectively organizes and highlights an individual's strongest qualities, personal accomplishments, and skills, as well as personal credentials and awards.

Self-Assessment: the process of reflecting on and evaluating personal characteristics, such as personality traits, learning habits, and personal strengths or weaknesses.

Self-Monitoring: the ability to watch yourself and maintain self-awareness of how you're learning, what you're learning, and whether you're learning.

Semester (Term) Grade Point Average: a GPA for one semester or academic term.

Service Learning: a form of experiential learning in which students serve or help others while they acquire skills through hands-on experience that can be used to strengthen their resumes and explore fields of work that may relate to their future career interests.

Shallow (Surface-Oriented) Learning: an approach to learning in which students spend most of their study time repeating and memorizing information in the exact form that it was presented to them.

Socially Constructed Knowledge: the acquisition of knowledge built through interaction and dialogue with others.

Stereotyping: viewing individuals of the same type (group) in the same (fixed) way.

Stigmatizing: associating inferior or unfavorable traits with people who belong to the same group.

Student Development (Co-Curricular) Transcript: an official document issued by the college that validates a student's co-curricular achievements, which the student can have sent to prospective employers or schools.

Student Development Services (Student Affairs): a division of the college that provides student support on issues relating to social and emotional adjustment, involvement in campus life outside the classroom, and leadership development.

Student Handbook: an official publication of a college or university that identifies student roles and responsibilities, violations of college rules and policies, and opportunities for student involvement in cocurricular programs, such as student clubs, campus organizations, and student leadership positions.

Summa Cum Laude: graduating with highest honors (e.g., achieving a cumulative GPA of at least 3.8).

Syllabus: an academic document that serves as a contract between instructor and student, which outlines course requirements, attendance policies, grading scale, course topic outlines by date, dates of tests and for completing reading and other assignments, and information about the instructor (e.g., office location and office hours).

Synthesis: a form of higher-level thinking that involves building up ideas by integrating (connecting) separate pieces of information to form a whole or more comprehensive product.

Test Anxiety: a state of emotional tension that can weaken test performance by interfering with memory and thinking.

Test Wise: being able to use the characteristics of the test question itself (such as its wording or format) to increase the probability of choosing the correct answer.

Theory: a body of conceptually related concepts and general principles that help in organizing, understanding, and applying knowledge that has been acquired in a particular field of study.

Transferable Skills: skills that can be transferred or applied across a range of subjects, careers, and life situations.

Values: what a person strongly believes in and cares about or feels is important to do and should be done.

Visual Aids: charts, graphs, diagrams, or concept maps that improve learning and memory by enabling the learner to visualize information as a picture or image and connect separate pieces of information to form a meaningful whole.

Visual Memory: memory that relies on the sense of vision.

Visualization: a memory-improvement strategy that involves creating a mental image or picture of what is to be remembered or imagining it being placed at a familiar site or location.

Vocational (Occupational) Development: exploring career options, making career choices wisely, and developing skills needed for career success.

Waive: to give up a right to access information (e.g., waiving the right to see a letter of recommendation).

Wellness: a state of optimal health, peak performance, and positive well-being that is produced when different dimensions of the self (body, spirit, and mind) are attended to and effectively integrated.

Work-Study Program: a federal program that supplies colleges and universities with funds to provide on-campus employment for students who are in financial need.

Written Communication Skills: the ability to write in a clear, creative, or persuasive manner.

Learning the Language of Higher Education

A Dictionary of College Vocabulary

Academic Affairs unit or division of the college that deals primarily with the college curriculum, course instruction, and campus services that support academic success (e.g., library and learning center).

Academic Calendar the scheduling system used by a college or university to divide the academic year into shorter terms (e.g., semesters, trimesters, or quarters).

Academic Credits (Units) what students are credited with after completing courses that are counted toward completion of their college degree; course credit is typically counted in terms of how many hours the class meets each week (e.g., a course that meets for three hours per week counts for three credits).

Academic Standing where a student stands academically (cumulative GPA) at a given point in their college experience (e.g., after one term or one year).

Academic Transcript a list of all courses a student has enrolled in, the grades received in those courses, and the student's grade point average.

Advanced Placement (AP) Tests tests designed to measure college-level work that are taken while a student is in high school; if the student scores high enough, then college credit is awarded in the subject area tested or the student is granted advanced placement in a college course.

Analysis (Analytical Thinking) a form of higher-level thinking skill that involves breaking down information, identifying its key parts or underlying elements, and detecting what is most important or relevant.

Associate Degree (A.A./A.S. Degree) two-year college degree that represents completion of general education requirements and prepares students for transfer to a four-year college or university.

Bachelor's (Baccalaureate) Degree degree awarded by four-year colleges and universities, which represents the completion of general education requirements plus completion of an academic specialization in a particular major.

Certificate credential received by students at a community college or technical college who have completed a one- or two-year vocational or occupational training program, which allows them entry into a specific occupation or career.

College Catalog (a.k.a., College Bulletin) an official publication of a college or university that identifies its mission, curriculum, academic policies, and procedures, as well as the names and educational background of the faculty.

Combined Bachelor Graduate Degree Program a program offered by some universities that allows students to apply for simultaneous admission to both undergraduate and graduate school in a particular field and to receive both a bachelor's degree and a graduate degree in that field after completing the combined program (e.g., a bachelor's and master's degree in physical therapy).

Counseling Services personal counseling provided by professionals on campus that is designed to promote self-awareness and self-development in emotional and social aspects of life.

Cross-Registration a collaborative program offered by two colleges or universities that allows students who are enrolled at one institution to register for and take courses at another institution.

Dean a college or university administrator who is responsible for running a particular unit of the college.

Distance Learning enrolling in and completing courses online rather than in person.

Doctoral Degree an advanced degree obtained after completion of the bachelor's (baccalaureate) degree, which typically requires five to six years of full-time study in graduate school, including completion of a thesis or doctoral dissertation.

Double Major attaining a bachelor's degree in two majors by meeting the course requirements of both academic fields.

Drop/Add the process of changing an academic schedule by dropping courses or adding courses to a pre-existing schedule; at most colleges and universities, adding and dropping courses can be done during the first week of the academic term.

Fine Arts a division of the liberal arts curriculum that focuses largely on artistic performance and appreciation of artistic expression by pursuing such questions as: What is beautiful? How do humans express and appreciate aesthetic (sensory) experiences, imagination, creativity, style, grace, and elegance?

Full-Time Student a student who typically enrolls and completes at least 24 units per academic year.

General-Education Curriculum collection of courses designed to provide a "general" or "broad" rather than narrow education, and develop skills needed for success in any major or career.

Graduate Record Examination (GRE) a standardized test for admission to graduate schools, which is used in a manner similar to the way that the SAT and ACT tests are used for admission to undergraduate colleges and universities.

Graduate Assistant (GA) a graduate student who receives financial assistance to pursue graduate studies by working in a university office or college professor.

Graduate Student student who has completed a four-year (bachelor's) degree and is enrolled in graduate school to obtain an advanced degree (e.g., master's or Ph.D.).

Health Services on-campus services provided to help students who are experiencing physical illnesses or injuries, and to educate students on matters relating to health and wellness.

Higher Education formal education beyond high school.

Honors Program a special program of courses and other learning experiences designed for college students who have demonstrated exceptionally high levels of academic achievement.

Humanities division of the liberal arts curriculum that focuses on the human experience, human culture, and questions that arise in a human's life, such as: Why are we here? What is the meaning or purpose of our existence? How should we live? What is the good life? Is there life after death?

Impacted Major an academic major in which there are more students wishing to enter the program than there are spaces available in the program; thus, students must formally apply and qualify for admission to the major by going through a competitive screening process.

Independent Study a project that allows a student to receive academic credit for an in-depth study of a topic of his or her choice by working independently with a faculty member without enrolling in a formal course that meets in a classroom according to a set schedule.

Interdisciplinary courses or programs that are designed to help students integrate knowledge from two or more academic disciplines (fields of study).

Inter-Term (a.k.a., January Interim or Maymester) a short academic term, typically running three to four weeks, during which students enroll in only one course, which is studied intensively.

Learning Habits the usual approaches, methods, or techniques a student uses while attempting to learn.

Lower-Division Courses courses taken by college students during their freshman and sophomore years.

Master's Degree degree obtained after completion of the bachelor's (baccalaureate) degree, which typically requires two to three years of full-time study in graduate school.

Matriculation the process of initially enrolling in or registering for college. (The term is derived from the term *matricula*—a list or register of persons belonging to a society or community.)

Multicultural Center place on campus that is designed to provide a place for interaction among and between members of diverse cultural groups.

Natural Sciences a division of the liberal arts curriculum that focuses on observing the physical world and explaining natural phenomena, asking such questions as: What causes physical events in the natural world? How can we predict and control physical events and improve the quality of interaction between humans and the natural environment?

Non-Resident Status out-of-state students who typically pay higher tuition than in-state students because they are not residents of the state in which their college is located.

Orientation an educational program designed to help students make a smooth transition to college that is delivered to students before their first academic term.

Part-Time Student a student who typically enrolls and completes less than 24 units per academic year.

Pass/Fail (Credit/No Credit) Grading a grading option offered in some courses whereby students do not receive a letter grade (A–F), but only a grade of "pass" (credit) or "fail" (no credit).

Phi Theta Kappa a national honor society that recognizes outstanding academic achievement of students at two-year colleges.

Placement Tests tests administered to new students upon entry to a college or university designed to assess their basic academic skills (e.g., reading, writing, mathematics) in order to place them in courses that are neither too advanced nor too elementary for their particular level of skill development.

Postsecondary Education formal education beyond secondary (high school) education.

Pre-professional Coursework undergraduate courses that are required or strongly recommended for gaining entry into professional school (e.g., medical school or law school).

Proficiency Tests tests given to college students before graduation that are designed to assess whether they can perform certain academic skills (e.g., writing) at a level advanced enough to qualify them for college graduation.

Quarter System a system for scheduling courses in which the academic year is divided into four quarters (fall, winter, spring, and summer terms), each of which lasts approximately 10–11 weeks.

Registrar's Office campus office that maintains college transcripts and other official records associated with student coursework and academic performance.

Resident Status in-state students who typically pay lower tuition than out-of-state students because they are residents of the state in which their college is located.

Residential Students students who live on campus or in a housing unit owned and operated by the college.

Semester System a system for scheduling courses in which the academic year is divided into two terms (fall and spring) that are approximately 15–16 weeks long.

Self-Regulation adjusting learning strategies in a way that best meets the specific demands of the subject being learned.

Senior Seminar (Capstone) Course course designed to put a "cap" or final touch on the college experience, helping seniors to tie ideas together in their major and/or make a smooth transition from college to life after college.

Shadow Majors students who have been admitted to their college or university, but have not yet been admitted to their intended major.

Social and Behavioral Sciences a division of the liberal arts curriculum that focuses on the observation of human behavior, individually and in groups, asking such questions as: What causes humans to behave the way they do? How can we predict, control, or improve human behavior and interpersonal interaction?

Student Activities cocurricular experiences offered outside the classroom that are designed to promote student learning and student involvement in campus life.

Student-Designed (Interdisciplinary) Major an academic program offered at some colleges and universities in which a student works with a college representative or committee to develop a major that is not officially offered by the institution.

Student Development Services (Student Affairs) division of the college that provides student support on issues relating to social and emotional adjustment, involvement in campus life outside the classroom, and leadership development.

Student Handbook an official publication of a college or university that identifies student roles and responsibilities, violations of college rules and policies, and opportunities for student involvement in cocurricular programs, such as student clubs, campus organizations, and student leadership positions.

Summer Session courses offered during the summer between spring and fall terms that typically run for four to six weeks.

Teaching Assistant (TA) a graduate student who receives financial assistance to pursue graduate studies by teaching undergraduate courses, leading course discussions, and/or helping professors grade papers or conduct labs.

Transfer Program two-year college program that provides general education and pre-major coursework to prepare students for successful transfer to a four-year college or university.

Trimester System a system for scheduling courses in which the academic year is divided into three terms (fall, winter, spring) that are approximately 12–13 weeks long.

Undeclared students who have not committed to a college major.

Undergraduate student who is enrolled in a two-year or four-year college.

University an educational institution that offers not only undergraduate degrees, but graduate degrees as well.

Upper-Division Courses courses taken by college students during their junior and senior years.

Vocational/Technical Programs community college programs of study that train students for a particular occupation or trade and immediate employment after completing a two-year associate degree (e.g., Associate of Applied Science) or a one-year certificate program.

Volunteerism volunteering personal time to help others.

Withdrawal dropping a class after the drop/add deadline, which results in a student receiving a "W" for the course and no academic credit.

Writing Center a campus support service where students can receive assistance at any stage of the writing process, whether it be collecting and organizing ideas, composing a first draft, or proofreading a final draft.

References

Academic Integrity at Princeton. (2003). *Examples of plagiarism.* Retrieved October 21, 2006, from http://www.princeton.edu/pr/pub/integrity/pages/plagiarism/

Acredolo, C., & O'Connor, J. (1991). On the difficulty of detecting cognitive uncertainty. *Human Development, 34,* 204–223.

Adler, R. B., & Towne, M. (2001). *Looking out, looking in: Interpersonal communication* (10th ed.). Orlando, FL: Harcourt Brace.

AhYun, K. (2002). Similarity and attraction. In M. Allen, R.W. Preiss, B.M. Gayle, & N.A. Burrell (Eds.), *Interpersonal communication research* (pp. 145–167). Mahwah, NJ: Erlbaum.

Ainslie, G. (1975). Specious reward: A behavioral theory of impulsiveness and impulse control. *Psychological Bulletin, 82,* 463–496.

Ainslie, G. (1992). *Picoeconomics: The strategic interaction of successive motivational states within the person.* New York, NY: Cambridge University Press.

Alkon, D. L. (1992). *Memory's voice: Deciphering the brain-mind code.* New York, NY: HarperCollins.

Allport, G. W. (1954). *The nature of prejudice.* Cambridge, MA: Addison-Wesley.

Amabile, T., Hadley, C. N., & Kramer, S. J. (2002). Creativity under the gun. *Harvard Business Review, 80*(8), 52–61.

American Association of Community Colleges 2009 Fact Sheet. (2009). Retrieved from http://www.aacc.nche.edu/About/Documents/factsheet2009.pdf

American College Testing. (2009). *National college dropout and graduation rates, 2008.* Retrieved June 4, 2009, from http://www.act.org/news

American Council on Education. (2008). *Making the case for affirmative action.* Retrieved January 13, 2007, from http://acenet.edu/bookstore/descsriptions/making_the_case/works/research.cfm

American Heart Association. (2006). *Fish, levels of mercury and omega-3 fatty acids.* Retrieved January 13, 2007, from http://americanheart.org/presenter.jthml?identifier=3013797

American Obesity Association. (2002). *Obesity in the U.S.* Retrieved April 26, 2006, from http://www.obesity.org/subs/fastfacts/obesity_US.shtml

American Psychiatric Association. (1994). *Diagnostic and statistical manual for mental disorders* (4th ed., DSM-IV). Washington, DC: American Psychiatric Press.

American Psychiatric Association: Work Group on Eating Disorders. (2000). Practice guidelines for the treatment of patients with eating disorders. *American Journal of Psychiatry, 157,* 1–39.

Amir, Y. (1976). The role of intergroup contact in change of prejudice and ethnic relations. In P. A. Katz (Ed.), *Towards the elimination of racism* (pp. 245–308). New York, NY: Pergamon Press.

Anderson, C. J. (2003). The psychology of doing nothing: Forms of decision avoidance result from reason and emotion. *Psychological Bulletin, 129,* 139–167.

Anderson, C. J., & Gates, C. (2002, August 8). Freshman absence-based intervention at the University of Mississippi. Electronic mailing list message. *First-Year Assessment Listserv (FYA) Series.*

Anderson, J. R., & Bower, G. H. (1974). Interference in memory for multiple contexts. *Memory and Cognition, 2,* 509–514.

Anderson, L.W., & Krathwohl, D.R. (Eds.). (2001). *A taxonomy for learning, teaching, and assessing: A revision of Bloom's taxonomy of educational objectives.* New York, NY: Addison Wesley Longman.

Anderson, M., & Fienberg, S. E. (2000). Race and ethnicity and the controversy over the U.S. census. *Current Sociology, 48*(3), 87–110.

Annual Social and Economic Supplement (ASEC). (2008). *Current population survey (CPS).* Retrieved January 18, 2010, from data-gov.tw.rpi.edu/…/ Current_Population_Survey_(CPS)_Annual_Survey

Appleby, D. C. (2008, June). *Diagnosing and treating the deadly 13th grade syndrome.* Paper presented at the Association of Psychological Science Convention, Chicago, IL.

Arnedt, J. T., Wilde, G. J. S., Munt, P. W., & MacLean, A. W. (2001). How do prolonged wakefulness and alcohol compare in the decrements they produce on a simulated driving task? *Accident Analysis and Prevention, 33,* 337–344.

Association of American Colleges and Universities (AAC&U). (2007). *College learning for the new global century.* Washington, DC: Author.

Astin, A. W. (1993). *What matters in college?* San Francisco, CA: Jossey-Bass.

Astin, A. W., Parrot, S. A., Korn, W. S., & Sax, L. J. (1997). *The American freshman: Thirty year trends, 1966–1996.* Los Angeles, CA: Higher Education Research Institute, University of California.

Ausubel, D. P. (1978). The facilitation of meaningful verbal learning in the classroom. *Educational Psychologist, 12,* 251–257.

Ausubel, D. P., Novak, J., & Hanesian, H. (1978). *Education psychology: A congnitive view* (2nd ed.). New York, NY: Holt, Rinehart & Winston.

Baddeley, A.D. (1999). *Essentials of human memory.* Hove, NY: Psychology.

Baer, J.M. (1993). *Creativity and divergent thinking.* Hillside, NJ: Erlbaum.

Bandura, A. (1986). *Social foundations of thought and action: A social cognitive theory.* Englewood Cliffs, NJ: Prentice Hall.

Bandura, A. (1994). Self-efficacy. In V. S. Ramachaudran (Ed.), *Encyclopedia of human behavior* (vol. 4, pp. 71–81). New York, NY: Academic Press.

Bandura, A. (1997). *Self-efficacy: The exercise of control.* New York, NY: Freeman.

Bandura, A., & Cervone, D. (1983). Self-evaluative and self-efficacy mechanisms governing the motivational effects of goal systems. *Journal of Personality and Social Psychology, 45*(5), 1017–1028.

Barefoot, B. O., Warnock, C. L., Dickinson, M. P., Richardson, S. E., & Roberts, M. R. (Eds.). (1998). *Exploring the evidence: Vol. 2. Reporting outcomes of first-year seminars* (Monograph No. 29). Columbia, OH: National Resource Center for the First-Year Experience and Students in Transition, University of South Carolina.

Bargdill, R. W. (2000). A phenomenological investigation of being bored with life. *Psychological Reports, 86,* 493–494.

Barker, L., & Watson, K. W. (2000). *Listen up: How to improve relationships, reduce stress, and be more productive by using the power of listening.* New York, NY: St. Martin's Press.

Bartels, A., & Zeki, S. (2000). The neural basis of romantic love. *European Journal of Neuroscience, 12,* 172–193.

Bartlett, T. (2002). Freshman pay, mentally and physically, as they adjust to college life. *Chronicle of Higher Education, 48,* 35–37.

Basadur, M., Runco, M. A., & Vega, L. A. (2000). Understanding how creative thinking skills, attitudes, and behaviors work together. *Journal of Creative Behavior, 34*(2), 77–100.

Bassham, G., Irwin, W., Nardone, H., & Wallace, J. M. (2005). *Critical thinking* (2nd ed.). New York, NY: McGraw-Hill.

Bates, G. A. (1994). *The next step: College.* Bloomington, IN: Phi Delta Kappa.

Bauer, D., Kopp, V., & Fischer, M.R. (2007). Answer changing in multiple choice assessment change that answer when in doubt—and spread the word! *BMC Medical Education, 7*, 28–32.

Baumeister, R. F., Heatherton, T. F., & Tice, D. M. (1994). *Losing control: How and why people fail at self-regulation.* San Diego, CA: Academic Press.

Bean, J. C. (2003). *Engaging ideas.* San Francisco, CA: Jossey-Bass.

Beck, B. L., Koons, S. R., & Milgram, D. L. (2000). Correlates and consequences of behavioral procrastination: The effects of academic procrastination, self-consciousness, self-esteem and self-handicapping. *Journal of Social Behavior and Personality, 15*, 3–13.

Beckett, W. (2003, September 5). What lies between the hookup and marriage? *The Chronicle.* Retrieved January 6, 2004, from http://www.dukechronicle.com/article/column-what-lies-between-hookup-and-marriage

Benedict, M.E., & Hoag, J. (2004). Seating location in large lectures: Are seating preferences or location related to course performance? *Journal of Economics Education, 35*, 215–231.

Benjamin, L. T., Jr., Cavell, T. A., & Shallenberger, W. R., III. (1984). Staying with initial answers on objective tests: Is it a myth? *Teaching of Psychology, 11*, 133–141.

Benjamin, M., McKeachie, W. J., Lin, Y.-G., & Holinger, D. (1981). Test anxiety: Deficits in information processing. *Journal of Educational Psychology, 73*, 816–824.

Bennet, W., & Gurin, J. (1983). *The dieter's dilemma.* New York, NY: Basic Books.

Benson, H., & Klipper, M. Z. (1990). *The relaxation response.* New York, NY: Avon.

Berndt, T. J. (1992). Friendship and friends' influence in adolescence. *Current Directions in Psychological Science, 1*(5), 156–159.

Biggs, J., & Tang, C. (2007). *Teaching for quality learning at university* (3rd ed.) Buckingham, UK: SRHE and Open University Press.

Biglan, A. (1973). The characteristics of subject matter in different academic areas. *Journal of Applied Psychology, 57*, 195–203.

Bjork, R. (1994). Memory and metamemory considerations in the training of human beings. In J. Metcalfe & A. P. Shimamura (Eds.), *Metacognition: Knowing about knowing* (pp. 185–206). Cambridge, MA: MIT Press.

Blakeslee, S. (1993, August 3). Mystery of sleep yields as studies reveal immune tie. *The New York Times*, pp. C1, C6.

Bligh, D.A. (2000). *What's the use of lectures?* San Francisco, CA: Jossey-Bass.

Boekaerts, M., Pintrich, P. R., & Zeidner, M. (2000). *Handbook of self-regulation.* San Diego, CA: Academic Press.

Bohme, K., & Budden, F. (2001). *The silent thief: Osteoporosis, exercises and strategies for prevention and treatment.* Buffalo, NY: Firefly.

Bok, D. (2006). *Our underachieving colleges.* Princeton, NJ: Princeton University Press.

Bolles, R. N. (1998). *The new quick job-hunting map.* Toronto, Ontario, Canada: Ten Speed Press.

Booth, F. W., & Vyas, D. R. (2001). Genes, environment, and exercise. *Advances in Experimental Medicine and Biology, 502*, 13–20.

Boudreau, C., & Kromrey, J. (1994). A longitudinal study of the retention and academic performance of participants in a freshman orientation course. *Journal of College Student Development, 35,* 444–449.

Bowen, H. R. (1977). *Investment in learning: The individual and social value of American higher education.* San Francisco, CA: Jossey-Bass.

Bowen, H. R. (1997). *Investment in learning: The individual and social value of American higher education* (2nd ed.). Baltimore, MD: Johns Hopkins Press.

Bowlby, J. (1980). *Attachment and loss: Vol. 3. Loss, sadness, and depression.* New York, NY: Basic Books.

Boyer, E. L. (1987). *College: The undergraduate experience in America.* New York, NY: Harper & Row.

Bradburn, E. M. (2002). *Short-term enrollment in postsecondary education: Student background and institutional differences in reasons for early departure, 1996–98.* Washington, DC: National Center for Education Statistics, U.S. Department of Education.

Bradshaw, D. (1995). Learning theory: Harnessing the strength of a neglected resource. In D. C. A. Bradshaw (Ed.), *Bringing learning to life: The learning revolution, the economy and the individual* (pp. 79–92). London, England: Falmer Press.

Bransford, J. D., Brown, A. L., & Cocking, R. R. (1999). *How people learn: Brain, mind, experience and school.* Washington, DC: National Academy Press.

Bridgeman, B. (2003). *Psychology and evolution: The origins of mind.* Thousand Oaks, CA: Sage.

Brody, J. E. (2003, August 18). Skipping a college course: Weight gain 101. *The New York Times,* p. D7.

Brooks, K. (2009). *You majored in what? Mapping your path from chaos to career.* New York, NY: Penguin.

Brown, R. D. (1988). Self-quiz on testing and grading issues. *Teaching at UNL (University of Nebraska–Lincoln), 10*(2), 1–3.

Brown, S. D., & Krane, N. E. R. (2000). Four (or five) sessions and a cloud of dust: Old assumptions and new observations about career counseling. In S. D. Brown & R. W. Lent (Eds.), *Handbook of counseling psychology* (3rd ed., pp. 740–766). New York, NY: Wiley.

Bruffee, K. A. (1993). *Collaborative learning: Higher education, interdependence, and the authority of knowledge.* Baltimore, MD: Johns Hopkins University Press.

Bruner, J. (1990). *Acts of meaning.* Cambridge, MA: Harvard University Press.

Burka, J. B., & Yuen, L. M. (1983). *Procrastination: Why you do it, what to do about it.* Reading, MA: Addison-Wesley.

Caine, R. N., & Caine, G. (1991). *Teaching and the human brain.* Alexandria, VA: Association for Supervision and Curriculum Development.

Cameron, L. (2003). *Metaphor in educational discourse.* London, England: Continuum.

Campbell, T. A., & Campbell, D. E. (1997, December). Faculty/student mentor program: Effects on academic performance and retention. *Research in Higher Education, 38,* 727–742.

Caplan, P. J., & Caplan, J. B. (1994). *Thinking critically about research on sex and gender.* New York, NY: HarperCollins College Publishers.

Carnegie, D. (1936). *How to win friends and influence people.* Simon and Schuster (1936) US.

Caroli, M., Argentieri, L., Cardone, M., & Masi, A. (2004). Role of television in childhood obesity prevention. *International Journal of Obesity Related Metabolic Disorders, 28*(Suppl. 3), S104–S108.

Carpenter, K. M., & Hasin, D. S. (1998). A prospective evaluation of the relationship between reasons for drinking and DSM-IV alcohol-use disorders. *Addictive Behaviors, 23*(1), 41–46.

Carter, R. (1998). *Mapping the mind.* Berkeley, CA: University of California Press.

Chan, Z. C. Y., & Ma, J. L. C. (2002, December). Anorexic eating: Two case studies in Hong Kong. *Qualitative Report, 7*(4). Retrieved October 24, 2009, from http://www.nova.edu/ssss/QR/QR7-4/chan.html

Chaney, W. (2007). *Dynamic mind.* Las Vegas, NV: Houghton-Brace Publishing.

Chi, M., de Leeuw, N., Chiu, M. H., & LaVancher, C. (1994). Eliciting self-explanations improves understanding. *Cognitive Science, 18,* 439–477.

Chickering, A. W., & Schlossberg, N. K. (1998). Moving on: Seniors as people in transition. In J. N. Gardner, G. Van der Veer, et al. (Eds.), *The senior year experience* (pp. 37–50). San Francisco, CA: Jossey-Bass.

Chronicle of Higher Education. (2003, August 30). Almanac 2003–04. *Chronicle of Higher Education, 49*(1).

Cianciotto, J. (2005). *Hispanic and latino same sex-couple households in the United States: A report from the 2000 Census.* New York, NY: The National Gay and Lesbian Task Force Policy Institute and the National Latino/a Coalition for Justice.

Claxton, C. S., & Murrell, P. H. (1988). *Learning styles: Implications for improving practice.* ASHE-ERIC Educational Report No. 4. Washington, DC: Association for the Study of Higher Education.

Coates, T. J. (1977). *How to sleep better: A drug-free program for overcoming insomnia.* Englewood Cliffs, NJ: Prentice Hall.

College Board. (2006). *Education pays update.* Washington, DC: Author.

College Board. (2008). *Education pays 2007.* Washington, DC: Author.

Collins, A. M., & Loftus, E. F. (1975). A spreading activation theory of semantic processing. *Psychological Review, 82,* 407–428.

Colombo, G., Cullen, R., & Lisle, B. (1995). *Rereading America: Cultural contexts for critical thinking and writing.* Boston, MA: Bedford Books of St. Martin's Press.

Conaway, M. A. (1982). Listening: Learning tool and retention agent. In A. S. Algier & K. W. Algier (Eds.), *Improving reading and study skills* (pp. 51–63). San Francisco, CA: Jossey-Bass.

Conley, D. T. (2005). *College knowledge: What it really takes for students to succeed and what we can do to get them ready.* San Francisco, CA: Jossey-Bass.

Corbin, C. B., Pangrazi, R. P., & Franks, B. D. (2000). Definitions: Health, fitness, and physical activity. *President's Council on Physical Fitness and Sports Research Digest, 3*(9), 1–8.

Covey, S. R. (1990). *Seven habits of highly effective people* (2nd ed.). New York, NY: Fireside.

Coward, A. (1990). *Pattern thinking.* New York, NY: Praeger.

Crawford, H. J., & Strapp, C. H. (1994). Effects of vocal and instrumental music on visuospatial and verbal performance as moderated by studying preference and personality. *Personality and Individual Differences, 16*(2), 237–245.

Crosby, O. (2002, Summer). Informational interviewing: Get the scoop on careers. *Occupational Outlook Quarterly,* 32–37.

Csikszentmihalyi, M. (1996). *Creativity: Flow and the psychology of discovery and invention.* New York, NY: HarperCollins.

Cude, B. J., Lawrence, F. C., Lyons, A. C., Metzger, K., LeJeune, E., Marks, L., & Machtmes, K. (2006). College students and financial literacy: What they know and what we need to learn. *Proceedings of the Eastern Family Economics and Resource Management Association Conference* (pp. 102–109).

Cuseo, J. B. (1996). *Cooperative learning: A pedagogy for addressing contemporary challenges and critical issues in higher education.* Stillwater, OK: New Forums Press.

Cuseo, J. B. (2003a). Comprehensive academic support for students during the first year of college. In G. L. Kramer, et al. (Eds.), *Student academic services: An integrated approach* (pp. 271–310). San Francisco, CA: Jossey-Bass.

Cuseo, J. B. (2003b, November). *The transfer transition.* Preconference workshop conducted at the Tenth National Conference on Students in Transition, Lake Buena Vista, FL.

Cuseo, J. B. (2005). "Decided," "undecided," and "in transition": Implications for academic advisement, career counseling, and student retention. In R. S. Feldman (Ed.), *Improving the first year of college: Research and practice* (pp. 27–50). Mahwah, NJ: Lawrence Erlbaum.

Cuseo, J. B., & Barefoot, B. O. (1996). A natural marriage: The extended orientation seminar and the community college. In J. Henkin (Ed.), *The community college: Opportunity and access for America's first-year students* (pp. 59–68). Columbia, OH: National Resource Center for the First-Year Experience and Students in Transition, University of South Carolina.

Damrad-Frye, R., & Laird, J. (1989). The experience of boredom: The role of self-perception of attention. *Journal of Personality & Social Psychology, 57,* 315–320.

Daniels, D., & Horowitz, L. J. (1997). *Being and caring: A psychology for living.* Prospect Heights, IL: Waveland Press.

De Bono, E. (2007). *How to have creative ideas.* London, England: Vermilion.

Dee, T. (2004). Are there civic returns to education? *Journal of Public Economics, 88,* 1697–1720.

DeJong, W., & Linkenback, J. (1999). Telling it like it is: Using social norms marketing campaigns to reduce student drinking. *AAHE Bulletin, 52*(4), pp. 11–13, 16.

Dement, W. C., & Vaughan, C. (1999). *The promise of sleep.* New York, NY: Delacorte Press.

Dement, W. C., & Vaughan, C. (2000). *The promise of sleep: A pioneer in sleep medicine explores the vital connection between health, happiness, and a good night's sleep.* New York, NY: Dell.

Demmert, W. G., Jr., & Towner, J. C. (2003). *A review of the research literature on the influences of culturally based education on the academic performance of Native American students.* Retrieved from the Northwest Regional Educational Laboratory, Portland, Oregon, Web site: http://www.nrel.org/indianaed/cbe.pdf

DesMaisons, K. (1998). *Potatoes not Prozac.* London, England: Simon & Schuster.

Devadoss, S., & Foltz, J. (1996). Evaluation of factors influencing student class attendance and performance. *American Journal of Agriculture Economics, vol. 78,* pp. 499–507.

Diaz, P. (1992). Effects of transfer on academic performance of community college students at the four-year institution. *Community Junior College Quarterly of Research and Practice, 16*(3), 279–291.

Donald, J.G. (2002). *Learning to think: Disciplinary perspectives.* San Francisco, CA: Jossey-Bass.

Doran, G.T. (1981). There's a S.M.A.R.T. way to write management's goals and objectives. *Management Review, 70*(11), 35–36.

Dorfman, J., Shames, J., & Kihlstrom, J.F. (1996). Intuition, incubation, and insight. In G. Underwood (Ed.), *Implicit cognition.* New York, NY: Oxford University Press.

Douglas, K. A., Collins, J. L., Warren, C., Kahn, L., Gold, R., Clayton, S., et al. (1997). Results from the 1995 national college health risk behavior survey. *Journal of American College Health, 46,* 55–66.

Doyle, S., Edison, M., & Pascarella, E. (1998). *The "seven principles of good practice in undergraduate education" as process indicators of cognitive development in college: A longitudinal study.* Paper presented at the annual meeting of the Association for the Study of Higher Education, Miami, FL.

Druckman, D., & Bjork, R. A. (Eds.). (1991). *In the mind's eye: Enhancing human performance.* Washington, DC: National Academy Press.

Dryden, G., & Vos, J. (1999). *The learning revolution: To change the way the world learns.* Torrance, CA: Learning Web.

Dunn, R., Dunn, K., & Price, G. (1990). *Learning style inventory.* Lawrence, KS: Price Systems.

Dupuy, G. M., & Vance, R. M. (1996, October). *Launching your career: A transition module for seniors.* Paper presented at the Second National Conference on Students in Transition, San Antonio, TX.

Eaton, S. B., & Konner, M. (1985). Paleolithic nutrition: A consideration of its nature and current implications. *New England Journal of Medicine, 312,* 283.

Eckman, P., & Friesen, W. V. (1969). Nonverbal leakage and clues to deception. *Psychiatry, 32,* 88–106.

Education Commission of the States. (1995). *Making quality count in undergraduate education.* Denver, CO: ECS Distribution Center.

Education Commission of the States. (1996). *Bridging the gap between neuroscience and education.* Denver, CO: Author.

Einstein, G. O., Morris, J., & Smith, S. (1985). Note-taking, individual differences, and memory for lecture information. *Journal of Educational Psychology, 77*(5), 522–532.

Ellin, A. (1993, September). Post-parchment depression. *Boston Phoenix.*

Ellis, A. (1995). Changing rational-emotive therapy (RET) to rational emotive behavior therapy (REBT). *Journal of Rational-Emotive & Cognitive Behavior Therapy, 13*(2), 85–89.

Ellis, A., & Knaus, W. J. (1977). *Overcoming procrastination.* New York, NY: Signet Books.

Elster, J., & Lowenstein, G. (Eds.). (1992). *Choice over time.* New York, NY: Russell Sage Foundation.

Entwistle, N.J., & Ramsden, P. (1983). *Understanding student learning.* London, England: Croom Helm.

Erasmus, U. (1993). *Fats that heal, fats that kill.* Burnaby, British Columbia, Canada: Alive Books.

Erickson, B. L., Peters, C. B., & Strommer, D. W. (2006). *Teaching first-year college students.* San Francisco, CA: Jossey-Bass.

Erickson, B. L., & Strommer, D. W. (1991). *Teaching college freshmen.* San Francisco, CA: Jossey-Bass.

Erickson, B. L., & Strommer, D. W. (2005). Inside the first-year classroom: Challenges and constraints. In J. L. Upcraft, J. N. Gardner, & B. O. Barefoot, *Challenging and supporting the first-year student* (pp. 241–256). San Francisco, CA: Jossey-Bass.

Ericsson, K. A. (2006). The influence of experience and deliberate practice on the development of superior expert performance. In K. A. Ericsson, N. Charness, P. Feltovich, & R. R. Hoffman (Eds.), *Cambridge handbook of expertise and expert performance* (pp. 685–706). Cambridge, England: Cambridge University Press.

Ericsson, K. A., & Charness, N. (1994). Expert performance. *American Psychologist, 49*(8), 725–747.

Everly, G. S. (1989). *A clinical guide to the treatment of the human stress response.* New York, NY: Plenum Press.

Ewell, P. T. (1997). Organizing for learning. *AAHE Bulletin, 50*(4), 3–6.

Fairbairn, G. J., & Winch, C. (1996). *Reading, writing and reasoning: A guide for students* (2nd ed.). Buckingham, UK: OU Press.

Family Care Foundation. (2005). *If the world were a village of 100 people.* Retrieved December 19, 2006, from http://www.familycare.org.news/if_the_world.htm

Feagin, J., & Feagin, C. (2007). *Racial and ethnic relations* (3rd ed.). Upper Saddle River, NJ: Prentice Hall.

Feldman, K. A., & Newcomb, T. M. (1994). *The impact of college on students.* New Brunswick, NJ: Transaction Publishers. (Original work published 1969).

Feldman, K. A., & Newcomb, T. M. (1997). The impact of college on students. New Brunswick, NJ: Transaction. (Original work published 1969).

Feskens, E. J., & Kromhout, D. (1993). Epidemiologic studies on Eskimos and fish intake. *Annals of the New York Academy of Science, 683,* 9–15.

Festinger, L. (1954). A theory of social comparison processes. *Human Relations,* 7, 117–140.

Fidler, P., & Godwin, M. (1994). Retaining African-American students through the freshman seminar. *Journal of Developmental Education, 17,* 34–41.

Fisher, J. L., Harris, J. L., & Harris, M. B. (1973). Effect of note-taking and review on recall. *Journal of Educational Psychology, 65*(3), 321–325.

Fixman, C. S. (1990). The foreign language needs of U.S.-based corporations. *Annals of the American Academy of Political and Social Science, 511,* 25–46.

Flavell, J. H. (1985). *Cognitive development* (2nd ed.). Englewood Cliffs, NJ: Prentice Hall.

Fletcher, A., Lamond, N., van den Heuvel, C. J., & Dawson, D. (2003). Prediction of performance during sleep deprivation and alcohol intoxication using a quantitative model of work-related fatigue. *Sleep Research Online, 5,* 67–75.

Flett, G. L., Blankstein, K. R., Hewitt, P. L., & Koledin, S. (1992). Components of perfectionism and procrastination in college students. *Social Behavior & Personality, 20,* 85–94.

Flippo, R. F., & Caverly, D. C. (2009). *Handbook of college reading and study strategy research* (2nd ed.). New York, NY: Lawrence Erlbaum Associates.

Flowers, L., Osterlind, S., Pascarella, E., & Pierson, C. (2001). How much do students learn in college? Cross-sectional estimates using the College Basic Academic Subjects Examination. *Journal of Higher Education, 72,* 565–583.

Foreman, J. (2009, March 2). Students, don't blame college for your misery. *Los Angeles Times,* p. F3.

Franklin, K. F. (2002). Conversations with Metropolitan University first-year students. *Journal of the First-Year Experience & Students in Transition, 14*(2), 57–88.

Fromm, E. (1970). *The art of loving.* New York, NY: Bantam.

Fromme, A. (1980). *The ability to love.* Chatsworth, CA: Wilshire Book Company.

Frost, S. H. (1991). *Academic advising for student success: A system of shared responsibility* (ASHE-ERIC Higher Education Report, No. 3). Washington, DC: School of Education and Human Development, George Washington University.

Furnham, A., & Argyle, M. (1998). *The psychology of money.* New York, NY: Routledge.

Gardner, H. (1983). *Frames of mind: The theory of multiple intelligences.* New York, NY: Basic Books.

Gardner, H. (1993). *Frames of mind: The theory of multiple intelligences* (2nd ed.). New York, NY: Basic Books.

Gardner, H. (1999). *Intelligence reframed: Multiple intelligences for the 21st century.* New York, NY: Basic Books.

Gardner, H. (2006). *Changing minds: The art and science of changing our own and other people's minds.* Boston, MA: Harvard Business School Press.

Gardner, P. D. (1991, March). *Learning the ropes: Socialization and assimilation into the workplace.* Paper presented at the Second National Conference on the Senior Year Experience, San Antonio, TX.

German, T. P., & Barrett, H. C. (2005). Functional fixedness in a technologically sparse culture. *Psychological Science, 16,* 1–5.

Gershoff, S., & Whitney, C. (1996). *The Tufts University guide to total nutrition.* New York, NY: Harper Perennial.

Gibb, H. R. (1991). *Trust: A new vision of human relationships for business, education, family, and personal living* (2nd ed.). North Hollywood, CA: Newcastle.

Gibb, J. R. (1961, September). Defensive communication. *Journal of Communication, 11,* 3.

Giles, L. C., Glonek, F. V., Luszcz, M. A., & Andrews, G. R. (2005). Effect of social networks on 10-year survival in very old Australians: The Australia longitudinal study of aging. *Journal of Epidemiology and Community Health, 59,* 574–579.

Gladwell, M. (2008). *Outliers: The story of success.* New York, NY: Little, Brown.

Glass, J., & Garrett, M. (1995). Student participation in a college orientation course: Retention, and grade point average. *Community College Journal of Research and Practice, 19,* 117–132.

Glenberg, A. M. (1997). What memory is for. *Behavioral and Brain Sciences, 20,* 1–55.

Glenberg, A. M., Bradley, M. M., Kraus, T. A., & Renzaglia, G. J. (1983). Studies of the long-term recency effect: Support for a contextually guided retrieval hypothesis. *Journal of Experimental Psychology: Learning, Memory, and Cognition, 9,* 231–255.

Glenberg, A. M., Schroeder, J. L., & Robertson, D. A. (1998). Averting the gaze disengages the environment and facilitates remembering. *Memory & Cognition, 26*(4), 651–658.

Godden, D., & Baddeley, A. (1975). Context dependent memory in two natural environments. *British Journal of Psychology, 66*(3), 325–331.

Goleman, D. (1995). *Emotional intelligence: Why it can matter more than IQ.* New York, NY: Random House.

Goleman, D. (2006). *Social intelligence: The new science of human relationships.* New York, NY: Dell.

Gordon, V. N., & Steele, G. E. (2003). Undecided first-year students: A 25-year longitudinal study. *Journal of the First-Year Experience and Students in Transition, 15*(1), 19–38.

Gottman, J. (1994). *Why marriages succeed and fail.* New York, NY: Fireside.

Graf, P. (1982). The memorial consequence of generation and transformation. *Journal of Verbal Learning and Verbal Behavior, 21,* 539–548.

Grandpre, E. (2000, September 21). First year attendance [Electronic mailing list message]. Retrieved from the First-Year Experience. Green, M. G. (Ed.). (1989). *Minorities on campus: A handbook for enhancing diversity.* Washington, DC: American Council on Education.

Greenberg, R., Pillard, R., & Pearlman, C. (1972). The effect of dream (stage REM) deprivation on adaptation to stress. *Psychosomatic Medicine, 34,* 257–262.

Grunder, P., & Hellmich, D. (1996). Academic persistence and achievement of remedial students in a community college's success program. *Community College Review, 24,* 21–33.

Guttmacher Institute (2009). *A real-time look at the impact of the recession on women's family planning and pregnancy decisions.* New York: Guttmacher Institute.

Haberman, S., & Luffey, D. (1998). Weighing in college students' diet and exercise behaviors. *Journal of American College Health, 46,* 189–191.

Hall, R. M., & Sandler, B. R. (1982). *The classroom climate: A chilly one for women.* Project on the Status of Women. Washington, DC: Association of American Colleges.

Hall, R. M., & Sandler, B. R. (1984). *Out of the classroom: A chilly campus climate for women.* Project on the Status of Women. Washington, DC: Association of American Colleges.

Halpern, D. F. (2003). *Thought & knowledge: An introduction to critical thinking* (4th ed.). Mahwah, NJ: Lawrence Erlbaum Associates.

Harriott, J., & Ferrari, J. R. (1996). Prevalence of procrastination among samples of adults. *Psychological Reports, 78,* 611–616.

Harris, M. B. (2000). Correlates and characteristics of boredom and proneness to boredom. *Journal of Applied Social Psychology, 30*(3), 576–598.

Harris, M. B. (2006). Correlates and characteristics of boredom proneness and boredom. Mary B. Harris. Aricle first published online: 31 Jul 2006. DOI: 10.1111/j.1559-1816.2000.tb02497.x.

Hartley, J. (1998). *Learning and studying: A research perspective.* London, England: Routledge.

Hartley, J., & Marshall, S. (1974). On notes and note taking. *Universities Quarterly, 28,* 225–235.

Hartman, H. J. (2001). *Metacognition in learning and instruction: Theory, research and practice.* Dordrecht, Holland: Kluwer Academic.

Harvey, L., Moon, S., Geall, V., & Bower, R. (1997). *Graduates work: Organizational change and students' attributes.* Birmingham, England: Centre for Research into Quality, University of Central England.

Hashaw, R. M., Hammond, C. J., & Rogers, P. H. (1990). Academic locus of control and the collegiate experience. *Research & Teaching in Developmental Education, 7*(1), 45–54.

Hatfield, E., & Walster, G. W. (1985). *A new look at love.* Lanham, MD: University Press of America.

Hauri, P., & Linde, S. (1996). *No more sleepless nights.* New York, NY: John Wiley & Sons.

Haven't filed yet? Tackle those taxes. (2003, April 11). *USA Today,* p. 3b.

Health, C., & Soll, J. (1996). Mental budgeting and consumer decisions. *Journal of Consumer Research, 23,* 40–52.

Heath, H. (1977). *Maturity and competence: A transcultural view.* New York, NY: Halsted Press.

Herman, R. E. (2000, November). Liberal arts: The key to the future. *USA Today Magazine, 129,* 34.

Higbee, K. L. (2001). *Your memory: How it works and how to improve it.* New York, NY: Marlowe.

Higher Education Institute (HERI). (2009). *The American college teacher: National norms for 2007–2008.* Los Angeles, CA: Author.

Higher Education Research Institute. (2004). *The spiritual life of college students: A national study of college students' search for meaning and purpose.* Los Angeles, CA: Author, Graduate School of Education & Information Studies, University of California.

Hildenbrand, M., & Gore, P. A., Jr. (2005). Career development in the first-year seminar: Best practice versus actual practice. In P. A. Gore (Ed.), *Facilitating the career development of students in transition* (Monograph No. 43, pp. 45–60). Columbia, OH: National Resource Center for the First-Year Experience and Students in Transition, University of South Carolina.

Hill, A. J. (2002). Developmental issues in attitudes toward food and diet. *Proceedings of the Nutrition Society, 61*(2), 259–268.

Hill, J. O., Wyat, H. R., Reed, G. W., & Peters, J. C. (2003). Obesity and environment: Where do we go from here? *Science, 299,* 853–855.

Hobson, J. A. (1988). *The dreaming brain.* New York, NY: Basic Books.

Hollenbeck, J. R., Williams, C. R., & Klein, H. J. (1989). An empirical examination of the antecedents of commitment to difficult goals. *Journal of Applied Psychology, 74*(1), 18–23.

Horne, J. (1988). *Why we sleep: The functions of sleep in humans and other mammals.* New York, NY: Oxford University Press.

Howard, P. J. (2000). *The owner's manual for the brain: Everyday applications of mind-brain research* (2nd ed.). Atlanta, GA: Bard Press.

Howe, M. J. (1970). Note-taking strategy, review, and long-term retention of verbal information. *Journal of Educational Psychology, 63,* 285.

Huck, S., & Bounds, W. (1972). Essay grades: An interaction between graders' handwriting clarity and the neatness of examination papers. *American Educational Research Journal, 9*(2), 279–283.

Hughes, D. C., Keeling, B., & Tuck, B. F. (1983). Effects of achievement expectations and handwriting quality on scoring essays. *Journal of Educational Measurement, 20*(1), 65–70.

Hunter, M. A., & Linder, C. W. (2005). First-year seminars. In M. L. Upcraft, J. N. Gardner, B. O. Barefoot, et al. (Eds.), *Challenging and supporting the first-year student: A handbook for improving the first year of college* (pp. 275–291). San Francisco, CA: Jossey-Bass.

Indiana University. (2004). *Selling your liberal arts degree to employers.* Retrieved July 7, 2004, from http://www.indiana.edu/~career/fulltime/selling_liberal_arts.html

Institute for Research on Higher Education. (1995). Connecting schools and employers: Work-related education and training. *Change, 27*(3), 39–46.

Internal Revenue Service. (2004). *Statistics of income 2001–2003.* Washington, DC: Author.

Jablonski, N. G., & Chaplin, G. (2002, October). Skin deep. *Scientific American,* 75–81.

Jacobs, W. J., & Nadel, L. (1985). Stress-induced recovery of fears and phobias. *Psychological Review, 92*(4), 512–531.

Jakubowski, P., & Lange, A. J. (1978). *The assertive option: Your rights and responsibilities.* Champaign, IL: Research Press.

Janis, I. L. (1982). *Groupthink: Psychological studies of policy decisions and fiascoes* (2nd ed.). Boston, MA: Houghton Mifflin.

Jemott, J. B., & Magloire, K. (1988). Academic stress, social support, and secretory immunoglobulin. *Journal of Personality and Social Psychology, 55,* 803–810.

Jenkins, J. G., & Dallenbach, K. M. (1924). Oblivescence during sleep and waking. *American Journal of Psychology, 35,* 605–612.

Jensen, E. (1998). *Teaching with the brain in mind.* Alexandria, VA: Association for Supervision and Curriculum Development.

Jensen, E. (2000). *Brain-based learning.* San Diego, CA: The Brain Store.

Johnsgard, K. W. (2004). *Conquering depression and anxiety through exercise.* New York, NY: Prometheus.

Johnstone, A. H., & Su, W. Y. (1994). Lectures: A learning experience? *Education in Chemistry, 31*(1), 65–76, 79.

Joint Science Academies Statement. (2005). *Global response to climate change.* Retrieved August 29, 2005, from http://nationalacademies.org/onpi/06072005.pdf

Jones, L., & Petruzzi, D. C. (1995). Test anxiety: A review of theory and current treatment. *Journal of College Student Psychotherapy, 10*(1), 3–15.

Kachgal, M. M., Hansen, L. S., & Nutter, K. J. (2001). Academic procrastination prevention/intervention: Strategies and recommendations. *Journal of Developmental Education, 25,* 14–24.

Kadison, R. D., & DiGeronimo, T. F. (2004). *College of the overwhelmed: The campus mental health crisis and what to do about it.* San Francisco, CA: Jossey-Bass.

Kagan, S., & Kagan, M. (1998). *Multiple intelligences: The complete MI book.* San Clemente, CA: Kagan Cooperative Learning.

Kasper, G. (2004, March). *Tax procrastination: Survey finds 29% have yet to begin taxes.* Retrieved June 6, 2006, from http://www.preweb.com/releases/2004/3/prweb114250.htm

Kaufman, J. C., & Baer, J. (2002). Could Steven Spielberg manage the Yankees? Creative thinking in different domains. *Korean Journal of Thinking & Problem Solving, 12*(2), 5–14.

Kelly, K. (1994). *Out of control: The new biology of machines, social systems, and the economic world.* Reading, MA: Addison-Wesley.

Khoshaba, D. M., & Maddi, S. R. (1999–2004). *HardiTraining: Managing stressful change.* Newport Beach, CA: Hardiness Institute.

Kielcolt-Glaser, J. K., & Glaser, R. (1986). Psychological influences on immunity. *Psychosomatics, 27,* 621–625.

Kiecolt, J. K., Glaser, R., Strain, E., Stout, J., Tarr, K., Holliday, J., & Speicher, C. (1986). Modulation of cellular immunity in medical students. *Journal of Behavioral Medicine, 9,* 5–21.

Kiewra, K. A. (1985). Students' note-taking behaviors and the efficacy of providing the instructor's notes for review. *Contemporary Educational Psychology, 10,* 378–386.

Kiewra, K. A. (2000). Fish giver or fishing teacher? The lure of strategy instruction. *Teaching at UNL (University of Nebraska–Lincoln), 22*(3), 1–3.

Kiewra, K. A. (2005). *Learn how to study and SOAR to success.* Upper Saddle River, NJ: Pearson Prentice Hall.

Kiewra, K. A., & DuBois, N. F. (1998). *Learning to learn: Making the transition from student to lifelong learner.* Needham Heights, MA: Allyn and Bacon.

Kiewra, K. A., & Fletcher, H. J. (1984). The relationship between notetaking variables and achievement measures. *Human Learning, 3,* 273–280.

Kiewra, K. A., DuBois, N., Christian, D., McShane, A., Meyerhoffer, M., & Roskelley, D. (1991). Note-taking functions and techniques. *Journal of Educational Psychology, 83*(2), 240–245.

Kiewra, K. A., Hart, K., Scoular, J., Stephen, M., Sterup, G., & Tyler, B. (2000). Fish giver or fishing teacher? The lure of strategy instruction. *Teaching at UNL (University of Nebraska–Lincoln), 22*(3).

King, A. (1990). Enhancing peer interaction and learning in the classroom through reciprocal questioning. *American Educational Research Journal, 27*(4), 664–687.

King, A. (1995). Guided peer questioning: A cooperative learning approach to critical thinking. *Cooperative Learning and College Teaching, 5*(2), 15–19.

King, J. E. (2002). *Crucial choices: How students' financial decisions affect their academic success.* Washington, DC: American Council on Education.

King, J. E. (2005). Academic success and financial decisions: Helping students make crucial choices. In R. S. Feldman (Ed.), *Improving the first year of college: Research and practice* (pp. 3–26). Mahwah, NJ: Lawrence Erlbaum.

Kintsch, W. (1968). Recognition and free recall of organized lists. *Journal of Experimental Psychology, 78,* 481–487.

Kintsch, W. (1970). *Learning, memory, and conceptual processes.* Hoboken, NJ: John Wiley & Sons.

Kintsch, W. (1994). Text comprehension, memory, and learning. *American Psychologist, 49,* 294–303.

Klein, S. P., & Hart, F. M. (1968). Chance and systematic factors affecting essay grades. *Journal of Educational Measurement, 5,* 197–206.

Knouse, S., Tanner, J., & Harris, E. (1999). The relation of college internships, college performance, and subsequent job opportunity. *Journal of Employment Counseling, 36,* 35–43.

Knox, S. (2004). *Financial basics: A money management guide for students.* Columbus, OH: State University Press.

Kolb, D. A. (1976). Management and learning process. *California Management Review, 18*(3), 21–31.

Kolb, D. A. (1985). *Learning styles inventory.* Boston, MA: McBer.

Kristof, K. M. (2008, December 27). Hooked on debt: Students learn too late the costs of private loans. *Los Angeles Times,* pp. A1, A18–A19.

Kruger, J., Wirtz, D., & Miller, D. (2005). Counterfactual thinking and the first instinct fallacy. *Journal of Personality and Social Psychology, 88,* 725–735.

Kucewicz, N. (2001, August 15). Ins and outs of the college dating game: Fun or forever? *The Rocky Mountain Collegian.* Retrieved January 3, 2004, from http://www.collegian.com/vnews/display.v/ART/2001/08/15/3d78c7cd538ef?in_archive=1

Kuh, G. D. (1993). In their own words: What students learn outside the classroom. *American Educational Research Journal, 30,* 277–304.

Kuh, G. D. (2005). Student engagement in the first year of college. In M. L. Upcraft, J. N. Gardner, B. O. Barefoot, et al. (Eds.), *Challenging and supporting the first-year student: A handbook for improving the first year of college* (pp. 86–107). San Francisco, CA: Jossey-Bass.

Kuh, G. D., Kinzie, J., Schuh, J. H., Whitt, E. J., et al. (2005). *Student success in college: Creating conditions that matter.* San Francisco, CA: Jossey-Bass.

Kuh, G. D., Schuh, J. H., Whitt, E. J., et al. (1991). *Involving colleges.* San Francisco, CA: Jossey-Bass.

Kuhn, L. (1988). What should we tell students about answer changing? *Research Serving Teaching, 1*(8).

Kurfiss, J. G. (1988). *Critical thinking: Theory, research, practice, and possibilities.* ASHE-ERIC, Report No. 2. Washington, DC: Association for the Study of Higher Education.

Ladas, H. S. (1980). Note-taking on lectures: An information-processing approach. *Educational Psychologist, 15*(1), 44–53.

Lakein, A. (1973). *How to get control of your time and your life.* New York, NY: New American Library.

Lancaster, L., & Stilman, D. (2002). *When generations collide: Who they are. Why they clash.* New York, NY: HarperCollins.

Latané, B., Liu, J. H., Nowak, A., Bonevento, N., & Zheng, L. (1995). Distance matters: Physical space and social impact. *Personality and Social Psychology Bulletin, 21,* 795–805.

Launius, M. H. (1997). College student attendance: Attitudes and academic performance. *College Student Journal, 31*(1) 86–93.

Lay, C. H., & Silverman, S. (1996). Trait procrastination, time management, and dilatory behavior. *Personality & Individual Differences, 21,* 61–67.

LeDoux, J. E. (1996). *The emotional brain: The mysterious underpinnings of emotional life.* New York, NY: Touchstone.

LeDoux, J. E. (1998). *The emotional brain: The mysterious underpinnings of emotional life.* New York, NY: Simon & Schuster.

Lefcourt, H. M. (1982). *Locus of control: Current trends in theory and research.* Hillsdale, NJ: Erlbaum.

Lehrer, P. M., & Woolfolk, R. L. (1993). *Principles and practice of stress management* (vol. 2). New York, NY: Guilford Press.

Leibel, R. L., Rosenbaum, M., & Hirsch, J. (1995). Changes in energy expenditure resulting from altered body weight. *New England Journal of Medicine, 332,* 621–628.

Letvin, D. J. (2006). *This is your brain on music: The science of a human obsession.* New York, NY: Dutton.

Leuwerke, W. C., Robbins, S. B., Sawyer, R., & Hovland, M. (2004). Predicting engineering major status from mathematics achievement and interest congruence. *Journal of Career Assessment, 12,* 135–149.

Levine, A., & Cureton, J. S. (1998). *When hopes and fears collide.* San Francisco, CA: Jossey-Bass.

Levitsky, D. A., Nussbaum, M., Halbmaier, C. A., & Mrdjenovic, G. (2003, July). *The freshman 15: A model for the study of techniques to curb the "epidemic" of obesity.* Annual meeting of the Society of the Study of Ingestive Behavior, University of Groningen, Haren, The Netherlands.

Lewin, K. (1935). *A dynamic theory of personality.* New York, NY: McGraw-Hill.

Liebertz, C. (2005a). Want clear thinking? Relax. *Scientific American Mind, 16*(3), 88–89.

Liebertz, C. (2005b). A healthy laugh. *Scientific American Mind, 16*(3), 90–91.

Light, R. L. (1990). *The Harvard assessment seminars.* Cambridge, MA: Harvard University Press.

Light, R. L. (1992). *The Harvard assessment seminars, second report.* Cambridge, MA: Harvard University Press.

Light, R. L. (2001). *Making the most of college: Students speak their minds.* Cambridge, MA: Harvard University Press.

Linn, R. L., & Gronlund, N. E. (1995). *Measurement and assessment in teaching* (7th ed.). Englewood Cliffs, NJ: Prentice Hall.

Lock, R. D. (2000). *Taking charge of your career direction* (4th ed.). Belmont, CA: Wadsworth/Thomson Learning.

Locke, E. A. (1977). An empirical study of lecture note-taking among college students. *Journal of Educational Research, 77,* 93–99.

Locke, E. A., & Latham, G. P. (1990). *A theory of goal setting and task performance.* Englewood Cliffs, NJ: Prentice Hall.

Locke, E.A., & Latham, G. P. (2005). Goal setting theory: Theory building by induction. In K. G. Smith & M. A. Mitt (Eds.), *Great minds in management: The process of theory development.* New York, NY: Oxford.

Love, P., & Love, A. G. (1995). *Enhancing student learning: Intellectual, social, and emotional integration.* ASHE-ERIC Higher Education Report No. 4. Washington, DC: Graduate School of Education and Human Development, George Washington University.

Maddi, S. R. (2002). The story of hardiness: Twenty years of theorizing, research, and practice. *Consulting Psychology Journal: Practice and Research, 54*(3), 175–185.

Mae, N. (2005). *Undergraduate students and credit cards in 2004: An analysis of usage rates and trend.* Wilkes-Barre, PA: Nellie Mae Corp.

Maes, J. D., Weldy, T. G., & Icenogle, M. L. (1997). A managerial perspective: Oral communication competency is most important for business students in the workplace. *Journal of Business Communication, 34*(1), 67–80.

Maier, N. R. F. (1970). *Problem solving and creativity in individuals and groups.* Belmont, CA: Brooks/Cole.

Malmberg, K. J., & Murnane, K. (2002). List composition and the word-frequency effect for recognition memory. *Journal of Experimental Psychology: Learning, Memory, and Cognition, 28,* 616–630.

Malvasi, M., Rudowsky, C., & Valencia, J. M. (2009). *Library Rx: Measuring and treating library anxiety, a research study.* Chicago, IL: Association of College and Research Libraries.

Marzano, R. J., Pickering, D. J., & Pollock, J. (2001). *Classroom instruction that works: Research-based strategies for increasing student achievement.* Alexandria, VA: Association for Supervision and Curriculum Development.

Maslow, A. H. (1954). *Motivation and personality.* New York, NY: Harper & Row.

Matsui, T., Okada, A., & Inoshita, O. (1983). Mechanism of feedback affecting task performance. *Organizational Behavior and Human Performance, 31,* 114–122.

Mayer, R. (2003). *Learning and instruction.* Upper Saddle River, NJ: Pearson Education.

McCance, N., & Pychyl, T. A. (2003, August). *From task avoidance to action: An experience sampling study of undergraduate students' thoughts, feelings and coping strategies in relation to academic procrastination.* Paper presented at the Third Annual Conference for Counseling Procrastinators in the Academic Context, University of Ohio, Columbus.

McGuiness, D., & Pribram, K. (1980). The neurophysiology of attention: Emotional and motivational controls. In M. D. Wittrock (Ed.), *The brain and psychology* (pp. 95–139). New York, NY: Academic Press.

Mehrabian, A. (1972). *Nonverbal communication.* Chicago, IL: Adline-Atherton.

Middleton, F., & Strick, P. (1994). Anatomical evidence for cerebellar and basal ganglia involvement in higher brain function. *Science, 226*(51584), 458–461.

Millard, B. (2004, November). *A purpose-based approach to navigating college transitions.* Preconference workshop presented at the Eleventh National Conference on Students in Transition, Nashville, TN.

Miller, M. A. (2003, September/October). The meaning of the baccalaureate. *About Campus,* 2–8.

Millman, J., Bishop, C., & Ebel, R. (1965). An analysis of test-wiseness. *Educational and Psychological Measurement, 25,* 707–727.

Milton, O. (1982). *Will that be on the final?* Springfield, IL: Charles C. Thomas.

Minninger, J. (1984). *Total recall: How to boost your memory power.* Emmaus, PA: Rodale.

Mitler, M. M., Dinges, D. F., & Dement, W. C. (1994). Sleep medicine, public policy, and public health. In M. H. Kryger, T. Roth, & W. C. Dement (Eds.), *Principles and practice of sleep medicine* (2nd ed.). Philadelphia, PA: Saunders.

Moeller, M. L. (1999). History, concept and position of self-help groups in Germany. *Group Analysis, 32*(2), 181–194.

Molnar, S. (1991). *Human variation: Race, type, and ethnic groups* (3rd ed.). Englewood Cliffs, NJ: Prentice Hall.

Monk, T. H. (2005). The post-lunch dip in performance. *Clinical Sports Medicine, 24*(2), 15–23.

Moor, R. (2003). Attendance and performance. *Journal of College Science Teaching, 32*(6), 367–371.

Moor, R. (2006). Class attendance. How students' attitudes about attendance relate to their academic performance in introductory science classes. *Research and Teaching in Developmental Education*, 19–33.

Moor, R., Jensen, M., Hatch, J., Duranczyk, I., Staats, S., & Koch, L. (2003). Showing up: The importance of class attendance for academic success in introductory science classes. *The American Biology Teacher, 65*(5), 325–329.

Multon, K. D., Brown, S. D., & Lent, R. W. (1991). Relation of self-efficacy beliefs to academic outcomes: A meta-analytic investigation. *Journal of Counseling Psychology, 38*(1), 30–38.

Murname, K., & Shiffrin, R. M. (1991). Interference and the representation of events in memory. *Journal of Experimental Psychology: Learning, Memory, & Cognition, 17*, 855–874.

Myers, D. G. (1993). *The pursuit of happiness: Who is happy—and why?* New York, NY: Morrow.

Myers, D. G., & McCaulley, N. H. (1985). *Manual: A guide to the development and use of the Myers-Briggs Type Indicator.* Palo Alto, CA: Consulting Psychologists Press.

Nagda, B. R., Gurin, P., & Johnson, S. M. (2005). Living, doing and thinking diversity: How does pre-college diversity experience affect first-year students' engagement with college diversity? In R. S. Feldman (Ed.), *Improving the first year of college: Research and practice* (pp. 73–110). Mahwah, NJ: Lawrence Erlbaum.

Narciso, J., & Burkett, D. (1975). *Disclose yourself: Discover the "me" in relationships.* Englewood Cliffs, NJ: Prentice Hall.

Natale, V., & Ciogna, P. (1996). Circadian regulation of subjective alertness in morning and evening types. *Environmental Design Research Association, 20*(4), 491–497.

National Alliance to End Homelessness. (2007). *Homelessness counts.* Retrieved from http://www.endhomelessness.org/content/general/detail/1440

National Association of Colleges & Employers. (2003). *Job Outlook 2003 survey.* Bethlehem, PA: Author.

National Institute of Mental Health. (2001). *Eating disorders: Facts about eating disorders and the search for solutions.* Retrieved August 7, 2006, from http://www.nimh.nih.gov/publicat/eating disorders.cfm

National Institute of Mental Health. (2006). *The numbers count: Mental disorders in America.* Retrieved December 16, 2006, from http://www.nimh.nih.gov.pulicat/numbers.cfm

National Institute of Mental Health. (2011). *Eating disorders.* Washington, DC: U.S. Department of Health and Human Services.

National Research Council. (1989). *Diet and health: Implications for reducing chronic disease risk.* Washington, DC: Committee on Diet and Health, National Academy Press.

National Resource Center for the First-Year Experience and Students in Transition. (2004). *The 2003 Your First College Year (YFCY) Survey.* Columbia, SC: Author.

National Resources Defense Council. (2012). *Global warming: An introduction to climate change.* Retrieved May 11, 2012, from http://www.nrdc.org/globalwarming

National Survey of Student Engagement. (2009). *NSSE Annual Results 2009. Assessment for improvement: Tracking student engagement over time.* Bloomington, IN: Author.

Newell, A., & Rosenbloom, P. S. (1981). Mechanisms of skill acquisition of the law of practice. In J. R. Anderson (Ed.), *Cognitive skills and their acquisition.* Hillsdale, NJ: Erlbaum.

Newell, A., & Simon, H. A. (1959). *The simulation of human thought.* Santa Monica, CA: Rand Corporation.

Newton, T. (1990, September). *Improving students' listening skills.* IDEA Paper No. 23. Manhattan, KS: Center for Faculty Evaluation and Development.

Nichols, M. P. (1995). *The lost art of listening.* New York, NY: Guilford Press.

Nichols, R. G., & Stevens, L. A. (1957). *Are you listening?* New York, NY: McGraw-Hill.

Niederjohn, M. S. (2008). First-year experience course improves students' financial literacy. *ESource for College Transitions* (electronic newsletter published by the National Resource Center for the First-Year Experience and Students in Transition), *6*(1), 9–11.

Norman, D. A. (1982). *Learning and memory.* San Francisco, CA: W. H. Freeman.

Nuñez, A. (2005). Negotiating ties: A qualitative study of first-generation female students' transitions to college. *Journal of the First-Year Experience & Students in Transition, 17*(2), 97–118.

Obama, B. (2006). *The audacity of hope: Thoughts on reclaiming the American dream.* New York, NY: Three Rivers Press.

Office of Research. (1994). *What employers expect of college graduates: International knowledge and second language skills.* Washington, DC: Office of Educational Research and Improvement (OERI), U.S. Department of Education.

O'Keefe, J., & Nadel, L. (1985). *The hippocampus as a cognitive map.* Oxford, England: Clarendon Press.

Okimoto, M., & Norman, D. A. (2010). *A comprehensive strategy for better reading, cognition and emotion.* Tokyo, Japan: Kaitakusha.

Onwuegbuzie, A. J. (2000). Academic procrastinators and perfectionistic tendencies among graduate students. *Journal of Social Behavior and Personality, 15,* 103–109.

Orszag, J. M., Orszag, P. R., & Whitmore, D. M. (2001). *Learning and earning: Working in college.* Retrieved July 19, 2006, from http://www.brockport. edu/career01/upromise.htm

Pace, C. R. (1990a). Measuring the quality of student effort [Monograph]. *Current Issues in Higher Education, 2*(1).

Pace, C. R. (1990b). *The undergraduates.* Los Angeles, CA: Center for the Study of Evaluation, University of California.

Paivio, A. (1990). *Mental representations: A dual coding approach.* New York, NY: Oxford University Press.

Palank, J. (2006, July 17). *Face it: "Book" no secret to employers.* Retrieved August 21, 2006, from http://www.washtimes.com/business/20060717-12942-1800r.htm

Park, O. (1984). Example comparison strategy versus attribute identification strategy in concept learning. *American Educational Research Journal, 21*(1), 145–162.

Pascarella, E. T. (2001, November/December). Cognitive growth in college: Surprising and reassuring findings from The National Study of Student Learning. *Change,* 21–27.

Pascarella, E. T., & Terenzini, P. (1991). *How college affects students: Findings and insights from twenty years of research.* San Francisco, CA: Jossey-Bass.

Pascarella, E. T., & Terenzini, P. (2005). *How college affects students: A third decade of research* (vol. 2). San Francisco, CA: Jossey-Bass.

Paul, R., & Elder, L. (2004). *The nature and functions of critical and creative thinking.* Dillon Beach, CA: Foundation for Critical Thinking.

Peele, S., & Brodsky, A. (1991). *Love and addiction.* New York, NY: Signet Books.

Peigneux, P. P., Laureys, S., Delbeuck, X., & Maquet, P. (2001, December 21). Sleeping brain, learning brain: The role of sleep for memory systems. *NeuroReport, 12*(18), A111–A124.

Pennsylvania State University. (2005). *How to avoid plagiarism.* Retrieved October 15, 2005, from http://tlt.its.psu/suggestions/cyberplag/cyberplagexamples.html

Peoples, J., & Bailey, G. (2008). *Humanity: An introduction to cultural anthropology.* Independence, KY: Cengage Learning.

Peter D. Hart Research Associates. (2006). *How should colleges prepare students to succeed in today's global economy?* Based on surveys among employers and recent college graduates conducted on behalf of the Association of American Colleges and Universities. Washington, DC: Author.

Peterson, C., & Seligman, M. E. P. (2004). *Character strengths and virtues: A handbook and classification.* New York, NY: Oxford University Press.

Pettigrew, T. F. (1998). Intergroup contact theory. *Annual Review of Psychology, 49,* 65–85.

Piaget, J. (1978). *Success and understanding.* Cambridge, MA: Harvard University Press.

Piaget, J. (1985). *The equilibration of cognitive structures: The central problem of intellectual development.* Chicago, IL: University of Chicago Press.

Pinker, S. (1994). *The language instinct.* New York, NY: HarperCollins.

Pintrich, P. R. (Ed.). (1995). *Understanding self-regulated learning.* (New Directions for Teaching and Learning No. 63). San Francisco, CA: Jossey-Bass.

Pope, L. (1990). *Looking beyond the Ivy League.* New York, NY: Penguin Press.

Porter, S. R., & Swing, R. L. (2006). Understanding how first-year seminars affect persistence. *Research in Higher Education, 47*(1), 89–109.

Potts, J. T. (1987). Predicting procrastination on academic tasks with self-report personality measures (Doctoral dissertation, Hofstra University). *Dissertation Abstracts International, 48,* 1543.

Pratt, B. (2008). *Extra credit: The 7 things every college student needs to know about credit, debt, and cash.* Keedysville, MD: ExtraCreditBook.com.

Pratto, F., Liu, J. H., Levin, S., Sidanius, J., Shih, M., Bachrach, H., & Hegarty, P. (2000). Social dominance orientation and the legitimization of inequality across cultures. *Journal of Cross-Cultural Psychology, 31,* 369–409.

Prentice, M., Storin, C., & Robinson, G. (2012). *Make it personal: How pregnancy planning and prevention help students complete college.* American Association of Community Colleges.

President's Council on Physical Fitness and Sports. (2001). Toward a uniform definition of wellness: A commentary. *Research Digest, 3*(15), 1–8.

Pribram, K. H. (1991). *Brain and perception: Holonomy and structure in figural processing.* Hillsdale, NJ: Erlbaum.

Price, R. H., Choi, J. N., & Vinokur, A. D. (2002). Links in the chain of adversity following job loss: How financial strain and loss of personal control lead to depression, impaired functioning, and poor health. *Journal of Occupational Health Psychology, 7*(4), 302–312.

Prinsell, C. P., Ramsey, P. H., & Ramsey, P. P. (1994). Score gains, attitudes, and behaviour changes due to answer-changing instruction. *Journal of Educational Measurement, 31,* 327–337.

Pryor, J. H., De Angelo, L., Palucki-Blake, B., Hurtado, S., & Tran, S. (2012). *The American freshman: National norms fall 2011.* Los Angeles, CA: Higher Education Research Institute, UCLA.

Public Service Enterprise Group (PSEG). (2009). *Diversity.* Retrieved January 6, 2009, from http://www.pseg.com/info/environment/sustainability/2009/people/diversity.jsp

Purdue University Online Writing Lab. (1995–2004). *Writing a research paper.* Retrieved August 18, 2005, from http://owl.english.purdue.edu/workshops/hypertext/ResearchW/notes.html

Purdy, M., & Borisoff, D. (Eds.). (1996). *Listening in everyday life: A personal and professional approach.* Lanham, MD: University Press of America.

Putman, R. D. (2000). *Bowling alone: The collapse and revival of American community.* New York, NY: Simon & Schuster.

Rader, P. E., & Hicks, R. A. (1987, April). *Jet lag desynchronization and self-assessment of business-related performance.* Paper presented at the meeting of the Western Psychological Association, Long Beach, CA.

Ramsden, P. (2003). *Learning to teach in higher education* (2nd ed.). London, England: RoutledgeFalmer.

Ramsden, P., & Entwistle, N. J. (1981). Effects of academic departments on students' approaches to studying. *British Journal of Educational Psychology, 51,* 368–383.

Rankin, H. A., Abrams, T., Barry, R. J., Bhatnagar, S., Clayton, D. F., Colombo, J., & Thompson, R. F. (2009). Habituation revisited: An updated and revised description of the behavioral characteristics of habituation. *Neurobiology of Learning and Memory, 92*(2), 135–138.

Reed, S. K. (1996). *Cognition: Theory and applications* (3rd ed.). Pacific Grove, CA: Brooks/Cole.

Rennels, M. R., & Chaudhair, R. B. (1988). Eye-contact and grade distribution. *Perceptual and Motor Skills, 67*(October), 627–632.

Resnick, L. B. (1986). *Education and learning to think, Special Report.* Pittsburgh, PA: Commission on Behavioral and Social Sciences Education, University of Pittsburgh.

Rhoads, J. (2005). *The transition to college: Top ten issues identified by students.* Retrieved June 30, 2006, from http://advising.wichita.edu/lasac/pubs/aah/trans.htm

Riesman, D., Glazer, N., & Denney, R. (2001). *The lonely crowd: A study of the changing American character* (rev. ed.). New Haven, CT: Yale University Press.

Ring, T. (1997, October). Issuers face a visit to the dean's office. *Credit Card Management, 10,* 34–39.

Riquelme, H. (2002). Can people creative in imagery interpret ambiguous figures faster than people less creative in imagery? *Journal of Creative Behavior, 36*(2), 105–116.

Rocdiger, H., & Karpicke, J. (2006). The power of testing memory: Basic research and implications for educational practice. *Perspectives on Psychological Science, 1*(3), 181–210.

Roffwarg, H. P., Muzio, J. N., & Dement, W. C. (1966). Ontogenetic development of the human sleep-dream cycle. *Science, 152,* 604–619.

Roos, L. L., Wise, S. L., Yoes, M. E., & Rocklin, T. R. (1996). Conducting self-adapted testing using MicroCAT. *Educational and Psychological Measurement, 56,* 821–827.

Rosenfield, I. (1988). *The invention of memory: A new view of the brain*. New York, NY: Basic Books.

Rothblum, E. D., Solomon, L. J., & Murakami, J. (1986). Affective, cognitive, and behavioral differences between high and low procrastinators. *Journal of Counseling Psychology, 33*(4), 387–394.

Rotter, J. (1966). Generalized expectancies for internal versus external controls of reinforcement. *Psychological Monographs: General and Applied, 80*(609), 1–28.

Ruggiero, V. R. (2004). *Beyond feelings: A guide to critical thinking*. New York, NY: McGraw-Hill.

Runco, M. A. (2004). Creativity. *Annual Review of Psychology, 55*, 657–687.

Saarni, C. (1999). *The development of emotional competence*. New York, NY: Guilford.

Sadker, M., & Sadker, D. (1994). *Failing at fairness: How America's schools cheat girls*. New York, NY: Charles Scribner's Sons.

Salovey, P., & Mayer, J. D. (1990). Emotional intelligence. *Imagination, Cognition, and Personality, 9*, 185–211.

Samuels, S. J., & Flor, R. F. (1997). The importance of automaticity for developing expertise in reading. *Reading & Writing Quarterly, 13*(2), 107–121.

Sapolsky, R. (2004). *Why zebras don't get ulcers*. New York, NY: W. H. Freeman.

Savitz, F. (1985). Effects of easy examination questions placed at the beginning of science multiple-choice examinations. *Journal of Instructional Psychology, 12*(1), 6–10.

Sax, L. J. (2003, July–August). Our incoming students: What are they like? *About Campus*, 15–20.

Sax, L. J., Astin, A. W., Korn, W. S., & Mahoney, K. M. (1999). *The American freshman: National norms for fall 1999*. Los Angeles, CA: Higher Education Research Institute, Graduate School of Education & Information Studies, University of California.

Sax, L. J., Bryant, A. N., & Gilmartin, S. K. (2004). A longitudinal investigation of emotional health among male and female first-year college students. *Journal of the First-Year Experience & Students in Transition, 16*(2), 29–65.

Sax, L. J., Lindholm, J. A., Astin, A. W., Korn, W. S., & Mahoney, K. M. (2004). *The American freshman: National norms for fall, 2004*. Los Angeles, CA: Higher Education Research Institute, University of California.

Schab, F. R. (1990). Odors and the remembrance of things past. *Journal of Experimental Psychology: Learning, Memory, and Cognition, 16*(4), 648–655.

Schacter, D. L. (1992). Understanding implicit memory. *American Psychologist, 47*(4), 559–569.

Schacter, D. L. (2001). *The seven sins of memory: How the mind forgets and remembers*. Boston, MA: Houghton Mifflin.

Schlosser, E. (2001). *Fast food nation: The dark side of the all-American meal*. Boston, MA: Houghton Mifflin.

Schneider, W., & Chein, J. M. (2003). Controlled and automatic processing: Behavior, theory, and biological mechanisms. *Cognitive Science, 27*, 525–559.

Schunk, D. H. (1995). Self-efficacy and education and instruction. In J. E. Maddux (Ed.), *Self-efficacy, adaptation, and adjustment: Theory, research, and application* (pp. 281–303). New York, NY: Plenum Press.

Schutte, N. S., Malouff, J. M., et al. (1998). Development and validation of emotional intelligence. *Personality and Individual Differences, 26*, 167–177.

Schutte, N. S., & Malouff, J. M. (2002). Incorporating emotional skills content in a college transition course enhances student retention. *Journal of the First-Year Experience, 14*(1), 7–21.

Seabrook, J. (2008). *Flash of genius and other true stories of invention.* New York, NY: St. Martin's Press.

Sedlacek, W. (1987). Black students on White campuses: 20 years of research. *Journal of College Student Personnel, 28,* 484–495.

Segall, M. H., Campbell, D. T., & Herskovits, M. J. (1966). *The influence of culture on visual perception.* Indianapolis, IN: Bobbs-Merrill.

Seirup, G. E. (2004). *College dating.* Retrieved January 2, 2004, from http://writing. colostate.edu/gallery/talkingback/v3.1/seirup.htm

Seligman, M. E. P. (1991). *Learned optimism.* New York, NY: Knopf.

Shah, A. (2008). Causes of poverty. *Global Issues.* Retrieved January 22, 2010, from http://www.globalissues.org/issue/2/causes-of-poverty

Shams, W., & Seitz, K. (2011). Influences of multisensory experience on subsequent unisensory processing. *Frontiers in Perception Science, 2*(264), 1–9.

Shanley, M., & Witten, C. (1990). University 101 freshman seminar course: A longitudinal study of persistence, retention, and graduation rates. *NASPA Journal, 27,* 344–352.

Shatz, M. A., & Best, J. B. (1987). Students' reasons for changing answers on objective tests. *Teaching of Psychology, 14*(4), 241–242.

Shelton, J. T., Elliot, E. M., Eaves, S. D., & Exner, A. L. (2009). The distracting effects of a ringing cell phone: An investigation of the laboratory and the classroom setting. *Journal of Environmental Psychology,* (March). Retrieved October 25, 2009, from http://news-info.wustl.edu/news/page/normal/14225.html

Shimoff, E., & Catania, C. A. (2001). Effects of recording attendance on grades in Introductory Psychology. *Teaching of Psychology, 23*(3), 192–195.

Sidanius, J., Levin, S., Liu, H., & Pratto, F. (2000). Social dominance orientation, anti-egalitarianism, and the political psychology of gender: An extension and cross-cultural replication. *European Journal of Social Psychology, 30,* 41–67.

Sidle, M., & McReynolds, J. (1999). The freshman year experience: Student retention and student success. *NASPA Journal, 36,* 288–300.

Simopoulos, A. P., & Pavlou, K. N. (Eds.). (1997). Genetic variation and dietary response. *World Review of Nutrition and Dietics.* Basel, Switzerland: S. Karger.

Simunek, M., Schutte, N. S., Hollander, S., & McKenley, J. (2000). *The relationship between ability to understand and regulate emotions, mood, and self-esteem.* Paper presented at the Conference of the American Psychological Society, Miami, FL.

Singh, N. A., Clements, K. M., & Fiatarone, M. A. (1997). A randomized controlled trial of the effect of exercise on sleep. *Sleep, 20,* 95–101.

Smith, D. (1997). How diversity influences learning. *Liberal Education, 83*(2), 42–48.

Smith, D. D. (2005). Experiential learning, service learning, and career development. In P. A. Gore (Ed.), *Facilitating the career development of students in transition* (Monograph No. 43, pp. 205–222). Columbia: National Resource Center for the First-Year Experience and Students in Transition, University of South Carolina.

Smith, R. L. (1994). The world of business. In W. C. Hartel, S. W. Schwartz, S. D. Blume, & J. N. Gardner (Eds.), *Ready for the real world* (pp. 123–135). Belmont, CA: Wadsworth Publishing.

Smith, S. M., Glenberg, A., & Bjork, R. A. (1978). Environmental context and human memory. *Memory & Cognition, 6,* 342–353.

Smith, T., Snyder, C. R., & Handelsman, M. M. (1982). On the self-serving function of an academic wooden leg: Test anxiety as a self-handicapping strategy. *Journal of Personality & Social Psychology, 42,* 314–321.

Snyder, C. R. (1994). *Psychology of hope: You can get from here to there.* New York, NY: Free Press.

Snyder, C. R. (1995). Conceptualizing, measuring, and nurturing hope. *Journal of Counseling and Development, 73*(January/February), 355–360.

Snyder, C. R., Harris, C., Anderson, J. R., Holleran, S. A., Irving, L. M., Sigmon, S. T., et al. (1991). The will and the ways: Development and validation of an individual-differences measure of hope. *Journal of Personality and Social Psychology, 60,* 570–585.

Soloman, L. J., & Rothblum, E. D. (1984). Academic procrastination: Frequency and cognitive-behavioral correlates. *Journal of Counseling Psychology, 31,* 503–509.

Southern Methodist University. (2006). *How is college different from high school?* Retrieved September 15, 2006, from http://www.smu.edu/alec/whyhighschool. html

Sprenger, M. (1999). *Learning and memory: The brain in action.* Alexandria, VA: Association for Supervision and Curriculum Development.

Stark, J. S., Lowther, R. J., Bentley, M. P., Ryan, G. G., Martens, M. L., Genthon, P. A., et al. (1990). *Planning introductory college courses: Influences on faculty.* Ann Arbor, MI: National Center for Research to Improve Postsecondary Teaching and Learning, University of Michigan. (ERIC Document Reproduction Services No. 330 277 370).

Starke, M. C., Harth, M., & Sirianni, F. (2001). Retention, bonding, and academic achievement: Success of a first-year seminar. *Journal of the First-Year Experience & Students in Transition, 13*(2), 7–35.

Staudinger, U. M. (2008). A psychology of wisdom: History and recent developments. *Research in Human Development, 5,* 107–120.

Staudinger, U. M., & Baltes, P. B. (1994). Psychology of wisdom. In R. J. Sternberg (Ed.), *Encyclopedia of intelligence* (vol. 1, pp. 143–152). New York, NY: Macmillan.

Steel, P. (2003). *The nature of procrastination: A meta-analytic and theoretical review of self-regulatory failure.* Retrieved June 28, 2006, from http://www.haskayne. ucalgary.ca/research/workingpapers

Steel, P. (2007). The nature of procrastination: A meta-analytic and theoretical review of quintessential self-regulatory failure. *Psychological Bulletin, 133*(1), 65–94.

Steel, P., Brothen, T., & Wambach, C. (2001). Procrastination and personality, performance, and mood. *Personality & Individual Differences, 30,* 95–106.

Stein, B. S. (1978). Depth of processing reexamined: The effects of the precision of encoding and testing appropriateness. *Journal of Verbal Learning and Verbal Behavior, 17,* 165–174.

Sternberg, R. J. (2001). What is the common thread of creativity? *American Psychologist, 56*(4), 360–362.

Strommer, D. W. (1993). Not quite good enough: Drifting about in higher education. *AAHE Bulletin, 45*(10), 14–15.

Sullivan, R. E. (1993, March 18). Greatly reduced expectations. *Rolling Stone,* pp. 2–4.

Suls, J., Martin, R., & Wheeler, L. (2002). Social comparison: Why, with whom and with what effect? *Current Directions in Psychological Science, 11*(5), 159–163.

Sundquist, J., & Winkleby, M. (2000, June). Country of birth, acculturation status and abdominal obesity in a national sample of Mexican-American women and men. *International Journal of Epidemiology, 29,* 470–477.

Susswein, R. (1995). College students and credit cards: A privilege earned? *Credit World, 83,* 21–23.

Svinicki, M. D., & Dixon, N. M. (1987). The Kolb model modified for classroom activities. *College Teaching, 35*(4), 141–146.

Szalavitz, M. (2003). Stand and deliver. *Psychology Today,* pp. 50–54.

Tagliacollo, V. A., Volpato, G. L., & Pereira, A., Jr. (2010). Association of student position in classroom and school performance. *Educational Research, 1*(6), 198–201.

Taylor, S. E., Peplau, L. A., & Sears, D. O. (2006). *Social psychology* (12th ed.). Upper Saddle River, NJ: Pearson/Prentice Hall.

Teigen, K. H. (1994). Yerkes-Dodson—A law for all seasons. *Theory & Psychology, 4,* 525–547.

Thomson, R. (1998). University of Vermont. In B. O. Barefoot, C. L. Warnock, M. P. Dickinson, S. E. Richardson, & M. R. Roberts (Eds.). (1998). *Exploring the evidence: Vol. 2. Reporting outcomes of first-year seminars* (Monograph No. 29, pp. 77–78). Columbia, OH: National Resource Center for the First-Year Experience and Students in Transition, University of South Carolina.

Tice, D. M., & Baumeister, R. F. (1997). Longitudinal study of procrastination, performance, stress, and health: The costs and benefits of dawdling. *Psychological Science, 8,* 454–458.

Tinto, V. (1993). *Leaving college: Rethinking the causes and cures of student attrition* (2nd ed.). Chicago, IL: University of Chicago Press.

Tinto, V. (1997). Classrooms as communities: Exploring the educational character of student persistence. *Journal of Higher Education, 68,* 599–623.

Tinto, V. (2000). Linking learning and leaving: Exploring the role of the college classroom in student departure. In J. M. Braxton (Ed.), *Reworking the student departure puzzle* (pp. 81–94). Nashville, TN: Vanderbilt University Press.

Tisdell, E. J. (2003). *Exploring spirituality and culture in adult and higher education.* San Francisco, CA: Jossey-Bass.

Titsworth, S., & Kiewra, K. A. (2004). Organizational lecture cues and student notetaking. *Contemporary Educational Psychology, 29,* 447–461.

Tobias, S. (1985). Test anxiety: Interference, defective skills, and cognitive capacity. *Educational Psychologist, 20*(3), 135–142.

Tomasho, R. (2009, April 22). Study tallies education gap's effect on GDP. *Wall Street Journal.*

Torrance, E. P. (1963). *Education and the creative potential.* Minneapolis, MN: University of Minnesota Press.

Tulving, E. (1983). *Elements of episodic memory.* Oxford, England: Clarendon Press/ Oxford University Press.

Tyson, E. (2003). *Personal finance for dummies.* Indianapolis, IN: IDG Books.

Underwood, B. J. (1983). *Attributes of memory.* Glenview, IL: Scott, Foresman.

University of New Hampshire Office of Residential Life. (2001). *The hate that hate produced.* Retrieved January 8, 2007, from http://www.unh.edu/residental-life/ diversity/kn_article6.pdf

U.S. Bureau of Labor Statistics. (2005). *Number of jobs, labor market experience, and earnings growth: Results from a longitudinal survey.* Retrieved September 24, 2005, from http://www.bls.gov/news.release/nlsoy.toc.htm

U.S. Census Bureau. (2000). *Racial and ethnic classifications in Census 2000 and beyond.* Retrieved December 19, 2006, from http://census.gov/population/www/ socdemo/race/racefactcb.html

U.S. Census Bureau. (2004). *The face of our population.* Retrieved December 12, 2006, from http://factfinder.census.gov/jsp/saff/SAFFInfojsp?_pageId=tp9_ race_ethnicity

U.S. Census Bureau. (2008). *Bureau of Labor Statistics.* Washington, DC: Author.

U.S. Census Bureau. (2010). *2010 census redistricting data (public law 94-171) summary file.* Retrieved April 7, 2012, from http://factfinder2 .census.gov/main. html

U.S. Department of Health & Human Services. (2000). *Healthy people 2010: Understanding and improving health.* Washington, DC: Government Printing Office.

Useem, M. (1989). *Liberal education and the corporation: The hiring and advancement of college graduates.* Piscataway, NJ: Aldine Transaction.

Van Dongen, H. P. A., Maislin, G., Mullington, J. M., & Dinges, D. F. (2003). The cumulative cost of additional wakefulness: Dose–response effects on neurobehavioral functions and sleep physiology from chronic sleep restriction and total sleep deprivation. *Sleep, 26,* 117–126.

Van Overwalle, F. I., Mervielde, I., & De Schuyer, J. (1995). Structural modeling of the relationships between attributional dimensions, emotions, and performance of college freshmen. *Cognition and Emotion, 9*(1), 59–85.

Viorst, J. (1998). *Necessary losses.* New York, NY: Fireside.

Voelker, R. (2004). Stress, sleep loss, and substance abuse create potent recipe for college depression. *Journal of the American Medical Association, 291,* 2177–2179.

Vygotsky, L. S. (1978). Internalization of higher cognitive functions. In M. Cole, V. John-Steiner, S. Scribner, & E. Souberman (Eds. & Trans.), *Mind in society: The development of higher psychological processes* (pp. 52–57). Cambridge, MA: Harvard University Press.

Waddington, P. (1996). *Dying for information: An investigation into the effects of information overload in the USA and worldwide.* London, England: Reuters.

Wade, C., & Tavris, C. (1990). Thinking critically and creatively. *Skeptical Inquirer, 14,* 372–377.

Walker, C. M. (1996). Financial management, coping, and debt in households under financial strain. *Journal of Economic Psychology, 17,* 789–807.

Walsh, K. (2005). *Suggestions from more experienced classmates.* Retrieved June 12, 2006, from http://www.uni.edu/walsh/introtips.html

Walter, T. W., Knudsbig, G. M., & Smith, D. E. P. (2003). *Critical thinking: Building the basics* (2nd ed.). Belmont, CA: Wadsworth.

Webber, R. A. (1991). *Breaking your time barriers: Becoming a strategic time manager.* Englewood Cliffs, NJ: Prentice Hall.

Weinstein, C. F. (1994). Students at risk for academic failure. In K. W. Prichard & R. M. Sawyer (Eds.), *Handbook of college teaching: Theory and applications* (pp. 375–385). Westport, CT: Greenwood Press.

Weinstein, C. F., & Meyer, D. K. (1991). Cognitive learning strategies. In R. J. Menges & M. D. Svinicki (Eds.), *College teaching: From theory to practice.* New Directions for Teaching and Learning No. 45, pp. 15–26. San Francisco, CA: Jossey-Bass.

Weinstein, C. E., & Underwood, V. L. (1985). Learning strategies: The how of learning. In J. W. Segal, S. F. Chapman, & R. Glaser (Eds.), *Thinking and learning skills* (pp. 241–258). Hillsdale, NJ: Erlbaum.

Wesley, J. C. (1994). Effects of ability, high school achievement, and procrastinatory behavior on college performance. *Educational & Psychological Measurement, 54,* 404–408.

Wheelright, J. (2005, March). Human, study thyself. *Discover,* pp. 39–45.

Wiederman, M. (2007). Why it's so hard to be happy. *Scientific American Mind, 18*(1), 36–43.

Wiley, C. (1992). Predicting business course grades from class attendance and other objective student characteristics. *College Student Journal, 26*(4), 497–501.

Wilhite, S. (1990). Self-efficacy, locus of control, self-assessment of memory ability, and student activities as predictors of college course achievement. *Journal of Educational Psychology, 82*(4), 696–700.

Wilkie, C. J., & Thompson, C. A. (1993). First-year reentry women's perceptions of their classroom experiences. *Journal of the Freshman Year Experience, 5*(2), 69–90.

Williams, J. M., Landers, D. M., & Boutcher, S. H. (1993). Arousal-performance relationships. *Sport Psychology: Personal Growth to Peak Performance, 3,* 173–184.

Willingham, D.B. (2001). *Cognition: The thinking animal.* Upper Saddle River, NJ: Prentice Hall.

Willingham, W. W. (1985). *Success in college: The role of personal qualities and academic ability.* New York, NY: College Entrance Examination Board.

Winsor, J. L., Curtis, D. B., & Stephens, R. D. (1997). National preferences in business and communication education: A survey update. *JACA, 3*(September), 170–179.

Wolvin, A. D., & Coakley, X. X. (1993). *Perspectives on listening.* Norwood, NJ: Ablex Publishing.

World Health Organization. (2012). *Obesity and overweight.* Retrieved May 29, 2012, from http://www.who.int/entity/mediacentre/factsheets/fs311/en/index.html

Wright, D. J. (Ed.). (1987). *Responding to the needs of today's minority students.* New Directions for Student Services, No. 38. San Francisco: Jossey-Bass.

Wyatt, G. (1992). Skipping class: An analysis of absenteeism among first-year college students. *Teaching Sociology, 20*(3), 201–207.

Wyckoff, S. C. (1999). The academic advising process in higher education: History, research, and improvement. *Recruitment & Retention in Higher Education, 13*(1), 1–3.

Yerkes, R. M., & Dodson, J. D. (1908). The relationship of strength and stimulus to rapidity of habit formation. *Journal of Neurological Psychology, 184,* 59–82.

Young, K. S. (1996, August). *Pathological Internet use: The emergence of a new clinical disorder.* Paper presented at the annual meeting of the American Psychological Association, Toronto, Ontario, Canada.

Zeidner, M. (1995). Adaptive coping with test situations: A review of the literature. *Educational Psychologist, 30*(3), 123–133.

Zimbardo, P. G., Johnson, R. L., & Weber, A. L. (2006). *Psychology: Core concepts* (5th ed.). Boston, MA: Allyn & Bacon.

Zimmerman, B. J. (1995). Self-efficacy and educational development. In A. Bandura (Ed.), *Self-efficacy in changing societies.* New York, NY: Cambridge University Press.

Zohar, D. (1998). An additive model of test anxiety: Role of exam-specific expectations. *Journal of Educational Psychology, 90,* 330–340.

Zull, J. E. (1998). The brain, the body, learning, and teaching. *National Teaching & Learning Forum, 7*(3), 1–5.

Zull, J. E. (2002). *The art of changing the brain: Enriching the practice of teaching by exploring the biology of learning.* Sterling, VA: Stylus.